Class Mark:

341.121 (415) KEN

Ireland and the League of Nations, 1919–1946

Ireland and the League of Nations, 1919–1946

International relations, diplomacy and politics

Michael Kennedy

IRISH ACADEMIC PRESS

This book was set in 10.5 on 12 point Ehrhardt for
IRISH ACADEMIC PRESS
Kill Lane, Blackrock, Co. Dublin, Ireland
and in North America for
IRISH ACADEMIC PRESS
5804 NE Hassalo St, Portland, Oregon 97213.

© Michael Kennedy 1996

A catalogue record for this title
is available from the British Library.

ISBN 0-7165-2549-6

All rights reserved. No part of this publication may be reproduced, stored in or introduced into a retrieval system, or transmitted, in any form or by any means (electronic, mechanical, photocopying, recording or otherwise), without the prior written permission of both the copyright owner and publisher of this book.

This book is printed on an acid-free and a wood-free paper

Printed in Great Britain
by Redwood Books, Trowbridge, Wiltshire

Contents

ABBREVIATIONS	9
PREFACE	11
INTRODUCTION	13

1 FROM APPLICATION TO ADMISSION, 1919–23   18

Sinn Féin and the League of Nations: 1919–21	18
January–July 1922: The role of George Gavan Duffy	21
League policy halted: July 1922–March 1923	23
The re-launch of League policy: March–September 1923	27
The Seanad's involvement and the Guarantee Bill	32
Final preparations	37
Admission	40
Conclusion	41

2 LEARNING THE ROPES, TYING UP LOOSE THREADS   43

The 1923 Assembly	43
The Corfu incident	44
The Article 393 controversy	46
The Protocol for the Pacific Settlement of International Disputes	48
The failure to develop policy: 1923–5	53
The registration of the Treaty: 1923–5	53
Why register?	55
September 1923: The League Assembly	58
October 1923 to January 1924: Getting the facts	60
June–July 1924: Registration	61
The British reaction: June 1924–March 1925	65
Conclusion	71

3 THE COUNCIL DISPUTE AND THE
  SEPTEMBER 1926 ASSEMBLY   73

  The Extraordinary Assembly   74
  The importance of the March 1926 Council crisis   75
  New enthusiasm: February–September 1926   75
  The Seventh Assembly: Autumn 1926   77
  The Council elections: 14–18 September 1926   81
  The last week of the Assembly: 18–25 September 1926   90
  Conclusion   91

4 THE RE-APPRAISAL AND RE-DIRECTION OF
  LEAGUE POLICY, 1927–9   93

  The Blythe memorandum   93
  The Walshe memorandum   94
  The March 1927 Council incident   96
  Patrick McGilligan and the stabilisation of League policy:
    1927–30   98
  Policy in action   105
  The general debate: 1928–31   106
  Internal reform of the League   108
  The Free State and the economic policy of the League   111
  The codification of International Law   114
  The ratification of League conventions   116
  The Optional Clause: September 1929   118
  Disarmament   121
  The General Act   124
  Conclusion   128

5 CANVASSING FOR A COUNCIL SEAT   129

  The canvass: September 1929–March 1930   129
  March–September 1930   134
  The Assembly   142
  The election   147
  Conclusion   149

6 COUNCIL MEMBER, SEPTEMBER 1930–SEPTEMBER 1933   150

  Council Member: January–September 1931   150
  Silesia and Disarmament   150
  The Sixty-Third Session of the Council: 18–23 May 1931   154

The Sixty-Fourth Session of the Council:
   1–14 September 1931   155
Manchuria: September 1931–September 1932   156
Cumann na nGaedheal and Manchuria   157
The Extraordinary Assembly   162
De Valera at the Thirteenth Assembly   164
Ireland and the Lytton Report   171
The Lytton Report at the Assembly: December 1932   173
The final round of the Manchurian Dispute   176
South America: Lester, Chaco and Leticia   177
Peru–Colombia Leticia: 1932–3   177
Bolivia–Paraguay, Chaco: The Council's moment   180
Ireland and the arms embargo: 1934–5   182
The re-eligibility debate and Ireland's departure
   from the Council   184
Conclusion   186

7 DE VALERA'S HEYDAY AT GENEVA,
   SEPTEMBER 1933–JULY 1936   189

The limits of Irish League policy:
   September 1933–September 1934   189
Europe in the run-up to the 15th Assembly:
   July–September 1934   194
The admission of Russia: September 1934   198
Abyssinia: 1934–6   202
   December 1934–October 1935: Armed stand-off   202
   The 1935 Assembly: Prelude to invasion   205
   Invasion and sanctions: October–November 1935   210
   The Hoare–Laval Pact: December 1935   214
   The impact of sanctions in an Irish context   215
   The end of sanctions: May–July 1936   219
Conclusion   222

8 THE RETREAT FROM GENEVA, 1936–46   226

The 1936 and 1937 Assemblies: A League without sanctions?   226
The League sidelined: The Spanish Civil War 1936–9   231
The 1938 Assembly: Munich   234
The descent to war   237
Cremins at Berne: 1940–6   243
The birth of the United Nations   247
Conclusion   250

9 THE LEAGUE, EUROPE AND IRISH FOREIGN POLICY
BETWEEN THE WARS   251

APPENDICES   258

1   The Covenant of the League of Nations   258
2   Letter of Application by the Irish Free State
    to the League of Nations   266
3   Delegation Personnel, 1923–46   267
4   Conventions Acceded to and Ratified by
    the Irish Free State, 1922–32   271

BIBLIOGRAPHY   273

INDEX   281

LIST OF FIGURES

1   Organisation of the League of Nations   14
2   Irish–Italian trade: 1929–37   217
3   Irish–Italian trade: September 1935–December 1936   218

LIST OF TABLES

1   Irish–Italian trade: 1929–37   217
2   Irish–Italian trade: September 1935–December 1936   218

Abbreviations

C1	D.F/A, BE, personal papers of Francis Cremins
D.F/A	Department of Foreign Affairs
DO	Dominions Office (PRO)
FLK	Franciscan Library, Killiney, Co. Dublin
FO	Foreign Office (PRO)
LAI	Eoin MacNeill Papers, UCDA
LONR	League of Nations Registry, Palais des Nations, Geneva
NA	National Archives, Dublin
NLI	National Library of Ireland, Dublin
P80	Desmond FitzGerald Papers, UCDA
P4	Hugh Kennedy Papers, UCDA
P35	Patrick McGilligan Papers, UCDA
P7	Richard Mulcahy Papers, UCDA
P24	Ernest Blythe Papers, UCDA
PRO	Public Record Office, Kew, London
S.	Department of the Taoiseach, S Series, National Archives, Dublin
UCDA	University College Dublin Archives
Dáil deb	Dáil Debates
Seanad deb	Seanad Debates
LNOJ	*League of Nations Official Journal* (Geneva, Monthly)
ISIA	*Irish Studies in International Affairs*

For my Mother and Father

Preface

I am indebted to a great many people for their help, support and encouragement as this book took shape from my post graduate work: my doctoral supervisor, Professor Ronan Fanning of University College Dublin; Dr Garret FitzGerald who read an early draft of this work; Dorothy and Douglas Gageby, and Stephen Barcroft, for their kind and very helpful insights into the careers of Sean Lester and Francis Cremins; Kathleen MacWhite for her help with research into the career of Michael MacWhite; and, of course, my parents without whom this book would have been impossible.

I would also like to thank Bernadette Chambers and Margaret McLoughlin, Archivists at Iveagh House, and Irene Dolan also of the Department of Foreign Affairs. The staff at the National Archives in Bishop Street, Dublin, the Archives Department of University College Dublin, Military Archives, Cathal Brugha Barracks, Dublin, the National Library of Ireland, the Manuscripts Department of Trinity College, Dublin, the Franciscan Library, Killiney, Co. Dublin, the Public Record Office, Kew, London and the League of Nations Archives, Geneva, were all unfailing in their efforts to produce what at times must have seemed like an unending stream of material from the largest to the most obscure collections.

Thanks are also due to Pauline Curry, Pauric Dempsey, Alan Kennedy, Mary Layden, Brian Lynch, Peter Lynch, Dr Alvin Jackson, Tracey Jury, Dr Michael Laffan, James I. McGuire, Peter MacDonagh, Dr Deirdre MacMahon, James P. McBride, Dr Joseph M. Skelly and James Whelan, all of whom provided guidance and assistance. I am very grateful for assistance received from the T.P. MacDonnell Fund and to the Mulcahy Trust for permission to quote from the papers of Richard Mulcahy. Inter-Library Loans at the Libraries of University College, Dublin and the Queen's University, Belfast provided an essential service by locating many obscure texts on the League of Nations. Finally I would like to thank Michael Adams and Martin Healy of Irish Academic Press who helped me prepare this manuscript for publication.

Introduction

This book analyses Ireland's role in the League of Nations and the intention, development, execution and consequence of Irish policy within that institution. The idea for a League of Nations to prevent war and foster peace grew out of the slaughter and destruction of World War I. In Ireland, Sinn Féin saw that the League would be an essential international podium from which to publicise their goal of an independent Irish state. Admission to the League was a prime concern of Sinn Féin and Free State foreign policy. From admission in 1923, and until 1937, when the League's failure was evident, the League of Nations was central to Irish foreign policy as the state defined its international position through the League and supported the League's efforts towards international peace and security. Ireland did not unquestioningly follow the League; the Department of External Affairs reconsidered Ireland's position and role in the League when it failed to effectively counter Italy's invasion of Abyssinia in October 1935. Following the lifting of economic sanctions on Italy in July 1936 the League diminished as an active element in Ireland's foreign policy. Through World War II the state adhered to the League ideal and kept up its contributions to the redundant organisation until the League's dissolution in April 1946.

The League had a wide importance in Irish foreign policy. Ireland had become a Dominion by the 1921 Anglo-Irish Treaty. Links between League of Nations policy and Ireland's role in the development of the international autonomy of the Dominions of the British Empire were very close and are examined in detail below. Inter-war Irish foreign policy was made up of three overlapping areas: League policy, Commonwealth policy and bilateral relations. Sometimes there is an overlap between two or all three of the areas, at other times League policy or aspects of bilateral relations function independently of each other. The crucial point is that inter-war Irish foreign policy must be viewed multi-dimensionally. The argument that Irish foreign policy stems solely from Anglo-Irish relations, or can be explained from analysing one viewpoint alone must be re-evaluated.

General overviews of Irish foreign policy must be re-examined in the light of the extensive array of primary resources available since 1991 and the release of the archives of the Department of Foreign Affairs. The analysis below seeks to examine Ireland's participation in the League of Nations using this material, nearly all of which has never before been the basis of research. The central object is to see the importance of the League in its own right as a factor in Irish foreign policy and to examine the League's inter-relationship with other areas of Irish foreign policy from 1919 to 1945.

Set up in 1920 as a result of the post-World War I peace treaties, the League of Nations was the major international institution of the inter-war period. It had a membership of 63 states but was far from universal as the majority of its members were European states, the strongest of which were France and Britain.[1] The League's basic institutions were an Assembly, which met yearly at Geneva, a Council made up of the Great Powers and a number of elected non-permanent members, which met quarterly, and a permanent Secretariat based at Geneva headed by a Secretary General. There were also a number of technical and ancillary organisations.

The League was viewed with special importance by small less powerful states such as Ireland. They hoped that the League would provide the basis of a peaceful world-order. Public opinion was regarded as a vital force in the development of the League. It would lead the world to choose peaceful methods for solving international disputes. Speaking in a radio broadcast from

Figure 1: *Organisation of the League of Nations*

---

[1] The United States was never a member, the Soviet Union only from 1934 to 1939.

Cork during a public relations visit to Ireland in 1930, Princess Radziwill, of the League Secretariat, summarised this view: 'no nation would dare declare war in face of the opinion behind the League'.[2] Desmond FitzGerald, Irish Minister for External Affairs from 1922 to 1927, professed this belief at the 1926 League Assembly: 'I hold the view that the conscience of the world as a whole is always going to be right.'[3] The League of Nations was the mechanism through which these idealistic and utopian hopes could be realised. It was to be a civilised forum through which disputes could be solved by what E.H. Carr calls a 'card-index' selection of solutions and without recourse to war.[4] The preamble of the League's Covenant puts it concisely: 'to promote international co-operation and to achieve international peace and security'.[5] The League was to be an association of governments, an international institution and a way of organising international life.

Some of the episodes analysed below may appear naive in light of the League's failure. Yet the League system was a rational response by those who had lived through a cataclysmic world war involving new technology, the fall of empires and the evolution of new political and state frameworks, that sought to ensure that a world war would never happen again. The League's eventual failure should not lead the historian immediately to discount it. The League of Nations and the role of Ireland in the League, can only be understood if analysed within a contemporary setting and as the first attempt at an international political institution.

Within that contemporary setting Ireland was one of the young small states of the inter-war period. Ireland arrived onto the European scene as part of a reawakening of popular nationalism across Europe and as part of a reorganisation of the power structure of the continent in the aftermath of World War I. The aim of the Anglo-Irish Treaty may have been to thrust Ireland into the Commonwealth, but the ideologies involved in Britain's settlement of its Irish problem related to the concept of self-determination that had developed from President Wilson's 14 points. The state was both European and Commonwealth oriented in its origins and outlook.

Ireland's world position was defined by her European geographical position before her political Commonwealth affiliation which was due solely to the terms of the 1921 Treaty. Ireland's heritage and national mentality led the state towards the European continent rather than towards the Atlantic states of Britain and the United States. Europe and hence the League were the most likely direction that Ireland foreign policy would take. There were few links between Ireland and the Commonwealth other than through the 1921 Treaty. Ireland would not unilaterally have joined the Commonwealth, although there

---

2 NA, D.F.A., LN85.
3 UCDA, P80/888.
4 Edward H. Carr, *The Twenty Years Crisis* (1989 edition, London) p.31.
5 The full text of the Covenant is contained in appendix one.

might have been some reciprocal trading agreements with Britain. The Irish percentage of the populations of the Dominions was declining rapidly in this period.[6] Ireland's natural tendency was towards a European-centred foreign policy. Thus, France, Britain, Spain, Germany, Italy and especially the small European states were Ireland's natural constituency in the international environment. This would have necessitated a rather large diplomatic network for a state of Ireland's size and limited resources. Membership of the League of Nations and diplomatic representation at Geneva, the seat of the League, would provide a catchall presence for the rest of Europe. Thus Ireland's foreign policy would demand a presence at the League. In reality this had to be put side by side with the practical necessity of Commonwealth membership. The analysis below maintains that the League and the Commonwealth form the dual basis of Irish foreign policy in the 1920s. The more European nature of Irish foreign policy is seen with de Valera's wholehearted support for the League in the 1930s.

The phases of Irish League policy permeate the political history of the inter-war period in Ireland. Until 1926 Ireland saw its international status as the major concern of League policy. From 1926, the development and stability of the League as an international grouping for the small powers was the goal of Irish League policy. This was not simply idealistic self-interest. It was for the benefit of the League as much as for Ireland itself that this end was followed, a peaceful world order and international stability would be to the benefit of all, but especially the small weak states like Ireland; this view was strongly held by Michael MacWhite, then Ireland's representitive at the League. The Department of External Affairs had by the late 1920s succeeded in developing an ambitious agenda for Ireland in the League and an active role for the League in Irish foreign policy. This culminated in Ireland's election to the League Council in September 1930 for three years.

Despite the change of government in Dublin in 1932, League policy was one of continuity. De Valera built Ireland's role in the League upon the basis developed by Cumann na nGaedheal. Due mainly to the internationalism of Sean Lester, Ireland's Permanent Representative at Geneva, de Valera used Ireland's Council membership from 1930 to 1933 to cast the state as a solid League supporter. Lester and de Valera championed the cause of the League and the primacy of the Covenant on the Council during the fraught discussions over Japan's invasion of Manchuria through 1931 and 1932. When Ireland left the Council in October 1933 her performance had ensured that the state ranked highly amongst the smaller powers at Geneva as a defender of the Covenant. The mid-1930s saw Ireland's role in League affairs widen as the state gained a greater influence in League activities. Symptomatic of this development was Lester's own promotion to the post of High Commissioner in the League-administered Free City of Danzig in 1934. His successor as

---

6 See the graph on p.356 of Roy Foster, *Modern Ireland 1600–1972* (London, 1988).

Irish representative to the League was Francis Cremins. Cremins's predilection towards balance of power politics, the League's inability to prevent Italy's invasion of Abyssinia in October 1935 and the resulting failure of economic sanctions on Italy led to a progressive downgrading of the League's importance for Ireland. De Valera's speeches became noticeably less pro-League as faith in collective security under the Covenant gave way to neutrality.

During the Economic War of 1932–38 when relations between Dublin and London were tense and at times frozen, the League provided a neutral ground on which both parties could meet. Though recourse to the League was considered to solve the annuities dispute, it was never considered a suitable framework within which to solve the totality of Anglo-Irish disputes. De Valera was aware that a solution would be found through bilateral talks.

Through the 1930s League membership gave the Free State a vital insight into the rise of Fascism and the decline to war in 1939. The League may have been increasingly redundant in its own right, but a Permanent Representative at Geneva, caught between Hitler's Reich and Mussolini's Italy, was in a central position to observe the tumultuous events of the late 1930s on the European continent.

From 1919 to 1946 an understanding of Ireland's policies and performance at the League of Nations is essential to an understanding of inter-war Irish foreign policy. Taken as part of inter-war Irish foreign policy it is perhaps the missing dimension that a lack of primary material and an overwhelming concern with Anglo-Irish relations and the Commonwealth link has obscured.

CHAPTER 1

From Application to Admission, 1919–23

Sinn Féin and the League of Nations: 1919–21

The first Dáil, which opened on 21 January 1919, aspired to gaining international recognition for Ireland through its 'Message to the free nations of the world'. Eamon de Valera[1] told the London *Daily Herald* on 2 April 1919 that the League was central to Ireland's claim for independence and recognition:

> So far are we from desiring isolation that our whole struggle is to get Ireland out of the cage in which the selfish statecraft of England would confine her ... to get Ireland back into the free world from which she was ravished ... to get her recognised as a free unit in a world league of nations.

In Sinn Féin policy, the League was a means to the end of gaining Ireland's international recognition.

De Valera spoke to the Dáil on 11 April 1919 about the League, praising its ideals and objectives. In his concluding remarks the real purpose of his argument emerged: 'we take up these principles because they are right, and we take them up particularly because the acceptance of these principles will mean that the long fight for Irish liberty is at an end'.[2] The Dáil then passed a resolution 'expressing Ireland's readiness 'to enter a World League of Nations based on equality of rights' and 'to accept all the duties, responsibilities and burdens which inclusion in such a League implies'.[3] The League was consistently viewed by Sinn Féin in the context of events in Ireland between

---

1 **Eamon de Valera** (1882–1975) Politician (Sinn Féin and Fianna Fáil). Commandant of Irish Volunteers in 1916 Rising, President of Dáil Éireann (1919–21), anti-Treaty in civil war of 1922–3, founder of Fianna Fáil 1926, President of the Executive Council (1932–37), Taoiseach (1937–48, 1951–4, 1957–9), Minister for External Affairs (1932–1948), President of the Republic of Ireland (1959–73).
2 Maurice Moynihan (ed.), *Speeches and Statements of Eamon de Valera: 1919–73* (Dublin, 1980), p. 26.
3 Ibid., p. 28.

1919 and 1921 and the struggle for independence. Sinn Féin hoped to gain legitimacy for their actions in Ireland and to publicise their case abroad through the League of Nations. Ireland's position within the League was not considered; it was the League's use to Ireland that conditioned Sinn Féin's approach to the new world organisation.

The Dáil sent a delegation, led by Sean T. O'Kelly, to the 1919–20 Paris Peace Conference.[4] George Gavan Duffy requested the nations attending the conference to press for Ireland to be given League membership.[5] On the instigation of British Prime Minister, David Lloyd George, the Paris conference became the first meeting of the League. The Irish appealed to the assembled victorious allied nations for recognition of Ireland's international status as an independent state. The United States delegate, President Woodrow Wilson, despite pressure from the United States Senate and the Irish Race Convention held at Philadelphia during February 1919, refused to meet the Irish delegation. Georges Clemenceau, the chief French delegate, considered that there was no way the Irish claim could come before the conference. The Allies would not consider the internal affairs of one of their own at the Paris conference. The Great Powers were at Paris to deal with the defeated Alliance powers. No favourable notice was given to the Irish delegation. The Irish manoeuvres were an irrelevant distraction to the Great Powers and ended in failure.

The rebuke at Paris soured Sinn Féin's view of the League of Nations. Interest in the League diminished after the Paris debacle. The focus of external relations moved away from the League. Sinn Féin diplomacy concentrated on establishing relations with single states rather than international groups. The League was seen in an increasingly negative light as a Great Power club that gave no protection to the interests of the smaller states. Protest letters about the Great Power basis of the League were sent to League officials by Sinn Féin diplomats. The Irish appealed, with others seeking national self determination, against the League; letters were counter-signed by Egyptian and Indian and at times Mexican nationalist movements along with Sinn Féin. A letter was sent to the first meeting of the League Council conveying a 'formal protest against this unreal English simulacrum of an international League of peace'.[6] The letter was anti-British and anti-Great Power in its

---

4 **Sean T. O'Kelly** (1888–1966). 1916 veteran, Irish delegation to Paris peace conference, 1919–22. Opposed Treaty in 1921, founder of Fianna Fáil, 1926. Vice-President of the Executive Council 1932–7; Minister for Health and Local Government 1932–9. Represented Ireland at the League of Nations Assembly in 1933. Tánaiste, 1939–1945. President of Éire 1945–9, President of the Republic of Ireland 1949–59.
5 **George Gavan Duffy** (1882–1951): Sinn Féin MP for Dublin South, 1918; member of Sinn Féin delegation to Paris Peace conference, 1919, last member of Treaty delegation to sign Treaty, 1921; Minister for Foreign Affairs, January–July 1922. Left politics to return to legal career. President of the High Court, 1946.
6 LONR, 40/2762/2762, Sean T. O'Kelly, to Eric Drummond, 16 January 1920.

scope and argued for the establishment of a democratic League of Nations free of Great Power influence. The plainly nationalistic motivation of Sinn Féin League policy is seen in this change of attitude. The League acknowledged the receipt of these letters but they had no impact. It gave no support to Sinn Féin's claim for international recognition for Ireland as an independent entity.

Sinn Féin did not again consider the League's role in Irish foreign policy until January 1922. De Valera spoke out against the League in the United States. In line with American opinion he criticised Article 10 of the League Covenant which preserved the existing territorial integrity of member states. It was an obvious relation of the Covenant to the partition of Ireland. Geneva could have been useful as a listening post or an information office to advance the Irish cause. A Department of Foreign Affairs report from August 1919 urged a presence in Geneva, however the lack of a suitable person lead to the post remaining empty.

Michael MacWhite began an Irish diplomatic presence in Geneva in September 1921.[7] He felt that the Genevese saw Ireland as 'a refractory part of England, [and] those who look on us as a distinct nation are few and far between'.[8] MacWhite was instructed to follow a policy of diplomatic reserve but to maintain a visible presence. He became more active once the Free State began to consider League membership. On 17 June 1923 he became Free State Permanent Representative to the League of Nations.

At Geneva from 1921 to 1929, MacWhite promoted an active Irish role at the League. He was an astute diplomat, observing and listening and with highly placed diplomatic connections. His value was not always noticed by his superior, Joseph Walshe, Secretary to the Department of External Affairs from 1922 to 1946.[9] In Walshe's eyes the post required 'an officer with fresher ideas and a training better calculated to promote a detailed interest in the intricacies of international negotiation and a clear perception of their import'.[10] However, MacWhite was competent, capable of taking his own initiative, and constantly with his finger on the pulse of European affairs. These are all factors which did not endear him to Walshe as MacWhite at times acted independently of instructions from Dublin. The despatch of MacWhite to Geneva was the most important result of Sinn Féin League policy. Follow-

---

7 **Michael MacWhite** (1882–1958): French foreign legion, 1914–18, Secretary to Irish delegation to Paris peace conference, 1920; Irish representative to Switzerland, 1921–3; Permanent Representative to League of Nations, 1923–9; Irish Minister at Washington, 1929–38; Irish Minister to Italy; 1938–50.
8 NA, D.F/A, miscellaneous papers, 1 November 1921.
9 **Joseph Walshe** (1886–1956): Former Jesuit seminarian, taught at Clongowes College. Member of Irish delegation to the Paris peace conference, 1919–20; Secretary to Dáil ministry of Foreign Affairs, 1922; Acting Secretary, Department of External Affairs, 1922–27, Secretary, Department of External Affairs, 1927–46; Ambassador to Holy See, 1951–4.
10 NA, S. 5337.

ing Irish admission to the League in 1923, MacWhite's ability and contacts were crucial in developing Ireland's role and position in the League in the mid to late 1920s.

January–July 1922: The role of George Gavan Duffy

Under the Treaty, a Provisional Government took office in Dublin on 14 January 1922. The new administration was uncertain whether it could play a part on the international stage as its mandate dealt solely with domestic affairs. In early January, MacWhite spoke to Eric Drummond on the possibility of Ireland gaining early membership of the League.[11] As the constitutional foundation of the Irish Free State was not yet fully in place, Drummond spoke of 'associate membership'. The date mentioned for full admission was September 1922. According to MacWhite, Drummond played down the need to have the Free State constitution ratified and in full operation, and thus the state legally exist in international law, before admission could be considered.

MacWhite reported his interviews with Drummond to George Gavan Duffy, Provisional Government Minister for Foreign Affairs from January to July 1922. Gavan Duffy rekindled Irish interest in the League and sought the immediate admission of the Irish Free State. Rather than seeing the League as a vehicle for Ireland's international recognition, Gavan Duffy began to define Ireland's role in the League. MacWhite's reports gave Gavan Duffy the impression that the Free State was entitled to immediate membership. Gavan Duffy failed to appreciate one crucial caveat. On 13 December 1921 Lloyd George had written to Arthur Griffith, spelling out clearly that

> it is our desire that Ireland shall rank co-equal with the other nations of the Commonwealth, and we are ready to support her claim to a similar place in the League of Nations as soon as her new constitution comes into effect.[12]

Application was not feasible before the constitution was enacted on 6 December 1922. The Free State then formally came into being and was fully self-governing as an international entity. Only then could the Free State join the League as determined by the Covenant.[13]

11 **James Eric Drummond** (1876–1951): Sixteenth earl of Perth, first Secretary General of the League of Nations (1919–33). Joined British Foreign Office, 1900, private secretary to Prime Minister H.H. Asquith (1912–15), and to Foreign Secretaries Grey and Baldwin. Member of British Delegation to Paris peace conference, 1919. Ambassador to Italy, 1933–9.
12 UCDA, P4/863.
13 Article 1 paragraph 2 states 'Any fully self governing State, Dominion or Colony not named in the Annex may become a Member of the League'.

Gavan Duffy was a law unto himself and disregarded League guidelines. He instead planned for Irish admission at the 1922 Assembly. During March 1922 Gavan Duffy wrote to the Chairman of the Provisional Government, Michael Collins, looking for advice on Irish membership of the Universal Postal Union and the International Telegraphic Union. Both institutions were affiliated to the League. Collins wrote back that 'it would probably be a wiser procedure to refrain altogether until we are in a stable position'.[14] The outbreak of civil war by 28 June meant that plans to join international organisations were officially mothballed. Gavan Duffy privately continued to plan for Irish admission to the League by September 1922.

The civil war was viewed uneasily abroad. It was detrimental to the state's international position. A definite announcement from Dublin on League membership was awaited in Geneva. Michael MacWhite wrote that the League Secretariat was 'growing increasingly anxious to know what are the intentions of the Irish Government with regard to that body. Even the Secretary General has been asking a friend of mine if the latter could get any information from me on the subject.'[15] The desire of international observers to see the Free State brought into the international community was evident at the March 1922 Genoa Economic Conference. The absence of an Irish delegation was noticed and MacWhite stated that there was

> disappointment that no Irish representative was present. As the Secretary of the conference called the roll, I was told that there was a moment of dramatic expectation when he came to Ireland. Everyone looked towards the seats for the Irish delegates only to find them empty.[16]

Officially, and on Collins's guidelines, the state was adopting a low international profile until its internal security problems were dealt with and the constitution in place. Only then could the Irish Free State develop its foreign policy and re-unite its fractured diplomatic service. League membership, which had looked so close in January, was no longer an option. Through 1922, Provisional Government cabinet minutes show the main concerns of the Government were the setting up of the institutions of state, the development of the Free State constitution and the progress of the civil war.

In June 1922 Gavan Duffy prepared a memorandum on the foreign policy objectives of the state entitled 'The position of Ireland's 'foreign affairs' at date of General Election, 1922'.[17] The memorandum proposed Geneva as a key Irish office abroad and made clear that admission to the League would be complete by September 1922. Gavan Duffy took for granted that the Free

14 NA, DE 2/449, 5 April 1922.
15 NA, D.F/A, Miscellaneous papers, MacWhite to Gavan Duffy, May 1922 report. Identity of friend unknown.
16 Ibid., MacWhite to Gavan Duffy, 1 June 1922.
17 UCDA, LAI /H/ 202.

State was eligible for admission to the League. His major concern was that the Assembly was 'the best opportunity to seize for our first appearance at a great international conference'. In a second memorandum on League policy of 22 July 1922, Gavan Duffy argued that as the Treaty was already ratified and contained the essence of the unratifed constitution the Free State fulfilled the League's admission requirements.[18] In fact, 'except in the unlikely event of an objection being raised by England, no opposition whatever to our admission is to be anticipated by the Assembly'. It did not occur to Gavan Duffy that there might be objections from other quarters, such as the League Secretariat. The situation had advanced down a blind alley. Gavan Duffy possessed little knowledge of the legal and political pre-requisites to mount an application for admission to the League.

League policy halted: July 1922–March 1923

Gavan Duffy resigned in late July 1922 due to internal tensions in the Government over the civil war. On 30 August 1922, Desmond FitzGerald replaced Gavan Duffy as Minister for External Affairs.[19] On 6 December 1922 FitzGerald became Minister for External Affairs in the first Executive Council. FitzGerald masterminded Ireland's eventual admission to the League, but his wider importance lies in his building up and safeguarding the Department of External Affairs. He prevented its assimilation into the Department of the President as occurred in other Dominions. As Minister he provided a bridge between the Sinn Féin Publicity Department and the Free State Department of External Affairs. Under FitzGerald the Free State took its first steps away from a propaganda-based foreign policy, to considering foreign policy as a means to safeguard national interests. During his term of office the state became aware of its position in the wider world. Under his guidance, Free State foreign policy widened from its initial concerns with the Treaty and British influence, to the development of Ireland's position within Europe and the League.

In mid-August 1922 MacWhite sent an important memorandum to Joseph Walshe as a primer for FitzGerald.[20] With Gavan Duffy's June memorandum it provided the backbone of FitzGerald's information on the League. MacWhite's drive is evident: 'immediate admission to membership of the League places in our hands trump cards the utility of which will be destroyed by delay.' The memorandum overwhelms its reader with the necessity and urgency of imme-

18 UCDA, P4/860.
19 **Desmond FitzGerald** (1889–1947): Politician (Sinn Féin, Cumann na nGaedheal, Fine Gael), journalist and philosopher. 1916 veteran; Director of Propaganda for Sinn Féin, 1919–21; Minister for External Affairs 1922–7, Minister for Defence, 1927–32. Fine Gael Senator 1938–47. Poet and dramatist, father of Garret FitzGerald.
20 UCDA, P4/860, 21 August 1922.

diate application. One of MacWhite's key points was that Ireland could help usher the disillusioned Americans into the League:

> I have been assured by the Democratic candidate for the presidency of the United States at the last election that if Ireland joins the League of Nations the admission of the United States will be but a matter of time ... Ireland is very much in favour at present times in League circles.

Such forces drove Gavan Duffy into seeking immediate admission and had overwhelmed the legal necessities of the application process. Initially FitzGerald was blinded by the hope of Gavan Duffy and the energy of MacWhite. The motivation was in part the burden of history. Ireland was a historic nation and admission to the League would re-integrate Ireland into the world community. The nationalist tradition was strongly linked into this view as the writer and biographer Patrick Sarsfield (P.S.) O'Hegarty wrote:

> our outlook and policy as members of the League would be those of a Nation with historical associations. [B]y virtue of our special history ... we can, through the League of Nations ... make the League a reality by going into it and supplying honesty and passion and decency in its councils. We can become a pivot for Europe and for America as well.[21]

Michael Cronin, Professor of Politics at University College, Dublin, considered that Ireland was a good site for the League headquarters because of Ireland's pacific tradition and its geographical position between the Old World and the New.[22] The historical necessity of Ireland's early admission to the League was clear.

P.S. O'Hegarty saw the importance of League membership in case of complications over the interpretation of the Treaty. A watch could be kept by the League on the operation of the Treaty: 'it would provide at once an arbitrary tribunal to which any dispute between Ireland and England or any disagreement over the Treaty could be referred'.[23] Such a move was considered in detail in the early 1930s by the de Valera administration during confrontations with Britain over land annuities. It was also an option considered in connection with the Boundary Commission. Gavan Duffy argued that 'the bigger our world position becomes, the more increasingly difficult it will be for England to attempt any undue interference with us'.[24] In 1922 the League was viewed by Ireland as 'insurance' against a possible British default on the terms of the Treaty.

---

21 Ibid., 15 September 1922.
22 Michael Cronin, 'The League of Nations Covenant', *Studies*, March, 1919, pp. 19–24.
23 UCDA, P4/860.
24 UCDA, LAI/H/59.

League membership would give credibility to the Free State's growing international sovereignty. Article 26 of the League Covenant asserted that membership of the League did not affect the sovereignty of members. The assumption was that a state admitted to the League was sovereign before admission. The League would thereby give a platform on which the Free State could pursue an independent foreign policy towards Great Britain and the Commonwealth. The assertion and vindication of international sovereignty, a central goal of any state's foreign policy, was the ultimate basis of Irish League policy before and immediately after admission. Sovereignty was the independence to pursue the national and international interests of the state unhindered in the international environment.

An Irish presence in the League would diminish the uncertainty caused by the civil war. It would underline the independent status of the state in the wider world and on the domestic front. This would vindicate the Treaty and bolster the support and confidence of the pro-Treaty side. Gavan Duffy felt that Ireland 'has lost heavily in prestige as a result of the violence and excesses of recent months'.[25] Contemporary events, primarily the Treaty and resultant civil war indicated that national considerations were paramount in Gavan Duffy's headlong rush towards admission.

MacWhite felt that Ireland could 'play a predominant part in international diplomacy and secure for herself an international status which would place her in the vanguard of European states'.[26] Gavan Duffy was more specific when he stated that 'it has often been said that Ireland in the League of Nations will be invaluable, because she may be expected to say plainly the things that everyone is thinking and that other powers are too cowardly to be the first to say'.[27] Gavan Duffy was perhaps a little extreme, but by the late twenties the Free State was not afraid to tell the Assembly or its various committees the faults Ireland perceived in the League system.

The force of opinion in favour of Irish League membership was so overwhelming and widely based that it led Gavan Duffy to forget legal necessities. FitzGerald was initially content to follow that line. On 1 September 1922 the Cabinet gave the go-ahead to approach the League Secretariat to seek admission. The move away from Gavan Duffy's plan began soon after and can be seen in a memorandum circulated on 15 September by P.S. O'Hegarty. Two options faced the Free State:

> (1) Membership at once. I do not think that this can be managed, or,
> (2) Application to be made now, and agreed to; membership to begin once the treaty is ratified.[28]

25 Ibid.
26 UCDA, P4/860. MacWhite to Walshe, 21 August 1922.
27 UCDA, LAI/H/59. June 1922.
28 UCDA, P24/552.

Policy had moved away from an immediate application. A letter from London from the former Assistant Under-Secretary for Ireland, Alfred Cope sealed the fate of the 1922 attempt. In an apologetic tone, he told Cosgrave that he had been told,

> that the Irish Free State when established by the enactment of their constitution is qualified for membership of the League of Nations. An application for admission prior to that time would, however, be referred by the League to the British Government, with an enquiry as to whether you came within the meaning of a fully self-governing Dominion as defined in Article 1 of the Covenant, and I am afraid the reply would have to be that when the constitution was passed you would be a fully self-governing Dominion but not until then.[29]

The letter was discussed at Cabinet and Hugh Kennedy, Legal Adviser to the Provisional Government noted some points arising from the British letter: 'have we [Provisional Government] any right to apply on behalf of the Irish Free State ... should [this] be decided by Saorstát itself when established ... Provisional Government can't bind Free State'.[30] The Free State's inability to comply with the Covenant was due to its constitutional position. That the Free State was not fully self-governing was now apparent. Gavan Duffy's reasoning was flawed and MacWhite's was just too hopeful. FitzGerald had initially been taken in but he now had the situation set out clearly before him due to Cope's letter and O'Hegarty's memorandum. He decided that admission could not be expected in 1922.

FitzGerald concluded the first application attempt in the Dáil on 18 September 1922 by countering a motion proposed by Gavan Duffy 'that it is the opinion of this Dáil that Ireland should join the League of Nations, and further that application for admission should be made forthwith'.[31] FitzGerald tabled an amendment 'that the application for admission to the League of Nations should be made as and when the Government find it advantageous'.[32] Considering the civil war, the amendment makes no reference to the legitimacy of the state and rested on the fact that the time was not yet right for admission to the League due to the state's incomplete constitutional position and League rules. The Free State had not yet reached a stage of full government:

> As soon as the constitution is passed and we have some real stable government—that is, a government whose position is absolutely clear

---

29 NA, S. 3332, 15 September 1922.
30 UCDA, P4/860, 16 September 1922.
31 *Dáil deb*: 1, 388; 18 September 1922.
32 Ibid.

and whose existence does not depend on the completing of an arrangement which is only half completed, then I think, it will be possible for us to make application for admission to the League of Nations.[33]

Kevin O'Higgins seconded FitzGerald's amendment, 'I have the feeling that this step is not one which should be undertaken by a Provisional Government or a Provisional Parliament'.[34] Those supporting Gavan Duffy said the Government were giving in to the British. The Government maintained that the time was not right to apply. FitzGerald starkly told Gavan Duffy where to find the Government's reason not to apply: 'I refer you to the constitution of the League'.[35] The matter was put to a vote, and the Dáil decided to adopt Desmond FitzGerald's amendment by 44 vote to 19. The conclusion that was in retrospect so likely to occur had finally been reached. Through September 1922 FitzGerald had manoeuvred out of a potentially damaging and embarrassing misinterpretation of the Free State's international position.

There was initial disappointment in Geneva when it was realised that the Free State had postponed its application to the League. The international pressure on the Free State to apply soon faded. By the winter of 1922 the Free State could continue unhindered with its League policy along the lines of FitzGerald's amendment. The constitution of the Irish Free State came into force on 6 December 1922. The state was finally legally entitled to apply for admission to the League of Nations.

The re-launch of League policy: March–September 1923

On 20 March 1923 the Executive Council voted to implement the Dáil resolution of 18 September 1922 and re-launch the admission of Saorstát Éireann to the League of Nations. Though this was a Cabinet decision, W.T. Cosgrave's role was more 'chief' than 'chairman'.[36] A note from Cosgrave to FitzGerald indicates Cosgrave's attitude to League membership: 'this question of our entry to the League of Nations ought to be definitely decided. Unless the state of war interferes with or prejudices our application we ought apply in my opinion'.[37] Cosgrave did not take de Valera's almost dictatorial attitude towards foreign policy. His involvement shows that he exerted an influence

33 Ibid., 1, 395.
34 Ibid., 1, 396.
35 Ibid., 1, 329; 18 September 1922.
36 **W.T. Cosgrave** (1880–1965). Member of the Irish volunteers; 1916 veteran, imprisoned after Rising; MP for Kilkenny, 1918; Minister for Local Government in the first Dáil. Succeeded Collins as Chairman of the Provisional Government, August 1922; President of the Executive Council, 1922–32. Founder of Cumann na nGaedheal, 1923. Joint President of Fine Gael, 1933–5, leader, 1935–44.
37 UCDA, P80/517.

when he felt the need and otherwise delegated responsibility to his Ministers. Cosgrave's interventions in the development of Irish foreign relations were few but of great significance.

Due to its recent establishment and insufficient numbers of personnel, the Department of External Affairs did not have the experience to undertake the League application unaided. The North Eastern Boundary Bureau, which was preparing the Free State's case for the Boundary Commission, was seconded to backup the Department. Two members of the bureau, Kevin O'Sheil, Assistant Legal Adviser to the Executive Council and Bolton C. Waller, later President of the League of Nations Society of Ireland, oversaw the admission process. The meticulous approach towards the application that they followed was very different from Gavan Duffy's actions in 1922.

The Boundary Bureau was more experienced and better equipped than the embryonic Department of External Affairs. Its personnel were already dealing in League of Nations matters as they had investigated international parallels to the 'Boundary Question' undertaken by the League. The Executive Council and the Department of External Affairs were expertly and efficiently briefed on the process and the progress of the Free State's application by the Bureau. By early 1924 External Affairs had developed sufficiently to undertake League policy unaided and the role of the Boundary Bureau diminished in League policy. The Boundary Commission was looming and the Bureau had to devote all its energy to its main task.

The application was re-launched during the final stages of the civil war when the victory of the Free State's forces was almost certain. With the security of the state assured and the operation of the Treaty enhanced, the state saw its foreign policy and external relations in a more positive light than in 1922. League policy was less like a revolutionary manifesto and was more considered in terms of policy and process.

Gaining international sovereignty was still an important reason behind the application. The state defined this as the ability to develop its own foreign policy and act on its own in the international arena rather than under any coercive influence. The Free State applied to the League as a fully self-governing state and not as a Dominion. This status was implicitly accepted by many nations. Waller was very conscious of this aspect: 'membership will see a new and world-wide recognition of the status achieved by the Irish Free State, membership being in fact at the present day one of the tests of the actions of full self-government ... Ireland will cease to be a name and will become a reality in world affairs.'[38] International sovereignty could not simply be declared, it had to be recognised by other states to be said to be effective.

Northern Ireland could not join the League as it was not fully self-governing as required by Article One of the Covenant. This made the Free State the

---

38 UCDA, P4/856, 29 March 1923.

dominant international entity in the island of Ireland. It was a point not lost on Kevin O'Sheil:

> by our joining, the sub-ordinate and petty status of Northern Ireland will become even more marked than at present. It is interesting to note in connection that Sir James Craig has always been most anxious to send representatives from the Six Counties to the League of Nations.[39]

This could prove useful in the case of a dispute over the delimitation of the border being brought to the League:

> Membership of the League marks very definitely before the world the immeasurable distance between the Saorstát and Northern Ireland. The admission of the Saorstát would make all the powers evident that it is a border dispute between a state internationally recognised and a province subordinate to another state.[40]

Until the sitting of the Boundary Commission the Free State had no definite Northern policy and simply wished Northern Ireland out of existence. League membership would emphasise the Free State's pre-eminence in a partitioned Ireland. Dublin wished to make clear to the Northern Irish Prime Minister, James Craig, that his statelet stood a better chance internationally within the sphere of Irish foreign policy where it would be of greater significance than as a forgotten part of Britain's imperial concerns. Once Northern Ireland became firmly established and the Boundary Commission failed, Northern Ireland almost vanished from Free State League policy. There were some veiled references in de Valera's speeches and Sean T. O'Kelly made desultory comments but they are only significant by their scarcity. At the League there was no foreshadowing of the policy of the 'Sore Thumb' that Ireland followed in the Council of Europe in the late 1940s.

Since 1922 emphasis had increased on Ireland's role in League affairs. It suited Ireland to support League activities as it would help her achieve a good international standing. If the League 'experiment' worked, the Free State would be the beneficiary of a stable world environment. Peaceful existence was for the general benefit of all. Waller and O'Sheil felt that with her place in the Assembly, Ireland could be a small but effective presence as a voice for world peace. Francis Hackett, a journalist friend of Senator James Douglas, a close observer of the Free State's foreign policy, summed up the role that Ireland could hope to play:

39 UCDA, P7/B/289, 29 March 1923.
40 UCDA, P7/B/288, memorandum from O'Sheil, 10 February 1923.

> I am sceptical about the big 'role', but I am certain that Ireland can make a place here so big, so influential, so effective, that no other chance it has had for years ... can compare to it.[41]

The Free State had an ability to give the League 'a clearminded and outspoken delegate who is disinterested, intrepid, informed and positive'.[42]

The relationship between Ireland, the Commonwealth and the League was beginning to make an impact on Irish League policy. In 1923, the Dominions were an unknown factor in international law. Tacit arrangements existed, like the *inter se* doctrine.[43] In Bolton Waller's opinion, 'in the actual working of the League it has been found that the Dominions have taken a very independent line, have acted with frequency and insight in the debates of the Assembly and elsewhere, and have greater influence than the majority of the States'.[44] The Free State took this position as a starting point in developing the Commonwealth dimension of League policy. It would continue and develop this role because 'Ireland as a member would be able to play a part not inferior to the smaller of the European countries, and in fact superior to many of them'.[45] Using the League to advance the international autonomy of the Dominions was to be a key theme of Irish League policy to the Statute of Westminster of 1931.

Britain was eager for the success of Ireland's application as it would give the British Empire an extra vote in the League Assembly. At a Cabinet meeting on 21 April 1923 Cosgrave read out a message from Lionel Curtis, Adviser on Irish Affairs at the Colonial Office[46] that London 'wished to be informed as to what attitude on their part would be most helpful to the Free State in connection to its application to the League of Nations'.[47]

But the British view was equivocal. Paul Canning has written that 'The British Government viewed Ireland's first tentative steps on the international stage ... with mixed feelings. The Foreign Office always tended to regard the assertion of independence in foreign affairs by any of the Dominions as a nuisance and an impediment to its ability to speak for a united empire; Ireland was no exception.'[48] However, the Foreign Office view should not be taken as representing policy across the administration. Canning's quotation indicates an inter-departmental divide regarding the place of the Dominions

---

41 UCDA, P4/861, Hackett to Douglas, 1 July 1923.
42 Ibid.
43 The 'inter se' doctrine stated that agreements between Dominions or parts of the Empire, or in which Dominions were parties were not 'inter se' (between themselves) international agreements, rather they were internal Commonwealth matters.
44 UCDA, P4/856, memorandum by Waller, 23 March 1923.
45 Ibid.
46 In 1925 a separate Dominions Office was set up with the accompanying post of Secretary of State for Dominion Affairs.
47 NA, Cabinet Minutes, G 2/2 (C 1/89), 21 April 1923.
48 Paul Canning, *British policy towards Ireland. 1921–1941* (Oxford, 1985), p. 95.

From Application to Admission 31

in British foreign policy. Lionel Curtis, although more pro-Free State than many of his colleagues, felt that all the Dominions were essential to the development of Britain as a world power. He was aware of the Foreign Office's attitude and highly critical of it. He felt that they were, 'prone to think that if the Dominions are left to go their own way they will soon learn their own impotence and be content to run like good dogs after the British coach.'[49] But perhaps sensing Britain's weaker position in the world post 1919, and without the supremacist views of the Foreign Office he gave more space to the Dominions need for independence, or at least co-equality:

> But the truth is that we need their driving power. We want them pulling willingly in team, not running obediently behind it. A false step at this juncture may stereotype a tendency that later will be impossible to correct.

Britain considered that the Free State would gain entry as a Dominion and not an independent state. Lionel Curtis felt that discretion was important; that, 'His Majesty's Government should abstain from offering any opinion on the subject, even when consulted indirectly, but make it clear that if the application is made it will be supported by the British representative on the Council of the League of Nations'.[50] Britain was in reality eager to have as little as possible to do with the Free State's admission. They did not want to give the impression that they were involving themselves in the Free State's external affairs. The question of new admissions to the League was one for the Assembly to decide, not for the British Government. With her progressive view on the development of Dominion status and her independent views on the position of small states in the League, Ireland was often to find herself at loggerheads with Britain at the League. Britain was deluding herself if it was really felt that Ireland would jump in line behind Great Britain as part of a united empire front at the League.

The letter of application was sent by FitzGerald on 17 April 1923.[51] MacWhite used the Geneva press corps to publicise the Free State's application. This did not meet with approval from FitzGerald or Walshe who were worried about unsympathetic foreign press reports on the civil war. MacWhite wrote to FitzGerald about the excited reaction to the arrival of the application letter in Geneva:

> To say it was welcomed would scarcely describe its reception for it was considered as the most important application that has been made since

---

49 PRO, CO 739/4/49361, Curtis to Devonshire, 5 September, 1923.
50 PRO, CO 739/4 Curtis to Secretary of State, 28 March, 1923.
51 See appendix 2.

the formulation of the League and moreso even, than if it came from Germany or Russia.[52]

The Seanad's involvement and the Guarantee Bill

The application process continued calmly through March and April 1923. The most controversial moment came in the Seanad in April when it was argued that the Executive Council had no right to apply for League membership without consulting both houses of the Oireachtas. The motion of September 1922 had only been passed by the Dáil. This action created a precedent in Irish foreign affairs by criticising the foreign policy formulation of the Cosgrave administration. The controversy was precipitated by a well-intentioned motion by Senator James Douglas with the desire to create 'public interest in the League and in the question as to whether Ireland should become a member or not'.[53] Douglas accepted that the Executive Council was entitled to apply on behalf of the Free State if and when the time suited it under the Dáil resolution of 18 September 1922. The earl of Wicklow declared that the method of application was flawed as it had been taken without any reference to the Seanad. Accordingly Wicklow moved a motion that 'the Seanad without expressing an opinion on the motion of Senator Douglas desires to record its conviction that the Government should take no steps to commit Saorstát Éireann to membership of the League of Nations without the sanction of the Oireachtas'.[54] Senator Douglas replied that matters of this type are normal matters of Executive concern in any state and anyway the matter had already come before the Dáil. Senator McLysaght caught the error in Wicklow's argument regarding the Seanad's part in the matter: 'we were not in existence then'.[55] There was no way that the Provisional Government could have taken the matter before the Seanad as it only came in to existence on the coming into operation of the Constitution. Despite the truth in this, Wicklow's motion was passed by sixteen votes to ten.

The episode was part of a power struggle between the Dáil and Seanad over the equality of the two houses. The Seanad felt that it had a right to intervene in this matter and was flexing its muscles. The Dáil considered that the Seanad had no right to intervene as it was an unrepresentative body. Those who spoke on the matter in the Seanad were generally ex-Unionists. They were interested in the League because membership would have implications for Irish sovereignty and Commonwealth membership. But it was their concern at the implied diminution of their status by the Dáil that angered

---

52 NA, BE, Box 6, 20 April 1923.
53 *Seanad deb*: 1, 590; 21 March 1923.
54 Ibid., 1, 980; 19 April 1923.
55 Ibid., 1, 984; 19 April 1923.

them. Wicklow's motion was a direct challenge to the foreign policy formulation of Cumann na nGaedheal.

Concerned that the result of his well intentioned debate might endanger the Government's position, Senator Douglas wrote to the Attorney General, Hugh Kennedy, on 20 April 1923. Douglas felt that 'the hasty and unexpected vote in the Seanad yesterday seems to raise a constitutional question between the Executive Council and the Seanad ... this resolution does not disprove the question that application for League of Nations membership is a matter of Executive Council action but it claims that the Government must consult the Seanad before taking important Executive action'.[56] This appears as an innocuous claim, but in the context of the Dáil–Seanad controversy over accountability it could 'snowball' if it became accepted as a precedent. It also made Cumann na nGaedheal look distinctly shaky in the penultimate phase of the civil war when its assertion of authority across the board was paramount.

The state's foundation was the result of a split over foreign policy in January 1922 and so the Attorney General was quick to dampen down any discontent. Kennedy dealt with the matter on three levels. Firstly he cleared the cause:

> the position you will see is rather curious. Before the passing of the Constitution, while we still had only one House of Parliament, a resolution was passed instructing the Executive Council to apply for admission to the League of Nations as soon as the Minister would think it practicable ... the papers for application were prepared, waiting for the appropriate moment and were eventually despatched. In these circumstances the Senate is certainly unfortunate.[57]

Wicklow had upset the application process but the Attorney General felt the Earl had a point, 'the application for admission is strictly an Executive act, and of course the Executive is responsible to the Parliament for its actions'. Kennedy decided that the best way out was to make room for the Seanad in the application process:

> the Seanad will have a more effective opportunity of discussing the matter, for one of the regulations of membership of the League of Nations is the giving of effective guarantees as regards international obligations ... these guarantees and undertakings will have to come before Parliament, in the shape of a bill, and therefore both Houses will have the fullest opportunity of discussing the whole matter.

56 UCDA, P4/852.
57 Ibid., Kennedy to Douglas, 23 April 1923.

The Attorney General had acted even-handedly. The dispute was defused by the League of Nations (Guarantee) Bill.

The application process required that the letter of application was backed up by documentary evidence that showed Ireland's conformity with the League Covenant. MacWhite suggested that the following documents be sent to uphold the application:

1 The Anglo-Irish Treaty (1921).
2 Letter from Lloyd George to Arthur Griffith dated 13 December 1921.
3 The act of the Dáil approving the Treaty 7 January 1922.
4 The Act of the British Parliament approving the treaty.
5 A copy of the Irish Free State Constitution.
6 Acts of Parliament enacting it.
7 A Proclamation of King George V with regard to the Irish Free State
8 FitzGerald's letter of application to the League.

In none of these documents was any watertight guarantee given covering Article One paragraph two of the Covenant, though possibly Article Eight of the Anglo-Irish Treaty or Article 49 of the Constitution were sufficient. These doubts and the problematic objection to application by the Seanad were resolved through the drafting of the League of Nations (Guarantee) Bill. The Irish application would be made watertight and the Senate would be pacified and get its say with this bill.

Waller and MacWhite brought the documents together as a stylishly propagandistic pamphlet: 'the Irish part should be in Gaelic type as otherwise it has no significance to foreigners'.[58] The opportunity of bringing the Irish Free State to the attention of the world through an otherwise mundane official action was not lost. It was a hallmark of MacWhite's method. He further suggested that 'a copy should be sent now by you (FitzGerald) to the Foreign Ministers of every country in the world, say about seventy, then to each delegate of the Assembly and the Representatives of the Press should get a copy, for this purpose about seventy will be required.'

In late June 1923 Joseph Walshe wrote to Arthur V. Matheson, the Parliamentary Draftsman to 'draft a short bill ... empowering the Government to give effective guarantees of its intention to preserve its international obligations and to accept such regulations as may be prescribed by the League'.[59] Hugh Kennedy wrote to Matheson as it occurred to him that 'if Parliament had not sanctioned the giving, by the Executive Council, of such guarantees and undertakings, anybody not well disposed to our admission to the League

---

58 UCDA, P4/858, MacWhite to FitzGerald, 12 July 1923.
59 UCDA, P4/859, 23 June 1923.

might raise it as an objection and cause the postponement of our admission for another year. I think therefore such a bill is required.'[60] The purpose of the Bill was to secure beyond doubt the Free State's application. With the recent domestic developments in mind, Kennedy added that the bill 'will enable each House of the Oireachtas by its vote on the bill to give its approval to the action of the Executive in applying for admission. The Senate has already shown some jealousy in the matter'.

The bill was to be short and to the point.

> PART ONE: It shall be lawful for the Executive Council of Saorstát Éireann, either as a condition precedent to the admission of Saorstát Éireann to the League of Nations or at any time after such admission, to give the League, in the name and on behalf of Saorstát Éireann, such guarantees as shall be thought proper by the Executive Council and be acceptable to the League, of the sincere intention of Saorstát Éireann to observe its international obligations
>
> PART TWO: It shall be lawful for the Executive Council of Saorstát Éireann; either as a condition precedent to the admission of Saorstát Éireann to the League of Nations or at any time after such admission, to accept in the name and on behalf of Saorstát Éireann, such regulations as are, or subject to ratification by the Oireachtas hereafter may be prescribed by the League of Nations in regard to its Military, Naval Air forces and Armaments.[61]

That Government could pass the Act would show domestic and foreign observers that the Government of the Irish Free State was in complete control of the state after the destabilising influence of the civil war. Control by the Executive Council of League affairs was established by the Act. It codified Cumann na nGaedheal's style of foreign policy and created a precedent as it put League affairs, and by extension foreign affairs, firmly under the control of the Executive Council.

The Act made clear that the Free State would comply with League demands for support of its policies. Although there were factors such as Article 49 of the constitution and the defence Articles of the Treaty that also dealt with the state's external defence, part one of the Act made the Free State liable to impose economic and even military sanctions in the name of the League and it was with the Executive Council that this power lay. Such factors would call into question the degree of actual neutrality in 1920s Irish foreign policy. The second half of the Act dealt exclusively with the armed forces of the Free State. Due to their increase in size during the civil war their

---

60 Ibid., 23 April 1923.
61 Public Statutes of the Oireachtas (1923) p. 1207, League of Nations (Guarantee) Act, 1923. [No. 41].

size led to concern from the League Secretariat that the Free State was over-armed. FitzGerald had informed Drummond that this level of armament was only short term:

> The members of the Permanent Advisory Commission will make allowances for the fact that the Free State Government has been compelled to raise a voluntary army of some 49,000 men to defend the State during a period of internal troubles. Happily these troubles are now over, and the soldiers are returning to civilian life as quickly as the labour force can absorb them. The Government is determined to reduce the army to the smallest force capable of fulfilling any requirements as soon as all danger to the state has been permanently removed.[62]

This was acceptable to the League and the Preparatory Commission which dealt with military matters found no reason to defer the state's membership on the grounds of its armed forces. The Guarantee Act codified the position of the Free State's armed forces in the eyes of the League.

FitzGerald outlined the Government's League policy when he introduced the Guarantee Bill in the Senate, 'the chief point is that Ireland as a free country, as a European country, takes her place with other countries in considering the interests of all of us'.[63] The debate was characterised by the normal discussion of the pros and cons of League membership and Ireland's place in the organisation but the Bill passed its stages with ease.

Irish journalists paid little attention to the application except where it infringed on Anglo-Irish relations. They continued to see Irish League policy in this narrow light through-out the twenties and thirties. The more cosmopolitan European press showed more interest in Ireland's admission to the League. In a letter to Cosgrave, Edward J. Phelan, indicated that, 'interest continues to be manifest in various quarters on the continent on the participation of the Free State in the Assembly'.[64] Phelan, an Irish national, was Chief of the Diplomatic Division of the International Labour Organisation. He was the eminence grise of Free State League policy. Primarily an international civil servant, he had a 'special relationship' with the Irish Permanent Representative to the League. Phelan appeared on the scene whenever the Free State was at any crucial juncture in its League policy, offering advice and help from the international and League viewpoints. The Department of External Affairs was always fully supportive of this relationship.

62 LNOJ, November 1923, p. 1479, 25 July 1923.
63 *Seanad deb*: 1, 1467–9; 27 July 1923.
64 NA, S. 5685, 24 July 1923. **Edward Phelan** (1888–1967) International civil servant. Civil servant at Board of Trade, National Health Insurance Commission. Ministry of Labour (1917), member of British delegation to Paris Peace Conference (1919), Chief of Diplomatic Division, ILO, 1920–38, Deputy Director General, ILO (1938–41). Director, ILO (1941–6), Director General, ILO (1946–8).

From Application to Admission 37

The Paris paper *L'Oeuvre*, commented that: 'Ireland is about to become an international power'.⁶⁵ It said that,

> Ireland is about to make her entry into the League of Nations. The next Assembly (which will be held in September) will admit her with all the respect due to her long martyrdom. Not only will Ireland be acclaimed; she will exercise influence. she will bring with her the prestige of a glorious past. It has been said of England that the Dominions, on entering the League, had followed Britain's footsteps like so many faithful vassals. Who will dare say so of Ireland!

The Irish were anticipated at the League with keen interest and expectation.

Final preparations

On 28 August 1923, the delegation to the Assembly was appointed by the Executive Council to 'negotiate the admission of the Irish Free State to the League of Nations and to represent the Country after admission'.⁶⁶ This was an important use of phrase. 'To negotiate' implies full international status and unimpeded international sovereignty, it was a very deliberate inclusion. The delegation consisted of:

> William Cosgrave: President of the Executive Council. First Delegate.
> Desmond FitzGerald: Minister for External Affairs. Delegate.
> Eoin Mac Neill: Minister for Education. Delegate.⁶⁷
> Hugh Kennedy: Attorney General. Delegate.
> Marquis MacSwiney of Mashonaglass: Member of the Royal Irish Academy. Delegate.
> Ormonde Grattan Esmonde: T.D. Delegate.
> Kevin O'Sheil: Substitute Delegate.
> Michael MacWhite: Secretary General.⁶⁸

---

65 *L'Oeuvre*, 6 July 1923 (translation), a paper Phelan also felt gave a good 'pan-European' view (he had written to Senator Douglas previously stating that the paper gave 'a fair balance of the general continental attitude)'
66 NA, Cabinet Minutes, G 2/12, (C 1/196), 28 August 1923.
67 **Eoin MacNeill** (1867–1945). Scholar and Politician (Sinn Féin and Cumann na nGaedheal). Founder of the Gaelic League in 1893, Professor of Early Medieval and Irish History (UCD) 1908, founder member of Irish Volunteers 1913 Attempted to halt 1916 Rising by countermanding orders issued by Pearse. Held Finance and Industries portfolios in the peroid 1919–21 Dáil governments. Minister for Education 1922–5. Free State representative on Boundary Commission 1924–5.
68 UCDA, P24/202.

The delegates insisted on using the Irish versions of their names at Geneva. This was sensible as a move to disassociate themselves from the British delegates but it created other problems. The Hungarian cartoonist Emery Kelen found the names a mouthful when he visited the delegation in September 1923 to sketch their portraits:

> The men of Erin came first to the League in an altogether unneighbourly spirit, bearing unreadable, unthinkable druidic names. My sketch-book was filled up with such anagrams as Marquis MacSuibhne Magh-Seanaghlas, and Aodh O. Cinnedigh. In later years, having proved to the whole world that the Irish can't spell, they dropped this habit so prejudicial to the brotherhood of man, and such names boiled down to Marquis MacSwiney of Mashonaglas and plain Hugh Kennedy.[69]

Joseph Walshe drew up a stringent timetable for the delegation. It was to be followed on all occasions because 'failure to do so will not only upset the arrangements made by foreign governments for their receptions, but will produce a very bad initial impression detrimental to our respect'.[70] In a document entitled 'Advice to Delegates' Walshe continued his schooling of the delegates: 'The Delegates are however respectfully urged to adapt themselves to cosmopolitan usages in all matters of dress, tenure and general decorum. French writers on the manner of Diplomatists insist on the necessity above all things of avoiding singularities and idiosyncrasies and of conforming in apparently trivial things to accepted customs and conventions'.[71] Walshe made clear that the Free State was to play a part at variance with the role expected of the Dominions at the League:

> Delegates will hold council amongst themselves about their attitude towards the other nations of the Commonwealth. It is the opinion of this Ministry that while relations with these latter should be most cordial, we should endeavour to associate for the most part with the Delegates of the other nations of Europe, especially the smaller nations.

The delegation left Dun Laoghaire on 29 August 1923. Eoin MacNeill chronicled the journey in letters to his wife. He noted how the delegation endured 'a very stormy passage to Holyhead. Only the Attorney General and myself, of all our party, succeeded in keeping out heads up'.[72] The delegation continued through England by train and on to France where they received a civic

69 Emery Kelen, *Peace in their time: The men who led us in and out of war 1914–1945* (London, 1964), p. 131.
70 UCDA, P4/869, 25 August 1923.
71 Ibid.
72 UCDA, LAI /H/ 215, 6 September 1923.

reception at Calais. They continued to Paris and to another reception. This was quite hectic according to Desmond FitzGerald: 'no time for anything in Paris, so many of us, always someone lost.'[73] On leaving Paris the delegation took the train to Culoz, north-east of Lyons. Here the Delegation was to split temporarily as the Presidential party left to attend celebrations in Bobbio in honour of the Irish missionary St. Columban. This left Kevin O'Sheil, Diarmuid O'Hegarty and Ormonde Grattan Esmonde as a depleted advance party. They arrived at Geneva on 31 August. The Presidential delegation arrived on 4 September.

Eoin MacNeill was ambivalent about the League on first impressions, though he recognised the value of the institution. On 7 September he wrote to his wife,

> I am still doubtful whether the League counts for much in the regulation of international troubles. The Italian–Greek crisis will help to show. But certainly it is a great institution for bringing people of various nations together and making them realise that the world is one place'.[74]

The complete delegation of eight was to be in Geneva until 12–13 September when Cosgrave accompanied by FitzGerald, Kennedy and Esmonde returned to Dublin. MacNeill then became Chief Delegate with O'Sheil, MacSwiney and MacWhite comprising a streamlined delegation who remained in Geneva until the close of the Assembly. Cosgrave was eager to get back to Dublin. The results of the August general election were coming through and placed a great strain on him and his health was suffering. Curtis felt that Cosgrave 'might crack at any moment, a change of leadership at this moment would ... be most disconcerting.'[75]

The Council received the Irish application from the Secretariat at its session on 31 August and referred it to the relevant committees. The Sixth Committee reported on 6 September 1923 and unanimously recommended that the Assembly should admit the Irish Free State to the League of Nations. The Permanent Advisory Committee followed declaring that the military, naval and air forces of the Irish Free State constituted no barrier to the admission of the Irish Free State to the League of Nations. Before they did so, FitzGerald and MacWhite had to appear before the committee to give another account of the state's armed forces. This matter was the only recurring problem that the Free State had to face in its admission to the League. Their statement was recorded in the League of Nations Official Journal:

> The demobilisation of the Army in Ireland has continued. In fact, Parliament has only passed a temporary Act to enable the army to

---

73 UCDA, P80/1404.
74 UCDA, LAI/G/216.
75 PRO, CO 739/4/49361 Curtis to Devonshire, 5–10 September 1923.

carry on for the period necessary to deal with the internal disturbances which have existed in the country[76]

With this minor obstacle cleared, the delegates had only to await Ireland's admission.

Admission

On Monday 10 September 1923 at 11am the fourth plenary meeting of the Fourth Assembly met to discuss the admission of the Irish Free State. The Vice-President of the Assembly, accompanied by the Rapporteur of the Sixth Committee, Mr Meierovics, recommended the admission of the Irish Free State to the League of Nations. A vote was taken and the Free State was duly unanimously elected. Cosgrave, MacNeill and FitzGerald then took their places in the Assembly Hall. According to MacWhite's report, there was 'an extraordinary outburst of applause from all parts of the Hall that did not subside until the Irish Delegates had taken their seats'.[77] The Free State was now a recognised international state, albeit a Dominion, but there were no codified rules as to what a Dominion was. Her international status was assured, if not fully understood. The Free State had received the international recognition that had been the goal of Irish foreign policy since 1918.

Cosgrave then addressed the meeting, beginning in Irish, or what the correspondent of the 'die-hard' conservative *Morning Post* thought at first was 'the French of Dublin'.[78] The correspondent then gave a view of the watching Assembly:

> during this proceeding the Assembly sat silent and solemn. It was evidently vastly impressed by the proof that just as Albania had an alphabet, so Ireland has a language. Mr Cosgrave then lapsed into common English.

Cosgrave's speech wound through Irish history: 'our ancient and historical Nation, after the lapse of many centuries and after many vicissitudes and misfortunes resumes as a free and securely established State her rightful place in the councils of her sister-nations of the world.'[79] As Eoin MacNeill, the speechwriter, had spent the previous days in Bobbio, Ireland's part in the preservation of Europe during the 'dark ages' was venerated:

---

76 LNOJ, November 1923, p. 1479.
77 NA, D.F/A 26/102.
78 *Morning Post*, 11 September 1923.
79 UCDA, P4/866.

Gentlemen, you are aware of the part that Ireland played in the early centuries of the present era on this continent. During the dark years that elapsed between the 7th and the 12th centuries ... men of our blood, trained in our Irish schools, kept alive the light of scholarship and culture and, at a very critical period, played a great part in the saving of modern civilisation.

The Free State was present in the modern era also, 'as one of the great mother countries of the world', a country possessing 'an Empire of the spirit ... very much in accord with the ideals which created the League of Nations and which we sincerely trust will always be its most powerful incentives, the ideals of liberty and peace'.

After praising the ideals behind the League, Cosgrave began a theme that was to pervade Ireland's membership of the League, the theme of 'Critical Support': 'we cannot say that we are satisfied with all its transactions. By some of its actions we have been profoundly impressed but, whether it was due to a too sanguine confidence in the beginning or a lack of knowledge of the entire facts we have on occasions been profoundly disappointed'. This was a direct reference to the Greco-Italian dispute that was to dog the 1923 Assembly. It was a theme that defined League policy through the 1920s and 1930s. The Irish would always support the League, but if there were faults in the League's operation they were the first to say so.

In conclusion Cosgrave became more hopeful, 'we realise that no human organisation can be perfect, and Ireland comes amongst you as an independent Nation, and as a co-equal member of the Community of Nations known as the British Commonwealth, resolved to play her part in making much of this great institution for peace as complete and efficient as possible.' On the conclusion of his speech, Cosgrave returned to his seat amid thunderous applause. With the state's successful admission to the League the delegation had fulfilled the state's initial League policy objective. Ireland had joined the League, as Cosgrave made clear, as an independent nation, and only secondly, as a member of the Commonwealth. There was much international expectation about the direction Irish League policy would follow; would it be directed against Britain, directed towards the Commonwealth or would the Free State side with the small European states that were members of the League?

Conclusion

Admission to the League of Nations was normally a mechanical procedure, painlessly carried out by the applicant state's diplomats. It was not so for Ireland. The change in Ireland's international status from colony to Dominion after the 1921 Treaty made the admission of the Irish Free State into the League a rite of passage into the international community. Admission was a vindication of Irish claims for national self-determination. It showed that the Anglo-Irish Treaty of December 1921 was flexible in its definition of Ireland's international status.

Underlying the application process is the theme of development and maturity in the Irish foreign service. From the rag-tag of the Sinn Féin diplomatic service, despite its near destruction during the civil war, there developed a small but professional diplomatic corps. The ideology of the Free State's foreign service developed dramatically during this period. The application to the League shows these ideas develop from vague revolutionary generalisations to realistic policies based on concrete domestic and international principles.

The process of Ireland's admission to the League is a microcosm of the early days of the state itself. The revolutionary theories of 1916 to 1921, the overwhelming influence behind the 1922 admission attempt was developed to provide an ideological basis to foreign policy based around Ireland's past and future position in the world order. The burden of history and the desire for recognition that empowered the 1922 attempt gave way to a reasoned, mature, and organised policy in 1923. Where the 1922 attempt was fuelled by revolutionary zeal and the certainty that Ireland deserved her rightful place amongst the nations, the 1923 admission procedure was based on the future development of Ireland's limited role in the League. The way had been sketched out by Cosgrave; the safeguarding of national policies and the development of international interests would be the key concerns of Irish League policy.

The care surrounding the 1923 attempt shows that the Cumann na nGaedheal Government viewed the League as an important addition to the state's foreign policy It would be of use to the state, firstly in its desire to prove its fledgling status against Britain and within the Commonwealth and as the inter-war years progressed, Irish Governments saw the state's international relations outside the traditional confines of Anglo-Irish relations and as part of a patchwork of European states. Perhaps it is best to leave the last word to Michael MacWhite:

> The unanimous admission of the Irish Free State to membership of the League of Nations has been considered by many keen observers to be the most important, as it certainly was the most popular, event of the Fourth Assembly. By this act, Ireland entered into a Treaty with 53 other members of the League, by virtue of which her independence is guaranteed against any possible interference from outside her own shores. In addition she has entered into the domain of international affairs and definitely broken down the isolation wall which caused her to be known on the Continent as an 'island behind an island'. Henceforward, she is a part of the European comity.[80]

80 NA, D.F/A 26/102.

CHAPTER 2

Learning the Ropes, Tying up Loose Threads

Irish involvement in the League to 1926 did not live up to the internationalist tones of Cosgrave's address to the 1923 Assembly or international expectations surrounding the admission of a supposedly activist new member. Ireland's League profile faded noticeably as, with the exception of one short speech by FitzGerald in 1924, no Irish delegate addressed the Assembly until September 1926. The fledgling Irish foreign service had its resources stretched trying to stay in existence. League policy, if it could be called such, was almost solely up to Michael MacWhite who was still learning how to operate within the League system. Irish policy at the League centred around the continued protection of Ireland's fledgling international sovereignty and the registration of the Anglo-Irish Treaty with the League as an international document.

The 1923 Assembly

The Irish were active at the 1923 Assembly as eager and popular newcomers. The delegates made themselves known by short speeches at the six Committees of the Assembly. They socialised widely in the cosmopolitan atmosphere of Geneva. Rumours that anti-Treaty elements would stage a protest at the Free State's admission never materialised. Neither did the expected ill feelings from the British delegation. Their report referred to the Irish admission as a normal event.[1] Free State sovereignty and status were accepted, if not wholly understood. Eoin Mac Neill wrote to his wife: 'I would like you to understand that every representative here regards our entry to the League as an international recognition that Ireland is a sovereign independent state. Quite a number of them speak of the Irish Republic and write to us as its delegates'.[2] With Ireland accepted as an entity within the League, the Irish delegates turned their attention to the controversies at the Assembly.

1 CMD 2015, League of Nations, Fourth Assembly Report of the British Delegation, Paragraph 133, p.34.
2 UCDA, LAI /G/ 217, 14 September 1923.

43

The Corfu incident

The great debate at the Fourth Assembly was the Italo-Greek crisis over the Greek island of Corfu that was triggered in August 1923 when a group of Italian officials were shot dead on the Greco-Albanian border whilst determining the frontiers of Albania. Mussolini blamed the Greek Government and demanded an apology and compensation. He subsequently shelled and invaded Corfu. The matter went to the League Council who passed it to the Conference of Ambassadors. In the end the Greek authorities had to pay compensation to Italy.

This was the first time that the Irish had to face an international crisis at the League. Lionel Curtis felt that it had a salutary effect on them, 'Kevin O'Sheil remarked to me that when one gets up against a crisis like the Greco-Italian question the abstract question of Irish sovereignty begins to loom rather small'.[3] The Irish delegation's report on the Assembly referred to the Corfu dispute as 'the first interference of Ireland in the Assembly'.[4] It highlighted Irish concern that the League work effectively to protect its members. It was the first of many attacks by the Free State on those who glossed over the League's failings. The Irish delegates felt that the League had shirked its responsibility by failing to act against Italy and passing the matter over to the Great Powers. The Corfu incident brought the delegation to the conclusion that, 'the Great Powers certainly cannot be said to control the League, although they naturally possess a considerable degree of influence in its Councils'.[5]

The Corfu crisis brought into question the position of small states within the League. Irish diplomats sought to make the League an equal and effective meeting place for all states. They argued that small states should be able to make their interests clearly heard against those of the powers. The Irish felt that the 'Assembly was remarkable for the activity of the Little Nations and the strong tendency amongst them to assert themselves on the big important issues ... [this] ... manifested itself very strongly during the debates on the Italo-Greek episode'.[6] The smaller nations had pressed for a more resolute solution of the conflict, not one that appeased Mussolini.

MacNeill spoke critically in the Assembly on the Corfu crisis. He was concerned that the Covenant was not followed and that there was not 're-course in the first instance to the means of settlement which the League can

---

3 PRO, CO 739/4/49361 10 September 1923.
4 UCDA. P4/202, Official Delegation Report p. 16.
5 UCDA, P24/202.
6 Ibid.
7 LONJ, Special Supplement No. 13 p. 137 (Geneva, 1923). All quotes from MacNeill's speech from this document.

afford'[7]. MacNeill was careful to point out the implications of the incident for the development of the League without apportioning blame to either party:

> The chief anxiety in the minds of the participants of this Assembly has been, not lest a particular set of events should result in a particular rupture of the peace, not that a solution might not be found for a particular difficulty, but that the work which we all had put our hands to should be undone, and the hopes which so many nations have placed in this great effort of goodwill to establishment of the foundations of peace, should be brought to nothing.

MacWhite considered that MacNeill's speech was in 'wide and general terms irrespective of the case under consideration' and that they, 'went further than those of any other delegate'. He concluded that, 'even the Italians were relieved by his (MacNeill) speech as, unlike the other delegates, he did not single them out as the only culprits'.[8] Yet between the lines MacNeill was telling the Italians and the powers that nothing like this crisis should again destabilise the League's pacific goal and that the League should be left to fulfil its role unhindered by outside interference.

On reflection MacNeill showed an understanding of the tricky position the Council was in when a member was the aggressor. However, he never supported its stance. He saw the League's action as 'an obvious facade—window dressing. Yet it was probably the wisest and most effective course that could have been taken in the circumstances'.[9] MacNeill 'excused the report [on Corfu] on the grounds that the League was still too immature to make full use of its formal powers'.[10] He might excuse the League for the action it had taken, but there was no forgiveness for the Corfu incident reducing the prominence given to the Free State's admission. MacNeill wrote to his wife that, 'we shall be glad if the problem is solved because ... the continuation of the aggravation over last week would have had some effect in diminishing the significance generally accredited to our accession to the League'.[11]

Cosgrave's speech on the state's admission showed the Free State's idealistic belief in the League. The Corfu crisis is evidence that there was underneath this an understanding of power politics. The Free State delegation observed this test of the League critically. MacNeill considered the Corfu incident a fiasco in which Greece was betrayed to keep a disgruntled Italy quiet. Lionel Curtis remarked that the 'small powers' were, 'in rage against Italy, and say not unnaturally, that if the League cannot bring her to book its

8 NA, D.F/A, Report by MacWhite on the Fourth Assembly.
9 UCDA, LAI /H/ 226, Report written by MacNeill. 4 October 1923.
10 Mark Tierney in *Eoin MacNeill: Scholar and Man of Action*, ed. F.X. Martin (Oxford, 1980).
11 UCDA, LAI /H/ 216, 8 September 1923.

use and interest to them is gone'.[12] The Free State report was clear that the League was powerless in the grip of the Great Power's desire to placate Italy. The Irish were not trying to be the champions of the small state as they were in the 1930s; they were reacting against the League's impotence. The episode was their first disillusionment with the grand ideals of Geneva.

The Article 393 controversy

On the close of the Assembly the members of the Free State delegation felt that they had performed well despite a few upsets and some nervousness. International sovereignty and international recognition had been achieved. The only loss to the Irish was to delegates themselves. At times *l'Espirit de Genève* was not too kind to their health: 'several of the Delegation have suffered from the changes of air and diet'.[13] The delegates carried out an unofficial analysis of their performance at Geneva in private correspondence between themselves and involving Edward Phelan, who knew the behind the scenes perspective from the I.L.O.

They agreed that 'things have gone well right up to the end of the Assembly ... it would have been difficult for a greater success to have been achieved'.[14] The successes of 1923 had to be built upon to consolidate Ireland's position and achievements. There was a feeling that these achievements would be contested by Britain. Kevin O'Sheil circulated a memorandum outlining private British reaction to Ireland's admission to the League: 'England, thoroughly alarmed at the success of our League venture will at once ... set about the task of endeavouring to bring us to boot.'[15] Britain was not prepared to stand silent while the Free State flouted the Commonwealth's supposedly united foreign policy.

The successes of the autumn were to suffer a set-back through the winter of 1923. The Colonial Office attempted to use the ratification of an amendment to Article 393 of the Treaty of Versailles to diminish Ireland's international position. The Article dealt with the make-up of the Governing Body of the International Labour Organisation. It originated from an I.L.O. conference of October 1922, a period during which the British felt that though the Irish Government had signified its intention in the Dáil of joining the League its attention was taken up by more pressing matters and so the British did not consult Dublin over the ratification of the amendment, though the other Dominions were informed. By October 1922 the Free State was a prospective League member and it did not take much foresight to see that by the time the

---

12 PRO, CO 739/4/49361, Curtis to Devonshire, 5–10 September, 1923.
13 UCDA, LAI /G/ 216, MacNeill to his wife, 7 September 1923.
14 UCDA, P4/894, Phelan to Kennedy 1 October 1923.
15 NA, S. 3332. Undated, probably September–October 1923.

amendment was due for ratification the Free State would be a League member in its own right. The Free State was made party to a group Dominion ratification behind its back. The Free State would have to redress the balance. Under the method of ratification the Free State was part of the British empire and not even a Dominion. It was a derogation of sovereignty due to the irregular circumstances arising out of the Free State's position on joining the League. The amendment made a precedent of Irish pre-membership League status as part of the United Kingdom. Britain was determined to use this to diminish the impression of independence the Free State had made at the 1923 Assembly. Matters stayed as such until the ratification was deposited at the beginning of the Fourth Assembly.

The British plan was that the deposition of the ratification would establish a precedent to re-assert Dominion and Commonwealth unity in the League. A delay occurred when the I.L.O. found a problem with the British Empire ratification. Though the Dominions had signed separately the Foreign Office countered them by a group ratification. Had the I.L.O. received one ratification or seven? Phelan was told by the Foreign Office that the ratification covered the Free State. External Affairs was told of this by Phelan, but could not act as Dublin had not been officially informed by London.

On 6 December 1923 the Colonial Secretary informed External Affairs of the intended ratification and presented the Irish with a fait accompli: 'the ratification applies to the whole Empire and this extends to the Irish Free State'.[16] The question of the Free State's ability to independently ratify Treaties was now in doubt as were the gains of the September Assembly. The Free State protested to the British that the Free State Government was 'responsible for the acts done in the name and on behalf of the Irish Free State and that a ratification of which they had no previous knowledge as in the present case could not bind the Irish Free State'.[17] The wrangling continued to no avail. The ratification was deposited and the Free State would have to take the consequences and fight back after losing round one.

The Department of External Affairs sent no response to the League or the Foreign Office about the ratification. They kept a low profile because they were uncertain how to respond. External Affairs saw the matter as final:

> there is no way of changing the past, as we are undoubtedly bound by certain conventions which we were under before the establishment of the State. The Barcelona Convention is one of these, it is just unfortunate that it is the first Convention into which the 'inter se clause' was inserted.[18]

---

16 NA, S. 4303, The duke Of Devonshire to Healy.
17 Ibid., Healy to the duke of Devonshire, 22 December 1923.
18 Ibid.

Rather than confronting the British head on with a rival precedent the Department of External Affairs preferred to play down the significance of the event and make the normal 'diplomatic' protests. The Department felt the circumstances were 'exceptional and are not likely to occur again'.[19] On 8 May 1925, Walshe instructed MacWhite to inform the I.L.O. that the Irish Free State wished to be included on the list of members who had accepted the amendment to Article 393.

This episode led the Department of External Affairs away from the creation of a League policy immediately after admission because they had to wait and see how British policy unfolded. They were dependent on short-term events and lost the impetus in developing League policy and the advantage of their active stance at the 1923 Assembly. While it may appear that the Free State was exaggerating the implications of the issue, the importance of Article 393 to the Free State authorities can be judged from the pursuance of their grievances over the ratification incident for almost two years. The registration of the Treaty as an international document between two sovereign states was an attempt to offset the impact of the Article 393 issue.

The Protocol for the Pacific Settlement of International Disputes

Under the Protocol, mutual assistance would be offered to a signatory state in the face of aggression by other signatories.[20] France and nine other states signed immediately. The British delegation side-stepped, saying that it had not the powers to sign. The British Labour administration of Ramsay MacDonald fell in November 1924 and the Conservatives returned to office. Austen Chamberlain became Foreign Secretary.[21] He would shape the uncertain future of the Geneva Protocol. Because of the uncertain political situation in Britain, months would elapse before the Free State's position on the Protocol became clear. The debate over the Protocol slowed down the development of a definite League policy because the Free State needed to know Britain's intentions for definite before Dublin could accept or reject the Protocol.

Anglo-Irish links were at their most tangible over military matters due to the Treaty. An Irish rejection of the Protocol would be pointless in the face of British acceptance as the military articles of the Anglo-Irish Treaty gave Britain naval facilities in Ireland. FitzGerald replied to a Dáil question from Major Bryan Cooper about the Protocol in a guarded fashion. The Executive Council was in agreement with the Geneva Protocol, 'but before signing they

19 Ibid., Attorney General to FitzGerald, 11 December 1924.
20 See Michael Kennedy, 'Candour and Chicanery: The Irish Free State and the Geneva Protocol, 1924–1925', *Irish Historical Studies*, No. 116, May 1995 (forthcoming) from which this section is largely drawn for a more detailed analysis.
21 Chamberlain was to hold the Foreign Affairs portfolio from 1924 to 1929.

wish to give serious consideration to each of the articles and, if necessary, to submit the Protocol for approval to the Oireachtas'.[22]

FitzGerald's 'wait and see' attitude curtailed the development of a long-term League policy. It was not appreciated by the Executive Council. On 19 February 1925, as the March 1925 League Council drew near and a British statement on the Protocol loomed, the Cabinet Secretary, Diarmuid O'Hegarty, wrote to FitzGerald that President Cosgrave and the Executive Council, 'consider it very unfortunate that we appear to be the only member of the Commonwealth who has not yet been able to reply to the British communications on the subject'.[23] Cosgrave wanted a definite response: 'the President thinks, in view of the importance of the question, and of the extent of documents which have gone through; that you should have a summary of the whole case prepared for the information of the members of the Council'.[24] FitzGerald now had strict orders to sort out the Free State's stance on the Protocol.

FitzGerald prepared a memorandum for a Cabinet meeting on 5 March 1925. The conclusion looked at the matter philosophically:

> To accept a Protocol which has no chance of universal acceptance would only increase our difficulties with Great Britain. It is obviously better to reject it for its defects than to consider it for its advantages which will never operate.[25]

An interesting perspective is contained in a note by Joe Walshe relating to the Protocol. Because of Walshe's belief that foreign policy should be secretive and because of his rather zealous nature, his comments are blunt and give away more than most because he never expected any person other than the recipient to read them. The note echoes the official memorandum quoted above:

> [W]e must either accept the Protocol with Britain or reject with her. We could not carry out an economic boycott of a state with which Britain continued her commercial intercourse, nor could we trade with a country with which a neighbour has severed all relations. These same principles apply to multilateral co-operation. Should Great Britain happen to be the aggressor state we should have no choice but to continue our ordinary relations with her no matter what obligations were imposed upon us by an international institution. Any other course would be suicide in our present lop-sided economic position.[26]

22 *Dáil deb*, 9; 869, 6 November 1924.
23 NA, S. 4040A.
24 Ibid.
25 UCDA, P24/180
26 NA, LN 95.

Walshe felt the state was limited in its actions towards the Protocol by the position of the Dominions, because no Dominion could be in a state of war with another country unless the empire as a whole was at war. These arguments led into a concerted attack on the failings of the Covenant and the French desire for certain security against a resurgent Germany: 'The Protocol is more definitely a military and economic pact and was framed chiefly by France with a view to keeping down the Central Powers.' The conclusion again related to how the Protocol affected the Free State's international position in the years 1924–5:

> [I]t has come much too early for the Saorstát which is not an independent state as far as the purposes of the Protocol are concerned. We can therefore reject it without having regard either to the motives of the framers or the advantages likely to accrue to them from it.

This is an interesting view. Politically the Free State was perceived to be internationally sovereign, its acceptance into the League of Nations acknowledged this, substance could be given to sovereignty in speeches or in actions at the League, but when it came to a matter like the Protocol the situation was clearly different. The Free State had clearly set out its position. The Protocol was to be rejected.

The ultimate position depended on Great Britain. The Free State would have to wait and see how Austen Chamberlain's speech to the Council developed the matter. Ireland did not want to appear anti-League by rejecting the Protocol and the state would let the British reject the Protocol first. The Free State's policy of rejection was not public knowledge until after Chamberlain had renounced the Protocol. Chamberlain made his speech on 12 March 1925. He vilified the Protocol on behalf of the British Government. MacWhite sat in on the Council meeting and reported the speech: 'It made a very bad impression. For the representatives of the mid-European states who were present, it felt like the pronouncement of a death sentence.'[27] The Protocol was dead. However, the Free State could not be implicated: 'Mr. Chamberlain in winding up his speech, stated that he was not in possession of the views of the Irish Free State on the question of the Protocol'.[28] MacWhite reported that 'there was a general murmur and everyone looked in my direction. The presumption was that the Saorstát Government held different views and the impact created was very favourable so far as we were concerned'.[29] In fact, the Free State was against the Protocol and would reject it. Chamberlain's actions gave the Irish a valuable propaganda victory. They appeared to support the Protocol and so kept their good League standing.

27 NA, LN 15. Report by MacWhite on the 33rd Session of the Council 16 March 1925.
28 Ibid.
29 NA, LN 95.

In the Dáil on 25 March 1925, arising from a question on general attitudes to the Geneva Protocol, FitzGerald made the Free State's stance clear. At the 1924 Assembly he argued that the delegates had accepted the principle of the Protocol, but 'they may alter their minds very considerably when they come back'.[30] As Britain had rejected the Protocol, FitzGerald revealed Ireland's response: 'we have arrived at no decision to sign or ratify, and are therefore not committed to the Protocol. As far as I am concerned I do not think that I could recommend its acceptance'.[31]

The official Free State rejection emerged during the Dáil debate on the External Affairs estimates on 13 May 1925. It formed the basis of a telegram that was sent to both the Secretary General of the League and the Secretary of State for Dominion Affairs officially confirming the Free State's rejection. The message was two-fold; general support but rejection due to specifics. The Irish Free State had,

> approached the subject with due advertance to the admirable intentions which animated the authors of that document, and with which we are in complete accord, namely, that a basis should be found which would enable differences arising between nations to be adjusted without recourse to arms, and thus remove from the sphere of international relations the menace of war.
>
> For this country—a small nation with no aspirations to territorial aggrandisement and no interests other than the social and economic welfare of our people and the maintenance of cordial intercourse with all other nations—the attractions of a scheme which has for its objective the maintenance of international peace are manifest.[32]

This was the sweet covering on the unpalatable truth. Though the Free State might 'wish to place on record that we are by no means of the opinion that the object of the framers of the Protocol is beyond the realm of achievement',[33] it felt that the machinery of the Covenant 'for dealing with disputes is somewhat unwieldy'. The kernel of the argument was that sanctions could be enforced against a smaller state, but not against a great power, and as the Geneva Protocol aimed at increasing security and disarmament through the increased use of sanctions, it was unacceptable. Extending a system that was flawed in the eyes of the Free State, was FitzGerald's first reason for rejecting the Protocol.

Siding with the 'Revisionists', FitzGerald continued: 'the expressed intention of the framers of the Protocol to exclude from the new system of pacific

---

30 *Dáil deb*, 10, 1354; 25 March 1925.
31 Ibid., 10, 1355.
32 *Dáil deb*, 10, 1417; 13 May 1925.
33 Ibid.

settlement any disputes which may arise regarding the existing territorial divisions appears to us to detract considerably from the value of the instrument'. This was conveyed in the context of the Versailles system and the resulting borders of the new European states. As this speech was also to form the basis of the rejection letter to the League, FitzGerald framed it in continental terms referring to the defeated Alliance powers who were either members or prospective members of the League:

> emphasising by implication the immutability of these frontiers and imposing upon members additional obligations, particularly by way of participating in disputes and in sanctions, is not calculated to induce them to accept the responsibilities of membership and is, therefore, likely to hinder rather than further the progress of world pacification and disarmament.

This was useful advice from an 'honest broker'. The Free State had no interest in the Protocol as its 'armed forces have been reduced to the minimum requisite for the maintenance of internal order.' When taken along with Article 49 of the Constitution it was clear that the Free State 'cannot be regarded as a material factor in the enforcement of sanctions'. These factors, leading to the actual rejection of the Protocol were 'dictated solely by our genuine desire that the League of Nations should realise the aspirations of its founders by uniting all nations in the common interest of world peace'. FitzGerald finished up by lauding the work of the League in its work for peace and especially concerning its social and humanitarian work.

FitzGerald could reject the Protocol and appear constructive, especially when taken against the British rejection. This would bolster the Free State's position as a supporter of the League. In a domestic context, it allowed FitzGerald to reject the Protocol without ever mentioning the potential regarding partition and the effect it might have regarding the military articles of the Treaty. This was astute and is reminiscent of the conclusion that it was better 'to reject the Protocol for its defects rather than to consider it for its advantages which will never operate'.

FitzGerald appears rather machiavellian in his attitude to the Protocol. The Free State had made up its mind well before Chamberlain's speech to reject the document. Yet he waited, despite Cabinet pressure, and revealed the Free State's position only after Chamberlain rejected the Protocol. As MacWhite's report showed, British rejection without the views of the Free State made Britain's loss the Free State's gain. Timing, conjecture and the use of the right phrase were the major elements of the Free State's policy regarding the Geneva Protocol.

The failure to develop policy: 1923–5

Due to the Article 393 controversy and the Geneva Protocol, policy developed with no long-term goal. From 1923 to 1926, the Free State failed to develop a co-ordinated League policy built on its achievements at the 1923 Assembly. This approach was compounded by a particularly unstable period in the Free State's domestic and external affairs. The Army Mutiny, the 1923 Imperial Conference and the opening of the Boundary Commission distracted Government attention from the League. The Department of External Affairs put much of its limited resources for League affairs into the registration of the 1921 Treaty at Geneva and so other areas of League policy suffered accordingly. Finally, the League itself was going through a period in which only a few areas on its agenda were of interest to the Free State. These factors combined to make the period following the state's admission the most disoriented in terms of League policy in the 1922–32 period.

The result was that by 1925 the delegation to the Assembly still held merely a watching brief. Irish involvement in the 1924 and 1925 Assemblies was low profile. Delegations were poorly briefed and made little impact even though such forceful personalities as Kevin O'Higgins were present. These years are a trough between the activist stance that accompanied the state's admission and the resurgence of an active interest in the League in 1926. The ad-hoc decisions the delegation took show that Ireland's natural constituency was within the League. Yet comparatively little time and attention was given by Dublin to League matters. In Geneva, MacWhite was left to his own devices. He attended conferences, built up diplomatic connections and facilitated information exchange between Geneva and Dublin. The registration of the Treaty provided the major direction to League involvement during these years and allowed the state to consolidate its entrance into the League.

The registration of the Treaty: 1923–5

The registration of the Anglo-Irish Treaty of December 1921 at the League of Nations Treaty Bureau on 11 July 1924 was more than an episode in Anglo-Irish relations. It was the culmination of a comprehensive two-year policy aimed at cementing the 1921 Treaty, the basis of the Free State, into international law. It was also aimed at raising the state's flagging stature at the League. Finally, it brought the League of Nations into the ongoing debate between the Free State, Britain and the Commonwealth over the definition of Dominion status.

Those who have written on the subject have positioned the registration within the development of Dominion status. This ignores the fact that the League and the Commonwealth were together the basis to Free State foreign policy in the 1920s. The registration had a rationale in both these dimensions.

David Harkness, in *The Restless Dominion*[34] has written the most comprehensive account of the Treaty registration to date. Due to his subject-matter, his argument is Commonwealth and Anglo-Irish oriented. Such an approach has led to the registration being interpreted as Irish Commonwealth policy undertaken through the League of Nations. This is enhanced by Harkness's emphasis on the Dublin–London correspondence of July 1924 to March 1925. It centred on the question of whether the Treaty was an international agreement covered by Article 18 of the League Covenant,[35] as the Irish maintained; or an inter-Commonwealth agreement by the *inter se* dogma, as the British maintained. The part played by the League has been played down, as have the implications for Irish League membership. The effect has been to place the registration in the Anglo-Irish interpretation of Irish foreign policy.

Since Harkness's book in 1969, Patrick Keatinge has implicitly reinforced this view in two articles. In the journal *Éire-Ireland* he argued that the development of Dominion status was 'the overriding objective pursued under the Cosgrave Government, through participation in the League of Nations and Imperial Conferences and in direct contacts with the British Government'.[36] In a prior article in *Studies* he argued that:

> the Cosgrave Government's role in the evolution of Dominion status has been examined at great length elsewhere [cf D.W. Harkness: *The Restless Dominion* MacMillan (London: 1969)] but some salient features within the League context may be mentioned here. The first bone of contention was the registration of the Anglo-Irish Treaty of 1921 ... this was only the opening shot in what became known as the 'inter se' dispute.[37]

Viewing the registration from the perspective of League policy shows that the registration had a wider rationale.

The article of the Covenant under which treaties were registered was Article 18. Its success can be seen from the League publication Ten years of international co-operation: 'by the end of May 1930, 2330 treaties or international understandings had been registered. About 300 are deposited for registration every year ... by June 1930, the Secretariat had published ... the texts of some 2160 treaties'.[38] From these statistics one can see that the registration

---

34 David Harkness, *The Restless Dominion: The Irish Free State and the British Commonwealth of Nations 1921–1931* (London, 1969). Hereafter cited as Harkness, *Restless Dominion*.
35 See appendix one.
36 Patrick Keatinge, 'The Formative Years of the Irish Diplomatic Service', *Éire-Ireland*, Volume 6, Number 3, 1971, pp. 57–71.
37 Patrick Keatinge, 'Ireland and the League of Nations' *Studies*, summer 1970, pp. 133–47.
38 League of Nations Secretariat, *Ten Years of International Co-operation* (Geneva, 1930), p. 16.

of a treaty was an important and frequent occurrence in the affairs of the League.

Why register?

The Free State's initial objective was to find out whether the Treaty could be registered and how the League and the British would react if the Treaty were registered. They put less weight on analysing why the Treaty ought to be registered. A problem in dealing with the viewpoints of contemporaries on the Treaty is that while one must assume that the implementation and safeguarding of the Treaty was foremost in their minds, this was not always stated in documents. The 'mental bond' amongst these statesmen was such that the Treaty was an all pervasive, if at times, unwritten concern. The Treaty was the basis of the state and, as such, the basis of the multi-dimensional foreign policy which the state followed.

The registration ended up in the Commonwealth arena, though this was not the explicit desire of the Department of External Affairs. The Free State attended the 1923 Imperial Conference as a newcomer and an observer. By 1924 the Free State had yet to join Canada and South Africa as 'radical Dominions'. Ireland was just realising the possibility of an active and progressive Dominion policy. Only after July 1924 was the registration pushed into the Commonwealth arena by British protests to the League that the registration of what it perceived to be an inter-Commonwealth agreement was not allowed under Article 18. The Free State had no direct reason to register the Treaty with the Commonwealth in mind. Its mind was on its League obligations and the domestic and international benefits of registration. It was not until 1926 at the earliest that the state, under the influence of Kevin O'Higgins, began to press strongly for the reform of the Commonwealth. The registration occurred too early for it to have had any explicit Commonwealth dimension.

It is likely that those involved in the registration realised its Commonwealth implications. The *inter se* controversy was never very far from the minds of those involved in Commonwealth affairs. The Free State was developing its view of the Dominions as a loose grouping of independent states and was seeking greater international autonomy. In terms of the desire to modernise the Commonwealth, one must read between the lines and look to an unstated but implied future Commonwealth dimension.

Closely related to the Free State's position in the Commonwealth was the question of sovereignty. However the registration was not concerned with the state's sovereignty within the Commonwealth, but rather sovereignty *vis-à-vis* Britain. The Treaty was to be registered so that the Free State could be shown to be an independent entity *vis-à-vis* Britain. Article 18 would implicitly establish this precedent. Bolton Waller considered the registration of the

Treaty as an enhancement of the Free State's international stature: 'the position in relation to Great Britain will be made plain, namely that the Treaty of 1921 is an international treaty between two countries internationally recognised'.[39] Registration was envisaged as a safety net for the Treaty in case the British failed to accept it as the international basis of the Free State and Anglo-Irish relations.

In a domestic context, the registration revolved around the legitimacy of the state. The Treaty split and the civil war created a position where the Cumann na nGaedheal administration used all methods to assert the legitimacy of the state created by the Treaty. After the civil war the Cosgrave administration was more determined than ever to stick to the terms of the Treaty. It became as sacrosanct to them as the ideal 'Republic' did to the anti-treaty side. The authorities would have a secure base for the foundation stone of the state if they had the Treaty registered. It would have more to back it up as the legitimate origin of the Irish state if accepted into the records of a pan-national organisation. The Treaty would be recognised throughout the world as the basis of the Free State. The registration would strengthen the position of a government that still had dissident elements to face.

Article 12 of the Treaty related to the delimitation of the north-eastern boundary between the Free State and Northern Ireland. The League was considered as an outside option if the commission failed to implement its mandate. A first step in this was to register the Treaty to create the basis on which to build an appeal to the League. The North-Eastern Boundary Bureau's part in the early period of Free State League policy made it likely that the boundary question would be interpreted in a League light. An appeal to the League of Nations was kept in reserve as a last resort: 'our idea is that in the event of a complication over the judgement of the Boundary Commission we should first take the matter before the Imperial Conference ... and in the event of no satisfaction there go to the League of Nations'.[40] It was necessary to register the Treaty with the League to avail properly of the arbitration articles of the Covenant. Article 13 covered the Free State case and as Waller noted 'it would be difficult to avoid the submitting to the League of a dispute arising out of a registered treaty, if the League or its members desired to take action'.[41] All this might however prove impossible as Article 15 forbade the League to get involved in domestic disputes. Registration would overcome this as it would show that the Treaty was an international document.

The Free State Government wanted to solve the boundary question within the context of the British Isles, but, 'even if Craig merely refused to nominate a representative, and Britain took no action, we will be given a valid reason for bringing the whole matter up before the League of Nations *or* the Impe-

39 UCDA, P4/856, Boundary Bureau memorandum on the League of Nations.
40 UCDA, P80/518, Waller memorandum on the Boundary question, 14 March 1923.
41 UCDA, P4/854, memorandum on joining the League of Nations.

rial Conference'.[42] As Kevin O'Sheil put it, 'it is obvious that the bigger the figure you make here (Geneva), so much greater will be your influence to bear on any Boundary Commission crux that may arise'.[43]

This line was not universally accepted: 'our Minister is in any case strongly of the opinion that the Boundary question cannot be regarded as having any practical relevance to the League of Nations. Reference to the League of the boundary question implies that all other means of settling this dispute with Great Britain have failed'.[44] This is all the more interesting as it is Joe Walshe giving the Minister's view. A curious point since the letter was written during a period in which Michael Hayes had caretaker responsibility for External Affairs between George Gavan Duffy's resignation and Desmond FitzGerald's appointment to the office. Walshe's argument is open to question if one remembers the League's success in the Silesian border referendum in 1921. Surely it was a precedent for the Boundary matter.

By registering the Treaty the Free State was being seen to implement its obligations under the League of Nations Guarantee Act and the Covenant. The state was giving tacit acceptance to the primacy of the burgeoning 'Geneva System' and stating her belief in this system. The small states were still an undefined entity at Geneva, but some such as the Scandinavian states, Norway in particular, stood out as independent members. Norway's approach appears to have been a guide to the Free State during the 1920s:

> countries like Norway manage to play a very prominent and creditable part in the work of the League of Nations ... If more of the small nation members of the League, discharged there functions as Norway does, the prospects for the League fulfilling the purpose for which it was established would be much brighter.[45]

This complemented the policy of 'critical support' in which the Free State, though actively supporting the League, would 'pull no punches' in criticising it, if it felt that the League had stepped out of line or adopted a policy with which the Free State disagreed. With the Treaty registered the Free State could adopt this role without hypocrisy as it could be said to have fulfilled its League obligations. However, the role took some time to get fully operational; the registration of the Treaty was a start off point.

By registration, the Free State was preparing the ground for any future disputes that might emerge involving the Free State over and above the boundary question. For example a dispute could emerge over certain provi-

42 UCDA, P24/171, memorandum by O'Sheil dated 21 April 1923. Quoted in J.J. Lee, *Ireland 1912–1985: Politics and Society* (Cambridge, 1989), p. 144.
43 UCDA, LAI /H/ 62, O'Sheil to Cosgrave, 9 August 1923.
44 NA, S 1367, Walshe to McGann, 1 August 1923.
45 UCDA, P24/157, memorandum on the League of Nations by Blythe, 20 October 1926.

sions of the Treaty like the Treaty Ports. There was the first resort to the Imperial Conference, but it was in the Free State's benefit to have an extra card up its sleeve. It could be used as a bargaining chip. If a dispute arose, for example, over the Treaty Ports, there would be more of an impulse to solve it quickly in an imperial setting rather than have the apparent disunity of the British Empire and the Commonwealth displayed before the whole world at the League. The Free State might never intend to bring a dispute before the League, but by registering, the potential was there.

Registration was a multi-purpose attempt at consolidating the Free State in the League of Nations while simultaneously sorting out some of the untidy ends left over from the creation of the state. The Treaty was registered for both League and Commonwealth reasons, not Commonwealth reasons alone as previous accounts have argued.

September 1923: The League Assembly

At the 1923 Assembly, the Irish implemented a twin-track policy on registration. Publicly they denied any move had been made (technically correct as the Executive Council had not dealt with the matter); while privately collecting information to get the Department of External Affairs acquainted with the registration process.

On 17 September MacWhite wrote to FitzGerald requesting permission to register. He made clear that the task facing him was far from a fait accompli: 'this matter should be seen to immediately so that we may be prepared for any eventuality'.[46] Storm warnings were sounding. On 19 September Eoin MacNeill wrote to Cosgrave informing him of the subterfuge and intrigue that existed due to rumours that registration was imminent. Quoted at length it gives an insight into the predicament of both the Irish and their opponents:

> [W]e have had no occasion to refer to the matter [registration] in any public way here. When it is mentioned to us in conversation we state the facts, namely that it is true that we have gone to extra trouble to provide everyone who seeks them with French versions not only of the Treaty but of all the principal documents that go to define or illustrate our position; seeing that the great majority understand such documents much better in French than English. That we for our part do not consider the similar work done by practically every delegation a matter for press telegrams, nor do we go about to collect information as to what other delegations may do in the late hours in their Hotels, and we do not desire that any reputable Irish journal would encourage this kind of thing. That the question of registering the Treaty is still

---

46 UCDA, P4/879, 17 September 1923.

one to be decided for us, even though the British press seem anxious to make a decision inevitable. That the League Covenant enables any Treaty or agreement between *members of the League* to be registered. That press opinions do not affect the facts of our status. That British Journals themselves must explain their assumption that a dispute exists between us and the British Government on the boundary clause, seeing that no such dispute has arisen, and that we have always experienced that this clause, like every other clause in the Treaty, will be fulfilled honestly and amicably on both sides.[47]

With mounting suspicion as to the Free State's intentions MacWhite wrote to Kennedy enclosing a League memorandum on the registration of Treaties and passing on the latest rumours about the Irish:

[T]he article published in the 'Times' last week regarding the registration of the Treaty and the Boundary Question was evidently inspired from official circles here and was meant to deter the Irish Government from taking any steps in the matter. It showed ... a certain amount of nervousness on the part of our friends which is easily to be understood, seeing their weakness on the matter.[48]

On 22 September, Dublin replied to MacWhite's letter. It outlined a cautious approach that was to become the basis of registration policy. MacWhite replied on 25 September that he was not in a position 'to make any authoritative statement as to the possible lines of action on the part of the League authorities following an attempt to register'.[49] MacWhite advised FitzGerald to postpone the registration until after the Assembly had closed. FitzGerald and Walshe were biding their time to select a suitable moment. They were trying to discover all the possible scenarios that could result from their action, and collect all available information on the reaction to the now theoretically possible registration.

In the Dáil on 3 October, Darrell Figgis questioned Cosgrave on the registration. The behind the scenes response of the Department of External Affairs illustrate just how jittery the authorities were about the difficult situation they had been put in by Figgis. It would mean a statement by President Cosgrave on a sensitive live issue, which had not been acknowledged publicly or voted on by the Executive Council. Figgis's question was 'to ask the President if it was the intention of the Executive Council to apply for the registration of the Irish–British treaty at Geneva in accordance with the regulations of the League'.[50] Joe Walshe was not pleased, he wrote to an unnamed

47 UCDA, P80/535, 19 September 1923.
48 UCDA, P4/886, 21 September 1923.
49 Ibid., MacWhite to FitzGerald, 25 September 1923.
50 UCDA, P4/879, 1 October 1923.

colleague, 'It is a mean question at the present moment as he [Figgis] must be fully aware of the difficulties. A direct answer must be avoided at all costs'.[51] The suggested answers were based on equivocation. Most revealing was, 'without admitting the importance of the question the subject is one which must obviously receive consideration in its due course and proper time'. Cosgrave actually replied that, 'the subject of the question is one which must obviously receive its consideration in due course and proper time'.[52] No one was going to give policy away.

The government had enough information to proceed with registration, but had not enough about the League's reaction, to give an answer to Figgis. It would also not be expedient for Anglo-Irish relations. The courses of action show that the Free State had no desire to annoy Great Britain in registering. Similarly it had no intention of running the risk of public humiliation and embarrassment at the loss of the status acquired at the 1923 Assembly by receiving a rebuke that this matter was not within the League's jurisdiction. The state would bide its time and wait until it was sure of the outcome before acting.

From the information gathered during the Assembly it was clear that the Treaty could be registered in theory under existing League guidelines. On 12 October 1923 MacWhite wrote to FitzGerald, 'there is no other course open to them [the League Secretariat] than to proceed with registration in the normal way'.[53] But beyond this the Irish were no wiser; the delegation had provided enough information for an opening move. In line with FitzGerald's desire to proceed with extreme caution, MacWhite next began to ascertain how the League would react to the treaty being offered for registration. This would give the Free State enough information to perceive the League's responding move. FitzGerald and Walshe did not want simply to be one move ahead of the League, they wanted to know they had 'game, set and match' in their favour before giving MacWhite instructions to proceed with registration.

October 1923 to January 1924: Getting the facts

The Executive Council gave the go-ahead for preparations for registration on 27 October.[54] It was considered necessary to find a precedent to which the decision to register the Treaty could be paralleled to counteract the problem of a League rejection. FitzGerald believed that Edward Phelan mentioned a suitable precedent to one of the delegates during the 1923. Phelan felt that,

51 NA, S. 3328, 3 October 1923.
52 *Dáil deb*, 5, 139, 3 October 1923.
53 NA, D.F/A, 417/105, 12 October 1923, MacWhite to FitzGerald.
54 NA, Cabinet Minutes, G2/3 (C2/4), 27 October 1923.

there are six precedents for the registration of a Treaty between two parts of the British Empire, or perhaps it would be better to say a six fold precedent. India and Great Britain have each ratified six of our labour conventions ... these conventions are all registered with the League under Article 18.[55]

These were of dubious value as precedents as they were League conventions and not treaties negotiated between two states, members of the Commonwealth and members of the League. On 13 December 1923 MacWhite wrote to FitzGerald with enough information to close the search for a precedent:

[S]trictly speaking no real precedent exists for the registration of the Treaty of 6 December 1921. I am also of the opinion that the British attitude is largely one of bluff ... it seems improbable that the British Government would intervene after a decision had formally been made to have the Treaty registered, as they desire at all costs to be able to show a united front in so far as the Commonwealth of nations is concerned. Besides if the League stretched a point or two in favour of Great Britain it would create a very bad impression especially in the United States.[56]

Thus matters stood in December 1923. It was definitely possible to register the Treaty, but in January 1924 all came to a standstill. MacWhite wrote to Desmond FitzGerald, 'I find it quite impossible to obtain any further informa-tion on the subject in League circles as, at the slightest mention of the Irish Treaty, all ears are alert and suspicions aroused and this, no matter how far removed from us the enquiry may be'.[57] Without having a precedent to the proposed registration the Irish were potentially on a weak footing. Yet with such a body of theoretical evidence based on official League documents behind their case it was beginning seem that they had nothing to fear from the League. Now it was a question of timing. Not until June 1924 was the atmosphere considered quiet enough to cautiously conclude the registration.

June–July 1924: Registration

The final move to register began with W.T. Cosgrave receiving a letter from Alfred O'Rahilly dated 16 June 1924, from Geneva. O'Rahilly was on the Irish delegation to an I.L.O. conference. He urged Cosgrave to immediately register the Treaty:

55 UCDA, P4/897, Phelan to Kennedy, 6 October 1923.
56 NA, D.F/A 417/105.
57 Ibid., 4 January 1924.

The matter is purely automatic though it might be best done when certain people have left Geneva. I quite realise that such an action may now seem rather a broad hint to Great Britain in connection with the Boundary Question but we have now surely come to the stage when such reminders are useful.[58]

This letter prompted Cosgrave to register as soon as possible. On 23 June 1924, Diarmuid O'Hegarty wrote to Joe Walshe in a note marked 'urgent' that 'the President is of the opinion that application should be made for registration and he proposes to write to Mr FitzGerald who is at present in London'.[59] Cosgrave took centre stage and took the decision on his own initiative, surprisingly, when FitzGerald was in London. Cosgrave also consulted the Attorney General, Hugh Kennedy. Kennedy replied that he was cautiously in favour of registration but urged vigilance:

If we applied and, through opposition from the British authorities or otherwise, the application was unsuccessful, I think it would have a very disastrous effect upon our whole position. For this reason, I think the application should be made only after careful enquiry and consideration.[60]

Monday 23 June was the key date for registration. Cosgrave took the decision to go ahead, Kennedy cautiously agreed; and finally Joe Walshe gave his perspective. He felt that the real difficulty was the attitude of Britain:

If they object, the machinery of the Council is at their disposal for making their objection effective and for proclaiming to the world that the Treaty is a domestic arrangement. It has always been the opinion of this department that the disadvantages following the rejection of our application would be far greater than those occurring from mere inaction. Mr MacWhite ... has been unable to find out what would there and then happen if the Treaty were presented to the registering authorities. He decided that it would be 'highly improbable' that the British would interfere after our formal application, but it is eminently a case for dealing in certainties.

Professor O'Rahilly says 'the matter is purely automatic' but he takes care to add 'it might best be done when certain people have left Geneva'; when he knows Geneva a little better he will find that it is never completely abandoned by at least 2 or 3 very capable certain people.[61]

58 NA, S. 3328.
59 Ibid.
60 Ibid., 23 June 1924.
61 Ibid., Walshe to O'Hegarty, 23 June 1924.

Walshe's memorandum marks one integral change in policy. He caught the deficiency of the policy to date when he stated that 'the real difficulty [is] the attitude of the British towards an attempt to register'. Prior to this, policy revolved around the League side. Like Kennedy, Walshe urged caution as the cost of failure in registering the Treaty would be very high to the Free State. Never before in Irish League policy had decisions been taken at such speed. Cosgrave's desire to implement the registration policy on his own initiative and with FitzGerald out of the country are two actions not in line with the accepted view of Cosgrave's character.

Walshe contacted FitzGerald and he replied with a memorandum on the possible scenarios that could occur if the British made a formal complaint against registration. FitzGerald expected the worst, that the Secretariat would respond that registration was invalid because the Treaty was a domestic Commonwealth matter. Then the Free State could appeal the matter to the Council, the Assembly and finally the Court of Justice. In any scenario FitzGerald felt that Britain could easily prevent registration:

> [T]he question therefore arises, should we proceed to register the Treaty without sounding England. In the event of its being returned to us by the Secretariat as non-registrable we should then be able to decide whether we should or should not appeal to the Council. It is to be remembered that the League is the greatest centre of gossip in Europe and that the return of the Treaty to us by the Secretariat would almost inevitably be public property. On the other hand we might sound England before taking steps for registration. I am agreeable to either course.
>
> It seems possible that although England might object in their hearts to the registration of the Treaty, they might consider it impolitic to take any action against its registration in view of the fact that she has claimed for the Dominions the right to membership of the League and the right to separate signature of Treaties, etc. ...
>
> Another possibility is that on presentation of the Treaty, the Secretariat, without deciding that it was non registrable, might inform us that there was a doubt as to whether or not it was registrable and to say that it would be preferred that it should be presented jointly by us and Great Britain.
>
> I think that in view of the explanation given above it would be well for each Minister to say if he thinks
> (1) that the Treaty should be presented for registration with the preliminaries; and
> (2) if he thinks we should approach the British beforehand.[62]

---

62 UCDA, LAI/F/304, 26 June 1924.

FitzGerald presented the situation as a gamble. It was a matter of collective responsibility, FitzGerald alone would not take the final decision. The Executive Council decided in favour of registration without first informing the British. On 28 June 'it was decided that application should be made at once to the Secretariat of the League of Nations for the registration of the Treaty.'[63]

For the next two weeks registration took on the utmost degree of secrecy. On 1 July FitzGerald wrote in a strictly confidential despatch to MacWhite that Dublin was sending two copies of the Treaty certified by the President, to be handed in to the registration office at the League of Nations for immediate registration. This was to be done quickly and unostentatiously. It was a confidential matter, there was to be no publicity:

> [I]f the League people make any questions about it refer to us immediately by code telegram if feasible. Otherwise by letter, and please keep us informed of everything relating to this matter. I am sure you will realise how important it is that these instructions be carried out literally.[64]

On 4 July MacWhite wrote to FitzGerald about his experiences with the Secretary General. Eric Drummond 'seemed to be a little surprised at first [and] said he was thankful that we had taken the necessary steps to have the Treaty registered'.[65] MacWhite insisted on secrecy, 'I hinted that so far as we were concerned we did not desire any undue publicity on the matter.'

The Treaty was registered on 11 July. The Free State had wrapped up the remaining loose thread from the state's creation and solidified her international position by fulfilling her obligations under the Covenant. MacWhite sent FitzGerald a short coded telegram 'handed documents secretary today, thanked us—take necessary steps. Only question asked do British know you register. League obliged publicity matters.'[66] It was not that simple. MacWhite followed the telegram with a letter. The League had not accepted the Free State's demand to register unquestioningly; 'it would seem that the League authorities spent three or four days discussing our demand for registration and its various phases, but, because of our membership of the League, no valid objection could be raised against the steps we have taken in the matter.'[67]

Eric Drummond wished the registration to be passed through the normal channels. The Secretariat was particularly concerned as to the exact legal nature of the Treaty in international terms. Van Hamill, Director of the Legal Section, had given it specific consideration:

63 NA, Cabinet Minutes G2/3.
64 NA, S. 3328.
65 Ibid.
66 Ibid., 11 July 1924.
67 NA, D.F/A, 417/105, MacWhite to FitzGerald, 11 July 1924.

> [A]s a matter of fact it does not seem to be a treaty between two independent Governments. From that point of view, the Irish-British treaty would be an internal act within the British Empire. The question therefore occurs whether the Secretariat, in registering the document, would not be open to the criticism of not truly and correctly applying Article 18 of the Covenant, which says that 'every treaty or international engagement entered into by any member of the League should be registered.'[68]

This seems to have been their first premise. From the immediate viewpoint, the Treaty was unsuitable for registration in the eyes of the League. What played into the hands of the Free State was the League's dependence on new precedents. Further on in his analysis quoted above, Van Hamill argued that there were a number of criticisms that could be made to refute the argument against registration. In relation to the actual document, 'the document being presented for registration by the Irish Free State, is evidently considered by that state as a treaty coming within the terms of Article 18 of the Covenant' and simply, 'the terms of the document constantly use the term "Treaty".' The lack of interpretation of the Covenant allowed even this simple argument based on the Treaty itself to refute the *inter se* doctrine. When taken along with the fact that the League's own guidelines on registration stated that registrable material 'comprises not only of every formal treaty of whatsoever character and every international convention, but also any other international engagement or act by which nations and their Governments intend to establish legal obligations between themselves and any other state or government', the Irish desire to register could not be refused. The Secretariat had no option but to comply with the terms of Article 18 and register the Treaty.

The British reaction: June 1924–March 1925

On 5 July Britain was informed *ex post facto* that the Free State intended to register the Treaty. The official British response did not materialise until 4 November 1924. In between the registration issue was dealt with in unofficial correspondence between Cosgrave and G.G. Whiskard of the Colonial Office. Whiskard had been in Dublin discussing compensation claims from the Anglo-Irish conflict of 1919–21. At an informal meeting he conveyed to Cosgrave the British view that the Treaty was unregistrable.

The Labour Government in Britain did not wish to rock the boat too much at Geneva. Prime Minister Ramsay MacDonald was a supporter of solving international difficulties through the League framework. There was no need for a direct or immediate confrontation at Geneva over the Treaty if

---

68 LONR, 17/49346/49346, Minute by Van Hamill, 9 July 1924.

it could be dealt with at a confidential level. Especially as it would confound the internationalism of the Geneva Protocol which MacDonald was sponsoring.

Whiskard's direct and private approach to Cosgrave on the registration issue may also have been due to the personality of the Secretary of State for the Colonies. J.H. Thomas had, in the words of Paul Canning 'always taken a keen interest in Irish affairs'; he also had 'a genuine sympathy for the Irish people', but, 'Thomas was like most Trade Union men, fundamentally conservative.'[69] Canning also points to MacDonald's preference to 'let Thomas handle Irish affairs almost singlehandedly'. This explains Whiskard's line of adopting a sympathetic approach to the Irish action by not going too hard on them, but ultimately adopting an inflexible attitude that the registration was not acceptable to Britain.

Cosgrave was given a chance to recant or suffer. Thomas's last chance stance failed when Cosgrave replied to his letter:

> I understood you to say to me that there was no objection and that there would be none to the registration of the Treaty. ... (I)t was obviously our duty to register the Treaty as the Treaty regulated relations between two states members of the League ... failure to register might rightly have been regarded as a breach of the Covenant.
>
> I understood that I pointed out to you how much this matter affected us here, that the Treaty was a matter between two nations and was as such regarded by those who supported it.[70]

Unofficially both sides had adopted the stances that they were to take throughout the Anglo-Irish controversy over the registration. No official correspondence exists until 4 November 1924. In light of the nature of the above correspondence, with the Labour administration adopting a softly-softly approach to the Free State and not wishing to get embroiled in a dispute in Geneva, what happened next is interesting. Rather than be accused of doing nothing with respect to the registration, the Whiskard–Cosgrave correspondence having been unofficial, J.H. Thomas wrote to T.M. Healy officially on 4 November with the Government's official objection to the registration. This was the day that the first Labour Government lost office, having lost its parliamentary majority in October. Labour could not now be said to have let the Free State away with registration or to have endangered Commonwealth unity by failing to act. If the Labour Government had stayed in power for longer there is a chance that the matter could have been sorted out in a confidential and low-key manner.

69 Paul Canning, *British Policy in Ireland, 1922–1941* (Oxford, 1985), p. 88. Thomas was Secretary of State for the Colonies in 1924, 1931 and 1935–6; he was Secretary of State for Dominion Affairs from 1930 to 1535.
70 NA, S. 3328, Cosgrave to Whiskard, 14 August 1924.

This was not to be. The new Colonial Secretary, Leopold Amery was determined to take a confrontational approach.[71] It was Conservative policy to emphasise the Dominions imperial position within the League. Amery asserted the primacy of the Commonwealth as a unit in the League of Nations and thus *inter se* Commonwealth relations, like the Anglo-Irish Treaty, were not covered by the League Covenant. J.H. Thomas might have started the ball rolling, but it was Amery who gave it the first kick. Amery's despatch of 4 November 1924 gave the rationale behind the British objection:

> since the Covenant of the League came into force, His Majesty's Government have consistently taken the view that neither it, nor any conventions concluded under the auspices of the League are intended to govern relations '*inter se*' of the various parts of the British Commonwealth. Having considered therefore, that the terms of Article 18 of the Covenant are not applicable to the Articles of Agreement of the Sixth of December 1921, we are informing the Secretary General of the League accordingly.[72]

This was the normal format that British rhetoric took until May 1925. An official letter was sent to Eric Drummond on 27 November 1924.[73] It stated that in the view of the British Government, the 1921 Treaty was a domestic Commonwealth affair. It was a very weak protest which simply stated the British position. There was no attempt to get the League to revoke the registration. The intention may have been to stop further registrations taking place. The British could not hope to make any response to a fait accompli, but they could prevent other Dominions using the Irish example as a precedent. The British protest was also aimed at reducing the popular perception of the Irish as more independent than the other Dominions.

Joe Walshe prepared a vigorous and vehement memorandum outlining possible responses to the British despatches. In a League context Walshe argued about the absurd notions held by the British about the Dominions at the League. He contrasted this with Britain's policy of apparently giving the Dominions equal stature at the League:

> [T]he British do not want to sacrifice their pet principle of the oneness of the sovereignty of the Commonwealth. They cannot allow two portions of the Commonwealth to bring a dispute before the League, the International Court, or any other external body. If a single member of the Commonwealth brings a dispute with an outside state before the League, the fiction of the whole acting for the part will save the situ-

---

71 Amery held the posts of Secretary of State for the Colonies from 1924 to 1929, and Secretary of State for Dominion Affairs, 1925–9.
72 UCDA, P35/204.
73 NA, S. 3328, Amery to Sir Eric Drummond, 27 November 1924.

ation. The effort to maintain this fiction at all costs is at the bottom of the present ridiculous position of the Dominions in the League. They are actually members twice over and have less power there than the smallest state in the League.

The British refusal to recognise the registration of the Treaty simply because Great Britain has always held the view that the Covenant does not apply to intra-Commonwealth relations is the most barefaced explicit denial of equality of which we have an instance. Up to this they had confined themselves to little manoeuvres more or less subtle and difficult to combat.[74]

Walshe outlined a two-point strategy. First, 'at the moment I can only suggest that we should emphatically declare that we joined the League of Nations believing the Covenant to be of universal application to all members without exception. We accepted the obligations of the Covenant fully believing that we were getting all the rights of member states.' This was probably sufficient to get a strong message across, but Walshe concluded with a high risk option: 'if at the mere wish of Great Britain the League decides that the Covenant does not apply to our relations with that Member State, we can give notice that we intend withdrawing [from the League] at an early date.'

This did not prove necessary, it may have been an approach designed to counter-bluff Britain's over-reaction to the registration. The Free State sent a note to the Secretary General to counter the British despatch of 4 November. This was dealt with at an Executive Council meeting on 8 December 1924.[75] The first draft was very blunt and it was toned down to a tactful rejection of the British objection:

[I]t is quite clear from Article 18 of the Covenant that it is binding upon States Members of the League to deposit for registration all treaties and international engagements. Inasmuch as Great Britain and the Irish Free State are Members of the League and as the Treaty is the basis of the relations between these two States, it was eminently the duty of the Irish Free State to register the Treaty.

An attempt now to obtain the withdrawal of this registration must necessarily be regarded as a disavowal of the Covenant or as a declaration that the Dominions are subject States to Great Britain, and in the latter case it must necessarily question the rights of the Dominions to membership of the League.

Therefore My Ministers cannot in any way agree to the action proposed in your despatch.[76]

74 UCDA, P35/204.
75 NA, Cabinet Minutes, G2/4 (C2/150).
76 UCDA, P35/204.

Whilst this was taking place the League reaction to the British objection was developing. Walshe had written to MacWhite for his opinion on the situation. He replied that,

> it would be idle to contend before an international tribunal that the Anglo-Irish Treaty was not an act intended to establish legal obligations between Great Britain and the Saorstát or between Great Britain and the Irish Government. ... [The Secretariat] had given their decision and that decision must stand if the fundamental principles on which the League is founded are to be observed.[77]

The growing opinion at Geneva was that the British were bluffing and that their protest was useless. The Treaty was registered and 'in this matter what applies to one member equally applies to all and the Saorstát in the League is on the same footing as any other member state.'[78] Edward Phelan wrote to MacWhite on 8 December 1924 about the British objection and the lines of action open to the British.[79] He argued that the registration could be contested on two grounds: 'that the Free State has neither the obligation nor the right to register the Treaty with the Secretariat in accordance with Article 18 [and] that the Treaty was not a treaty within the meaning of Article 18.' However, 'the terms of Article 18 are explicit ... [and] ... the obligation is binding ... therefore, the Irish Free State is not only entitled but obliged to register any treaty or international engagement which it may have entered into'. Phelan went on to argue why the Free State, as a Dominion, was correct in registering the Treaty:

> there are not different categories of members of the League [and] all members have the same rights and obligations. [A] state, on entering the League cannot, if it wanted, contract out of certain obligations. It is either admitted as a member or not.

Phelan argued that the Covenant allowed the Free State to register the Treaty. Article 15 paragraph 8 could be used to counter Article 18 but 'the rights of a member remain unprejudiced until such time as the Council has pronounced ... therefore Article 15 cannot be invoked against Article 18'. More subtly, as Great Britain had supported Free State membership of the League, she had implicitly declared that the Free State had 'no obligation inconsistent with the terms of the Covenant.' He finished up with Article 21 that stated that 'nothing in this Covenant shall be deemed to affect the validity of international engagements, such as treaties of arbitration or re-

---

77 NA, D.F/A, 417/105, 6 December 1924.
78 Ibid.
79 NA, D.F/A, 417/105.

gional understandings like the Monroe doctrine, for securing the maintenance of peace.' This had been included in the Covenant to tempt the United States into League membership. This it failed to do but it could have helped Great Britain except that A.B. Keith, the constitutional lawyer, had written that 'disputes 'between different parts of the Empire can be brought to the cognisance of the League' and that the Court of International Justice is 'open to the Dominions.'' From this Phelan concluded that 'the Free State as a member of the League has the same rights and obligations under Article 18 as other members of the League.'

Phelan finished up with some comments of his own. It was his opinion that the Free State and the Secretariat were in the right. Regarding the British protest, 'if any protest has been made it is either in the nature of a political bluff or it is a confused ... method of protesting against an appeal to the League concerning the application of the Treaty, which is quite another and a hypothetical matter.'

On 18 December Joe Walshe replied to the British despatch to the Secretary General by informing Sir Eric Drummond that,

> [T]he Government of the Irish Free State cannot see that any useful purpose would be served by the initiation of a controversy as to the intentions of any individual signatories to the Covenant. The obligations contained in Article 18 are, in their opinion, imposed in the most specific terms on every member of the League and they are unable to accept the contention that the clear and unequivocal language of that Article is susceptible to any of the interpretations compatible with the limitations which the British Government now seek to read into it.
>
> They accordingly dissent from the view expressed by the British Government that the terms of Article 18 are not applicable to the Treaty of 6 December 1921.[80]

Walshe made it clear that the Free State was in no way different to any other League member. The matter was firmly set in the cast of relations between two sovereign states and the British had no power to say that the actions of the Irish were out of bounds. He was well supported by the majority of League members and those in Geneva as a report from MacWhite to FitzGerald dated 18 December showed. The Free State was quite unassailable in its stance on the Treaty and the bulk of opinion was behind it whilst mystified by the British stance:

> The highest officials at the Secretariat of the League are naturally somewhat reluctant to talk of the situation that has arisen as a result of the British note concerning the registration of the Anglo-Irish Treaty.

80 NA, S. 3328.

Nevertheless, I have reason to know that they fully hold the view that the registration is well within the conditions laid down by Article 18 of the Covenant.

It is generally felt, not only in League circles, but amongst the enlightened public, that the English Tory Government attempted to strike a blow at the prestige of the League and the Saorstát at the same time, but that they will very likely be hoist on their own petard because of the energetic way in which the Irish Government took up the challenge and refused to be bullied in the matter. Your attitude meets with universal approval and sympathy.[81]

By now it was obvious to the British that they were protesting in vain. The despatches to Dublin indicate that the Free State representatives knew that they had carried the day, especially after a despatch from MacWhite to FitzGerald on 23 December: 'In discussing the British note with the Secretary General he said between ourselves that it was a most extraordinary step for the Foreign Office to take, as they have no ground to stand on.'[82] This had filtered through to the British as Phelan informed Patrick McGilligan on 29 December:' I think they must have realised that their action was a blunder, that I gather is the impression of the British here.'[83]

Finally on 9 March 1925 the final episode of the registration of the Treaty ended with the British still objecting and refusing to accept the registration but deciding that 'His Majesty's Government doubt whether any advantage is to be gained by the prolonging of the present correspondence, and gather that in the letter addressed to the League of Nations on behalf of the Government of the Irish Free State on the 18th of December 1924 that your Ministers share this feeling.'[84] The registration issue was now finally at an end; the British still did not accept that the Treaty was fit to be registered, but the Irish had kept their dominant position.

Conclusion

The League had firmly, if unofficially, supported the Irish Free State throughout in its plan to register the Treaty. The Free State could now turn its attention to other matters. In the desire to attain their prime objective in registering the Treaty the Irish had not progressed very far in their involvement in other League matters. The wider issues of League membership were now to take higher priority as the state began, from 1926 on, projecting herself outward and into the live issues of League membership. The registration gave the Free

81 Ibid.
82 NA, D.F/A, 417/105.
83 UCDA, P35/204.
84 NA, S. 3328, Amery to T.M. Healy, 9 March 1925.

State confidence in international relations. MacWhite wrote to his colleague Professor Timothy A. Smiddy, 'a few weeks ago I had the Anglo-Irish Treaty registered with the League. Our people expected some opposition, but there was none. They are, by force of circumstance, growing out of this timidity'.[85] The Free State authorities viewed the act of registration in a global sense as giving the state confidence in the totality of its foreign relations.

This was the practical importance of the registration. Despite the lack lustre performance at the Assembly from 1924 to 1925, the state had copper-fastened itself into the League. The fundamental document relating to the state's creation and basis had been accepted by the League as an international agreement. Ireland accordingly had accepted the League as the umbrella under which her foreign relations would be carried out. As MacWhite said, it had given the Free State the basis and more importantly, the confidence to develop those relations through the League. Following registration the Free State began to reassert herself in the League. From 1926 on the League began to play a more prominent role in Irish foreign policy and figure more prominently beside the Commonwealth as the second track in what was fast becoming a two-track League and Commonwealth driven foreign policy.

---

85 NA, BE, Box 6, 28 July 1924. **Timothy A. Smiddy**: Minister in Washington, 1922–9; High Commissioner in London, 1929–30; Tariff Commission, Dublin, 1930–3; Head of Combined Purchasing Section, Department of Local Government, 1933–45.

CHAPTER 3

The Council Dispute and the September 1926 Assembly

In spring 1926 a smouldering dispute blazed up over the composition of the Council and the election of non-permanent members.[1] They were theoretically the elected representatives of the Assembly on the Council but selfishly guarded their seats as additions to national prestige. In early 1926 the dispute became entangled with the admission of Germany to the League. This was to take place at an Extraordinary Assembly opening on 8 March. Spain and Brazil threatened to veto German admission and her permanent seat if they did not also receive a permanent seat. Both MacWhite and Desmond FitzGerald saw the dispute as antithetical to their democratic view of the League. Their concern led to the development of a forceful Irish response to the Council crisis from March to September 1926.

The Irish were concerned at the negative effect any increase in the number of permanent seats would have on the size and efficiency of the Council. The Free State wanted the League to work democratically and to the rules of the Covenant and to do so in favour of small states like itself. In the opinion of the Free State, the only task for the Extraordinary Assembly was the admission of Germany to the League; the Council question was a matter to be dealt with at the September Assembly. It was essential that Germany be brought into the international community. This became the Free State's policy for the extraordinary Assembly. It was close to adopting the line taken by the Dominions. But the Free State's approach was different from the other Dominions because she was a European state. While the Irish diplomats agreed with some of the Dominion complaints about an increase in Council membership decreasing its efficiency, it was not so concerned about the perceived 'Europeanisation' of the Council as South Africa or Australia were. To this extent, the Free State's policy was an independent one. It leant more towards solidarity with the small European states than the Dominions. On 2 March, the Executive Council approved the delegation of FitzGerald and MacWhite to the Extraordinary Assembly. The small delegation was due to the limited agenda set for the Assembly.

1 The Council was composed of the Great Powers: Britain, France, Italy, Japan and six elected non-permanent members.

73

The Extraordinary Assembly

Spain and Brazil vetoed German admission when the Assembly opened. The Locarno powers brokered solutions outside the League. Brazil and Spain remained obstinate.[2] Attempts at a compromise failed. The Assembly met on 17 March, put Germany's entry off until September and admitted defeat. The League set up a Commission of Inquiry into the Council issue.

FitzGerald reported to the Dáil on 6 May 1926. The delegation's report presented a balanced view of the crisis and indicated where the problems lay. FitzGerald was on the commission discussing the political aspects of German entry. He reported that it was 'unanimously in favour of Germany but this report was not presented to the Assembly, as one of the conditions on which Germany's demand was based, i.e. the allocation to her of a permanent seat on the Council, could not be met, owing to the opposition of Brazil'.[3] The report covered the failure of Germany to gain admission and the Council crisis. It outlined the resulting impasse and Irish concerns that the Assembly should resolve the issue in public and not in secret as the Great Powers had attempted: 'many ... were of the opinion that the Assembly alone could provide a solution to the difficulty with which the League was confronted'.[4]

The Saorstát pointed out that the League was not living up to the rules of the Covenant or the Assembly. The final paragraph of the report summed up the Free State's argument on the Council:

> the Assembly because of its sovereignty, was quite competent to take an immediate decision [on the crisis]. The Assembly, by asserting its sovereignty, may save the prestige of the League and increase its own authority at the expense of that of the Council by declaring all non-permanent seats to be vacant and preceding forthwith to the election of new members to fill the vacancies thus created.

By doing this Brazil and Spain would lose their seats and this would remove the block to Germany's entry. The Assembly could reassert its position by making it clear that the non-permanent seats were filled by its representatives on the Council. The Free State could not condone the side-stepping of League institutions in solving disputes so crucial to the League. The League was to act as the sum of all its members, generally this only meant the most active ones, but it did not mean solely the Great Powers acting in concert outside the parameters of the League.

---

2 Brazil and Spain withdrew from the League over this issue in 1926. They were the first members of significance to withdraw until Japan in 1933. The withdrawals did not become binding for two years. In 1928 Spain reconsidered and returned to Geneva, Brazil's withdrawal was final.
3 NA, S. 8176, March 1926.
4 Ibid.

On 20 May MacWhite informed FitzGerald of the progress of the Commission of Inquiry into the composition of the Council. He felt that, 'the majority of the members of the commission seem favourable to the status quo, that is to maintain the present number with the addition of Germany'.[5] It would be the task of the Irish delegation to the September Assembly to deal with the conclusion of the Council dispute.

The importance of the March 1926 Council crisis

The March Council crisis falls outside the interpretations of Irish foreign policy normally taken by historians as it had no explicit Anglo-Irish dimension. The active stance taken by the Department of External Affairs in an overtly international and European issue questions the historiographical convenience that all Irish external affairs in the 1920s and 1930s were a product of Anglo-Irish affairs. The crisis saw the department involved in an international crisis with world wide ramifications as it involved the future of the League system. With FitzGerald, Walshe developed a balanced and impartial response to a crisis that was in danger of destabilising the League. The crisis, with its European dimension, shows that the Department of External Affairs had a wider scope to its operations than it has been credited with by historians.

The issue involved the Free State directly as a League member. The state's position as a small state in the League was under threat. The non-permanent seats on the Council were the only opportunity that states like the Free State had of representation on the League's higher bodies. This was to receive its most spectacular vindication through Free State actions at the September 1926 Assembly.

New enthusiasm: February–September 1926

The Council Crisis and the Extraordinary Assembly re-kindled the Free State's enthusiasm for the League. There was a new desire for the state to actively participate in its work and development. The registration of the treaty had cleared the way and the Council crisis provided the impetus. A more vigorous approach to planning was evident in the Department of External Affairs for the September 1926 Assembly. In early February, Walshe wrote to O'Hegarty:

> It is hoped this year to get the delegation appointed two or three months beforehand and to allocate the committees so that there may be

---

5 NA, LN 15.

ample time to prepare the matter and consequently to take a more effective part in the discussions.[6]

This view was heightened by the Irish interest in the Extraordinary Assembly. The crisis over Germany's admission led the Free State to realise that the League was only as good as its members made it and it was up to those members to make the League a workable force. This is not as idealistic as it sounds. The Free State's own interests were bound up in the continued success of the League. As a small state it needed the League as a democratising force in the world order to allow small states such as itself participate in the international environment which would otherwise be the sole preserve of the Great Powers.

Walshe wrote to O'Hegarty on 1 June that, 'the Minister considers the work of preparing for the League Assembly and the Imperial Conference would be greatly facilitated if the delegates for both meetings were appointed forthwith'.[7] This was early by previous standards. It shows that the link was strengthening between League and Commonwealth policy. Walshe developed this in a memorandum marked 'private and confidential: not for circulation':

> it will not be possible to establish here an exclusively League of Nations section. Nor is it advisable to do so. The League for us is too closely connected with status within and without the Commonwealth to allow of efficient work being done in connection with it by an officer who is not in constant touch with the whole trend of intra-Commonwealth relations.[8]

This seems to suggest that Walshe had very little place for the League in his plans, that it was 'too closely connected to status within and without the Commonwealth' to be of importance as an area itself. Rather, Walshe did not want an exclusive League of Nations section because to have a separate branch dealing with both League and Commonwealth policies would destroy the essential overlap between them at the core of Free State foreign policy. 1926 was a key year in the development of a structured Irish League and Commonwealth policy. Walshe had identified the two-track nature of the state's foreign policy and that future development should be in that direction. The state had found its feet in the international arena with an increasingly structured approach to the central aspects of its foreign relations. The vital importance of the League in the external affairs of the Free State had been realised.

The first indication of this change came with the choice of a delegation for the 1926 Assembly. At a Cabinet meeting on 7 June the delegation was

6 NA, LN 1-3, 8 February 1926.
7 NA, S. 8176.
8 NA, S. 5337.

appointed. This was earlier than other years. It was to consist of Desmond FitzGerald, Ernest Blythe, and Eoin MacNeill, whose growing antipathy to the events and workings of the Assembly, and politics in general, was evident by the note of 'if he consents' by his name.[9]

MacNeill was losing interest in public life after the failure of the Boundary Commission; the reason for his inclusion can be seen from a letter he wrote to Cosgrave whilst at the 1923 Assembly: 'The fact that I am a Minister counts here, both within our delegation and outside. I am also something of a dark horse and nobody tries to pull my leg'.[10] He was not to be as active a member of the delegation in 1926 as he had been in 1923. He was on the delegation for prestige reasons, as an Irish elder statesman. Daniel Binchy, Professor of International Law at the National University of Ireland, was included as a substitute delegate.[11] Joe Walshe served as secretary.

The Seventh Assembly: Autumn 1926

The Seventh Assembly is of interest because from the personal papers of Ernest Blythe, Desmond FitzGerald and Eoin MacNeill a picture can be constructed of the Irish delegation at Geneva throughout the Assembly. The attitudes of three different men emerge. Blythe was observant and critical of the Assembly, especially the lack of Irish involvement in it; FitzGerald, as Chief Delegate, was exhausted by his chairmanship of the Second Committee, Ireland's attempt to gain election to a temporary seat on the reconstituted Council and the heavy round of social engagements. MacNeill became disenchanted with Geneva and returned to Ireland early.

This gives an insight into the two sides of the League Assembly; the social side: dinner and luncheon parties, motor drives, late nights; and the business side: FitzGerald up until all hours on the Second Committee, the hurried writing of speeches and, most importantly, the heated discussion amongst the Irish delegates as to whether the Free State should go up for election to the Council. This took place against the backdrop of German entry to the League.

9 **Ernest Blythe** (1889–1975): politician and writer. Born in Antrim, former Irish Volunteer, member of Sinn Féin executive in 1917, elected for Monaghan in the first Dáil. Minister for Trade and Commerce (1919–22), Provisional Government Minister for Local Government (1922), Minister for Health and Local Government (1922–3), Minister for Finance (1923–32), Vice-President of the Executive Council (1927–32). He wrote poetry, history and autobiographical works. He was Director of the Abbey theatre from 1939 to 1967. Blythe was a prominent member of Irish delegations to the League for the period 1926–32.
10 NA, S. 3332, 20 September 1923.
11 **Daniel Binchy** (1900–89): Professor of Law National University of Ireland, 1925–45, Department of External Affairs, Minister Plenipotentiary to Germany (1929–32), Dublin Institute of Advanced Studies, 1948–75. Binchy was an outstanding scholar in early Irish law.

It was a hectic schedule for the Irish. FitzGerald wrote to his wife that, 'I think Ernest will at least go back and press that this job is not a holiday for me'.¹² It was crucial to have the Minister for Finance on the side of a small department like External Affairs. Typical of FitzGerald's comments was: 'one unceasing rush for me. Perhaps more time next week. Any way it should be less worrying. Am sometimes nearly fainting from nervous exhaustion'.¹³

This snapshot of the Irish delegation begins with the land and sea crossing to France through Britain. In his first letter to his wife Blythe revealed that all did not go as expected:

> In Paris four of us went to the Moulin Rouge at about 9.30 ... We had to leave however in about an hour as we found that four unprotected men were subject to too frequent attention to remain any length of time. We got a train at 8 o'clock on Saturday morning. It was the train in which we had seats booked but not the train for which we had tickets. Cooks must have stuck our seat vouchers in other people's tickets and vice-versa. We were ejected from the train at Dijon where we had lunch and waited three and a half hours, visiting Cathedral, Park etc. We did not get to Geneva until after 12.30.¹⁴

The serious and jovial mixed during the Assembly in the cosmopolitan atmosphere of Geneva. Plenary sessions took place in the Salle de la Reformation, in intense heat and through the buzz of talking and movement. They were followed by long lunches which left the remainder of the afternoon to be taken up by meetings of Committees or plenary sessions of the Assembly. The evenings were occupied by lengthy formal dinners. The delegates would rarely retire before midnight.

In the elections to fill the official posts of the Assembly, Desmond FitzGerald stood for the chair of the Second Committee. These elections were facades as canvassing before made the result certain. FitzGerald made no pretence at hiding this: 'I am to be, I am told, Chairman of the Second Committee. I don't know anything about it except that it deals with everything I am least interested in'.¹⁵ His view changed some days later: 'The Committee is the Second Committee, it deals with all sorts of things, settlement of Greek refugees, Hungarian finance, Austrian economic conference, epidemiological institutes etc. It is not as political as the First—but it performs some of the best work of the League such as the restoration of Austria and Hungary'.¹⁶ He was writing whilst the elections were taking place, preferring not to be present as, 'it may mean voting for myself'. He had to finish up because 'J.[oe]

12 UCDA, P80/1407, undated letter, postmark 22 September 1926.
13 Ibid., undated letter, postmark 18 September 1926.
14 UCDA, P24/2252, 6 September 1926.
15 UCDA, P80/1407, 7 September.
16 Ibid., letter, postmark 21 September 1926.

W.[alshe] has just come in to say that I have been elected with great éclat and that he said a few words of thanks on my behalf. I have now to go off and get the Secretary of the Committee who is at my service for the session. He will do everything for me including telling me what to say and when to say it'.[17] FitzGerald thus became the most prominent Irish delegate at the Assembly. His task was vast and his election also made him one of the ex-officio Vice-Presidents of the Assembly. Along with the President of the Assembly and the Secretary General this group was known as the General Committee of the Assembly. It was a sign of Ireland's increasing presence in the League only three years after her entry.

In light of the pending report of the Commission of Inquiry into the Council, the most important committee at the 1926 Assembly was the First Committee (Constitutional and Legal questions). The Irish representative was Ernest Blythe. Its progress was held up until Germany took her seat in the Assembly on 10 September. According to Blythe, 'It is expected that the German delegation will be here on Friday. Everything, practically speaking is held up pending their arrival'.[18]

During the final week of the Assembly, the Committees reported back to it with a summary of their work completed. They held their meetings parallel to those of the Assembly so delegates generally attended the Assembly, or skipped it if their Committees were sitting. Blythe attended both and was critical of behaviour in the Assembly:

> The Assembly on the whole is disorderly and unimpressive. A buzz of talk goes on continuously. French is really the language of the Assembly and when speeches are being translated into English nobody pretends to listen and talks at the top of his voice to his neighbours about almost anything that interests him or goes around and picks up long lost friends amongst the other delegations.[19]

If the morning session of the Assembly finished early some of the Irish delegation would go down to the shores of Lake Geneva, to swim, sunbathe and eat lunch on the waterfront at a lake-side stall. Blythe was quite self-conscious 'we four are conspicuously white skinned ... nearly all the others are the colour of coffee'.[20] A spell of sunbathing remedied this and Blythe's next letter tells the result: 'I am sitting in my room with nothing on the upper half of my body but a thick coating of cold-cream ... my shoulders and the upper half of my body have the colour of a lobster and the feel of a hot linseed poultice'.[21]

17 Ibid., letter, 7 September.
18 Op. cit. P24, letter, 8 September 1926.
19 Ibid., letter, 7 September 1926.
20 Op. cit. P24, undated letter.
21 Op. cit. P24.

Germany was voted into the League on 8 September On the afternoon of 10 September 1926 the German delegation took its alphabetically allocated place in the Salle de la Reformation. Blythe looked on:

> the Germans were brought into the hall at the beginning of the sitting, ... (w)hen we were admitted all the delegates rose to their feet and applauded. On Friday however the British and French kept their seats and remained silent, about half the Assembly followed this example. The remainder rose and applauded. Briand got up after Stresemann and certainly made a wonderful and courageous speech. Stresemann made his speech in a fairly even voice without a single gesture. Briand ... walked up and down the platform, made jokes at one moment, spoke in a trembling voice at an other and incessantly moved his hands in the greatest variety of gestures. When he had finished there was a roar of applause and a lot of the delegates got up and waved their hats and handkerchiefs.[22]

With Germany admitted, the Assembly could get down to business. The First Committee began an analysis of the report of the Commission of Inquiry into the structure of the Council with the intention of presenting it to the Assembly for approval. The crucial meetings took place on 14 September. Here the officially titled 'Draft resolution concerning the election of the non-permanent members of the Council, their terms of office and the conditions of re-eligibility' was discussed. The plan was that the non-permanent membership would be increased by three, to nine. Three of these nine would be elected every year for a three year term. Re-eligibility was not possible for another consecutive term without the candidate getting at least a two thirds majority of a vote in the Assembly. The Assembly had full powers to remove the mandate of all the non-permanent members and call for a total re-election if it thought fit. These provisions were discussed article by article. Blythe argued that the draft resolution had flaws as it 'contained no procedure for allowing the Assembly to withdraw the mandate of a non-permanent member of the Council.'[23] He was afraid that this could place an uncooperative state on the Council for three years with no way of revoking the mandate. The need to remove a single mandate, rather than the block power to remove all and call for total re-election, was crucial because, 'the possibility of a withdrawal would decrease the disadvantages ... inherent in a Council of too large a size'. Blythe offered the solution that a non-permanent member of the Council could be deprived of his seat by a decision of the Assembly taken on a two-thirds majority.

Blythe was acting on his own initiative and not on instructions from the Department of External Affairs. The speech does contain the attitudes of the

22 UCDA, P24/2252, letter, 11 September 1926.
23 UCDA, P24/603 League of Nations Official Journal. Special Supplement Number 25 (Geneva, 1926).

Free State towards the League, but they were mixed with Blythe's personal feelings. He expressed the Department of External Affairs concern at the increase in the number of Council seats and mingled it with his own criticism of the behaviour of Brazil and Spain. The most striking aspect of the speech is this implicit criticism of the actions of Spain and Brazil. If they could have been held in check by the revocation of their mandate Germany would have been admitted to the League in March 1926.

In line with Free State policy, Blythe felt that the Assembly should have greater power over the Council. This would limit the actions of the Great Powers on the Council as there would be a nine to five majority of non-permanent members over permanent members. As the non-permanent members were the elected representatives of the Assembly, the Assembly should at least have the power to get rid of any particular representatives that would not toe the line. The only case covered was the wholesale revocation of all the temporary Council seats and totally new elections. Blythe was not arguing against this, he was arguing for a refinement of the process, a process he implicitly supported in his speech. The only comfort offered to Blythe was that the provisions given in the articles for agreement would cover his case.

Blythe argued that although the new provisions were acceptable, they should not be regarded as a final solution to Council reform. There were still flaws; the Assembly could not prevent a situation where non-permanent members would hold up the League's work due to their own narrow national policies. The draft terms of the resolution were passed on 14 September and sent to the Assembly for general debate and a final vote on 15 September. Blythe's remarks were taken up and continued by FitzGerald's speech to the Assembly on 15 September. FitzGerald argued that though the resolution was the best solution available it might make the Council more unwieldy. The Irish were taking a co-ordinated approach as they had decided unofficially to go up for election to the Council if the chance arose. It was a covert canvass. From the speech it would be evident where the state stood when it announced its candidature. MacWhite was already aware from conversations he had at the monthly dinner of Permanent Representatives that a degreee of sentiment existed in favour of an Irish candidature. The delegation felt that they should capitalise on this sentiment.

The Council elections: 14–18 September 1926

On the afternoon of 14 September the Free State announced its candidature for a non-permanent seat on the reconstituted Council. The state went forward representing the Assembly and against the notion of geographical constituencies in the elections, and factors that impeded the Assembly's freedom to choose the non-permanent members of the Council. The Saorstát was standing up for the rights of the small states, stressing the need for all states, however powerful, to have equal use of their vote. States should be free to choose and should not have to do so under the grasp of the powers, who could agree on candidates amongst themselves.

It is important to stress this 'League oriented' view of the Free State's decision. It was misconstrued at the time, and historians since have continued the misconception that the Free State went up for election solely to prove Dominion autonomy. There was a dual reason for standing: to assert any League member's freedom to stand for election and to assert the freedom of the Dominions, as League members in the Assembly. This has been misinterpreted by Irish historians who emphasise the Dominion reason to the exclusion of the League dimension. In the definitive work on the League, F.P. Walters states that in 1926 'the Free State stood unsuccessfully, as an independent candidate'.[24]

FitzGerald met the Dominion delegations and the British Foreign Secretary Sir Austen Chamberlain on the afternoon of 14 September and announced that the Free State was standing as a candidate. The Dominions were, according to Chamberlain, 'unexpectedly confronted with a problem of great difficulty'.[25] The Dominions and Britain would not support the Free State. FitzGerald refused to budge. The meeting ended amicably, 'no decision was taken and none was sought, but we all left under the impression that Mr. FitzGerald would not proceed with the Free State candidature in the circumstances'.[26] Chamberlain believed that he had made FitzGerald agree to withdraw the candidature. FitzGerald simply fudged the issue by giving the impression that the Irish would withdraw.

When FitzGerald returned to inform the Irish delegation, whom he had not consulted in advance, about the outcome of the meeting, they overruled him. The Free State would run for election without British Empire support. Details of this turn about are contained in an interview given to Michael Tierney by Michael MacWhite. According to Tierney there was:

> a prolonged discussion with the British, in the course of which Desmond FitzGerald ... was persuaded by Austen Chamberlain to withdraw Ireland's claim. When he reported his decision to his colleagues, there was a tremendous argument, in which MacNeill, according to an account later given to the present writer by Michael MacWhite, towered over FitzGerald and Blythe who supported him, and forced them to withdraw the withdrawal.[27]

Two Ministers and senior delegates, Blythe and FitzGerald were forced to change their mind by the other members of the delegation. This is backed up

---

24 Walters, *History*, p. 336.
25 PRO, DO 117/27, CP 334 (26) Memo by Austen Chamberlain, 15 September 1926.
26 Ibid.
27 Michael Tierney, *Eoin MacNeill: Scholar and Man of Action, 1867–1945* (Oxford, 1980), ed. F.X. Martin, p. 356.

by a letter from FitzGerald to Austen Chamberlain. The letter, dated 14 September sets out the Irish rethink:

> My delegation has very carefully considered the position reviewed at the meeting this afternoon, and on the grounds that I did my best to set out at that meeting they have decided that we should let Ireland's name go forward as a candidate in the Council election.
>
> We regret exceedingly that in this opinion we differ from the opinion of the British and the other Dominion delegates, ... we are moved entirely by what we conceive to be the best interests of the Dominions.[28]

At least that was what the Irish told the Dominion and British delegates. The interests of the Assembly and the position of the small states affected by the new rules for election were the basis of the candidature. Chamberlain received the letter in the Assembly on the morning of 15 September. The decision was final; Joe Walshe sent a letter to each Dominion delegation stating that 'it has been definitely decided to proceed with our candidature for a seat on the Council'.[29] Events moved so quickly that British delegation member E.J. Harding prefaced a despatch of 15 September to London with the apology that, 'the situation with regard to a Dominion seat on the Council undergoes such rapid changes that it is difficult to keep pace with it'.[30] Dublin was informed by telegram, on 15 September; Walshe told Paul Banim of the President's Office that, owing to the situation in Geneva, the delegation had decided that the Free State should offer itself as a candidate for a seat on the Council 'to assert equal status, as much as to seek election'.[31]

At the final Dominion meeting during the early evening of 15 September FitzGerald stuck to his position saying that it had been reaffirmed by Dublin and he could now not alter it. South Africa stated that it would support the Irish, but the other Dominions and Britain referred to previous commitments that stopped them changing their vote in favour of the Free State. Chamberlain appealed to FitzGerald to reconsider. FitzGerald's reluctance to change the Irish position brought the meeting to an end.

Few of the Irish delegates expected the state to be elected. It was the fact that the state was standing for election that the delegates expected to be most effective. By standing for election the Free State would publicise the position of the small and powerless states at the Assembly, especially as they were affected by the new Council rules. A state that appeared on the scene the day before the election could not expect many votes. FitzGerald's speech at the

28 UCDA, P24/157.
29 Ibid., 14 September 1926.
30 PRO, DO 117/28.
31 NA S. 5166.

Assembly became a massive canvassing speech. Blythe was not expectant of success, yet he was expectant of the Irish creating a stir:

> As a result of a great lot of discussion we decided to put the Saorstát forward for the Council. I don't think that there is any possibility of success though others are not of that opinion. We feel however that there is a very general opinion in the Assembly that the Dominions do hold a somewhat subordinate status and that Great Britain represents them on the Council.
>
> Some of the others thought that the Dominions should simply be in the Assembly ... [O]ur view was that this would be so weak that it would be quite useless. As none of the others would go forward we decided to go on ... [W]e have created a small sensation and will prevent at any rate the arranged election from going through as a formality and the Dominions being regarded as of no account.[32]

Blythe's last comment shows that League reasoning mattered as much as the Dominion rationale in the state's election attempt. Desmond FitzGerald put less emphasis on the Dominion side when he wrote, 'we did not go up representing the Dominions but the Assembly',[33] and 'the Irish papers quite misunderstood our going up for the Council. We did not only defend Dominion rights but also countries like Austria, Hungary and Abyssinia etc.'.[34] The double rationale behind the election attempt is clear. By the evening of 14 September the stage was set. The Free State, against the wishes of Britain and the Dominions, was preparing to contest the elections to the Council of the League.

The Assembly debate on the new rules for non-permanent members took place at the tenth plenary meeting of the Assembly on the morning of 15 September 1926. FitzGerald's speech was of key importance to the Irish election bid and is a good synopsis of Free State League policy. He outlined the Free State's policy of critical support of the League, accepting the new rules with unease:

> I do not think that, in principle, the proposals are desirable. For instance, fourteen is too large a number for the Council, seeing that each member possesses a veto. I think also that the provision debarring elected members from re-election is theoretically undesirable, as it limits the Assembly's choice in selecting representatives.[35]

32 UCDA, P24/2252, Blythe letter, 15 September 1926.
33 UCDA, P80/1407, letter, postmark 18 September 1926.
34 Ibid., letter, 19 September 1926.
35 All quotes from speech from, UCDA, File P80/540. Extract from verbatim records of the 7th ordinary session of the Assembly of the League of Nations.

He was not fooled by idealism, he asserted that in theory there should be no need to have a non-eligibility clause, however practice, as shown by the events of the previous March, dictated that there should be such a clause. Such caustic comments contained in FitzGerald's speech were interpreted as, 'sarcastic references to Brazil and Spain who quit the League because they were not granted permanent seats (on the Council)'.[36]

FitzGerald then made the Free State's position clear. The state would support the new rules, though with caution:

> It is, on the whole, better to limit our power of choice rather than to have the elected members regarding themselves as permanent members who are merely to go through the formality of an election from time to time, with the threat of withdrawing from the League if the Assembly exercises its undoubted right to change its representatives. On the face of it, then, I agree with the resolution as practically worthy of support.

The Free State would not let the League and the supporters of the new plan away with their revised rules lightly. Attacking the unwritten plans to create a geographical basis to non-permanent Council seats, and continuing on the message begun by Blythe, took up the rest of FitzGerald's speech. FitzGerald began by attacking the fact that, 'there seems to be behind the present proposals a proposal which may be interpreted as giving a right to certain seats to particular groups of states, geographical groups or groups based on alliances or undertakings'. This, and the lack of choice created by it, was the kernel of the new situation, according to FitzGerald. The Council problem had been solved, but it must not create a situation where the knock-on effect on the other organs of the League would be to their detriment. FitzGerald conveyed this plainly:

> We recognise the desirability of having a Council in which there is representation of the different states and civilisations comprised in the League. At the same time, we think that we must never loose sight of the fact that the Assembly as a whole elects the non-permanent members and accordingly the non-permanent members must represent the Assembly as a whole. Every effort must be made to preserve for the Assembly the greatest possible freedom of choice as to the states that shall from time to time be appointed to the Council. Accordingly, while we hold that all shades of opinion and every sort of interest in the League should from time to time be represented on the Council, we deny the right of particular groups to be at any time represented thereon in any specified proportion, we deny more emphatically still

36 NA, LN 1–5, press clipping contained in file from the *Chicago Tribune*, 16 September 1926.

the right of any group to choose from among themselves a state which the Assembly would be under an obligation to elect.

Such an arrangement means that not only will there be a hierarchy on the Council, itself undesirable but practically necessary, but a hierarchy in the Assembly. The Assembly will be divided into a hierarchy of states which are due to be members of the Council once every 2 years or every 3 years or every 4 years and states that are only due to be members of the Council every 10 years, and those others which, with those states revolving in their orbits will never get a seat at all.

I say that we cannot stand by now and see such a situation created either by resolution or by the establishment of a precedent. It may be said that no such arrangement is made; but last March we saw a situation arise whereby a country deemed that because it had been elected by the Assembly on a number of occasions for a number of years, it had its seat by prescriptive rights.

The whole history of the League shows that the establishment of prescriptive rights tends to take away entirely all the powers of the Council. What is the chief power of the Assembly? We know perfectly well that we have come here every year unorganised. We have only one power that is really vital and that is really great, and that is our power to control the Council. We control the Council by our power to elect the majority of its members. That I consider to be the greatest and most important power possessed by the Assembly.

FitzGerald attacked the basis on which the Council was being reconstituted. The new proposals removed the Assembly's freedom to choose their candidates. It put the election and the choice of candidates into the hands of the 'Great Powers'. FitzGerald then took a final swipe at Brazil and Spain and ended with a stark portrayal of what the new rules and the situation they would create meant:

for the proper exercise of the Assembly's power, for proper implementation of the world conscience, the Assembly must retain as one body, representing almost all nations of the world, the power to choose freely from year to year without any consideration of established prescriptive right, whatever representatives it elects. It must also, at any time be able to say that it is not entirely satisfied with its members or members of the elected powers on the Council and to tell those members that they must make way for another. It must be able to do that with a perfectly free hand and not be called upon to weigh the possibility of fresh crises, the possibility of the League breaking up as a result of its actions or a weakening of the League and of the power of the League through crises arising when nations—because they have a grievance or they feel that they have a grievance which we consider imaginary but which they, with a certain amount of right, consider to be real, decide that they want nothing more to do with the League because the Assembly has not voted for them. To our minds the very essence of voting is choosing, and it seems to us that behind all these arrangements is an attempt to let us veto but not to let us choose those who are to represent us on the Council.

In the immediate situation, the speech was an indictment of the cause, the method of resolution, and possibly of the consequences of the new rules. The Free State only supported the new rules, as FitzGerald made clear in his speech, because there was no other choice. FitzGerald made no attempt to laud the rules. Instead he outlined the flaws in the new system. It was food for thought for any of those who saw Geneva in a utopian light.

The Free State indicated to the assembled nations that it could not allow the Assembly to have its power usurped by other states. In this sense, the election that followed can be seen as the Free State practically applying the message contained in the speech. FitzGerald was pleased with the speech and its effect: '[at the] Assembly everybody was coming up to me. we were the big event ... very satisfied with what we have done'.[37] The Free State delegates spent the late evening of 15 September canvassing at a reception given in honour of the President of the Assembly. The talking was over and all that remained was for the Free State delegation to see how their shock tactics fared in the Council elections taking place the next day.

On the morning of 16 September Desmond FitzGerald announced to the British that, 'as a result of his canvassing he would "not let the Dominions down".'[38] Nine seats were to be filled by a roll-call vote. Ballot one would choose the nine non-permanent members and a further three ballots would be held to find out who would be elected for three years, two years, or one year. Eighteen countries went forward for ballot one. Forty-nine states voted and the majority necessary for a seat was 25 votes. In ballot one 8 states were elected. The Free State received ten votes. A supplementary ballot was called to fill the remaining seat. The contenders were the Free State, Finland, Uruguay and Czechoslovakia. Czechoslovakia was elected with 27 votes and the Free State came in last place, receiving 2 votes, one her own and the other from Canada.

The Free State had done well considering its late showing and the delegation's knowledge that the state's reasons for entering the elections had been in the competing and not the winning. Rather than applaud an apparent moral victory by the Irish, it is more appropriate to analyse how the delegation themselves felt that they had fared. FitzGerald's letters show that he was

---

37 UCDA, P80/1407, letter, postmark 18 September 1926.
38 PRO, DO 117/27, Batterbee to Harding, 16 September 1926.

quite pleased except that the newspapers had got the Free State's intentions all wrong:

> [We] did very well with ten votes. In spite of the opposition of the big ones—Britain etc. ... the Irish newspapers that I have seen here have been worthy of themselves. They seem to get the wrong end of everything with perfect genius. We probably got a better share from every other press. We have been one of the most prominent countries here—a thing that means nothing but suffering for me personally—and those damn fools haven't the sense enough to make anything of it. But of course it doesn't really matter whether they do or not. The foreign papers have done well by us, and from the point of view of prestige that matters much more. We got ten votes with Britain against us. And only appearing on the scene the day before the election. I am quite satisfied that we could have been elected with a proper canvass and in good time. Quite a lot practically blamed me for not telling them before they had promised their votes. But of course it was only when Spain definitely went out that we could do anything and if another had gone up on our principle we should have left the field for them.[39]

FitzGerald got the episode off his chest with these letters. A muted sense of satisfaction coupled with anger at the way the press reacted pervaded his outlook. Ernest Blythe was more satisfied. He felt that

> yesterday was from our point of view quite satisfactory. In spite of the British discouragement this morning saying that we should not get two. In any case we regard it as certain that a Dominion will be elected next year.[40]

Daniel Binchy was one of the most extreme supporters of the election bid. His fervour indicates that feelings must have been running very high after the meeting between FitzGerald and Chamberlain. Writing in retrospect he felt that it was,

> the only possible one under the circumstances. A definite challenge had been given by Sir Austen to the principle that a Dominion was entitled to separate representation on the Council. That challenge had to be met, and I may add the principle had to be asserted. As a result of our action, although our candidature was heavily defeated, the fight was won and the election of Canada in the next year was entirely due to our action in 1926.[41]

39 UCDA, P80/1407, letters, 18 and 19 September.
40 UCDA, P24/2252, letter, 17 September 1926.
41 NA, D.F/A 29/95, Binchy to Walshe, 15 January 1930.

The linkage that Binchy puts on the election decision may be misleading. As we shall see, the Canadian election in 1927 owed more to Austen Chamberlain's actions the following March than they did to his actions in September 1926.

This 'definite challenge' may be a reference to more sinister events. Terence de Vere White mentions in passing some interesting backroom dealing initiated by Austen Chamberlain. The source was an interview with MacWhite, an account that mirrors that given above to Michael Tierney. He states that, 'When the Irish decision was known, a hasty agreement was reached between Sir Austen and Briand, with the result that Czechoslovakia received overwhelming and unexpected support at the elections'.[42] This turn of events indicates two things. Firstly, the British were worried that the Free State's candidature would be successful. Ten votes, with Britain against was not bad going, what if the Irish had enjoyed British support? The British were happy with the outcome. Batterbee wrote,

> this is the most satisfactory account that could have been hoped for. The Irish Free State has not got in and would not have got in if all the Empire delegates had voted for her—a nasty situation would have arisen if she had obtained sufficient foreign votes to enable her to say that had she got the votes of the British block she would have been successful.[43]

Secondly, FitzGerald's speech must have hit its desired target. The Free State's approach had not fallen on deaf ears. Their criticism of the reconstituted Council had been so effective that the powers had to resort to exactly those tactics that the Irish deplored to remove an irritating fly in the ointment.

Edward Phelan felt that the Free State had done well. In early October he wrote to Cosgrave that:

> as regards our candidature for a seat on that body I think we have every reason to be well satisfied with the number of votes we obtained. If we had gone forward earlier we should have undoubtedly secured more votes. I think also our sudden appearance as a candidate was somewhat unexpected in view of our rather passive attitude at past sessions. If our record in this respect is better in the future, as no doubt it will become, our chances of election on another occasion will be correspondingly increased.[44]

---

42 Terence de Vere White, *Kevin O'Higgins* (Dublin, 1986 edition), p. 190.
43 PRO, DO 117/27, Batterbee to Harding, 16 September 1926.
44 NA, S. 5685, 7 October 1926.

Phelan also wrote to Eoin MacNeill that 'as I look back on the Assembly I am more than ever convinced that the line we took was the right one and that both the Free State and the League owe the delegation a debt'.[45]

The last week of the Assembly: 18–25 September 1926

By 18 September, with the elections over, the delegation returned to the more mundane aspects of the Assembly. FitzGerald returned to the chair of the Second Committee. The rest of the delegation continued at their Committees and at the plenary meetings of the Assembly. The social scene was still going strong and a much more relaxed atmosphere was apparent in the behaviour of the delegation after the elections:

> We spend our evenings mostly in lounging over dinner. We go out to the restaurant about half seven or eight and leave about half nine for a Cafe where we have coffee. We leave the Café for home about eleven, except when we go to a function.[46]

On 17 September a meeting took place at Thoiry in the French Jura. It was a supposedly secret meeting between Briand and Stresemann to discuss the future of Franco-German relations. Desmond FitzGerald was curious about the meeting, and along with the cartoonist Emery Kelen, set off to Thoiry. Kelen left an account of his trip with FitzGerald in his autobiography:

> There was in Geneva a certain D. FitzGerald, foreign minister of the Irish Free State in Cosgrave's Cabinet, who differed from all other foreign ministers in that he didn't possess a hat. Like Jack Kennedy, he had one of those great Irish death to hats growths of hair. The day after Thoiry, he proposed that we should go and inspect the suddenly renowned establishment of Mère Leger.
>
> She showed us the room where the historic luncheon had taken place. I asked Mère Leger to prepare for us exactly the same dishes she had served to the foreign ministers, and she brought in saucisson chaud, truite meuniere, civet de lievre, poule au pot, pigeon, compote and cheese. There was some difference of opinion over the dessert, which FitzGerald solved after the fashion of foreign ministers, by tossing a coin. He won; they always do.[47]

---

45 UCDA, LAI/H/63, 16 October 1926.
46 UCDA, P24/2252, letter, 17 September 1926.
47 Emery Kelen, *Peace in their time: the men who led us in and out of war 1914–1945* (London, 1964), p. 166–8.

The last week of the Assembly saw significant ideas for future Irish League policy develop. These were to be the basis of a coherent Irish League policy. Developed privately in Blythe's letters they aimed to put the ad-hoc decisions of the September Assembly onto an official footing. Blythe outlined his views in a letter to his wife on 15 September; just as the state was going up for election:

> [D]uring the last two years Ireland has been absolutely negligible at the Assembly neither saying or doing anything whatsoever; except correcting a small British mistake. I am satisfied that we had better stay at home than play the role of last year and the year before. On the other hand good results can be got from our playing an independent and active part.[48]

He continued two days later: 'In order to play the part which we ought to play and which it would be valuable to play at the League we must in other years make much better preparations in advance. Also I think one or two people in External Affairs must be put onto League work all year round'.[49] Blythe returned to Ireland with these thoughts on his mind. The following chapter will show how the official acceptance of this outline led to the adoption of a more widespread and resolute League policy.

Conclusion

The September 1926 Assembly shows the widening scope of 1920s Free State foreign policy. External affairs were beginning to signify more than Anglo-Irish affairs. The stance taken at the Assembly and the Council elections was European and international. The Seventh Assembly was a turning point in the Free State's League membership. Through actively criticising the new rules for the election of non-permanent members to the Council and showing displeasure at them by offering her candidature to upset the pre-arranged lists of candidates, the Free State became the media personality of the Assembly. This approach portrayed the Irish delegates as representatives of the small states who could not hope to gain a Council seat due to Great Power unwillingness to choose them as desirable candidates. It was the event that allowed the Free State to make a new start at the League. The state was placed in a position from which she could make or break her League policy. It was not in itself the beginning of a redefinition, but the proof to back up Walshe's assertion of the previous February that the League was a basic foundation of Free State foreign policy. From this, the desire to develop a coherent long-

---

48 UCDA, P24/2252.
49 Ibid., letter, 21 September 1926.

term policy emerged, based initially on Ernest Blythe's criticisms of the Irish performance at the 1926 Assembly. The 1926 Assembly gave reassurance that the Free State had a part to play in the workings of the League. It also showed the Free State that it had a part to play in the wider world.

The election was a judgement of the Free State's position in the wider world as seen through the eyes of the League's members. The results show that there was support for Ireland's concerns over the Council and the Assembly and a belief in them as candidates. The election result shows that a new state, unsupported by the major powers and on its own steam, could prevent an arranged election from going ahead. It also showed that the Free State was accepted as a small power of some ability in the eyes of some of the other League members. This could only be a good start. By 1926 the Free State was at a cross-roads with its League policy. Either the prominent stance taken at the 1926 Assembly could be built upon, or the state could relapse into the slumber that had characterised League policy in 1925.

CHAPTER 4

The Re-appraisal and Re-direction of League Policy, 1927–9

The Blythe memorandum

On returning to Dublin after the 1926 Assembly Ernest Blythe formally set out his thoughts on the development of League policy. The resulting memorandum was the first time since 1923 that a member of the Executive Council had put forward a comprehensive approach to the organisation and implementation of Irish League policy. His ideas arose from his personal experiences at the 1926 Assembly and were not related to his post as Minister for Finance:

> I am of the opinion that it would be to the advantage of this country to take the work of the League more seriously than in the past. I feel satisfied that the general work of the League may be of enormous value to the world at large and indirectly, (if not directly), to this country.[1]

Blythe advocated that the Irish follow a high profile, comprehensively structured League policy. The seven points that the memorandum argued were:

> Delegation to be consulted 12 months in advance.
> Same delegation every year.
> Special League of Nations staff in the Department of External Affairs.
> Delegates to be briefed 1 month in advance.
> Meetings of delegates to be held during previous 2 to 3 months.
> Following these meetings delegates to receive instructions from the
>   Executive Council on all important matters.
> Social activities to be planned well in advance.[2]

The League and the Department of External Affairs were considered by Blythe to be assets to the Free State's foreign policy worth developing. He did

1 UCDA, P24/157.
2 NA, S. 8176.

not consider the League to be a drain on the exchequer as the Department of Finance contended. He proposed a dual stance for the state:

> The League generally would be strengthened by the existence of another state which took up an intelligent and independent line on every question which arose and, the status of the Saorstát itself both in the League and in the British Commonwealth of Nations would be very substantially improved.[3]

An independent Irish policy would help develop the League's stature and Ireland's place within the League system. The League would also be an ideal forum for the six Dominions to assert their growing international autonomy. From 1926 to 1931 these principles were central to the Free State's foreign relations. FitzGerald's comment that, 'at least Ernest will go back and press that this job is not a holiday for me' and Blythe's placement on the delegation suggests External Affairs was trying to sell the League to Finance.[4] Blythe was successfully won over as he concluded:

> The carrying out of such a change as I suggest may involve some additional expense but in my view there is no satisfactory half-way-house between taking the League seriously (which involves endeavouring to acquit ourselves creditably in the Commissions and the Assembly) and abstaining from sending any delegation to Geneva.[5]

Blythe's guidelines were to be augmented by Walshe and later MacWhite. By December 1926 a new phase in Irish League policy had begun.

The Walshe memorandum

In December 1926, Walshe circulated a memorandum on the need to increase the Department's staff to allow greater flexibility in the department and to increase its stature.[6] A significant portion was given over to League policy. Walshe argued that the League was central to Free State external relations. The equality conferred on the Dominions by the Balfour Declaration[7] of the 1926 Imperial Conference and its redefinition of the Dominions role in inter-

---

3 Op. cit., P24/157.
4 UCDA, P80/1407.
5 Op. cit. P24/157.
6 NA, S.5337.
7 This stated that the dominions 'are autonomous communities within the British Empire, equal in status, in no way sub ordinate to one another in any aspect of their domestic or external affairs, though united by their common allegiance to the crown, and fully associated as members of the British Commonwealth'.

national relations, led Walshe to link the Commonwealth and League as the core concerns of Irish foreign relations. Walshe began:

> The Dominions will have to depend largely on their position and activities in the League to complete their recognition as international entities. The acquisition of a position of prestige in the League is a possibility well within the reach of a country situated as we are without the need of backstairs intrigue. The post of representative at the League should therefore be maintained ... The League representative more than any other of our representatives abroad has an opportunity of getting the active goodwill of all countries including Great Britain for the Saorstát, and of studying their methods of diplomacy. He has to defeat these methods with friendly correctness when they tend to manifest themselves in conclusions derogatory to the status of the Dominions. He has to keep his Department at home in detailed and constant touch with every aspect of the League's activities so that our Delegates may be prepared long beforehand to take an active part in all the discussions of the Assembly.[8]

Walshe knew that the League was being neglected by Ireland, and that this was due to the lack of resources, both human and logistical, in his department:

> The Department has been understaffed since the beginning ... We have largely been obliged to leave our missions abroad largely to their own devices, and have been, consequently, in part responsible for their mistakes and for the smallness of the positive results achieved by them ... We have almost entirely neglected the League of Nations ... *We are at a point where things vitally affecting our international and internal situation can happen without our knowledge.*

These are not the words of a civil servant who desired to neglect League policy or Irish involvement at the League. It is symptomatic of Walshe's desire to improve departmental procedures relating to the League and devote more of the scarce resources available to External Affairs to upgrade League policy.

By the end of 1926, Walshe, a senior member of the administration and Blythe, a senior member of the Executive Council had emphasised the need to develop League policy.[9] This positive fallout from the 1926 Assembly marks the beginning of a slow and deliberate reappraisal of Irish League policy. These developments were soon disrupted by events in Geneva.

8 NA, S. 5337.
9 The absence of any documentation from Desmond FitzGerald may be because he was immediately involved in the Imperial Conference after the League Assembly

The March 1927 Council incident

At the March 1927 Council session, Sir Austen Chamberlain implied that only Great Britain could represent the Dominions on the League Council. A new form of treaty signature would be implemented which would subordinate the Dominions to Great Britain. This attacked Dominion equality with other League members. If accepted as a precedent it would damage the Free State's increasingly independent League policy.

The Free State was aware that Chamberlain would make a statement, but was not aware of how damaging its content would be. On 11 February 1927, MacWhite wrote to Desmond FitzGerald that the Irish representative should sit in whilst Sir Austen spoke, 'otherwise, Sir Austen Chamberlain can get up ... and announce that he is speaking in the name of seven Governments'.[10] The Free State tried to make sure Sir Austen made clear in the statement that he was 'acting on request of the other members of the Commonwealth'.[11] Yet Chamberlain implied that a Dominion could not sit on the Council in its own right and that Great Britain represented them as the sole imperial representative. It was a clear sign of subordination. MacWhite reported to FitzGerald that

> if it is generally accepted, the status of the Saorstát as a member of the League will be considered affected. Our inequality with all the other members of the League cannot escape the notice of international jurists and other interested parties.[12]

Chamberlain's most damaging comments surfaced once the minutes were published. MacWhite wrote to FitzGerald, on 15 March 1927:

> [Y]ou will note that Sir Austen is made to say that he sits there [the Council] 'as a representative of Great Britain and the Dominions.' Sir Austen did not mention the Dominions at the Council meeting in this context, although he left it to be implied that he represents them, but the minutes which were written leave no shadow of a doubt as to what he meant.[13]

The need to redress the impact of Chamberlain's statement sent League policy off on a Commonwealth tangent through 1927. League policy was intertwined with Commonwealth policy as the basis of the Free State external relations.

---

10 NA, LN 65.
11 Ibid., Governor General to Secretary of State for the Dominions, 3 March 1927.
12 NA, LN 65.
13 Ibid.

Edward Phelan was incensed by Chamberlain's behaviour and wrote to Desmond FitzGerald that:

> Sir Austen made the following statements: ... 'I sit here as the representative of Great Britain and the Dominions, *but the Dominions sit in the Assembly in their own name.*' The underlining is mine. As this was prefaced by the statement:- 'I make this statement at the express desire of all the Governments represented at the Imperial Conference', it seems to me that either he or I or you must have gone mad. I cannot believe that he was authorised to make any such statement by your self and Kevin.[14]

The short-term option was to write to the League authorities and get them to verify the error by including an erratum slip with the reports stating the true meaning of Chamberlain's statement. Directly the Free State told London,

> His Majesty's Government in the Irish Free State have no doubt that the obvious note takers errors in the statement quoted have already been corrected by the Foreign office, but they feel that such a fundamental departure from the principle of co-equality of all the members of the Commonwealth is implied ... in the description of Sir Austen as the representative of Great Britain and the Dominions instead of as representative of Great Britain alone ... (these) should be brought formally to the notice of His Majesty's Government so that the responsible section of the secretariat may be warned to exercise greater care in future.[15]

It was all the Free State could do until the September Assembly.

Walshe wrote to MacWhite on 25 March 1927 proposing a solution: '[the British] have gone so far that the Canadians, if they wish to maintain the right of the Dominions to separate membership of the Council, will be obliged to go up for election themselves this year or to give us their open support'.[16] Chamberlain had to be refuted by creating the precedent of Dominion membership of the Council. By informing the Canadians the Free State was trying to co-ordinate action between the Dominions to rectify the situation. Walshe telegraphed Deasy, his opposite number in Ottawa that, 'we have officially drawn [the] British Government's attention to [the] use [of] words ["]Her Dominions["] and also [the British] claim to represent Dominions on Council as [a] fundamental departure [from the] principle [of] co-equality. Have assured due to note-taker's error and require immediate public correction'.[17]

14 UCDA, P80/557, 21 March 1927.
15 Ibid., T.M. Healy to Amery, 25 March 1927.
16 NA, LN 65.
17 Ibid., 29 March 1927.

The importance of this incident for Free State League policy was outlined by MacWhite in a report to FitzGerald dated 29 March 1927:'[If] the Saorstát should go up for election to the Council in September next she would make but a very poor show unless something is done to dispel the error that now prevails in League circles as a result of Sir Austen Chamberlain's statement.'[18]

The British denied the accuracy of the minutes and stated that Chamberlain was the representative of Britain only, not the Dominions. The incident had soured Irish relations within the Commonwealth. The British added that 'the Secretariat of the League have been asked to make the necessary corrections in the minutes of the meetings', but Dublin was not so sure and instructed MacWhite to, 'secure that the Secretariat would give adequate publicity to the correction'.[19] Chamberlain had created a situation out of which the Dominions could only extract themselves by getting one of their number elected to the Council.

Sir Eric Drummond subtly gave MacWhite his opinion on the matter: 'I pretended to Sir Eric that the error was due to the carelessness of some of his office, but he only shook his head and smiled'.[20] There had been a definite move by elements within the Secretariat to redraft Chamberlain's statement to the detriment of the Dominions. The Free State, with the help of Canada, would create such a precedent to reverse Chamberlain's damaging statement to the ultimate benefit of Free State League and Commonwealth policy. The Irish response would accentuate the changes in the Dominion's external status from the 1926 Imperial Conference and would make the equality of all League members clear. The effect of this would be to again increase the Free State's position in the League.

Patrick McGilligan and the stabilisation of League policy: 1927–30

It was imperative to the state that a Dominion be elected to reaffirm the Dominions independent position in the League. Walshe considered that,

> the feeling that Great Britain ('British Empire') represents all the Commonwealth states on the Council is still very strong and though it has been somewhat weakened ... it is never the less clear that only the actual election of another Commonwealth state to the Council will make our independent status at the League apparent at home and abroad.[21]

---

18 Ibid.
19 NA, D.F/A, LB, Walshe to MacWhite, 27 April 1927.
20 Ibid.
21 NA, S. 5166.

The Executive Council decided that, 'the Saorstát should offer itself as a candidate for one of the non-permanent seats on the Council, but that if Canada decided to go forward the Saorstát should withdraw in its favour.'[22] League policy was adapted to fit the different circumstances of 1927. In 1926 the state had adopted an independent position relative to the crisis over the composition of the Council. In 1927 the Free State was again insisting upon the equality of League members and vindicating the equality given to the Dominions by the Balfour Declaration.

At the Assembly the Irish delegates concentrated on getting either Canada or the Free State elected to the Council. Canada was successfully elected, with Free State help, for three years. The Dominions had reasserted their position as equal members of the League.

Canada's election was the subject of a memorandum prepared by Walshe to acquaint the new Minister for External Affairs, Patrick McGilligan, with Free State League policy.[23] It argued that the League was an organisation in which small states could increase their status within the world community and this was of particular value to the Dominions. Walshe felt that the League was worth 'serious and constant attention' as Irish status could suffer most at the League from Foreign Office attacks on Dominions desiring to make their status clear to the world and to obtain recognition for their increasing autonomy.

The memorandum highlights the inter-relationship between the League and the Commonwealth as the fundamental elements of Free State foreign policy. In Walshe's opinion, the Free State was almost entirely responsible for Canada's candidature. He wrote that: 'without the pressure exercised from the Free State between June and September, Canada would not have become a candidate.' This episode shows how the Dominions could work together at the League to assert their independence. From the memorandum it appears, or at least Walshe wanted to make it appear to McGilligan, that Canada was little more than a front for the Free State. As a near contemporary account put it, 'the sudden incursion of Canada into world politics was rather unexpected ... the Canadians might have deferred for some time but for the initiative taken by the Free State'.[24] It was a sign of the growing stature of the Free State in the League. The Canadians did procrastinate and were lackadaisical in their approach to the elections when left without Free State support. Walshe felt that:

22 NA, Cabinet Minutes G2/6 (C3/14).
23 UCDA, P35/B/117. **Patrick McGilligan** (1889–1979): Politician (Cumann na nGaedheal and Fine Gael). Minister for Industry and Commerce (1924–32) where he was responsible for the first national loan and the Shannon Scheme. As Minister for External Affairs (1927–32), in addition to his role in League of Nations policy, he led the Free State's delegation to Imperial Conferences and was responsible for the final drafting of the statute of Westminster (1931). He was Minister for Finance in the 1948–51 Inter-Party Government and Attorney General from 1954 to 1957.
24 Arthur B. Keith, *The Sovereignty of the British Dominions* (London, 1929), p. 331.

> Canada would not have been a candidate without pressure from the Irish Free State. It is equally true that her candidature would not have been successful without the work done on her behalf by the Irish Free State delegation. It was of the utmost importance that Belgium should not succeed in her request for re-eligibility to the Council. Had she succeeded, Canada would have been rejected. The Irish Free State delegation had to urge strongly on Canada herself as well as the other Dominions to vote against Belgium on the question ... In the whole matter Mr. MacWhite's knowledge of League affairs and his friendly relations with some members of almost every delegation were a deciding factor.[25]

For Free State policy to succeed in the backroom dealing surrounding the elections shows the state's increasing stature and influence at Geneva. The link with Chamberlain's statements to the March meeting of the Council is evident:

> Canada's election to the Council puts an end to Great Britain's pretence to represent the other states of the Commonwealth. Canada was elected to represent the Assembly like all the other non-permanent members and theoretically there should be no difficulty in having other states of the Commonwealth elected during Canada's periods of office, though in practice there would be serious difficulty.
>
> The 8th Assembly therefore marks another step forward in the evolution of the Dominions and no occasion should be lost to emphasise its significance. Our status will only be recognised by the world in proportion as we exercise the power of a sovereign state through concrete actions.[26]

The state had no qualms about using others and the mechanisms of the League to its own ends. It was preparing the ground for a future attempt at election to the Council by nullifying Austen Chamberlain's statement and setting a precedent that the Dominions could sit on the Council as independent members.

On 14 April 1928 Michael MacWhite sent the new Minister a report on the state's position at Geneva with guidelines on future policy. His opening theme was that though the state was a League member since 1923,

> the prestige of the Saorstát amongst the League members is less to-day than it was five or six years ago. Six Assemblies have come and gone

25 UCDA, P35/B/117.
26 Ibid.

since she became a Member of the League, nevertheless the voice of the Saorstát has been scarcely heard in the Reformation Hall.[27]

Yet there were more positive points,

> From this, however, it must not be inferred that their action on matters under discussion has been insignificant. On the contrary, it has on many occasions been appreciable for influence may be exercised in conversations with other delegates, in supporting proposals corresponding to our ideas and by a discriminating use of the vote.

MacWhite argued that the long-term position of Ireland within the League depended on her representatives participating actively and openly in the general work of the Assembly and its committees. The Saorstát should cultivate its international relations using the League. He considered that the Free State would only have a future in the international system if it exploited the options open to it at Geneva. MacWhite had tried to follow this line, but needed increased resources to intervene effectively in League affairs. He asked for more elaborate instructions and an opportunity of discussing policy development with the departments concerned.

MacWhite did not intend McGilligan to give up in despair. He ended the memorandum on an optimistic note that gave McGilligan ideas on where future policy would lead to:

> The question of Canada's successor on the Council must be of first class importance to the Saorstát. Canada's mandate will not expire before 1930 and if the Saorstát should aspire to it, and her prestige both at home and abroad requires that she should, it is imperative that she should make her candidature known at an early date.
>
> The Saorstát's chances of success will depend to a high degree on her action in League matters during the next two years.
>
> If this clause (the Optional Clause of the Statute of the Permanent Court of International court of Justice) could be signed on behalf of the Saorstát before the 1930 Assembly her chances of election to a seat on the League Council would be considerably enhanced.
>
> The question of the limitation of armaments is becoming day by day of greater importance to the League and its members. It is one on which the Saorstát could take up a very strong attitude in view of the reductions that have been effected in this domain in the Saorstát Army since 1924.

---

27 NA, LN 1–7, though, with regard to the state's prominent stance at the 1926 Assembly, this was hardly true.

> Humanitarian questions, such as traffic in drugs, traffic in Women and Children and Hygiene should also receive attention, as many States attach perhaps more importance to this side of the League(s) activities, where practical work can be accomplished, than to those which they regard as more or less chimerical.

MacWhite had been intentionally scathing making no mention of the 1926 election attempt or the effect that the registration of the treaty had in League circles. He was pressing for more than a holding operation; for the Free State to make active use of the League to develop policy coherently rather than just having a transient presence. He wanted definite instructions from Dublin as to his future policy at Geneva. As a prompt MacWhite had set the agenda through describing the various areas open to the Free State, now he wanted guidance in the direction he could follow to improve the state's interests and position at the League. This memorandum, along with the policy inherited from FitzGerald, became the basis of McGilligan's League policy. MacWhite had ultimately set the agenda for League policy for the remainder of the decade. Policy would concentrate on improving the state's position at the League and in increasing its role in League affairs with the ultimate objective of election to the Council. McGilligan acted in the spirit of MacWhite's memorandum. It is noteworthy that he left his own comments about what MacWhite had proposed:

> These points of consequence arise on this: Arbitration, Limitation of Armaments and the Commonwealth caucus system at Geneva. On all three we must have our minds cleared before the delegation for this years Assembly leaves. File this for later on and meanwhile ask Mr. McDunphy to list '8 Assembly League of Nations: delegates' for an early meeting of the Executive Council. For that meeting you must prepare and circulate the usual memos, indicate the points likely to come up for discussion this year at Geneva. I shall discuss personnel with you very soon. PMG 24 April 1928.[28]

McGilligan actively implemented MacWhite's proposals. This was a far more explicit memorandum than Blythe's. Blythe had been the harbinger of the new approach; Walshe and MacWhite had provided the basis to the new active League policy. Policy combined critical support with an active stance at the League and a desire to work Ireland's international affairs along League guidelines. This was integral to the ability to pursue an active stance at the League. As Sean Murphy, Assistant Secretary at External Affairs, wrote to Patrick McGilligan, 'in order to get any advantage internationally from the League it is necessary to take a definite "stand" on the question under discus-

---

28 Ibid., McGilligan to Walshe dated 24 April 1928.

sion. That brings you into the market so to speak'.²⁹ Increasingly well prepared and well briefed, if somewhat under-resourced, the Free State's diplomats were to position themselves at the centre of that 'market'.

Preparations for the 1928 Assembly indicated how quickly the new approach was taken onboard. The Assembly was discussed on 3 July, early by previous standards, and the delegation was selected. It was to comprise of Ernest Blythe: Minister for Finance and Vice President of the Executive Council: Primary Delegate; Desmond FitzGerald: Minister for Defence; John M. O'Sullivan: Minister for Health;³⁰ John A. Costello: Attorney General;³¹ Michael MacWhite: Irish Free State Permanent Delegate at Geneva; and Sean Murphy: Assistant Secretary at the Department of External Affairs.

McGilligan would attend the Assembly if possible but put more energy into Commonwealth affairs as the decade progressed, leaving the more experienced Blythe and FitzGerald to League matters. The primary delegates would alternate between the Minister for External Affairs and the Vice-President of the Executive Council. At the more junior levels of the delegation the intention was to widen the number of members of the administration, both political and civil service, that had League experience. The personnel of the delegation stabilised and took on support staff such as secretaries. The Committees of the Assembly were assigned in a manner best suited to the individual interests of the delegates. For example, Minister for Defence, Desmond FitzGerald sat on the Disarmament Committee, John M. O'Sullivan, Minister for Health contributed to the Health and Social Questions Committee. The Department of External Affairs took an optimistic position, for example, regarding the 1929 Assembly: 'we must, in any case, continue our policy of taking a more prominent part each year'.³² Other departments were getting interested. For the first time there was interest in a cross-departmental delegation. In 1930 the Department of Industry and Commerce suggested one of its members should be part of the delegation. In 1931, John Leydon, of the Department of Finance, was a substitute member of the delegation.

29 NA, LN 1–7, 19 September 1928. **Sean Murphy** (1896–1964), Solicitor, Secretary of Irish mission to Paris, 1920; represented Free State in Paris, 1923; Administrative Officer, Department of External Affairs, 1925–8, Assistant Secretary, 1928–38. Minister to France, 1938–50. Ambassador to Canada, 1950–5. Secretary of Department, 1955–7.
30 **John Marcus O'Sullivan** (1891–1948): Academic and politician (Cumann na nGaedheal) Former Professor of Modern History at University College Dublin, TD for North Kerry (1924–32), Parliamentary Secretary for the Minister for Finance (1924–6), Minister for Education (1926–32).
31 **John A. Costello** (1891–1976) Barrister, Politician (Cumann na nGaedheal, Fine Gael). Attorney General, 1926–32; represented Free State at many League of Nations and Commonwealth Conferences in late twenties, entered Dáil, 1933. Compromise Taoiseach as leader of 1948–51 Inter-Party Government. Led second Inter-Party Government, 1954–7.
32 NA, LN 1–9, note by Walshe dated 8 July 1929.

One of the potentially most damaging constraints on League policy was the replacement of Michael MacWhite by Sean Lester in April 1929.[33] It was a badly timed move. As the state was becoming more active in the League, Walshe removed an experienced diplomat with widespread connections and replaced him with a man who, on his own account, had little experience with foreign relations and foreign languages. MacWhite was resourceful and independent, able to make his own mind up about policy, and suitable for a post towards which the department could not give its fullest attention. That is not to fault Lester who held the League together during World War II and was to become its last Secretary General.[34] However it took him at least a year to get settled in and despite his ability, he never seems to have been happy under the service of the Irish Government, eventually leaving the Irish foreign service in 1934 for service with the League as High Commissioner in Danzig.

In April 1929 MacWhite was moved to Washington as part of a general shake-up and a concurrent expansion in the foreign service instituted by McGilligan.[35] Perhaps Walshe wanted to sweep clean before beginning the canvass for election to the League of Nations Council, the state's most adventurous League policy to date. In any case it seems a strange option to take so close to this demarche, the new Ministers abroad had little time to settle in and make contacts before starting to implement an arduous and high profile policy. According to Stephen Barcroft, 'Lester was at first reluctant to go'.[36] There were some rumours that his appointment was to be temporary and that Desmond FitzGerald was to replace him once he had finished his reform of the Free State's Defence Forces. Lester cannot be blamed for the fact that he was unfamiliar with the League. MacWhite's removal left the Free State for a temporary but crucial period with an inexperienced diplomat in an important office.

A major development was McGilligan's use of both Lester and MacWhite to brief him on the situation at Geneva before the Assembly. In 1928, MacWhite was recalled to Dublin for consultation with the delegation before the Assembly. Each year Francis Cremins wrote to Lester that, 'the Minister would be glad to bring to his notice as early as possible any matter which you consider

---

33 Sean Lester (1889–1959) Former *Freeman's Journal* news editor who drifted into Sinn Féin. Worked in publicity section of the Department of External Affairs (1923–9), representative to League of Nations (1929–33), seconded to League as High Commissioner for Danzig (1934–7), returned to Geneva as Deputy Secretary General of the League (1937–40), Secretary General of the League of Nations (1940–7).
34 A detailed account of Lester as Secretary General, from 1940 to 1947, is given in Arthur W. Rovine, *The First 50 Years: The Secretary General in World Politics 1920–1970* (Leyden, 1970), pp. 172–99.
35 In the autumn of 1928 it was rumoured that MacWhite's next post would be to set up the Free State's legation in Paris.
36 Stephen Barcroft, 'The International Civil Servant: The League of Nations Career of Sean Lester'. Ph.D. Thesis Trinity College Dublin, 1972, p. 6.

the delegation could usefully deal with in the discussion at the Assembly'.[37] Walshe and his staff at Headquarters had remoulded their preparations for the Assembly with a greater emphasis on the ability of a well-briefed delegation to actively participate in the working of the Assembly. Dublin-Geneva links assumed a higher profile and level of communication as Minister and Permanent Representative co-operated on the Assembly preparations and shared intelligence. An active League policy was finally in place with a constant eye on the future and especially election to the Council.

Policy in action

Devising a new approach to League policy was one matter, implementing it was another. It was within the Assembly that the Free State pursued its newly devised policy as it was not a member of any other League body.[38] In the League hierarchy, the Council got the prestigious tasks, the Assembly the more humdrum affairs. Delegation reports and archive records indicate a wider area of activity and results after 1928 as Patrick McGilligan remodelled League policy.

Each Assembly began with a general debate which discussed the League's work over the previous year. It was a launching board for the Irish to introduce their policies. These views were developed in the committees where the Assembly's most practical work took place. Not all of the six committees presented windows of opportunity for the Irish. Some of their affairs necessitated intricate technical briefings that External Affairs could not provide. But where action was possible Irish delegates could be outspoken, potentially rebellious and at least constructive in their actions. The areas targeted by the Irish were,

- Internal Reform of the League
- Economic Policy of the League
- The Codification of International Law
- The Ratification of League Conventions
- The Optional Clause: September 1929
- Disarmament
- The General Act

---

37 NA, LN 1-9, 24 July 1929. **Francis T. Cremins** (1885–1975): Diplomat and Civil Servant. General Post Office, 1900–20; External Affairs, 1922–5; Lands and Fisheries, 1925–9; Head of League of Nations Section, External Affairs, 1929–34; Permanent Representative at Geneva, 1934–40, Chargé d'Affaires at Berne, 1940–9.
38 The International Labour Organisation and the other ancillary League organs are not within the scope of this work.

The general debate: 1928–31

The Irish used the general debate to give qualified support to the League. It underlined the Irish presence and allowed the delegation to begin each Assembly on a prominent note. The tone of the delegate's speeches tells much about them. They were younger than most present and lacked the stolidity of some of the older delegates. They had in the last ten years been part of an independence movement in a country undergoing a national revolution. A rebellious zeal and idealism was evident in their speeches.

The speaker was the Chief Delegate, either Blythe or McGilligan. The exception was Daniel Binchy, Free State Minister in Berlin who addressed the Assembly in 1931. There were few references to Dominion affairs in Free State League policy in the speeches. Instead the Free State asserted its independence. The most important message was 'critical support'. The Free State would support the League, but was not afraid to criticise it when it stepped out of line or if it was not living up to its functions or the Covenant.

In 1928, Blythe illustrated this tactic when speaking on the choice of officials in the Secretariat. He hoped that great care would be taken by the Secretary General that nothing was done to suggest that certain states had rights to particular posts in the Secretariat. A time might come when Secretariat officials were 'appointed and promoted solely on their personal merits and qualifications, without reference to any question of nationality.'[39] Blythe recognised that this was impossible due to 'national jealousies and suspicions'.

MacWhite wrote to Blythe in late September 1928 and informed him, with characteristic optimism that the Irish delegation had made a good impression:

> The independent attitude it invariably adopted both in the Assembly and in the Commissions has been favourably commented on in diplomatic circles. With better preparation next year we could manage that no important negotiations could go on during the Assembly without our views being considered.[40]

In 1929, Patrick McGilligan followed Blythe, reminding the League about its plans for security and disarmament. The Free State was not optimistic about the moral pronouncements and the lack of action that was stalling the disarmament process. McGilligan argued that words on their own were not enough, they had to be followed by effective action, otherwise

> they lose their effectiveness and, eventually, can become harmful as conveying to the public interested in these matters that words and

---

39 UCDA, P24/203, League of Nations Ninth Assembly, Report of the Delegation of Saorstát Éireann, pp. 52–3.
40 UCDA, P24/472, MacWhite to Blythe 28 September 1928.

> actions have here no bond, that statements are not seriously meant, or that the League is so ineffective that even in one of the principle tasks laid upon it by the Covenant it can and ought to be ignored. It would be dangerous to accustom our peoples to couple together the ideas of 'League work for disarmament' and 'futility' ... We cannot close our eyes to the fact that although during the past ten years there has been a considerable increase in general security, due to the work of the League, there has been no corresponding decrease in the implements of war.[41]

This speech went down well, Cremins informed Walshe that, 'the Minister was very well received, and the Assembly was unusually attentive, several points being loudly applauded'.[42] The Free State was pulling no punches. The Irish indicated their support for the League and its agenda but not of how it was being implemented.

The following year Blythe was as critical and under no illusion that the Geneva system was failing to live up to its goals. This was effectively set against the League's tenth birthday. Whilst the existence of the League was again praised as a worthwhile institution Blythe made clear that it could not to sit back on its laurels. Ten years old, the League was still young in an international system that had been controlled by nation-states for over 250 years. The Irish urged caution:

> we must realise the danger of not maintaining a satisfactory rate of progress in every field of the League's activity, particularly in those spheres, such as disarmament, which, in popular mind, are the special concern of the League. The League has not yet become a part of the daily political thought of our time through out the world. In the mind of the masses, it is still on trial. A feeling of disillusionment in regard to it may grow up if, within a very short time, much more cannot be done towards limiting the preparation for war.[43]

By 1931, after the Japanese invasion of Manchuria, faith in the League was an increasingly difficult stance. The Free State was not turning from the League; it was still worthy of support, but the world climate was increasingly difficult for international organisations to be effective. If anything, the Irish, now Council members, were more resolutely in support of the League than ever before. Binchy outlined the future facing the League in his 1931 speech:

> [I]f groups and blocks of States are formed outside the auspices of the League of Nations; if the State's concerned take up the attitude that

---

41 NA, S. 8179.
42 NA, LN 1-9, 11 October 1929.
43 NA, S. 8180.

the internal arrangements of those groups and their policy towards other States are solely their own concern, outside the jurisdiction of the League and its organs, then I think the League will have become an empty framework outside of which will be found the realities of international life. If, on the other hand, the members of the League are prepared to adapt and to bring within a universal framework of methods which they have devised to meet their particular international needs, the League of Nations will have become the real international framework.[44]

Such was the Free State's ideal of the League through the 1920s. As the 1930s opened and the international climate became more troubled it looked increasingly doubtful that this view would prevail. Whilst the Saorstát was willing to support the aims and methods of the League, support was incompatible with a League that functioned inefficiently.

Internal reform of the League

An international civil service was a novel idea. A non-partisan organisation would administer the affairs of the League. Its employees would be equally picked from amongst member nations. There was jealousy over appointments. Defects existed in the structure of the organisation as it lacked regularised pension and promotion schemes.

The Free State spoke out on this issue as a 'good League member' to improve the League for all, especially the smaller states. The League had to be seen to get its own house in order before it could claim to be able to do the same for that of anybody else. This promoted the state's image as part of its plan for election to the Council. In 1928 Ernest Blythe outlined the approach: 'the time has arrived when precautions should be deliberately taken to ensure that the international character and outlook of the civil service of the League, and its undivided loyalty to this great international organisation will be permanently maintained.'[45] He then advocated a system with equality and internationalism at the centre of the promotions and staff policy of the Secretariat. It advocated the replacement of officials by those of other nations so as to prevent any League official from thinking that they held their office as a sinecure of their national government. This would increase the calibre of those applying for posts and the Secretary General would not be 'hampered by the growth of a tradition which gave a preponderating importance to national claims'.[46]

44 NA, S 8181.
45 UCDA, P24/ 203, League of Nations, Ninth Assembly, Report of the Delegation of Saorstát Éireann. p. 53.
46 Ibid.

The international character of the Secretariat was paramount. Blythe's line was similar to FitzGerald's speech at the 1926 Assembly where he stated that though there should be freedom of choice in elections to the Council, international jealousies necessitated some codified system. This was a live issue; the concept of 'supra-nationality' was new to international affairs. Its first attempt in practice was the League Secretariat.

Through the 1929 Assembly the Free State delegates attacked internal League deficiencies. They would not allow the emotion of an anniversary to cloud rational judgement; there was little point in a celebration if it had no substance. McGilligan picked up Blythe's argument of 1928. It was

> essential to the proper carrying out of the work of the Secretariat that the League should take definite and early steps to ensure that the Secretariat will be a body of international Civil Servants who will have proper security of tenure, and whose advancement in the League service will, in all cases, depend on individual merit rather than on the incident of nationality.[47]

The Irish wanted to see the Secretariat work better. It was the Free State's normal line, 'what we have will do for the present, but there must be improvements'.

Sean Lester, less than half a year in the post and lacking adequate French, was left to argue the Irish case for reform of the Secretariat in the Fourth Committee. Stephen Barcroft sums it up, 'The 4th Committee held twelve meetings but Lester, still feeling his way around and unknown to his colleagues, neither spoke nor found himself on any of the sub-committees set up to deal with specific points.'[48] Thus the MacWhite–Lester shift was detrimental to performance at Geneva.

The Irish position changed by 1930. Rather than regulating the intake of the Secretariat to prevent national jealousies arising, the role of the Great Powers had to be reduced in favour of the smaller states. By giving the smaller League members a greater role, the organisation would run better because it was in the interests of the small states that it should do so.

Blythe discussed the report of the 'Committee of 13' on the Secretariat. He argued that the solution was acceptable but by no means ideal. Its most welcoming factor was that it allowed appointment and promotion on merit but also allowed regulation of the nationalities of those holding posts. This would help the selection of incumbents from small states who could balance out the overwhelming Great Power influence.

In the general debate the Free State agreed with the report, but there was still discussion in the 4th Committee. This year Sean Lester had prepared his

47 NA, S. 8179.
48 Stephen A. Barcroft, 'The International Civil servant: The League of Nations Career of Sean Lester', Ph.D. thesis, Trinity College Dublin, 1972, p. 9.

ground in a memorandum entitled 'Reorganisation of the Secretariat of the League of Nations'.[49] He argued a reduction in Great Power influence in the Secretariat. Lester had definite views on how League officials should behave when dealing with their home country:

> The official who transmits information about his own country must be careful not to become an instrument of its policy ... I would be inclined to take the line that such close contact between the official and his Government is undesirable and that information and opinion should be obtained by other means.

This was Lester's personal philosophy of the role of the international civil servant in relation to his mother country. The Free State opposed attempts to make it the duty of League officials to deal with their home country as Permanent Representatives were for this purpose. The former plan gave the Great Powers a direct route into the Secretariat and a convenient channel. Lester urged that,

> our policy should be to oppose (the above) ... and to urge that the proper line of communication with governments is not in any way through officials, but through accredited representatives. I believe that we would have support from a man like Hambro in this line.[50]

Lester brought these points to the Fourth Committee. The report being discussed was unanimous that the organisation of the Secretariat gave rise to international dissatisfaction and administrative dissent. The Great Powers were too numerous in the organisation of the higher staff of the Secretariat and there existed a feeling of insecurity and instability among the staff due to a lack of proper pension arrangements. Lester got his point across in the final report:

> In future there shall, as a general rule, be no appointment of more than one national of any state among the higher officials of the Secretariat, from and including ... Director of Section upwards. It is understood that, in principle, the successor of any of these high officials shall not be chosen from amongst the compatriots of his predecessor.[51]

---

49 NA, LN 99, 29 August 1930.
50 The Free State had the best of both, it had a permanent representative and also had Edward Phelan in the I.L.O. Phelan, however, was not approached by the Dublin administration but rather gave his own views when he thought necessary. He felt it was his duty rather than Dublin telling him that it was.
51 Report of the Irish Delegation to the 11th Assembly of the League of Nations 1930, p. 94.

The Great Powers continued to dominate the League Secretariat whilst they had a use for it. The equal distribution of posts to nationals of all member states remained a live issue. It would take some time to achieve a fully equal distribution. The Irish had drawn attention to a problem which the United Nations subsequently handled with greater success.

The Free State and the economic policy of the League

Accounts of Cumann na nGaedheal economic policy take the view that 'the overall prosperity of the economy depended on agriculture',[52] and on 'the Tariff Commission's singular lack of enthusiasm for recommending the imposition of tariffs'.[53] They pursued a free trade policy due to the agricultural basis of the state. Up to 1930-1 when the Depression hit the Free State it was 'virtually the only free trade economy in western Europe'.[54] Cumann na nGaedheal policies became protectionist in response to the economic nationalism of the 1930s. At least so it seems until analysing the state's arguments during economic discussions at the League.

Free State economic policy at Geneva did not rest on the agricultural basis of the Irish economy, or frown on tariffs. It aimed at creating within the economic plans of the League an ability for less developed countries to use tariffs to develop industrial and agricultural sectors. The League, they argued, should take account of their needs and not call for the complete reduction and removal of tariffs.

The Economic and Financial Committee (EFC) dealt with the League's economic affairs. It followed the World Economic Conference of May 1927 in aiming to remove all barriers to free economic relations between states. This was a blanket ban on tariffs. The Free State felt obliged to accept international and League conventions, but an indiscriminate ban on tariffs would damage the Free State's economic development. The League viewed tariff reduction as 'economic disarmament'; tariffs were a weapon. The Free State saw tariffs more positively. Through the late twenties in Assembly debates and in the Second Committee, Irish delegates argued that developing states needed to maintain a certain level of tariff protection to aid their growing economies.

At the 1928 Assembly, Blythe cautiously welcomed the reduction of tariffs as it removed one of the causes of international disputes. However he argued that across the board tariff restrictions were detrimental to the growth of less developed economies. He supported League policy,

---

52 Kieran A. Kennedy, Thomas Giblin, Deirdre McHugh, *The Economic Development of Ireland in the Twentieth Century* (London, 1988), p. 34.
53 Ronan Fanning, *The Irish Department of Finance: 1922–1958* (Dublin, 1978), p. 205.
54 Ibid.

so long as it is clear that it is not intended to prevent the development of countries which historical circumstances have left economically backward. It is unfortunate that the recommendation of the Economic Conference in regard to tariffs should have been so worded as to call on countries which have low tariffs, equally with countries which have excessively high tariffs, to move in the direction of reduction. Such a recommendation is unacceptable to my country.[55]

Blythe outlined the need for the League to remember less developed countries, like the Free State, which needed tariffs. He urged the League to direct its attention to only those tariffs which 'are called bargaining tariffs, as well as retaliatory tariffs and tariffs which have a political object.' The needs of less-developed nations should not be subordinated to the more economically developed in a free trade system.

John M. O'Sullivan developed the theme at the Second Committee. O'Sullivan drew attention to developing nations and argued that the League neglected the need for tariffs to aid their economies. He thus outlined the Free State's case to the Assembly:

> We are not a doctrinaire protectionist country, we are not doctrinaire Free Trade. If we feel called upon ... to transform that agricultural country, into a more industrialised country ... what policy has the League to suggest for us except the lowering of our tariffs? ... I have searched and I can find none. That is the reason why I should like to say again in regard to these small States, not that an effort was made to crush them–far from it—but that they were simply forgotten ... What we ask is that special attention should be given to the problem presented by the economically weaker countries.[56]

He went on to say that otherwise, his government had 'nothing but admiration for the excellent work that has been done by the League organisations.' The Irish had realised since the 1926 Assembly that some League members, especially the less powerful, were more equal than others. Speaking up for the rights of the small states was the only way the Great Powers would be reminded that these states had a place in the League and a right to be heard.

The Tenth Assembly proposed that the economic work of the League towards tariff reduction should be developed. A report and plan for tariff reduction was presented by the EFC. This did not take account of the Free State's line. The delegation was prepared to tackle the question; McGilligan was Minister for Industry and Commerce as well as for External Affairs, and O'Sullivan, quite a polymath, represented the state on the Second Committee.

55 UCDA, P24/203.
56 Ibid.

McGilligan took up where Blythe left off. He expressed the fear that the 'underdeveloped countries would be doomed to stagnation, or, worse still, to comparative retrogression in this respect.'[57] He thanked members of the EFC who had made clear 'the exception which these countries must constitute. This was the soft side to the hard line taken by O'Sullivan in the Second Committee. He had attacked the EFC for not outlining any solutions for states whose industrial policy was in its infancy: 'the truth was that so far it [the report] had asked them to deprive themselves of their only means of protection. If all free trade was not formally the doctrine of the League, in practise the present drive in certain quarters was towards full free trade.'[58] The League had developed its policy in blanket terms; all tariffs must be reduced, a general policy that did not suit all League members. The end that the EFC had in mind was a tariff truce. O'Sullivan did not support the truce as it would hamper the state's development and would tie the hands of successive governments. The Free State's tariffs had always been as low as possible and O'Sullivan felt that 'the suggestion now made to states whose economic and industrial development was in its infancy, that they should renounce protective tariffs was neither more nor less than an invitation to commit economic hari kiri'. League economic policy was against the spirit of internationalism. It proposed to exclude certain nations whose economic position meant that they had no option for their continued economic development but to resort to protective tariffs for 'infant industry' purposes. The Free State was arguing against the then accepted classical economic interpretation of trade theory that all states profited from free trade and that comparative advantage was to the benefit of all.

O'Sullivan was back in fighting form at the 1930 Assembly, it was his third year as Free State representative on the Second Committee. He again attacked the approach to economic policy taken by the League:

> occasionally the League has seemed inclined to plunge into methods of solving what was undoubtedly a grave condition, without full examination of the actual facts in the different countries, and was inclined also to keep too rigidly to one particular straight line, and to see salvation in that alone.[59]

His speech also dealt with the plight of agricultural areas under the depressed economic conditions of the period and the fact that the policies advocated by the League either aimed at keeping the status quo between peripheral agricultural areas and core industrialised zones.

As the 1930s dawned it became clear that total free trade was succumbing to economic nationalism. The League continued to 'shoot itself in the foot' by

57 NA, S. 8179.
58 Ibid.
59 NA, S 8180.

failing to agree on any realistic plans. Inter-war commentators failed to see the links between politics and economics. If the League had been less theoretical and seen its environment in a more practical light, its inability to deal with economic matters might not appear as all the more glaring.

From 1928 to 1930 the state's economic policy at the League was coherent and forceful against that theoretically supported by the League. The Free State was not seen at the League to be a totally free trade state; protection was perceived as vital to the future of industrial and economic development. Looking at Free State economic policy relative to that of the League, shows that the 'Free Trade' label cannot simply be slapped on the economic policy of Cumann na nGaedheal. F.S.L. Lyons has written that: 'the attitude of the Free State Government was one of extreme caution towards the whole concept of industrial protection'.[60] This was not the case in the League context. O'Sullivan, McGilligan and Blythe were three members of the same Government and formed a sizeable number, including the Minister for Finance, who did not advocate the orthodoxy followed by the Civil Service. Cumann na nGaedheal's tariff policy was never as clearly defined as to suggest a doctrinaire belief in free trade. It is necessary to take this under-emphasised protectionist streak into account when analysing Cumann na nGaedheal's economic policies to 1932.

The codification of International Law

Codification sought to make international law clearer, more precise, and more unified. The Free State felt the success of codification would allow the League to develop by letting the Permanent Court of International Justice (PCIJ) act with increased authority in international disputes. The strengthening of international law would provide the Dominions with a body over and above the Privy Council to which they could bring cases relating to inter-Dominion affairs. Codification would aid the removal of the *inter se* issue facing the Dominions

By the 1927 Assembly a 'short-list' of three areas had been decided upon for the first codification conference: Conflicts of laws on Nationality; Territorial Waters; Responsibility of states for damage suffered within their territories by foreigners. The Conference was to meet on 13 March 1930. The territorial waters issue might have aroused more interest on account of the articles and annexe of the Treaty dealing with this issue. It may have suited the Free State not to mention these articles as the provision of coastal defence provided by the Treaty was a large financial burden off the mind of the Free State Government. There was some unease that British claims to territorial waters might damage the Free State's fishing grounds but in general there

---

60 F.S.L. Lyons, *Ireland since the Famine* (London, 1971), p. 600.

were no proposals to be put forward by the Saorstát. The Conference failed to produce a draft convention.

The League wanted the work of codification to continue by asking member governments to discuss the continuance of codification. The Free State agreed that the work of codification should continue. The Great Powers took a different view. Costello had to fight hard to get the Free State's case accepted at the First Committee against a resolution put down by Britain, Germany, Greece, France and Italy that intended to quietly shelve codification. These five states argued that the codification process should only be continued 'after a full opportunity has been allowed to all the members of the League to examine the results of the experience already acquired.'[61] This put no time scale on the issue, or created no institution to guide these new deliberations. Costello argued that this 'could mean nothing else except that all projects of codification were to be shelved for all time.'

Before introducing the Irish resolution, Costello made a speech which, according to the Irish report, 'attracted considerable attention' and set out a new approach on codification. It was prompted by a rumour 'to the effect that an attempt was to be made to abandon or postpone indefinitely, the work of progressive codification. Such a course was quite unthinkable'. The Irish resolution aimed at thwarting this, and getting the question of codification reviewed. The speech outlines four proposals which the Free state felt integral to the continual codification:

> The codification must embrace the formulation of new rules, and the modification or adaptation of existing rules ... The experts concerned in the preparatory work must be under constant political guidance. The work of codification must be continuous—new efforts must be continually made to define new subjects for codification ... Account must be taken of the fact that under modern conditions international law is in a state of flux and evolution. for that reason, the codes of international law, should contain revision Clauses.

The Committee proposed by Costello was to be a flexible organisation to respond to the changes in international law and to integrate it into League documents such as the General Acts. The Irish resolution proposed that codification 'should be continued and directed in a manner most likely to produce the best possible results.' It requested the Council to appoint a committee to examine other measures that would facilitate and encourage codification. The committee would report to the 1931 Assembly.

The Polish delegate supported Costello: 'The ground should be prepared first and for that reason he was in favour of the Irish proposal which would

---

61 *Report of the Delegation of the Irish Free State to the League of Nations Assembly* (Stationary Office, Dublin, 1930). All subsequent quotes in this section from this document.

help the solution of the main question, namely, the extent of codification which the League of Nations should attempt. The Irish resolution would create a spirit of optimism. A sub-committee was set up and a new resolution combining the Irish and the joint resolution was submitted to the Assembly. This read 'The Assembly accepted demands to adjourn the question to its next session, and required the Council, in the meanwhile, to invite the members of the League of Nations, to communicate to it, their observations on these suggestions, in order that these observations may be taken into consideration by the Assembly'.

The Free State had helped the progress of codification at the Assembly. Great Power indifference had been overcome. The action of the small states had helped ensure that the codification of international law, a tricky topic at the best of times, did not fall foul of Great Power disapproval. It is an example of the power of a small state to influence larger powers.

The ratification of League conventions

League Conventions were non-obligatory instruments dealing with matters such as the prohibition of the use of poisonous gas (The Geneva Gas Protocol, 1925), the better known Opium Convention (1925), and Obscene Publications Convention (1923). It was an area in which initially the Free State fared badly. By February 1928 the Free State had only signed and ratified one; the 'Protocol of Signature for the Permanent Court of International Justice', and had signed but not yet ratified 'The Obscene Publications Convention'. On 3 April 1928, Sir Eric Drummond wrote to McGilligan about the lack of Free State ratifications as part of a general League policy to increase the number of states that were implementing League conventions. He informed the Minister of 'the importance which the Council attaches to an increase in the number of ratifications'.[62]

The 1929 Assembly saw the Free State sign the 'Optional Clause', Article 36, of the Statute of the Permanent Court of International Justice.[63] After speaking on this matter McGilligan turned to the question of ratifications. He began by explaining the Free State's poor record, 'We ourselves cannot claim a fully satisfactory certificate in this respect, but our comparatively late entry into the League, and the necessity we were under of creating an entire political system, can be pleaded in excuse.'[64]

What McGilligan advocated next can be seen in two ways; either it was a call supporting the League and the need for it to be effective, or it was electioneering to show the Free State as a concerned League member, adopt-

---

62 NA, LN 70.
63 See next section.
64 NA, S. 8179, Speech by McGilligan to the Assembly, 1929.

ing a high profile and stating its credentials in order to put its name in for the 1930 elections to the Council:

> We are convinced that it is harmful to the League, tending to bring it into disrepute, if the number of Conventions signed but not ratified is permitted to increase. This is a matter to which we propose to give early attention, and I hope that when the Assembly meets again we shall have a better record to show.[65]

McGilligan then urged other states to ratify and implement League Conventions because even though,

> the decision to take no action in the way of ratification may be taken on the grounds that the convention has no direct relevancy to national conditions. States perhaps forget that whereas the protection of a convention may not be required within its own territory, it may be of greatest value to those of its citizens who work in other countries.[66]

Referring to the Free State, McGilligan concluded, 'we have come to the conclusion that this consideration is not for us a valid excuse for failure to ratify, and that our loyalty to the League requires that we should display an interest in all the activities of the League, though we may not be directly concerned.' This laid the Free State's cards on the table for the Council election. It indicated the state's commitment to the League. McGilligan's speech stands out as one of the state's most intense at the Assembly. He was practically dictating a policy to be followed, urging all members to consider the League instead of national aspirations.

On 4 March 1930, the Executive Council approved the submission to the Dáil of nine conventions, seven of them relating to the League. They were approved in May and June 1930. Speaking on the slavery convention, McGilligan outlined why the Free State was taking this step:

> The accession of a country like Switzerland, although clearly it was accepting the obligations, and clearly not directly concerned in passing anything of the sort, would be a big moral asset towards ensuring the general application of the convention and, with that in view, we bring this convention forward here.[67]

The Free State lived up to its intentions and fulfilled its obligations relating to seven conventions before the 1930 Assembly. The League had tried to

65 Ibid.
66 Ibid., McGilligan may have been specifically referring to Free State workers in Northern Ireland.
67 *Dáil deb*, 35; 172–3, 29 May 1930.

increase the number of ratifications so Blythe, following McGilligan, was in vogue as he spoke of the interest his government felt in the report of the Committee on the Speeding up of Ratifications. Referring to McGilligan's promise Blythe stated:

> I am glad to be able to announce that, in execution of this promise, the Irish Free State has, since the last session of the Assembly, finally accepted no less than seven League Conventions. I may add to this record the fact that the Irish Free State stands third in the list of ratifications of International Labour Office Conventions, having ratified no less than eleven of these conventions in the past twelve months.[68]

The record was set straight, the state was accepting the obligations of League membership. On an international level and in supporting the League this was a good record. There was a sense of self-gratification in Blythe's 'look at us' approach and exhorting the rest of the world to follow suit. Was the Free State trying to set an example, or was it again posturing as a potential Council member? 1930 and 1931 show a large increase in the number of conventions ratified. 1931 saw the League again try to increase the number of ratified conventions. The Free State received another list of Conventions it had not yet ratified. When replying to a request to accept the 'Convention regulating the Measurement of Vessels employed in Inland Navigation (1925)', Lester replied that 'this does not appear to have any application to the existing circumstances of the Irish Free State'.[69] The high point of 1930 was never again repeated. Fianna Fáil never adopted such a prominent policy to Conventions, though they did accept a small number. By the mid 1930s and the demise of the League, the perceived need to ratify its conventions had passed. It was for a brief period at the end of the 1920s when it was felt that the League would succeed that the Free State gave its greatest attention to conventions.

The Optional Clause: September 1929

The Optional Clause gave the Permanent Court of International Justice (PCIJ) compulsory jurisdiction over disputes in which the signatory state was involved. The court was unproven in action and the international arbitration of disputes had not evolved sufficiently to warrant the widespread signature of Article 36. The Kellogg–Briand Pact of August 1928 changed this. With war 'illegal' as a manner of solving international disputes, states turned to the

---

68 NA, S. 8180.
69 NA, GE, S. 5/31, 10 February 1932.

PCIJ to solve future international disputes, and declared their intention to sign the Optional Clause at the 1929 League Assembly.

For the Free State this was another overlap between League and Commonwealth policy. Events within the Commonwealth set the backdrop to Ireland's signature. No Commonwealth state had signed the Optional Clause and Great Britain refused to sign. It was not until the return of Labour and Ramsay MacDonald to government in 1929 that Britain decided to sign.

This change of attitude opened the way for Free State signature. To sign the clause prior to this change of British policy would have been ridiculous. Great Britain was, in reality, the only state against which the Free State might have a case. Unless Great Britain adhered to the clause there was no reason for the Free State to do so. A premature signature of the Optional Clause would have triggered off a divisive inter-Dominion row. It was Cumann na nGaedheal policy to help the Dominions international evolution, not to make this more difficult. The Free State took its cue from the British decision in the middle of 1929.

There were other factors which led to the Free State decision to sign the optional Clause. The state's growing stature in international relations and its attempt to maximise its position in the League made signature likely. The change in the international climate following the signature of the Kellogg–Briand pact created a perfect reason. As McGilligan put it in the Dáil:

> We had signed that (the Kellogg–Briand Pact) amongst others and when it came to a decision in this matter we felt that having declared that war was no longer any part of national policy in relation to other States we must give further proof of good faith in the matter by indicating that we were prepared to have recourse to this method of judicial settlement in all cases where judicial settlement seemed to be the proper thing.[70]

By September 1929, it was clear that British Prime Minister Ramsay MacDonald, and Arthur Henderson, his Foreign Secretary, would sign the clause, but with reservations covering its application to inter-Dominion disputes. Dominions Office records indicate that the British expected, as early as summer 1929, the Free State to sign without such reservations.[71]

The Dominions were being given the trappings, but not the substance, of statehood in the international community. The Commonwealth delegates got caught up in rounds of meetings and negotiations as to the form of their adhesions to the Optional Clause. The meetings attempted to forge a compromise, but the Free State stuck to its line that it would not accept any reservations. Tempers flared during the difficult negotiations at these meetings as

---

70 Dáil deb, 33; 884, 26 February 1930.
71 See PRO DO 117/153 and DO 35/95/1/4021/14.

Costello turned down re-draft after re-draft. The British felt that he was being put up to this by O'Sullivan and McGilligan. By 14 September the British had become reconciled to the Free State's opting out of the Empire signature.

McGilligan outlined the Free State's approach in his address to the Assembly:

> I shall have the honour during the course of this Assembly of making the declaration accepting this Clause on behalf of the Irish Free State, confident that by this act the Irish Free State will be helping to promote the peaceful settlement of all disputes of a legal character between members of the League and other States who accept the compulsory jurisdiction of the Permanent Court of International Justice.[72]

He made no mention of reservations or conditions, the state would accept and sign the Optional Clause without them. The Dominions continued to squabble amongst themselves. On 14 September, the Free State pre-empted them and signed the clause itself with no reservations and on the sole condition of reciprocity. McGilligan made blunt references to those states, who, like the British, would only accept the Optional Clause with reservation:

> Reservations clearly cannot be made to any convention or protocol except in so far as the convention or protocol expressly provides for them. It is to be hoped, therefore, that during the coming decade League conventions will not be nullified by the practice of attaching their acceptance to such reservations.[73]

A report dated 12 September, two days before the Free State signature, outlined why the state had decided to take this independent course:

> The present government of the Irish Free State had persuaded the majority of the Irish people that they had attained, or that at least they could attain by virtue of the Treaty, full national status as a member of the comity of nations. ... [I]f we were to give away even a mere theoretic right of resort to the Permanent Court in the case of a dispute with Great Britain, it would be held that we had surrendered a fundamental principle of our sovereignty.[74]

By signing the clause without reservations the Free State was striking a blow for the League and showing the importance of the League to the Do-

---

72 NA, S. 8179.
73 Ibid.
74 UCDA, P24/187.

minions in their search for international autonomy. The Irish signature without reservations showed that unlike the British, they could accept the primacy of League guidelines before national interest. Reservations clogged up the international work of the League and with special reference to the 'Optional Clause', they removed the chance of any truly international legal system emerging.

The state benefited more from the fallout from an independent signature with no reservations, than from any potential protection offered by the clause. There are similarities to the 1927 Council incident. The Free State was creating a precedent to pre-empt that to be created by the British and the Dominions, by signing independently and in advance. There was very little chance that the state would ever bring a dispute before the Permanent Court, the best alternative was that it offered an alternative or a balance to the Privy Council. McGilligan gave a concise summary of Free State policy in the Dáil:

> We would pretty well exhaust every other method of settlement before we would take the decision to try to force a dispute before the Permanent Court of International Justice. (T)here should and very probably would be other methods of settlement more available to us, ones that we would more readily avail of, before we would go to the Permanent Court of International Justice ... I would state as the policy of this Government that the Court would be the last resort.[75]

Rather like the registration of the Treaty in 1924, the Free state signed the 'Optional Clause' in the hope that the benefits thereby incurred would never have to be used. The actual benefits accrued by the act of signature far outweighed those potential benefits gained in theory by the operation of the clause.

Disarmament

To 1930 the Free State's part in the disarmament process was limited. Ireland had to rely on speeches at the Assembly to develop its views on disarmament. The state could only follow and offer general support. As some rough notes in Patrick McGilligan's papers, probably for a Dáil speech, state:

> We have no responsibility except to take part in every movement for peace and the reduction of armaments. ... We have a special interest in joining in any movement destined to lessen the danger of war between the United States and Great Britain.[76]

75 *Dáil deb*, 33; 893, 26 February 1930.
76 UCDA, P35/B/118.

Words had to speak louder than actions. Ireland did not hold a seat on the Preparatory Commission until its last session from 6 November 1930 until 9 December 1930. This was as a result of election to the Council; all Council members were members of the Preparatory Commission.

In 1928 the Free State attempted a concerted disarmament-security policy at the Assembly. The Kellogg–Briand Pact (Pact of Paris) of August 1928, was an ideal pick-me-up for the League. Discussing the League's goal of world peace Blythe spoke in support of the Pact, describing it as a 'great and impressive effort to save humanity from a possible renewal of the horrors of war ... a new summons to the nations to bestir themselves in solving their gravest problems'.[77] The League should take heed and pursue its duty to disarmament with renewed vigour:

> The answer to the League should be plain. The general Disarmament Conference has been too long postponed ... There can be no approach to the certainty of peace until a serious beginning has been made with general disarmament ... A definite limit, in time, should be set to the work of the Preparatory Commission, and the Assembly should be requested to call the Disarmament Conference before the next ordinary session of the Assembly.

The Irish wanted the Preparatory Commission to forget its bickering and get back to work in light of the massive popular sentiment in favour of peace that was indicated by the Kellogg Pact. Desmond FitzGerald, now Minister for Defence, was not so forthright. He was Free State representative on the disarmament Committee of the Assembly. His section of the Delegation's report makes clear the total lack of agreement on the question of disarmament amongst both the members of the Committee and the members of the Preparatory Commission itself. The bulk of the discussion was amongst the Great Powers, the Free State had little room to manoeuvre and could only state support of disarmament in general and watch the powers work out the details.

The highly critical attitude adopted by Blythe was upheld by McGilligan the following year. He stressed the need to call the Disarmament Conference before public opinion gave up on the League. McGilligan felt that the result of the Preparatory Commission's work towards disarmament was, 'to the good; but I think that in the eleventh year after the world war, and a year after the Kellogg Pact, some more definite result might have been expected. ... One can hardly be charged with impatience for drawing attention to the slow progress that has been made.'[78] Again the Free State called for the immediate meeting of a Disarmament Conference, 'without waiting for agreement on technical points, in order that the political aspects may be made

77 UCDA, P24/203.
78 NA S. 8179.

apparent, and that efforts may be made to discover what concessions can be offered by all parties, in the general interest.'

The Free State was unconvinced by the endless technical debates over gun calibre and whether the tonnage of individual ships or the tonnage of individual classes of ships should be set. The underlying reason for delay was political, over and above the military covering. If states could see eye to eye politically, it was more likely that they would be able to agree militarily. Endless technical argument was turning public opinion from the League and its work, McGilligan's key point was that, 'it would be dangerous to accustom our peoples to couple together the ideas of "League work for Disarmament" and "futility".'

The Free State wanted the Disarmament Conference to be called as soon as possible. This was similar to attitudes held by Germany and the Soviet Union. The political must overcome the technical, this way the real barriers to disarmament would be broken down and agreement on the technical grounds would soon follow. McGilligan cited the Free State as an example of disarmament by one state:

> I bring forward the action of my own country which in this matter has acted in closest accordance with the spirit of the League. Five years ago we, comparatively speaking, made an enormous decrease in the armaments of the Free State and had reached a position of something approaching normality. Since then, however, we have further reduced our annual expenditure on arms from about £2,800,000 to less than £1,500,000.

This was evidently aimed at earning the Free State 'brownie points' as a good League member. The reduction in national armaments can be explained by the end of the civil war in 1923 and the drastic economies in government finances that were commonplace in the early years of the state. However they fitted in with the context of the speech and gave visible proof that the Free State was putting action to its words.

1929 was the last year that the state had to watch from the ringside. By September 1930 it was a member of the Council with a place on the Preparatory Commission. Irish options to speak on disarmament were thereby greatly enhanced. The state became involved in the technical side of the Disarmament process at the 'eleventh hour'. By late 1930 the slow work of the Preparatory Commission, helped on by the success of the London Naval Conference of January to April 1930, had led to the adoption of a Draft Disarmament Convention. Few had any belief in it, as Lord Cecil wrote, 'until the figures have been filled in, it is impossible to estimate how complete will be the first general disarmament treaty'.[79] This convention was, by all

---

79 *Survey of International Affairs, 1930* (London, 1931), p. 123.

accounts, a pale shadow of the level and effectiveness of the League's powers for disarmament expected in 1920. The sixty-second session of the Council accepted the Convention in January 1931. It resolved that the Disarmament Conference was to open in Geneva on 2 February 1932.

The General Act

The League, moved by the spirit of the failed Geneva Protocol, tried to build a security and arbitration framework for the late 1920s. States could disarm secure in the knowledge that their disputes could be solved peacefully by a League mechanism. If there was a danger of war, the League could step in and help the victim through new powers given to the Council. This resulted in a number of 'Model Treaties' which covered arbitration and conciliation and represented a flexible and sophisticated attempt to be a 'guide to all those who might wish, or be persuaded to join in constructing a still more extensive system of safeguards'.[80]

The 1928 Assembly took the treaties dealing with the Pacific Settlement of International Disputes and moulded them into, 'The General Act for the Pacific Settlement of International Disputes', henceforth, 'The General Act'. It created a system for solving international disputes by judicial settlement, arbitration and conciliation. The League had finally created a fairly viable security system. The General Act was left open for signature from 26 September 1928.

The Free State supported the General Act from the beginning. In order to disassociate itself from the negative remarks of Britain and Australia on the matter, the Attorney General, John A. Costello made the state's position clear:

> The Irish Free State accepted the scheme embodied in the General Act and considered it to be a serious effort at simplifying and facilitating the process of Arbitration and as satisfying a world wide public demand for some practical result on the part of the League in the development of the Pacific Settlement of International Disputes.[81]

This point was reinforced by Ernest Blythe at the Assembly:

> I do not hesitate to say that the Irish Free State is no less strongly in favour of arbitration than Canada It is the duty of all the governments which have signed the Kellogg Pact to endeavour to bring about the conditions under which it can most surely achieve its objective. They

---

80 Walters, *History*, p. 383.
81 NA, LN 1–7, 25 September 1928.

must work for the establishment of goodwill and the removal of mistrust among nations.[82]

But by the end of the Assembly the General Act remained without a single signature.

At the 1929 Assembly, Patrick McGilligan announced that the Free State intended to sign the General Act. This was an independent decision, the Commonwealth did not decide to sign until after discussions held at the 1930 Imperial Conference. McGilligan linked the signature in with the signing by the Free State of the Optional Clause:

> We feel, however, that acceptance of the Optional Clause is hardly enough. It is in our view necessary to have some means of settling those types of disputes which are not strictly legal in character. The Committee on Arbitration and Security has provided us with a means of achieving this. The General Act, as well as model bilateral treaties in regard to arbitration, conciliation and judicial settlement are now open to accession by all members of the League. It is my intention to seek, during the next Session of Parliament, approval for the acceptance of the General Act by the Irish Free State.[83]

That session of parliament passed without the acceptance of the Act. Francis Cremins puts this down to a time constraint: 'it was not found possible, owing to the pressure of the demands on parliamentary time, to submit the question of our accession to the General Act to the Dáil before the commencement of the Summer recess'.[84] Ernest Blythe returned to the Act in his 1930 address to the Assembly. Opening on the link between the Kellogg–Briand Pact and the Covenant in the pacific settlement of international disputes, Blythe continued:

> The acceptance of this general obligation must necessarily lead to the conclusion of agreements between all Members of the League, establishing the machinery necessary to give practical effect to it, if the case should arise. The Committee on Arbitration and Security have provided us with a large variety of agreements of this kind. For those who prefer them, there are the model bilateral treaties on conciliation, arbitration and judicial settlement and, in addition to these, there are the model multi-lateral treaties dealing with the same subjects which have been amalgamated into the General Act. The attitude which we have

---

82 UCDA, P24\203.
83 NA, S. 8179.
84 NA, GE Series, S. 7/2, 14 August 1930, Cremins to Lester.

already declared with regard to the principles declared in the General Act remains unchanged.[85]

The following June, Patrick McGilligan introduced the General Act in the Dáil. McGilligan used his introductory speech as a résumé of developments to date in the construction of a League security mechanism in which the Free State had been involved:

> We may take another step along the rather difficult and tortuous way that leads to the settlement of disputes by means other than warlike ones ... We have incurred obligations with regard to the pacific settlement of disputes in a variety of ways, under the Covenant of the League of Nations, the Kellogg Pact, the Optional clause with regard to the Permanent Court of International Justice, and in a variety of Treaties which have specific clauses attached to them from time to time[86]

By the time McGilligan had finished his introduction, the state's adherence to the concept of peacefully settling disputes between nations by arbitration or conciliation was in no doubt. He continued by fully outlining the system contained in the General Act, 'the General Act really applies to all classes of disputes, whether legal or those that could not be brought within the category of legal disputes'.[87] The state was to accede to all the provisions of the act for a period of five years[88], this would expand on the Optional Clause. Even so McGilligan may have been adopting an 'in for a penny, in for a pound' attitude:

> It seems better that we should have the whole procedure with regard to both judicial settlement and arbitration as well as conciliation. Having accepted or put ourselves in a position that we may accept the decision of the Permanent Court in regard to legal disputes, there seems no reason why we should stop short at this, and refrain from having disputes, whether of a legal type or a non-legal type, also submitted, in default of conciliation, to either the process of judicial settlement or arbitration.[89]

This rather cavalier attitude was directly the line proposed by the Department of External Affairs on the General Act. In a memorandum written

85 NA, S. 8180.
86 *Dáil deb*, 39; 1136–7, 26 June 1931.
87 Ibid., 39; 1139.
88 The Act would be revoked only if the party in question said so, otherwise it would constantly renew itself.
89 *Dáil Deb*, 39; 1141.

Re-appraisal and Re-direction of League Policy 127

shortly before McGilligan's Dáil speech[90] it was argued that to accept the act with reservations, as chapter four of the General Act allowed, would be contrary to Free State League policy:

> At many meetings of the Assembly when this Act was being discussed we announced that we were in favour of an all-round pacific policy and to limit our accession to any one of the chapters and not accept the Act as a whole would be somewhat in contrariety to what has been said at the League on many occasions by Irish representatives.[91]

The opposition parties accepted the act, though with cynicism. Fianna Fáil TD, Sean T. O'Kelly, replying to McGilligan, supported his actions:

> There is a considerable amount of real belief, if not enthusiasm, in the League of Nations method and machinery for the purpose of ending disputes. The more that spirit can be cultivated, the more it can grow and develop, the better it will be for the world. If our signature can help in that direction, and if our belief, even modified and conditional as it may be, in the machinery to be utilised is of any value, then I think we ought to give it.[92]

The Free State accession was deposited at Geneva on 26 September 1931. It signified the state's belief in the League's ideas for a security system. Such a belief in arbitration/conciliation is strange after the boundary fiasco of 1925. Other interpretations could see it as naked self-interest, though actual election to the Council before the matter went to the Dáil seems to remove this as an option. The effect of the accession on Commonwealth policy is another spin-off. McGilligan mentioned it only in reference to the state's non-acceptance of reservations and not as playing any part in the state's ultimate acceptance of the ideals of the General Act. The Act was accepted because the state felt that it could believe in it and that any viable security option was worth trying. It was, however, unfortunate that the State's acceptance, along with that of the others whose accessions were deposited in September 1931 were marred by the Japanese invasion of Manchuria. The General Act stood, but it lacked public support. The League had completed its Security/Arbitration system, but it lacked a suitable world climate in which to operate.

90 NA, S. 4040A, 11 June 1931.
91 Op. cit., *Dáil deb.*
92 Ibid., 1146–7.

Conclusion

A coherent League policy was developed and implemented between 1926 and 1931. The Free State became more prominent on the international stage as the state made its presence felt at the League Assemblies and in its Committees. This is not to suggest that Ireland was in any sense 'punching above its weight' at the League. The Irish delegates held limited influence, but since 1926 had been using this influence more advantageously. They were now involved in the Assembly's debates and contributing to the work of the Assembly Committees. This led the League team in External Affairs towards a greater understanding of the League and a sense of collegiality with the members of other League delegations. This increased Irish presence and involvement in the League's work drew Ireland's diplomats out of the Anglo-Irish core that represented Irish foreign policy since the 1921 Treaty. They were moving in the European as well as the Commonwealth mainstream.

Taking this combined European and Commonwealth mainstream as the overall context of Irish external affairs shows that, by 1929, the Free State had become a state with a small, though well developed, external relations network built on the dual foundations of the League and the Commonwealth. Along with the developments at the League, the Free State was, with Canada and South Africa, forging the new Commonwealth. McGilligan's term of office saw increased Irish overseas representation, this expansion of Ireland's diplomatic network made certain the survival of the Department of External Affairs, the future of which had looked so uncertain under FitzGerald. Possibly because the world system under which these successes were made was to be destroyed in the 1930s, these developments have been overlooked. Irish League policy had dramatically revised itself since 1926. The scope of policy was still small, the department under-resourced, but Irish League policy now had coherent aims and objectives. Election to the Council was the central objective.

CHAPTER 5

Canvassing for a Council Seat

The canvass: September 1929–March 1930

Election to the League Council was the goal of Free State late 1920s League policy. Its origins were in the pyrrhic victory of 1926 in the council elections, the management of the Canadian candidature in 1927 and the active Irish stance at the Assembly since 1928. At the 1929 Assembly McGilligan made it clear that the Free State would stand for election in 1930 for the seat vacated by Canada. Though the Irish faced criticism that they were seeking to turn the Canadian seat into a 'Commonwealth seat' they stressed that their candidature was independent of any grouping.

Sean Lester agreed with McGilligan's early announcement of Ireland's candidature in order to pre-empt other contenders. The most likely competitor and the greatest threat was Australia. Lester argued that the Irish should play hard to get and made sure that when Irish support was solicited at the 1929 Assembly it was given as a quid pro quo for supporting the Free State at the Council elections in 1930. Ireland would then survey the emerging field of candidates before committing herself fully to running. In preparation, Lester began to consolidate his personal contacts with other representatives at Geneva.

These moves were the beginning of a co-ordinated canvass that began in earnest in January 1930 and lasted up to the eve of the election. It involved all the contemporary Irish diplomatic network and was structured around a Paris–Geneva axis which was overseen from Dublin by Joe Walshe and Patrick McGilligan. The Paris legation had opened in 1929 with the charismatic socialite Count Gerald O'Kelly de Gallagh as Minister.[1] O'Kelly began by seeking support from League members who had legations in Paris. Paris was sufficiently removed from Geneva to be outside League gossip circles and was the diplomatic capital of Europe. Sean Murphy made O'Kelly's brief clear:

---

1 **Gerald O'Kelly de Gallagh** (1890–1968): Diplomat. Irish representative to Belgium (1921–9); Minister Plenipotentiary to France (1929–35); Special Counsellor at Paris and Brussels Legations (1935–48), Chargé d'Affaires at Lisbon (1948–68).

Where it would do well to do so, use your personal influence with your colleagues to get the support of their governments. Informally you could point out that we are a mother country: that since our entry into the League we have taken an independent attitude on League matters. You can say that you understand that Australia is also likely to be a candidate and the inference will , I think, be clear. I understand that if Australia goes forward, the British will support her against us. So we are particularly anxious to secure all the votes possible.[2]

The opening balance gave the Free State little certain support but many contacts to be developed. Most interesting is the degree of support that the Latin American states, especially Uruguay and El Salvador, gave the Free State. They remembered the role of Irish volunteers and emigrants in their own national revolutions during the nineteenth century and came out in support of Ireland's candidature due to this historical link.[3] The young nations of Latin America were solidly in favour of Ireland's election and urged the young states of eastern and central Europe to support the Free State as one of the active members of the League. Such support would be crucial in fighting off an Australian candidature.

The structure of the canvass shows the degree of co-ordination in the Irish foreign service. Though the department was understaffed and under-resourced it had the ability to mount a continent-wide operation by using strategically placed offices such as Paris and Geneva. A subsidiary role was played by the Vatican and Berlin offices where Charles Bewley and Daniel Binchy respectively were Ministers.[4] In London, Timothy A. Smiddy solicited crucial support from Britain. As the United States was not a League member, Michael MacWhite played a background role in Washington. The number of personnel involved, the degree of co-operation between them and the high stakes in question make the Council election bid the most detailed and large-scale policy that the Irish foreign service undertook since the Treaty negotiations in 1921.

In Paris, O'Kelly found varying support for Ireland. At one extreme was the Swedish Minister who saw the Irish candidature as a second seat for the Commonwealth and not as an independent seat backed by the smaller members of the Assembly. The Hungarian Minister was in little doubt; he said that his country's support was almost a foregone conclusion. The canvass was

2 NA, D.F/A, 26/95, 19 December 1929. All unattributed references are from this file.
3 See Peadar Kirby, *Ireland and Latin America: Links and Lessons* (Dublin, 1992). Kirby does not mention the close ties between Ireland and Latin America at the League of Nations.
4 **Charles Bewley** (1888–1969). Barrister, Diplomat and Author. As a Barrister, defended Republican prisoners 1916–21, Irish Trade Representative in Berlin, 1921–3; returned to legal profession, 1923–9; Minister to Holy See, 1929–33; Minister to Berlin, 1933–9.

going so well that O'Kelly wrote to Sean Lester that, 'I'm in the midst of my canvassing and so far have met nothing but encouragement.'[5] To Walshe he wrote that,

> from my experience so far it would appear that ... our candidature will be popular amongst most European states ... if there could be such a thing as a completely free vote on the subject we would have an overwhelming majority. Unfortunately completely free votes are non-existent in politics.[6]

O'Kelly continued with impressive speed. By 27 January, he had canvassed 17 states from the Latin American and Little Entente groupings or the non-aligned states.[7] The Salvadorian Minister, M. Guerrero, enthusiastically informed him that

> when Mr Dandurand was elected for Canada, it was largely because of his personal popularity with his colleagues, there being considerable misgivings among the members of the Assembly as to whether the election of Canada did not in fact mean the election of a second seat for Britain. He added that it was quite obvious that there could be no such misgivings concerning our candidature. Our record was conclusive on the point.[8]

Less certain was Daniel Binchy. He felt the Free State should wait until 1933 when it would have a better chance. Binchy was disillusioned with the Free State's bid which he felt was based on tactical considerations rather than principles as it had been in 1926. In a long personal memorandum to Walshe he argued that Australia was the stronger candidate and that Ireland was sure to lose a Council election for the second time. Binchy felt that this would do untold damage to Ireland's position within the League and equally affect the domestic political situation in the build-up to the 1932 election.

Such attacks on League policy were rare. Binchy prefaced his comments remarking that if he were in Dublin he could have had a private conversation with Walshe on the subject. Binchy had thought over the question of opposing Australia and openly told Walshe that 'I am afraid I can't regard it as anything but the most serious mistake'.[9] Binchy's concerns were without foundation. He was overestimating Australia who had a poor League record. Binchy was pulling his punches in advocating that the state wait until 1933 to

5 13 January 1930.
6 O'Kelly de Gallagh to Walshe, 15 January 1930.
7 These were, Norway, Persia, China, Portugal, Sweden, Switzerland, Cuba, Latvia, Siam, Holland, Romania, Hungary, Salvador, Paraguay, Chile, Austria, Denmark.
8 O'Kelly de Gallagh to Walshe, 22 January 1930.
9 Binchy to Walshe, 15 January 1930.

challenge New Zealand. Australia was senior next to Canada, and with British support might seem assured of a seat. The seniority argument would only hold water in a Commonwealth environment. A solid and direct Irish canvass based on her League record might tip the balance. Australia might be senior to the Free State in the Dominions, but the Free State was senior to Australia in the League. Australia's League record was poor, and Ireland's record as an independent small state would have far greater support as a candidate.

Binchy's pessimism was unwarranted, he took too little regard of the Free State's standing in the League, and overestimated the Commonwealth dimension. By 1930, the Irish had made a niche for themselves in the League. They had a specific stance and a defined approach to the League, a far cry from the explosive newcomers that they must have appeared as in 1926. Binchy changed his tune as the canvass continued. By April, Binchy was contributing with a new found faith. Perhaps in retrospect this memorandum should be seen as initial nervousness towards a new departure.

In Washington, ex-Permanent Representative at Geneva, Michael MacWhite, felt that he was in a bad position to have a positive influence on policy. Few Americans were interested in the League. He suggested that it, 'would be far more effective to approach the members of the diplomatic corps in Paris and other European capitals who have been, themselves, delegates to the last Assembly, as they will most probably, be also to the next'.[10] MacWhite simply reported on American press reports on the Council elections and their views on the Free State's chances. It was unfortunate that a diplomat who knew Geneva intimately and had so many contacts in the European diplomatic network should be left on the side as the canvass progressed.

The attitude of the Great Powers who were permanent, or semi-permanent Council members had to be gauged. The British and German Governments could be approached directly by the Irish representatives in London and Berlin. It was up to O'Kelly to meet the representatives of France, Italy and Japan as well as some of the more powerful semi-permanent Council members. O'Kelly first met the Japanese representative, M. Adacti. As a Pacific power, the Japanese were moving towards support of Australia, directly contrary to the Free State's interests. This was Realpolitik: 'My own impression is that while he might be genuinely pleased to see us on the League Council, his oriental prudence made him fear all sorts of complications with Australia and Britain'.[11] The Free State was now exposed to the vagaries of strategic notions. Being a good world citizen just was not enough, when it came to the crunch, interests rather than ideals were of greater importance.

Sean Lester found increasing obstacles to the Free State's candidature. It was likely that Australia would now back out but that with her seat becoming

---

10 MacWhite to Walshe, 27 January 1930.
11 O'Kelly de Gallagh to Walshe, 31 January 1930.

a non-group seat the League Secretariat, with the support of the Secretary General, would support a Chinese candidature. This would greatly increase the odds against the Free State and make the need to canvass effectively more urgent. Lester prophesied the price of failure: 'If in any circumstances we are a defeated candidate at the next Assembly, I fear our prospects for election will recede for the next ten years or more'.[12] The rising stakes made success crucial.

Lester then met Eric Drummond. The need to keep the final seat 'open', the needs of the non-aligned states and most importantly, the predicament faced by China, were the factors outlined by the Secretary General as reasons for the Free State withholding its candidature until 1931. His only word of encouragement was that the Chinese bid depended on their paying off their accumulated outstanding contributions. Lester was not swayed. He told Drummond 'not to expect any change in the Saorstát's position'.[13] Against these obstacles the Free State could play its trump card of independence. The small states were unlikely to vote for China's re-eligibility, and the Irish would not be seen as a Dominion. Despite Drummond's fears, the Saorstát was perceived in most quarters as a candidate fit to hold an 'open' seat.

The situation was still very fluid. China was the greatest long term threat. British support was distant but likely, depending on the attitude of Australia. The line-up facing the Free State was still not clear. Although the state had a clear idea of its strategy, it was still unsure where to aim its sights. Francis Cremins wrote to O'Kelly, on Walshe's behalf, informing him that he was to postpone any further canvassing due to the difficulty of identifying other potential candidates and until the Australians position became clear:

> The Council difficulty is likely to be solved within the next fortnight. Australia will not go forward. If not we shall have the support of Great Britain. Meanwhile you need not do anything until you hear further from us.[14]

O'Kelly agreed that he would be in a much stronger situation if he were able to state directly that Australia was not a candidate. With Australia out the Irish were more likely to get support from Britain and this would bring the other less independent Dominions in line behind Britain in support of the Free State. Attention could then be focused on the growing Chinese threat. On 3 March Smiddy informed Walshe that Australia had withdrawn for certain. No reason was given, more than likely it was due to a lack of interest rather than a deliberate move in favour of the Free State.

12 Ibid.
13 Lester to Walshe, 13 February 1930.
14 Cremins to O'Kelly, 25 February 1930.

March–September 1930

In Paris and Geneva, O'Kelly and Lester restarted their canvassing. Primary attention turned to Great Britain. Walshe telegraphed Smiddy to obtain a meeting with Lord Passfield, the Secretary of State for Dominion Affairs to seek British support for the Free State's candidature.[15] Walshe felt that Drummond might try to persuade the British not to look favourably on a Dominion candidate so as to leave the field open for China. He told Smiddy that 'Messrs Henderson and Dalton were hostile at Geneva, rather openly so, that they would throw all their weight against us but second thoughts will probably bring them to a wiser decision'.[16] It was Smiddy's role to provide the second thoughts.

Smiddy met Passfield who was purposely vague, saying that he knew very little of the situation. The matter would be discussed by the Foreign Office in consultation with the other Dominions, then London would make up its mind. The approach to Britain was the opening move in informing all the Dominions of the Free State's candidature on 24 March. Smiddy's approach was intended to soften the impact on the British. In the first weeks of April the Dominion responses drifted in. First Canada, then Australia and South Africa and finally, on 15 April, New Zealand. They all promised their support. This put more pressure on Britain to give a definite pledge of support.

A sinister element was becoming apparent. There seemed to be a scheme afoot to force the Irish to withdraw their election bid. It had begun in early February when Michael MacWhite drew Walshe's attention to a piece in the American newspaper *The World*. It stated that either Canada, seeking re-election, or South Africa would be favoured for election to the Council by Britain and probably not the Free State. Backing up the report in *The World* in late January, it was reported that, 'South Africa will actually succeed in getting a non-permanent seat as a successor to Canada and the Dominion representatives.' These later reports all surfaced at the same time as Smiddy was approaching Passfield. It was an attempt to see whether the Free State would withdraw her candidature, or whether it would lessen the levels of support that the canvass was creating. Cremins felt that, 'a deliberate attempt is being made in some quarter of Geneva to confuse the issue with regard to our candidature. As we understand the matter their is no intention on the part of South Africa to seek election in September next. We are relying on that country's support for our candidature'.[17]

Britain was now the odd one out having failed to respond to the Free State's telegram of 24 March. There was some uncertainty as to what was the

15 Passfield (Sidney James Webb) was Secretary of State for Dominion affairs from 1929 to 1930 and Secretary of State for the Colonies from 1929 to 1931.
16 Walshe to Smiddy 18 March, 1930. Arthur Henderson (Foreign Secretary) and Hugh Dalton (Under-Secretary for Foreign Affairs).
17 11 April 1930.

Foreign Office attitude. Walshe felt that Passfield had suggested that the Free State would, 'oppose the British on the Council for the sake of appearing more independent'.[18] He was incensed at this opinion,

> we intend to be guided in each case by the individual merits as we always have been at the League. Any attempt on the part of the Foreign Office to get other members of the Commonwealth to vote against us will hardly promote a good feeling of co-operation. If the opportunity arises you should express your amazement at the attitude of mind you have described.

Smiddy took stock of this, replying that he felt that he had probably over emphasised the opinions prevalent in London. In early May he saw Lord Passfield again. This time there was a more positive response that 'His Majesty's Government would be in no way adverse to our candidature'[19] but that the situation would be reviewed in September at the Assembly.

The British Government took the Free State's candidature very seriously. Lord Robert Cecil took charge of a specific Dominion Office committee to consider Britain's response. The line-up suggests the importance that the British attached to the issue: Robert Cecil, Hugh Dalton, Philip Noel-Baker, Alexander Cadogan, Harry Batterbee. Geo-politics was the main concern of the Cecil Committee's first meeting on 2 April 1930. China was the significant obstacle to immediate support of the Free State: 'if she were re-elected she might ask the League of Nations to undertake a reconstruction scheme, which would be of immense importance not only to China, but to the British Empire'.[20] None of those present wanted to tie their hands too early. They decided to work to gain time and fudge the issue by sending no immediate response to Dublin. Following inter-departmental discussions between the Dominions Office and the Foreign Office the Committee held a further meeting on 23 May. The Free State now had the support of all members of the Commonwealth, except the United Kingdom. In considering a response to McGilligan the committee indicated that there was no set reason for holding back on immediate support, but an amalgam of differing reasons. Noel-Baker felt that the Free State should not be supported as she would be beaten and he was also concerned where China would turn for international support if she lost her seat. Cecil felt that it would be better if the Free State waited until 1933 before standing for election. The diverse elements reached common ground when they hit on the term 'certain important considerations of a general League nature' to explain their desire to wait until September before choosing which candidates to support.[21] This was the message of a despatch

18 Ibid.
19 2 May 1930.
20 PRO, DO. 35/168/1/6276/9.
21 Ibid., DO. 35/168/1/6276/22, Minutes of meeting of 23 May 1930.

of 3 June from Passfield to McGilligan. It did nothing further than solidify the already known sentiments of the British administration. The matter would be reviewed at Geneva and if the other members of the Commonwealth were supporting the Free State, then so would Britain.

McGilligan responded on 18 June to Passfield's successor, J.H. Thomas. He pointed out to the British that the Irish were not trying to create a Dominion group. Their views on the Council had been set out at the 1926 Assembly. He hit out at the British for suggesting that the Irish candidature was anything other than an independent one. Clearly this was a purely British opinion:

> It seems evident from foreign press reports—not all of them helpful to the Irish candidature—that the fact that this country is seeking election not as a natural successor of Canada, but solely as a member of the League of Nations, is well recognised abroad.[22]

With this despatch having no impact on the British it was followed up two weeks later in more forceful terms. The Chinese were berated, 'The question of China's election this year is so unlikely to have any real bearing on the Chinese situation that it must not be allowed to present any obstacle to the consideration of other matters which are of the utmost importance'.[23] In other words, the Irish candidature. Again, more forcefully, it was the independent nature of the Irish scheme which McGilligan backed up strongly with arguments on the international character of Ireland and her positive input into League affairs. In his two concluding paragraphs, McGilligan lost his patience with the British:

> you can quite easily understand that abstract reasoning about the possible effect of the election of China on a situation created by—and only to be healed by—the passage of centuries, fails to rouse our enthusiasm. As you are aware, the other members of the Commonwealth have promised us their support and I hope your Government will find it possible to do likewise. It would, I fear, be quite impracticable to postpone the consideration of the question until we meet at Geneva.

It was impossible to get any further consideration of the matter from the British. The likelihood, if the Irish read between the lines, was that the British would support Ireland. As a Great Power, they could not show their hand immediately and so the Free State would have to wait.

Sean Lester had been looking beyond the election by examining the expansion needed at the Geneva Legation to cater for Council membership.

22 McGilligan to Thomas, 3 June 1930.
23 McGilligan to Thomas, 18 June 1930.

The Irish Legation was already overworked and understaffed. Lester urged Sean Murphy to expand the legation to the level of the Canadian operation which had a staff of seven, including the Permanent Representative. With this Lester felt that Canada had, 'been able to make some justifications of her election to the Council'.[24] If the Irish, with their staff of two, hoped to completely and quickly justify their election what levels would they need?

A secretary to the legation was the first part of any expansion. This would help reduce the considerable pressure that Lester was under:

> since June last, the Representative has been a delegate at five international conferences, involving daily attendance for five and a half months, apart from preparatory work. In addition, there are numerous meetings of important League committees which should be attended even if the Saorstát is not represented on the Council.

A military attaché was also necessary, as would an additional typist/secretary. These were suggestions likely to give Walshe a heart attack. Lester offered what little comfort he could, 'you will notice that even with the appointments, the Irish staff would be smaller than the Canadian'. Lester regarded this as the minimum staff with which he could operate the legation in Geneva.

By 1930 a sign of the League's growing importance to the Irish was that there were two staff dealing with League matters, Sean Murphy, the Assistant Secretary, and Francis Cremins. Lester implored that this core be strengthened so that Ireland should, 'not be classified as a passenger on the Council'. Lester identified the central nature of the League to Irish foreign policy when he states that, 'The direction at home would no doubt gain substantially through the more specialised study and closer contact with the problems made possible by the increased staff as Geneva, but you would find, I suggest, that even in this case it would be no substitute for the work peculiar to Headquarters.'

Our understanding of the position in Geneva is expanded further by a picture of the physical conditions that Lester and his secretary had to work in. The entire operation was run from two rooms, his own office and a general typing-filing-indexing-mail room. The legation was too small to expand under any circumstances. Lester carefully mentioned that the Canadian offices consisted of six rooms and a reception hall. Joseph Walshe, not to mention the Department of Finance was in danger of disintegrating into complete apoplexy on receipt of this memorandum.

The cost might be high, but they were the bare minimum necessary to reap the benefits of Council membership; 'the Saorstát would gain immediate prestige from election, but unless we can "make good" in a modest way, the state would ultimately lose in status'. If this were not to be the case, and his

24 Lester to Walshe, 22 March 1930.

proposal fell on deaf ears, Lester concluded that it 'would be better to postpone our candidature, and take what we can in a gesture towards China'.

Back in Paris, O'Kelly de Gallagh began again in earnest. With the Australians out of the way and the still indefinite British hinting at support between the lines the canvass was again on target. In Berlin, Daniel Binchy was also more upbeat in his views. In a far cry from his uncertain remarks of the previous January, Binchy planned to approach the German Government and call on the Permanent Head of the German Foreign Office Herr Schubert. An Irish–German Treaty of Navigation and Commerce had been signed on 12 May 1930. McGilligan, Walshe reported, was fully in favour of Binchy's proposed demarche. Walshe indicated how he was the night-watchman over the canvass in Dublin in his reply to Binchy, 'having no definite support from the United Kingdom, we are hardly in a position to seek such a definite promise from Germany, as it appears to be your view that the attitude of Germany would be influenced by that of Great Britain.'[25] Either Walshe knew better, or he was leaving all to Binchy and simply responding in turn to Binchy's more informed position. He urged Binchy to make a formal approach, to mention the British attitude and leave it at that. With the Berlin Legation in action, the three major Irish offices on the European mainland were involved in the canvass, along with Smiddy in London.

In May the Chinese Minister in Paris, M. Kao visited O'Kelly to announce his state's candidature. O'Kelly feigned a 'diplomatic illness': 'I am not replying thereto on the plan of being out of town'.[26] Dublin urged a more 'tactful' approach. O'Kelly was to reply that the matter had been 'transmitted to our government for most sympathetic consideration'.[27] Evidently Dublin was going to give little sympathy to this demand. Observers felt that the Free State must overcome the threats of a Chinese candidature, as an unnamed eastern European diplomat made clear to O'Kelly at a Paris Chamber of Commerce Dinner:

> He volunteered the information that China was our most dangerous rival in the forthcoming elections ... My colleague stated quite categorically that the Chinese Minister here informed him that Sir Eric Drummond had promised China last year that she would be elected in 1930. Of course such a statement from the Chinese Minister may be an exaggeration in as much as I am inclined to doubt whether there was any formal promise on Sir Eric Drummond's part, but I think that there can be no doubt that there was a declaration of sympathy to the Chinese candidature on the part of the Secretariat.[28]

25 Walshe to Binchy, 15 May 1930.
26 O'Kelly de Gallagh to Walshe, 13 May 1930.
27 Murphy to O'Kelly de Gallagh, 17 May 1930.
28 Ibid. O'Kelly de Gallagh to Murphy.

O'Kelly followed Dublin's instructions and kept an even keel. M. Guerrero urged the Free State to adopt a style of canvassing that was aimed at attacking other candidates as well as increasing Free State support. O'Kelly de Gallagh replied to him, 'I was careful to point out that ... we were very desirous of avoiding coming into direct confrontation with any given candidate and that we were going forward simply as a member of the League without laying claim to any particular succession.'[29] This illustrates the consistency of Free State League policy, even from before 1927. The state saw its part in the League as 'international', not as a means to extend national prestige. The state was standing for election to keep the final non-permanent Council seat independent and non-group. This continued the policy of 1926 and was similar to Ireland's statements on joining the League in 1923. The Irish felt that an independent and pro-League candidate would benefit the League system. The state was determined not to get its candidature mixed up in inter-state rivalry and jealousy at the League. It shows Walshe's constant belief that the Saorstát should not get involved in the politics of international relations.

By May, 21 countries had been canvassed including the Dominions and Britain. Direct support had only been received from the four Dominions, promises of support of varying natures were otherwise given. Only the responses of the Austrian, Paraguayan and Salvadorian representatives were regarded as reliable. Cremins felt that the next move ought to be towards the powers, specifically Germany and France.

Attention returned to Geneva. The 14th Session of the International Labour Conference opened on 10 June, 1930. It was a rich hunting ground for Sean Lester as he searched for further information on the Chinese candidature. The question of whether China would go forward was still uncertain. China was committed, as O'Kelly had recently discovered, but few other states appeared to aspire to Chinese ideals and rally to her support. A crucial Irish contact was the Siamese Minister in Geneva, Prince Varvaidya. The Siamese Minister in Paris had said his country would support the Free State, the Prince was not so sure:

> If China is defeated in the re-eligibility vote, one of the three votes will be given to Ireland ... He said that he regretted very much that China had decided to go forward ... While the revolutionary conditions prevailed in China, he thought that they would be foolish to claim a Council seat, but the Chinese Government was making it a question of prestige. He felt quite confident that China would not get the votes of a sufficient number of small states to establish re-eligibility.[30]

29 O'Kelly de Gallagh to Walshe, 20 June 1930.
30 Lester to Walshe, 14 June 1930.

Through regional and realpolitik interests the Siamese were faced with the predicament of having to support the Chinese. The South-East Asian states had shifted their voting dilemma from Australia to China. Both states had dubious League records but had a geo-political influence that could not be ignored. With two of the seats that were being vacated already allotted to a Scandinavian and a South American state, there was an atmosphere of rivalry being created between the Eastern states and the Free State. The contest was hotting up between the Free State and China. The Irish had to redouble their efforts to gain support.

Binchy made contact with officials in the German Foreign Office and was given a favourable reception. He approached a Herr de Hass at a lunch party given at the Irish Legation. In asking for an interview to see Herr von Bulow, head of the German Foreign Office, he was assured that Germany was not committed and that 'it was practically certain that we should secure their vote'.[31] Binchy did not hold this promise too highly, telling Walshe that he forwarded it to him, 'for what it is worth, my own experience has perhaps made me too sceptical.' Herr von Bulow was 'practically certain that Germany would support' the Free State.[32]

In Paris, O'Kelly met Briand on 27 June 1930. The Irish Minister stressed the independence of the Free State's candidature, but Briand hooked onto the Dominion line. O'Kelly indicated that Ireland had Dominion support. Briand replied, 'Alors, je crois que cela ira seul'.[33] O'Kelly felt that France would support the Free State but Briand would not at this stage commit himself. Such support for Ireland would be at the expense of French support for Norway.

The views of the Italians were less clear. This was within O'Kelly's brief as Bewley was Minister to the Vatican, not to Italy. The Italian Minister's response fits in with the vague foreign policy that Mussolini followed up to 1935 and O'Kelly remarked that he could 'hazard no kind of opinion as to what the outcome of the demarche will be'.[34]

The position of Japan, the other permanent member of the League Council, was still unclear, but more likely to be favourable towards the Free State following the withdrawal of Australia. The Free State had therefore a realistic belief in the support of the permanent members of the Council, the Great Powers. This was good going, along with the support of two of the League's groups and the definite support of the Dominions, though Britain was still pending. There had been no completely negative responses to date.

The holiday period was beginning and it would be difficult for Lester and O'Kelly to make further inroads. The Irish Minister in Paris approached some of the remaining Latin American states and completed his canvass of

31 Binchy to Walshe, 20 June 1930.
32 Confidential memorandum, 15 August 1930.
33 O'Kelly de Gallagh to Walshe, 27 June 1930
34 O'Kelly de Gallagh to Walshe, 24 June 1930.

the small European nations. O'Kelly finished his canvass in early August. He was still getting many favourable responses. His contacts whilst canvassing the Latin American and Little Entente groups had paid off. The Colombian Minister, M. Cobo felt that, 'as between China, a Scandinavian country and Ireland, Ireland stood by far the greatest chance of election'.[35] O'Kelly's final despatch to Walshe was positive in tone:

> While you notice that hardly in any case was a promise of a vote forthcoming ... the reception given to the announcement of our candidature was in the vast majority of cases characterised by a cordiality which it was felt to be spontaneous and sincere and was in no way mere evidence of courtesy. Of course these expressions of friendship do not bind governments, but state a feeling which they indicate is certainly very favourable and, while I have no means of judging the practical value of such manifestations before the election has taken place, I should not think that it is unreasonably optimistic to state that the Irish candidature will be a popular candidature in practically all sections of Geneva.[36]

A memorandum by Cremins of 15 August projected China as the main rival. Forty-four states had been canvassed, seven, the four Dominions and Columbia, Paraguay and Salvador had definitely promised their votes. Of the remaining thirty-seven states canvassed, the strongest support had come from Latin America and the 'Little Entente' states of Eastern Europe. All of the 'Great Powers' were still undecided, this is not surprising, they would hardly reveal their hands so soon. The memorandum was an upbeat conclusion to the canvass. It had been an episode of great uncertainty with ups and downs and moments of immense tension. The Free State ended its greatest international manoeuvre so far with its prominent position at the League vindicated.

The Irish press had been silent about Irish chances in the election. On 19 August the *Irish Independent* printed an article arguing that the Free State's chances were lessening as the election day drew nearer. The establishment of a Commonwealth seat was viewed with disdain in some quarters, and this, the *Independent* argued, was lessening the Free State's chances of election. A likely explanation for this article is that some one in government circles wished to dampen down over optimistic expectation on the state's candidature. The article was founded on pure speculation, or at least disinformation. Most telling was the statement that both South Africa and Canada were going to support other nations in place of Ireland. Perhaps it was a return by elements hostile to the Free State to the tactics followed the previous spring. How the field was developing can be seen in a memorandum sent to Dublin

---

35 O'Kelly de Gallagh to Walshe, 28 July 1930.
36 O'Kelly de Gallagh to Walshe, 9 August 1930.

by Lester. Lester's view was that 'my own opinion would have to be that the Chinese candidature is becoming less threatening than it was a few months ago'.[37] Few were willing to predict the outcome, Lord Robert Cecil was 'close as a clam' regarding the result.[38]

The British press restarted their campaign against the Irish as the opening of the Assembly drew near. Within two days of each other, *The Observer* and the *Daily Express* both hit out at the Irish candidature:

> The Irish Free State is not so confident now that it will secure the non-permanent seat on the Council of the League of Nations which is to be vacated by Canada. Not two months ago its chances of election were good. China has now put forward an opposition and it appears that the vote of the British delegation and a number of the Dominion's will go to China.[39]

The intentions of China were becoming clearer. On 26 August, Lester received a visit from the Chinese Minister in Geneva, Dr Woo Kai Seng. Lester assured the Chinese Minister that, 'we had very optimistic reports, and that as far as could be gauged, we were very optimistic of election'.[40] Dr Woo replied that he had heard likewise for his own country. Dr Woo then suggested a collaboration between the Free State and the Chinese, that the two delegations hold a joint meeting after the Assembly commenced. Lester made it clear to Dr Woo that the Free State could not be pressured in any way and that it would be master of its own destiny: 'I said that it would be unfair to him if I left him under any misapprehension regarding the Irish position. That my government had been putting forward all their energy to seeking election and that there would be absolutely no prospect of withdrawal.'

Lester felt that the Chinese canvass might be losing steam: 'The fact that he did not withdraw his proposal of a meeting after I had twice emphasised the irrevocable decision of the Saorstát leaves me with a little hope that they have found the going too heavy'. Lester left the ball in the Chinese court, they could come back and do the running.

The Assembly

As the final scenes of the pre-election power play took place in Geneva, the discussion in Dublin was of the delegation to send to Geneva to execute policy. The eventual delegation is interesting:

37 Lester–Walshe, 21 August 1930.
38 Ibid., Lester to Walshe, 22 August 1930.
39 *Daily Express*, 24 August 1930.
40 Lester to Walshe, 26 August 1930.

Ernest Blythe: Minister for Finance
John Marcus O'Sullivan: Minister for Health
John A. Costello: Attorney General
Daniel Binchy: Free State Minister in Berlin
Gerald O'Kelly: Free State Minister in Paris
Sean Lester: Free State Permanent Representative in Geneva

Francis Cremins was in attendance as delegation secretary. McGilligan did not attend on account of the impending Imperial Conference.[41] The delegation was high-powered. All were League 'veterans' except O'Kelly. His inclusion, and Binchy's was aimed at increasing the capability of the Free State Ministers on the continent. Blythe and O'Sullivan were forceful in previous Assemblies and Blythe and Binchy were on the 1926 Delegation and so had experienced the Free State's election attempt that year. The skills of all the members indicate a diverse and well-chosen delegation from the Executive Council and the diplomatic service.

Also apparent is a definite 'tailoring' of personnel for specific tasks. Not only were the Commissions handed out on ability grounds within the League Delegation, but when contrasted with the delegation for the October 1930 Imperial Conference, we see a definite 'League' and 'Commonwealth' choice. The Imperial Conference delegation was similarly made up of those with the greatest Dominion experience; FitzGerald, now the doyen of the Dominion negotiators, McGilligan, along with the top two at External Affairs: Walshe and Murphy complemented by Diarmuid O'Hegarty and John Hearne. Like the League delegation they were veterans of the Imperial Conference and were used to working together as a team.[42]

In a letter to Walshe on 29 August, Lester mentioned he had discussed the Assembly and the election with Sir Eric Drummond's private secretary. This had revealed other possibilities and scenarios. Belgium could announce her candidature and Portugal was definitely going forward. China was still the greatest problem facing the Free State. If China succeeded in a re-eligibility vote, all the months of planning would be in vain.

The Free State was in a strong position with the support of the Latin American, Little Entente and elements of the Scandinavian groupings. Her stance as an independent candidate gave her a wide-ranging platform of support amongst the 'non-aligned' states which were not part of any group. Thus the Free State was not perceived as a Dominion candidate, even though the Dominions and Britain were also supporting her. This was quite a coup for the Irish who, as we saw above in the case of France, had previously found it

---

41 Not all approved of this move, O'Kelly de Gallagh felt that 'Mr McGilligan's absence from Geneva will be interpreted in a sense unfavourable to our candidature'. O'Kelly to Walshe, 28 August 1930.

42 **John Hearne** (1893–1968): Diplomat. Legal Adviser, External Affairs, 1929–39; High Commissioner to Canada, 1939–50; Ambassador to USA, 1950–60.

difficult in some quarters to sell their independent position at the League to other members.

Instrumental in the widespread acceptance of this 'independent' view was a statement by McGilligan nailing the Free State's independent candidature firmly to the mast. McGilligan left no doubt as to his country's intentions. On this document the progress of the final fortnight of the campaign rested. It was direct and to the point, pulling no punches:

> The only, 'British Empire' group recognised in the League of Nations is the group consisting of Great Britain and Northern Ireland and all parts of the British Empire not separate members of the League. The Irish Free State is not a member of that, nor of any group within the League, and in connection with elections to the Council, as in every other matter, the Irish Free State, like the other members of the Commonwealth, acts solely on its own initiative and represents nobody but itself.
>
> Accordingly, the Irish Free State offers itself for election this year, not in the capacity of one of the members of the British Commonwealth, but as a Member of the League, having equal rights to representation with other members.
>
> In practically all the notices of the Irish candidature which have appeared in the foreign press—not all of them intended to be helpful—the point is especially emphasised that the Irish candidature is independent of any group, and that we go forward for a seat on the Council simply as a member of the League and as nothing else.[43]

The Irish did not disassociate themselves from the much sought after Commonwealth vote by this statement. But it indicated where the state drew its rationale for contesting the election.

Delegations from Romania and South Africa paid angry visits to Sean Lester. Both felt that their support for Ireland had been undermined by the 'Anti-Group' declaration. Lester visited the Romanian Minister, M. Antoniade, on 3 September. The discussion ostensibly wove around the question of who the Irish declaration had been aimed at. Lester was careful to point out that it was in fact aimed at removing the notion that the Free State was trying to create a 'Commonwealth' group in the League. The Romanians felt that McGilligan had directed his venom at the Little Entente group of states alone. From his report, it seems that Lester succeeded in calming the Romanian Minister. Not all group members took the statement in this manner. Denmark, one of the 'Baltic Group', would first vote for Norway and then the Free State.

43 Undated.

The Free State did not want a seat if in doing so it was considered to have consolidated a Dominion group seat by replacing Canada. Thus McGilligan was killing two birds with the one stone. The acceptance by the League of the Free State by electing her on her own agenda would consolidate her place in the League by copper fastening Ireland as an independent state. It would also send signals from the League to the Dominions relating to the upcoming Statute of Westminster that the Dominions were independent on the world stage. They could now set their own independent agenda and policy separate to that of Britain.

With less than a fortnight left before the Council elections, Cremins began sending daily reports to Walshe. On 6 September he felt that the state's position was 'fair'. There were now five European states going for election: Norway, Belgium, Portugal, Greece, and the Irish Free State. Portugal was the greatest threat. She had undertaken a campaign of negative canvassing, along the lines that Ireland was a British vassal.

O'Kelly discussed the Irish position with M Guerrero who was more optimistic than Cremins, feeling that Ireland was on course for victory. He also visited the Portuguese delegate, M. Vasconcellos, to see how concrete the rumours about Portugal were. He was left in no doubt; on meeting him, Vasconcellos 'threw up his arms and exclaimed "Cher ami, je suis vraiment desole et tres malheureux de notre situation vis-a-vis l'un de l'autre".'[44] Despite their friendship, the Portuguese delegate remained stubborn, castigating the Irish as trying to change the seat to a Dominion one: 'Vous avez beau faire et dire tout ce que vous voudrez, mon cher O'Kelly; tout le monde sait que vous etes le candidat du Commonwealth'. O'Kelly made no headway into this argument, though Vasconcellos said that he would support Ireland in the event of Portugal not standing for election.

With both Portugal and Ireland as candidates the possibility arose of a split in the South American vote. A unified South American vote was central to the success of the Irish candidature, such dissension would gravely destabilise the Irish campaign and reduce her chances of election. Talk of voting arrangements with Portugal was an attempt to defuse the confrontation. Ireland would attempt to canvass the Dominion states to support Portugal. This was simply a tactic to waste time and keep the Portuguese happy, the Irish had no intention of fulfilling this bargain.

This was the situation before the delegation set off. The implications of this episode are important in their relation to the state's performance at the League from 1923. The support promised to the state and the expressions of those canvassed show that, for practical purposes the state had achieved international sovereignty and had carved out a position of some esteem for itself in the world community. The state was not seen as a vassal Dominion but an active, independent and fully integrated member of the League. The

---

44 Cremins to Walshe, 7 September 1930.

international role of the Irish Free State was seen and deemed to be valuable by the other members of the League. They felt that the state had the potential and the credentials to be a Council member. The state itself had progressed admirably in its own management of international affairs since its entry to the League in 1923. The delegation would prepare the ground in Geneva as the Assembly started, and then see if their careful canvass had paid off.

Support was still coming in yet it was hard for the Irish delegation to formulate a stable picture of the field. They were courting the support of both South America and Scandinavia, both enemies of each other. Each would appear to support the Irish. Portugal still remained the barrier between the Free State and certain election. The Irish policy of fudging a definite response on a deal with the Portuguese was working as a delaying tactic. It added to general uncertainty from Lisbon on Portugal's intentions.

By Thursday, 11 September, Cremins was uncertain but optimistic, writing that 'all members of the Commonwealth voting for us and supporting us. Candidature seems strong.'[45] Yet he struck a cautious note: 'would not however encourage public optimism in case of possible setbacks.' As always in Geneva, anything could happen at the last minute. A sign of this tension was Cremins telegraphing Dublin to see if Michael MacWhite would be able to assist at Geneva for the duration of the candidature.[46] An experienced hand might prove neccessary.

Cremins last long report was written on 13 September, four days before the election. Portugal was still cockily asserting that she had at least 36 votes. Portugal was canvassing against the Free State, stating that the Irish, despite all claims to the contrary, were a Dominion and completely under British dominance. The Chinese re-eligibility vote loomed. It seemed that all the powers except Italy would vote for China's re-eligibility, but not all would vote for her in the election. Cremins was uncertain if this compromise would work: 'if many states gave their individual votes in the first case as a gesture a sufficient number might conceivably go the whole way and China might secure election'.[47] He still felt certain enough to conclude his despatch on a note expectant of China's inevitable failure.

The election

Up to the last minute there was uncertainty. A telegram on 16 September, less than twenty-four hours before the election took place struck an ominous note, 'prospects seem worse owing to defections from South American group. Have

---

45 Cremins to Walshe, 11 September 1930.
46 Cremins to Walshe, 12 September 1930.
47 Cremins to Walshe, 13 September 1930.

doubtful note sounded in morning papers if possible. Competition between Norway, Portugal, China and ourselves very keen.'[48]

The election was the culmination of Free State League policy since 1926. It was an acceptance by the wider world of the message of the Free State's speeches, interventions and stance at Geneva. The Irish delegation at Geneva had to keep up sufficient support and keep a high profile in the first weeks of the Assembly. The state was on the verge of its most auspicious international role. Once the Assembly opened the delegates delivered a series of aggressive speeches. Blythe made the main speech to the Assembly. It was a traditional Free State 'critical support' of the League outpouring. Blythe presented the Free State's League as the small state independent candidate as he outlined the positive and progressive approach the state took towards the League. The state's ratification of League conventions, its acceptance of the Optional Clause, the desire for the League to work democratically and effectively so as to retain public support were all mentioned. It was an admirable election manifesto. Blythe concluded by supporting Aristide Briand's call for a Federal States of Europe, but in doing so portrayed the Free State as a world nation: 'Though a European country, the Irish Free State has close ties with countries in other Continents. In some cases those ties are political. In other cases, they are ties of friendship and gratitude'.[49] The state was thus in a good position to represent the rest of the world, as members of the Assembly, in the Council.

China failed to get the necessary majority to secure re-eligibility. With the main contender out of the way, the Irish were almost assured of election. Its rivals were, Guatemala, Norway and Portugal. If Norway and Guatemala were assured of seats as group candidates, then the contest would be between Ireland and Portugal for the final 'non-group' seat. In light of the previously mentioned Portuguese ambivalence towards the election, the Irish were in a good position.

The election took place on the 17 September. The *Irish Times* saw the Free State as the 'odds on favourite'.[50] Voting took place at the Fourteenth Plenary meeting of the Assembly. The results were:

Norway: 38 Votes
Guatemala: 41 Votes
Irish Free State: 36 Votes

Portugal got 30 votes and so failed in her election bid. The 4 Dominion votes and that of Britain could arguably be seen to hold the balance. But only had they decided to give their votes to Portugal to oust the Free State. Assuming Britain voted for Portugal due to the two states friendship since

---

48 Cremins to Walshe, 16 September 1930.
49 NA, S. 8180.
50 *Irish Times*, 16 September 1930.

early modern times and not for the Free State, the Free State did not vote for Portugal and South Africa supported the Free State as in 1926, *ceteris paribus*, it would take the votes of Canada, Australia and New Zealand all to go against the Free State just to tie the vote for the last seat 33 to 33. It would seem that it was the bulk of the support that the canvass had generated through all the members of the League that secured the state's election. The Dominion vote was part of this. It shows Dominion unity, the Free State's position as a Dominion and how the Dominions were capable of working together in international relations.

A list of thirty-six states possibly offering support was drawn up in Dublin and reflects the outline given above. There was definitely good overall support. The most interesting section of this document is the 'doubtful' category. Norway, Liberia, Italy, Germany, and France were down as doubtful but likely. This is understandable in light of the fact that the Great Powers, who predominated this group would not show their hands too early, Norway was a prospective candidate and the Liberians were, according to Lester, not to be trusted. Denmark, Finland, Czechoslovakia, Yugoslavia and Spain were doubtful and unlikely. This could be due to 'enemies' of these states supporting the Free State, for example Poland and Czechoslovakia and Finland and Norway. Spain may have been indicating a grudge against the Free State for the attitude the Irish took towards her at the 1926 elections and because Spain did not agree with the Council election procedure. A year's work had proved successful. This was one hurdle over, but the state had now to vindicate itself as a member of the League's highest body. The new Council line-up was:

Permanent Members	*Semi-Permanent Members*	*Non-Permanent Members*
Great Britain	Poland	Yugoslavia
France		Persia
Italy		Chile
Japan		Irish Free State
Germany		Norway
		Guatemala

As with the 1926 election, this election was interpreted differently by the various observers. The *Irish Times* took a normal 'pro-British' stance and wrote about the election as a 'signal honour for the youngest Dominion'.[51] But from the canvass and the views of other states consulted, it is apparent that the League members considered the Free State as an independent candidate. The following year, John Hearne made it clear how the Free State saw itself:

51 *Irish Times*, 18 September 1930.

The Irish Free State had made it perfectly clear, both before and at the time of its election to the Council that it sought election as a member of the Assembly and that it did not seek election on the grounds that it had associations with other states.[52]

Blythe attended a Council meeting within half an hour of the election result being announced. This was simply a honorary visit at which he said a few words of thanks and introduction. At later meetings he presented some reports. Ireland had been appointed Council Rapporteur for the areas of Rural Health and Child Welfare.

Conclusion

It had been as close a run contest as Cremins had expected. Blythe felt that 'although we had six votes to spare, the contest was still close enough, and if we had not carried out an exhaustive canvass, I feel we should certainly have been beaten'.[53]

The preparation and detail which the Irish foreign service exhibited in preparation for the state's election bid indicates that the Irish Free State did possess an organised diplomatic service. The service could design, implement and successfully conclude a high profile multi-dimensional foreign policy. A considerable degree of cohesion existed between Dublin, Geneva, Paris and the other Irish offices on the continent. Whilst External Affairs was under-resourced, it was not inactive or incapable.

The election victory was a symbol of the success of Irish League policy since 1926. It marked the state's elevation to a higher plane of League activity. A member of the Assembly, the Irish had built themselves a niche as an active League member. That the Assembly gave Ireland a mandate to continue their policy in the Council is even more striking when set against their 'non-group' position. The Irish did not have the backing of any historic group to work from. Their possible association with the Dominion group was, if anything, a set-back. Ireland had to build up international support through a widespread canvass. The nature of this support indicates that the Irish were a 'catch-all' candidate, appealing to each state's views on the League and Ireland's past role there, rather than national rivalries and jealousies. The Free State had a high profile in the League in the view of other states. They judged the Irish as a worthwhile candidate and her diplomats as capable Council members who would be as active in the Council as the Assembly. It was a vindication of the stance taken by the Irish delegation to the League Assembly since 1926.

52 League of Nations Assembly Records, First Committee 1931, pp. 16–17. Quoted in Barcroft, 'Lester' p. 12.
53 NA, 26/95, Blythe to McGilligan, 18 September 1930.

CHAPTER 6

Council Member, September 1930–September 1933

Council Member: January–September 1931

W.T. Cosgrave stressed the increased recognition that election to the Council gave the Free State in his address to the Cumann na nGaedheal annual convention in the Mansion House in May 1931. Election, he considered, 'may justly be claimed as a vindication of the degree of prestige acknowledged for this country among the other nations of the world'.[1] No longer was Irish League policy aimed solely at the September Assembly, it had to send a well-briefed delegation to the quarterly Council sessions. Council policy aimed to consolidate and build upon Ireland's position in the Assembly. However, the state was still in no position to make an immediate impact among the League and Great Power heavyweights on the Council. Through 1930 Ireland dealt with relatively minor non-political matters on the Council agenda. The Council was entering a troublesome period. Walters writes that, 'by the autumn of 1930 the period of short and easy Council sessions was over, never to return.'[2] From September 1931 the League was on 'crisis footing' after the invasion of Manchuria.

Silesia and Disarmament

For the January session Walshe briefed the delegation on 'two questions of a serious political nature on which a definite stand may have to be taken.'[3] These were the German–Polish dispute over the discrimination of German minorities in Silesia by the Polish authorities, and the setting of a date for the opening of the Disarmament Conference.

The Silesian problem concerned allegations of electoral discrimination in regional elections in the territory. It was brought to the Council as a violation

1 *Irish Times*, 6 May 1931.
2 Walters, *History*, p. 446.
3 NA, S. 8181, Walshe to O'Hegarty, 5 January 1931.

of the Silesian Convention by the Germans. Walshe has been portrayed as an over-zealous diplomat: 'Walshe tended to allow himself to become too involved. He found it difficult to stand back from political situations about which he held strong views.'[4] But over Silesia he was quite impartial. He supported the Germans, but through analysis rather than conviction:

> If the German case is as irrefutable as it appears, there is no other conclusion to be drawn from it than that the Polish Government are guilty of a breach of their treaty obligations, and of a series of acts which could lead to war in Europe.[5]

Walshe supported a resolute and impartial approach by the Council to dampen down the threat of war. He urged McGilligan to press the Council towards an immediate elimination of the causes of the dispute and to oppose attempts by the Council to shirk the issue. The memorandum shows Walshe's belief that the League was an effective instrument if it could be made to work to the Covenant. The Irish would aim to further the 'immediate removal of causes of friction between Germany and Poland'.[6] This approach would introduce the Free State to the Council as a moderating influence intended to broker solutions in line with the Covenant. Walshe was emphatic, the Irish were to avoid 'a strong uncompromising attitude on the general question of Polish–German relations which would immediately stamp us as being in favour of a revision of the Versailles Treaty'. As the thirties continued, the Irish became more 'Revisionist'. When Ireland had made an initial impression, Walshe felt it could make its position clear, 'at a later stage of our membership of the Council we may have acquired a position which will enable us to favour revision, at present we cannot afford to do so.'

Continuity was the theme in Irish disarmament policy. The Disarmament Conference was to take place as soon as possible, preferably at the end of 1931. McGilligan would stress that the settlement of outstanding international differences would not be helped by further postponement. The early commencement of the conference would provide an impetus for the settlement of international differences.

The Irish delegation for the session was extremely high-powered. McGilligan headed it, making up for his absence in September 1930. He was accompanied by Walshe and his foil, the departmental Legal Adviser, John Hearne. A sign of his quick ascendancy was the inclusion of Frederick Boland, who like Hearne, had joined the Department in 1929.[7] They were joined in Geneva by Sean Lester.

4 Dermot Keogh, 'Profile of Joseph Walshe, Secretary, Department of Foreign Affairs, 1922–1946', in *ISIA*, Vol. 3, No. 2 (1990) pp. 59–80, p. 68.
5 NA, S. 8181, 5 January 1931.
6 Ibid.
7 F.H. Boland (1905–85). Diplomat. Joined External Affairs in 1929; First posting to

Silesia took up the main work of the Council. The Japanese Rapporteur presented a report that was acceptable to both sides, but subtly laid the blame on Poland. The Irish report on the Council session is quite impartial in its views on the resolution of the Silesian problem, though the crisis was solved along the lines preferred by Walshe.

McGilligan attacked the petty squabbles of the Preparatory Commission and spoke out on the need to keep the draft disarmament convention in perspective:

> At last, after ten years we seem to be at the beginning of our real task, but we should not deceive ourselves by thinking that the beginning is even relatively satisfactory. Nothwithstanding its zealous and admirable efforts, the Preparatory Commission has merely enabled us to see more clearly the difficulties in the way.[8]

McGilligan regarded the Convention as only, 'a first step towards a solution'.[9] He argued the need for political consensus: 'the Irish Government earnestly hope that the relations between states will have so improved by the date of the conference that it will be possible to introduce improvements which alone can make the convention of permanent value'.[10] But as with disarmament in the previous chapter, the Irish could only comment and aspire to have an indirect influence.

The codification of international law was different. Costello had made quite an impact on the second commission at the 1930 Assembly. The Irish would again argue that the codification process should continue. McGilligan secured from the Council that the Secretary General should secure the views of various governments on the route that future codification would take. If the governments were left to themselves, they would quietly shelve the issue.

The most direct Irish involvement in the work of the Council was in the sphere of League social policy. McGilligan presented reports on the work of the Health Committee and on the work of the Preparatory Commission for the European Conference on Rural Hygiene. He also made presentations on the question of child welfare. They are part of the hard slog of international relations to construct small links between states that in their entirety provide closer international ties.

During a secret meeting of the Council the Irish made an independent suggestion for the President of the Disarmament Conference. Lester sent a

---

Paris, 1932–4; Head of League of Nations Section, External Affairs, 1934–6, Department of Industry and Commerce (overseas trade section), 1936–8, Assistant Secretary, External Affairs, 1938–46; Secretary, External Affairs, 1946–50, Ambassador, London, 1950–5; Permanent representative to United Nations, 1955–64.
8 NA, S. 8181, telegram to Dublin, 20 January 1931.
9 Ibid.
10 Ibid.

secret dispatch to Dublin that, 'the Irish representative made a suggestion which according to a leading French journalist changed the course of events. Rumours of the activities of the Irish representative on the Council had attracted attention of newspapers from Moscow to Washington'.[11] McGilligan instructed Lester to propose an independent president. Lester asked the Council to consider, 'whether it would not be well to look outside Europe for a president. They all knew that the only difficulty about appointing a European president was the political difficulty.' The Minister for External Affairs had suggested an American president, either former United States Secretary of State Frank Kellogg or General Dawes, the United States Ambassador in London. The reason was that 'the gentleman in question has a great deal of European experience and had taken part in most important judicial work'.[12]

The Irish démarche was not the result of any official contacts with the Americans. Rather like the 1926 Council elections, it was an on the spur of the moment decision in the face of certain circumstances. The Irish had heard a 'Gentleman's' name mentioned and had seen it in the Press. They were not sure, 'if the statesman they had in mind was personally willing'.[13] The proposal was only a suggestion and was, 'brought to the attention of the Council (so that) it might prove to be a way out of the difficulty'.[14] It had the effect of making the Great Powers aware that the Free State was present at the Council table. It was received with alarm. Arthur Henderson, Acting President of the Council balked and 'understood that the American Government did not at this stage wish to be associated with the question of the president'. Briand took a similar stance. Quite whether it was the League or the Americans who did not want an American involved is unclear. At the conclusion, the matter was blamed on the Americans: 'I [Lester] then asked whether I was right in understanding that the American Government did not want to have an American Chairman and the President, Mr. Henderson replied that was his information and that it also applied to the Vice-Presidency.'[15]

This move was aimed at stirring the Council out of lethargy. The Free State had seen rumours of an American candidate in the press and realised that if they mentioned it, the Council would move to scotch these rumours and select a president from Europe. An apparent Irish defeat over the candidate would be a strategic victory as the momentum towards the Disarmament Conference was increased by the appointment of a President.

It had been a very successful session for the League and for the Free State. Lester was very optimistic in his conclusion to an article for The League of Nations Society of Ireland journal, *Concord*: 'the success of the Sixty Second session of the Council was great, therefore, because it was

11 Ibid., confidential verbatim report, Lester to Walshe, January 1931.
12 Ibid.
13 Ibid.
14 Ibid.
15 Ibid.

unexpected. It existed in a better atmosphere than has existed in Europe perhaps since 1928.'

The Sixty-Third Session of the Council: 18–23 May 1931

Few areas on this session's agenda were of direct importance to the Irish. Policy in these instances was to actively show interest. Walshe argued that this 'makes for prestige to play a worthy part in international affairs.'[16] At this session, the Irish read reports on Child Welfare and Rural Health. The delegation comprised McGilligan, Walshe, Cremins and Boland. They arrived at Geneva on 15 May.

A discussion took place on Briand's plan for a European Union. This plan is often seen as a precursor to the integration movements of the 1950s. Ireland's rush to accept EEC membership in 1961 and 1973 was not mirrored in 1931. Support was lukewarm from most European states, though the plan earned Briand much praise. Ireland was uncertain how the plan might effect its vital Commonwealth trading links and the state's newly won international sovereignty. Cumann na nGaedheal had worked hard since the civil war to exert the state's influence on the world, a plan like Briand's would be contrary to this objective.

McGilligan suggested a compromise when a row broke out between Britain and Germany over the furnishing of information on weapons to the Disarmament Conference. The German's wanted to provide information beyond the scope of the draft disarmament convention, the British preferred to stick to the convention. The Rapporteur, in submitting his report, advised acceptance of the British model. McGilligan stepped in at this point to make his state's position clear. He stated that though the German proposal was widely based, the Irish did not see it as too idealistic. McGilligan's purpose was to make clear that the Irish Government saw the convention as little more than a starting point, reference to it as an end in itself circumscribed the concept of disarmament. He gently implied this by stating,

> the non-acceptance by the Council of the German proposal should not be taken to mean that it desired in any sense to restrict the work of the General Disarmament Conference to the limits proposed by the draft convention, or that it would not be possible at a later stage to go beyond them.[17]

This was an example of the role a small state could play on the Council by making small points of order or mentioning procedural matters. It reminded

16 NA, S. 8182, 14 July 1932.
17 League of Nations, *Sixty-Third Session of the Council, Report* (Dublin, 1931), p. 10.

the larger powers that they were not the sole arbiters of the work of the Council.

The Treaties of Versailles and St Germain had forbidden an Anschluss between Austria and Germany. When a plan for an Austro-German Customs Union emerged, it was viewed negatively by France, Britain, Italy and Czechoslovakia who felt it would impede Austrian independence. The scheme went to the Council for further analysis and a legal interpretation. The Germans desired that the Irish be kept fully abreast of developments in the situation. Leo McCauley informed Walshe that this was, 'chiefly because Ireland had a seat on the League Council and, at the same time could view the question impartially as she was not likely to be affected by the union if it took place'.[18] If the Irish could be directed towards a neutral role, it would leave Germany with at least one less barrier to the proposed plan. The Germans did not want the Customs Union plan to be brought to the Council as it would certainly reduce the chances of the scheme coming into operation.

Walshe was anxious to carefully prepare the ground for McGilligan before the Council session opened. Ireland would not be an easily won over small state, as Germany wished. McGilligan had no sympathy for the German Foreign Minister, Dr Curtius adopting a cautionary stance towards bringing the issue to the Council. According to Walshe, 'the Minister takes the view that the Council is the most appropriate body for the consideration of the proposed Customs Union and that the first step in the consideration of the proposed Customs Union must be to deal with the doubts which have arisen as to its legality under the provisions of existing treaties'.[19] McGilligan desired the Council to undertake to examine the dispute under the Covenant, rather than through the constraints of power-politics. The Customs Union project became the subject of an inquiry by the Permanent Court of International Justice. But by the next Council session in September 1931, the German and Austrian Governments had dropped the plan due to adverse international pressure.

The Sixty-Fourth Session of the Council: 1–14 September 1931

The League was meeting at a time of unparalleled economic crisis to which it had no response. Alexander Cadogan wrote to Permanent Under-Secretary at the British Foreign Office, Robert Vansittart that, 'the Assembly has opened

---

18 NA, D.F/A, 26/14, 20 April 1931. Leo T. McCauley (1895–1974): Academic and Diplomat. Lecturer in Classics at UCD. Entered Department of Finance and in late twenties transferred to External Affairs. First Secretary in Berlin, 1929–33; Chargé at Vatican, 1933–4; Consul, New York, 1934–6; Assistant Secretary, External Affairs, 1946–9; Ambassador to Spain, 1949–55; Ambassador to Canada, 1955–6; Ambassador at Vatican, 1956–62.
19 Ibid., Walshe to McCauley, 20 April 1931.

in a mood of gloom and futility ... this is the dullest and most depressing Assembly that has ever met.'[20] The Council meeting was more successful, dealing with its agenda in a lively manner. For the Irish it involved reading more reports on the issue of Rural Hygiene, and dealing with a Brazilian plan for a centre for the study of leprosy in Rio de Janeiro. This was Council work, as laid down by the League, not part of national policy. There was little else 'official' for the delegation of McGilligan, Sean Murphy, Francis Cremins, Freddie Boland and John Leydon to do.

Council membership would change for the 65th Session, following elections for new non-permanent members. Rapporteurs for 1931-2 were to be chosen. The Irish wanted a more prominent part in the proceedings of the Council by becoming Rapporteur for a higher profile issue. The rationale was that it would, 'increase our influence and prestige in League circles.'[21] It would be good for the League because any matter which,

> falls to be discharged by Rapporteurs on the more important subjects dealt with by the Council can instead be performed by the representative of a state with such a reputation for impartiality and independence as the Irish Free State can justly claim to have achieved.

Ireland had served its apprenticeship on the Council, they were ready for a larger role in the proceedings. Murphy listed some areas: Economic Questions; Financial Questions; International Law; Mandates; Minorities; Danzig and Armaments. Economics, International Law and Armaments were all issues with which the Irish were familiar due to the Free State's Assembly policy of the late twenties. League finance fell each year to Sean Lester at the Assembly Committees, hence it was another area with which the Irish were no strangers. Ireland eventually became Rapporteur for Health and Opium questions and in March 1933 took up the minorities post.

Manchuria: September 1931–September 1932

The Japanese invasion of the northern Chinese province of Manchuria on 18 September 1931 ended the harmony on the Council. China involved the League in the dispute under Article 11 of the Covenant. The League could appeal to the parties to settle their differences peacefully under Article 11; it did not have to intervene as Articles 15 or 16 required. This reaction typified the Council's uncertainty towards Manchuria in the initial stage of the conflict. The crisis was on the other side of the globe and its seriousness was diffused as the British stock market was in financial trouble.

20 PRO, FO 371/15733/W 10526/10526/98, 9 September 1931.
21 NA, D.F/A, 26/16, Murphy to Lester, 10 August 1931.

Cumann na nGaedheal and Manchuria

Without instructions from McGilligan, Lester attempted to steer the discussion on Manchuria into a pan-Council rather than a great power context. A Great Power dominated 'Committee' had met separately to discuss Manchuria. Its existence would divide the Council between permanent and non-permanent members. Lester reported on the Committee to the Irish delegation. McGilligan's reaction is interesting: '[I]mmediately after the meeting, I reported the incident to the Minister (and the other members of the delegation), *but he did not express any opinion on my action*'.[22] McGilligan was not interested in Lester's interventions.

In the absence of official direction, Lester adopted a policy of non-intervention. It was not the reaction to be expected from a state 'recognised at Geneva as one of the main upholders of the complete independence of the smaller states'.[23] Ireland's response to the Manchurian issue during the last months of 1931 lacked vigour. McGilligan's attendance at Council meetings became sporadic as government business took up his time. At the 1931 Assembly it was Daniel Binchy, then Irish Minister in Berlin, who spoke for the Irish at the general debate, not McGilligan, though he was Chief Delegate. McGilligan was beginning to lose touch with Ireland's policy at the Council as the depression began to affect Ireland and as the 1932 general election loomed.

The conflict escalated and China called a special meeting of the Council. Lester was told by Walshe not get involved. The Council reformed under the presidency of French Foreign Minister, Aristide Briand, and with the American consul, Prentiss Gilbert, present. This unprecedented move created a fragile American–League front against Japan with the implementation of the Kellogg–Briand Pact (1928) for the renunciation of war. The Free State informed Japan and China of their obligations under this treaty which made war illegal for the solution of disputes and warned them that 'public opinion throughout the world expects the two governments to adhere to undertakings thus assumed'.[24] It was a bi-lateral action taken under the auspices of the League by each member state of the Council. Lester felt that Japan was beginning to feel the pressure of world opinion. To Lester's annoyance, the inclusion of the American consul led to the re-surfacing of the Great Power committee.

Lester planned to 'kill-off' the committee by questioning its purpose at a secret session of the Council on 22 October 1931. It was a personal initiative that had not been sanctioned by Dublin. McGilligan's inaction had given him room to manoeuvre and Walshe had only issued the vaguest of instructions.

22 NA, D. F/A 22/18, Lester–Walshe, 7 October 1931. All unattributed references are from this file. my italics.
23 Patrick McGilligan, *Dáil deb*, 39; 128.
24 PRO FO 371/15494/ F 5919/1391/10.

Lester considered that the committee 'which includes all the permanent and excludes representatives of the non-permanent members creates a breach in the Council which is not in accord with the spirit of equality in this remarkable organisation'.[25] He asked the Secretary General to make sure that the committee that had been formed did not become a precedent. Lester was uncertain about criticising the Committee but Briand and Drummond agreed that the Committee had outlived its usefulness and agreed to end meetings. Lester's action killed the divisive committee and earned him praise from great and small powers alike. The small powers, generally non-permanent members, were glad to have a strong voice and potential leader figure in their ranks. Lester felt that the Free State had, 'acted as the spokesman of seven and probably earned the respect of the others'.

The Council session ended with a resolution calling for an immediate Japanese withdrawal and the beginning of negotiations between the two parties. Though the resolution was vetoed by Japan and was not binding, Japan suffered a moral defeat. The Council was to meet again on 16 November. The interim allowed Lester to seek detailed instructions from Dublin. He argued that Ireland should adopt a higher profile over Manchuria after the 'committee of five' episode, as an activist policy over Manchuria would bolster the Council. Walshe was against an activist policy and stepped into McGilligan's place to keep Lester in order.[26] Walshe aimed to protect Ireland from an impassioned demarche that Irish diplomatic resources could not follow up.[27] He felt that the state should lead from the front in any Council initiative she lent her name to. Without officials, interests or claims in the Far East the Free State could not, in Walshe's opinion, successfully implement Lester's activist approach.

Lester urged that the Minister or Walshe be present at the November Council session to indicate that Ireland attached great importance to the League's intervention in Manchuria. Failing that, Lester wanted Walshe to allow the permanent delegate to take 'a cautious but positive line'.[28] This would also signify the increased Irish interest. It was not, as Walshe feared, a first step to dragging Ireland into the centre of the crisis. Walshe interpreted a cautious line as non-involvement as opposed to Lester's pro-active and assertive interpretation.

Lester found the sense of powerlessness and of letting policy options slip through the Council trying and exasperating. He had been controlled and quiet in his initial pleas to Walshe to follow an active policy. However on

25 22 October 1931.
26 See Michael Kennedy, 'Principle seasoned with the sauce of realism: Sean Lester, Joseph Walshe and the definition of Irish policy towards Manchuria', *ISIA*, Vol. 6, 1995 (forthcoming) for a discussion of this area in greater detail. This section is in part drawn from this article.
27 Walshe–Lester, 14 November 1931.
28 Lester–Walshe, 28 October 1931.

realising the impotence of Walshe's preferred line he lost his patience. Lester's journalistic experience stood him credit as he despatched a measured but scathing attack. With irony he wrote,

> I am to do nothing until my vote or opinion is specifically demanded and, if possible, am to defer giving it until I have consulted you. If a postponement is impossible, I am to try to follow the majority. This will certainly relieve my task of responsibility. Nevertheless I feel bound to express my disappointment that I should not at least be instructed to uphold the moral authority of the League in the greatest crisis it has yet faced.[29]

This was most unusual for the Irish diplomatic service which sought a consensus approach to policy. Lester attacked Walshe by stating that protecting China through an active League policy was also the best protection against the spread of Bolshevism in the area. Locking a wayward China into the League system, as her election as a non-permanent member of the Council had attempted to do, would create another League bastion in the Far East if the powers put their support behind China. In Lester's view, Dublin's instructions would only worsen an already dangerous situation by playing into the hands of Japan and the Soviet Union. He favoured a policy of support of the League. His conclusion illustrates his overall predicament:

> You will agree that for a representative to be effective he should not only obey mechanically the Minister's instructions, but that he should have the opportunity of understanding the reasoning that has lead to the Minister's decisions.

With the Minister lacking interest in the crisis and Walshe and Lester arguing over policy rather than seeking consensus, Free State Council policy lost all direction during winter 1931. With his mind set on following the letter of the Covenant and upholding Ireland's position as an assertive middle-ranking Council member it was only Lester who provided any degree of action and continuity. Lester was willing to take the gamble, he knew the future of the League was at stake. The Free State gained nothing due to McGilligan's opting out of Council policy and Walshe's caution. Lester kept the Free State's position clear: support of the League's involvement and the desire for a peaceful solution to the dispute facilitated by the Council. It was a holding operation and the Free State's prestige was slipping. Edward Phelan noticed that the Free State was lacking her usual vitality on the Council over the Manchurian issue. He wrote with exasperation to McGilligan, that the Free State had,

29 Lester–Walshe, 16 November 1931.

a definite duty to the states who voted for us for a seat on the Council: we represent all the states which have no permanent seats: we asked for their suffrage on the grounds that we were under nobody's thumb and that precisely in such a crisis as this we would be free to take an independent League stand. We shall have to render an account to the Assembly and in the Assembly there will be severe criticism of the Council. The Assembly will be unable to do anything—the Japanese will still be in Manchuria for centuries to come unless I am much mistaken.[30]

With an election looming in the Free State McGilligan had his mind elsewhere. Lester's holding operation brought him to the attention of the British Dominions Office who noticed that Lester was becoming 'internationally minded rather in the sense of regarding the League as a self-sufficient organisation (even if not a super-state)'.[31]

With Lester and Walshe at loggerheads over the direction of policy, the Council re-convened in Paris. The meetings lacked direction. Lester felt that a resumé of events to date might focus attention and was prepared to call for a map to be drawn up outlining the Japanese front lines on crucial dates. Dublin ruled out this line of action. Lester was told again to 'take no positive action in the way of asking for a map or otherwise'.[32] Lester could not play any role and his despatches make clear the impotence of the Council which could not bring itself to discuss the matter of sanctions. In a sulky manner he showed his distaste at his enforced inability to act: 'Every member of the committee spoke today with the exception of Mr Lerroux, the three South American delegates and, of course, I followed my instructions.'[33]

Lester made occasional interventions in the December session. He contributed to the wording of resolutions, making sure they did not give Japan any right of initiative in Manchuria with the blessing of the League. Otherwise he felt that Colban of Norway and his friend the Spanish representative, Madariaga, were intervening on the lines he himself would have followed and considered his own intervention unnecessary. Lester did not want to annoy Walshe any more and was conscious that Dublin was not going to take on board his activist approach.

As the Council neared its end, Lester realised that he was the only delegate unlikely to speak at the final public session. This would prove fatal to the Free State's standing on the Council. Lester telegraphed Walshe to see if the Minister desired he should speak, 'if so does he wish to give me general

30 UCDA, P35B/121, Phelan–McGilligan, 26 December 1931.
31 Stephen Barcroft, 'Irish foreign policy at the League of Nations', *ISIA*, Vol. 1, No. 1, pp. 19–29. p. 20.
32 Walshe–Lester, 16 November 1931, telegram marked 'very urgent'.
33 Lester–Walshe, 18 November 1931.

line or to leave matter to me'.[34] The uninspiring response from Dublin was to speak only if others were doing so and to 'take no line which might be at variance with the final resolution'.[35] Lester was to keep urging negotiation and a speedy conclusion to the dispute within the structures of the League.

These instructions were of little value as Lester could only observe events as they occurred and react accordingly. The speeches on the proposed Commission of Inquiry to be despatched to Manchuria that the Council had spent the December session discussing were mere platitudes. A speech would look like lip service congratulations to the League for a commission of dubious value that had been suggested by the Japanese to waste time as they increased their hold on Manchuria. Lester was also concerned that the Commission's personnel were chosen solely from amongst the great powers. Lester discussed these points with Colban and Fotitch (Yugoslavia) and as a cumulative silence would show the unease of the non-permanent members towards the Commission, the three delegates remained silent. Lester's primary concern was that the standing of the League remain as untarnished as possible.

On 10 December the League constituted its Commission of Inquiry into Manchuria. It was to study and report on the threat to good relations between Japan and China but had no power to control military movements or initiate negotiations. It was hoped the Commission would have an influence greater than its remit. The Commission, which was responsible to the Council was headed by Lord Lytton and departed for the Far East on 3 February 1932, finally reaching Manchuria in April. With that the Council adjourned.

The sixty-sixth session of the Council opened on 25 January. Japanese troops invaded Shanghai on 28 January adding an extra complication to Chinese affairs. With McGilligan involved with domestic issues it was left to Lester to define policy through the November 1931 instructions laid down by Walshe. Lester and Hearne represented the Free State. They did not attempt to lead the Council's discussions by setting an agenda but aimed to engender an environment conducive to the evolution of the Council's discussions. Lester made sure that the whole Council was involved, not just the powers using the facade of the Council. He helped to facilitate what little movement there was on the Council during this session. There was a sense of hopelessness and lack of confidence at the meetings. Lester watched as Japan and China slogged it out.

On 29 January China invoked Article 15 of the Covenant. The Chinese later asked for the dispute to be referred to the Assembly from the Council. Lester supported the move as it would give extra moral support to the League's work over Manchuria. Lester was redefining the Free State's lacklustre Manchurian policy and was beginning to make a more prominent and influential place for the Free State on the Council. It was due to Lester's single-minded

34 Lester–Walshe, 7 December 1931.
35 Walshe–Lester, 8 December 1931.

approach that the Free State was increasingly seen as a supporter of the League's central role in Manchuria. His constant presence and his advocacy role did not define League policy rather they smoothed the path for its progress and prevented it drifting to the whims of the Great Powers. Lester increasingly acted on his own initiative, stating that he was not always able to contact Dublin as events moved quickly. He endeavoured to maintain Ireland's reputation for independence and courage on the Council.

The Extraordinary Assembly

The Irish parliament was dissolved on 29 January and a general election on 16 February 1932 returned a minority Fianna Fáil Government. Eamon de Valera took the post of External Affairs in the new administration. Initial fears, based on his criticisms of the League in the United States in 1919, that de Valera would pay little attention to League affairs proved ill-founded. De Valera developed a high profile at the League and was soon renowned as a statesman of world repute. Through his actions on the Council in early 1932 Lester laid the basis for de Valera's first appearances at the League in September of that year.

Despite the change of government, no new approach to Manchuria immediately evolved. Lester's desire for a strong Council line towards Japan was still blocked by Walshe, whilst de Valera's first actions in the External Affairs portfolio concerned Anglo-Irish relations. The Extraordinary Assembly opened on 3 March, clashing with the first meeting of the new Executive Council in Dublin. Lester used the interregnum to speak freely for the Free State and establish a more aggressive and progressive footing for the incoming administration. The Extraordinary Assembly took over the investigation of the dispute from the Council. Hearne and Lester again represented the Free State. Lester stressed Ireland's belief that the League was the forum in which a solution to the crisis lay. His speech to the Assembly on 8 March allowed him to draw a veil over the lacklustre Irish response to Manchuria since September 1931. He was concerned by reports in the *Journal de Genève* that mentioned 'the significant silence of the smaller members of the Council', and assumed that they referred to Ireland. Ireland was the only Council member who had not yet spoken at the Extraordinary Assembly. Walshe's cautious policy was not furthering Ireland's position on the Council or in the eyes of the world media.

Lester maintained that Ireland had no direct interest in the dispute other than as a League member. Ireland's concern was the safeguarding of world peace and the development of the League as an institution to safeguard that peace. Lester declared that it was the duty of signatories to use the Covenant to solve disputes. He stressed that the territorial integrity of members was guaranteed by Article 10 of the Covenant which must be used to the limit to solve disputes. Lester made Ireland's position clear by ending on a high point:

> It is clear that the duty of the Assembly is not only to settle the dispute between two members of the League, but also and above all to uphold the sanctity of the Covenant ... we must not only settle this dispute: we must settle it right. [It is the] hardest task that the League has ever been called to undertake, but that is the purpose of its existence.[36]

The speech projected Ireland as strongly loyal to League principles. Yet in line with Walshe's instructions Lester had in effect said nothing new. He received applause from those who supported a strong League role and the less enthusiastic representatives of the Great Powers. The Spanish representative, Madariaga, told Lester that it was 'what he had always expected of Ireland'.[37] Ireland was, according to Lester, 'on the right side' of League opinion.[38] British Foreign Secretary, Sir John Simon, apologising to Lester for stating that states on the Council were only in favour of sanctions in reverse proportion to having to implement them, made a point of praising the speech.[39] Lester's remarks did not go further than the ultimate terms of the Assembly's final resolution, yet they had an impact greater than their content and revived Ireland's flagging position on the Council. The London *Times* caught another aspect of Lester's speech when it remarked that if the League were content with half measures over Manchuria, 'the smaller nations will revise their views about its protective value'.[40]

On 11 March the Assembly reaffirmed the League's involvement in the dispute. It resolved to set up a Committee to work towards a settlement in Manchuria and establish a truce in Shanghai. This 'Committee of 19' would keep a watch on the situation in Manchuria and try to bring both parties together; it would be the Assembly's eyes and ears. However, it would wait for the Lytton Commission to report. Lester, because of his membership of the Council, was automatically on this committee.

The Committee of Nineteen met through the summer, dealing with the incursion in Shanghai and following a cease-fire in Shanghai in early May, with Manchuria. Lester felt that the Council could not shirk the responsibility of Manchuria whilst dealing with Shanghai. He agreed with the Chinese that the parties should give information on the steps they had taken to implement the two Council resolutions on Manchuria. All other Council members considered this an appropriate response. Lester operated a twin-track strategy on the Committee. His long term policy was to prepare the ground for the

36 NA, D.F/A 27/18A.
37 Ibid., Lester–Walshe, 9 March 1932.
38 Ibid.
39 Simon was Foreign Secretary from 1931 to 1935.
40 9 March 1932.

Irish delegation at the September Assembly, whilst in the short term he continued his policy of keeping the Committee of Nineteen on course to deal with Manchuria. Lester made timely interventions over the form of the resolution for the truce in Shanghai, making sure that the Japanese did not have any loopholes through which to prolong the period their troops were present in the area. Lester also made sure that there was a considerable Irish input into the Committee's report.

De Valera at the Thirteenth Assembly

As the summer progressed, preparation for the Thirteenth Assembly began. Ireland would hold the rotating Presidency of the Council between September 1932 and January 1933. De Valera would make the opening speech to the Assembly as Acting President. He would also chair the Council session at which the Lytton Report would be presented. De Valera was a novice at Geneva compared to Lester and Cremins. They undertook careful preparation to ensure de Valera's entry onto the international stage was flawless.

Shortly after de Valera became Minister, Lester suggested that the Minister should pay a short trip to Geneva to get accustomed to the atmosphere. He mentioned that 'the Minister would come into close personal contact with the leading members of the League'[41] if he attended the Committee of Nineteen. This would prepare him for the prestigious yet onerous task of chairing the Council. Lester pointed out that Ireland would not be a Council member for 'more than twenty years'[42] and wished to use the remaining 18 months to ensure that when Ireland left the Council, she would do so with her 'national reputation placed on a higher level and thus be able to reap future advantage for national purpose when we are "reduced to the ranks".'

De Valera did not go to Geneva, but he still had to be made aware of the machinations of the Geneva system: 'it would be an added handicap if his first appearance were on the day he became President of the Council (succeeding men here like Briand and Paul-Boncour)'.[43] This would have the added dimension of being the occasion on which de Valera addressed the Assembly for the first time. As with the Council election, Walshe and the headquarters staff in Dublin used the entire Irish diplomatic network to provide press and private information about the September Assembly and the Lytton report. Cremins contacted Lester for suggestions on topics to be included in de Valera's opening address to the Assembly.

The historiographical (and hagiographical) tendency has been to focus on de Valera to the exclusion of the other members of the high-profile delegation

---

41 NA, D.F/A, 27/18A, Lester–Walshe, 11 March 1932.
42 NA, D.F/A, 26/27, Lester–Walshe, 9 March 1932.
43 Ibid.

which included the best and the brightest in the Irish diplomatic service.⁴⁴ A narrow perspective centring solely on de Valera, his speech and the international reaction to it, misses the many dimensions to the Assembly.

As the Assembly was due to open, there was increasing speculation about de Valera's intentions. The United States press expected de Valera to make Anglo-Irish relations, especially the annuities dispute, a key theme. The Japanese were worried that de Valera would play into the hands of the United States by embarrassing Britain. Japan considered that the British were more inclined to adopt a friendly attitude towards Tokyo over Manchuria than America.

The Dominions Office were apprehensive about de Valera's intentions as C.W. Dixon felt that if de Valera were to mention the ongoing Anglo-Irish antagonism at the Council he would 'probably have a friendly audience to convince ... quite a number of the smaller states might be prepared to show sympathy with the Irish Free State as another small state engaged in a dispute with a larger one'.⁴⁵ However, the Irish delegation were always careful to separate the disputes with Britain from their actions at Geneva where Irish and British met in a cordial and workmanlike atmosphere through the 1930s.

It is surprising how well the two delegations got on at Geneva. It provided the two states with their only neutral meeting place. The Irish did not exploit their position on the Council to Britain's disadvantage as many in both the Foreign and Dominions offices expected. In 1932 a Dominions Office despatch made clear that, 'personal relations between the United Kingdom and the Irish Free State delegates at Geneva have been excellent'.⁴⁶ The Irish might not attend joint Commonwealth meetings or attend British dinners where a toast was to be proposed to the King, but in non-official matters and affairs directly related to the Assembly, both parties continued to interact. At the 1934 Assembly, Price, of the Dominions Office wrote to London that, 'the Free State delegation in no way hold themselves aloof personally and are quite ready to discuss what is going on'.⁴⁷ Throughout the Economic War and until the April 1938 tripartite agreements, the normal mode of interaction of the Irish delegates with their British counterparts was accurately summarised by Ben Cockram of the Dominions Office in 1935: 'the Irish Free State delegates, of course, find it easier to co-operate when that co-operation is not proclaimed to the world'.⁴⁸ While not always seeing eye-to-eye over de Valera's attempts to gain elected higher office at the Assembly (Anthony Eden saw de Valera as a dangerous 'firebrand' out to secure personal publicity) Anglo-Irish relations at Geneva in the 1930s were social and co-operative at personal level between delegates.

44 See appendix 3 for delegation personnel.
45 PRO, DO 35/397/12/11111/332, C.E. Dixon–E.J. Harding, 15 August 1932.
46 Ibid., undated minute.
47 PRO, DO 35/185/11/6942/1A/1, Price–Wiseman, 12 September 1934.
48 PRO, DO 35/186A/1/6942/2/19.

At official level there was more of a stand off, but as will be shown below, this also did not stop greater co-operation than the troubled Anglo-Irish climate might initially suggest. There were occasional clashes. In 1934 there was heightened Anglo-French pressure to prevent de Valera from standing for President of the Assembly. The French, alone, also opposed de Valera running for Chairman of the Sixth Committee, which would deal with minority matters. Though the British did not get involved in the Sixth Committee vote, and made no attempt to align with French opposition, Price wrote to London that 'we did not give any very active support. Perhaps there was some connection between this and the fact that the same afternoon we received refusals to attend the United Kingdom dinner from the whole Free State delegation!'[49]

Before the Assembly commenced the Council held its sixty-eighth session. The Japanese called for a delay of at least six weeks between the reception of the Lytton report at the Council and its reference to a special session of the Assembly. It was the first occasion de Valera chaired a Council session dealing with Manchuria.[50] Lester had already informed Cremins that references to Manchuria 'should be treated with caution, patience and forbearance, but to the spirit and letter of the Covenant.'[51] De Valera was an unknown in international relations. He had been portrayed as a romantic revolutionary by the local press. The Council chamber was crowded to see how de Valera dealt with the Japanese request. Without fuss he accepted a Japanese call for a delay and the reception of the Lytton report was put forward to 14 November. In the process, he spoke out against this delaying action and Japan's signature of a treaty of union with their puppet state of Manchukuo. He felt that it prejudiced the settlement of the dispute. The statement was carefully balanced by an acknowledgement that the delay was indicative of the importance that Japan attached to settling the dispute. The strongly anti-Japanese line that some commentators at Geneva had rumoured de Valera would take did not materialise. De Valera enhanced the role of the Assembly in the dispute by stressing that the Council must not impede the Assembly's workings by putting off the discussion of the Lytton report. It is clear that he considered the Assembly as the more competent body to deal with such a dispute. De Valera's unexpectedly mild behaviour impressed those at the Council meeting. There was no impression that de Valera intended to embarrass the Great Powers. De Valera's calmness may have been disappointing, but it was a continuation of Ireland's mediatory role, not taking sides between adversaries and above all supporting the League. The Council and its onlookers expected an amateur, a romantic and a rebel. Careful preparation by Lester and Cremins ensured that de Valera had been coached in the ways of Geneva, so that he

49 PRO DO 35/185/11/6942/1A/1, Price–Wiseman, 12 September 1934.
50 De Valera first chaired a Council session on 23 September. This session did not deal with Manchuria, but with the question of slavery and League finances.
51 NA, S. 8182, Lester–Cremins, 1 July 1932.

appeared very much the international statesman. Following on from Paul-Boncour and with the tradition of Briand to live up to, the world press should have guessed that the propagandistic outpourings of 1919–21 against the League in America would be replaced by a more mature and controlled demeanour. The expectation of pyrotechnics had proved false and de Valera's handling of the debate with calm efficiency marked him, according to the *New York Times*, as 'one of the ablest presiding officers that the Council has had'.[52]

Following the normal round of dinners and lunch parties, the moment Lester and Cremins had spent six months planning for arrived. The morning of 26 September saw de Valera address the Assembly as Acting-President. The speech was relayed from Geneva by the BBC and carried on the Irish broadcasting service. His speech had been planned by Cremins in conjunction with Lester and Frederick Boland and members of the League Secretariat. A note attached that it 'may be modified as you wish'[53] gave de Valera *carte blanche* to develop it as he saw fit. It is the moment that biographers of de Valera have chosen to launch into their various chapters on his international reputation. It is more a development, than a beginning. The themes were a more aggressively worded attack on the failings of the League to live up to the Covenant and public opinion than those of McGilligan and FitzGerald. Stressing international peace and security and international co-operation, but overwhelmingly conscious of the League's shortcomings, the speech is a continuation of critical support. It gives praise where praise is due. After mentioning the League's achievements in the difficult year of 1931–2 de Valera made clear that they represented a 'record of no mean achievement'. In the tradition of critical support he then changed tone to one reminiscent of Cosgrave's after Ireland's admission. De Valera argued that the League could not prosper on commendations alone. It might know its own difficulties, but as it had no moral sanction other than world public opinion, 'it is time for us to ask ourselves what is the attitude of the outsider—the average man and woman—to the League and to all this activity at Geneva?' Whereas Cosgrave in 1923 could speak of the League's relative youth to explain its poor performance de Valera, speaking nine years later could not magic away the evident failure. He spoke of rising international 'complaint, criticism and suspicion' as the League failed to deal with the pressing problems of the day.[54]

The speech shows elements of Lester's experiences over the past year on the Council. De Valera spoke of how the equality of states was ignored and how the powers papered over the cracks to provide cosmetic solutions to deep seated problems. De Valera had removed the carnival mask of Geneva from the Assembly and shown it the grim truth that the Assembly refused to

---

52 *New York Times*, 26 September 1932.
53 NA, D.F/A, 26/31, 20 September 1932.
54 All quotes from this speech, unless otherwise referenced, are from the version contained in Eamon de Valera, *Peace and War* (Dublin, 1944), pp. 5–14. Hereafter referred to as *Peace and War*.

believe. The League was floundering because national interests were overtaking the Covenant as the ruling factor in international relations. Speaking for the small state and the ordinary man alike, de Valera argued that action and adherence to the Covenant, not volumes of statistics and surveys were the way to dispel the notions of criticism and growing disinterest in the League that were now pervading the world's public. Building on Lester's speeches at the Council, de Valera argued the primacy of the Covenant,

> the one effective way of silencing criticism of the League, of bringing to its support millions who stand aside in apathy, or look at its activities with undisguised cynicism, is to show unmistakably that the Covenant of the League is a solemn pact, the obligations of which no state, great or small, will find it possible to ignore.

In a draft this came out more forcefully:

> If therefore the League is today threatened with extinction, it is not because there is anything wrong with the Covenant or the objects which the League was founded to fulfil. It is because for twelve years, the objects of the League have been lost sight of. It is because for the last twelve years the Covenant of the League has remained a dead letter.[55]

This version was not published in *Peace and War*. It is a perspective that both Lester and de Valera were to hold to the end of the League's existence in 1946. Lester, as Secretary General, wrote 'it was not the League that failed, it was the nations which failed to use it'.[56] Lester had been trying to use the Covenant to the letter over Manchuria; perhaps if he had been more successful, de Valera's point that 'no state is powerful enough to stand for long against the League if the governments in the League and their peoples are determined that the Covenant shall be upheld' would not ring so hollow today. In the version delivered to the Assembly, de Valera spun out his conclusion. He spoke out for the success of the Disarmament Conference, the need to look after the well-being of the world's population in the face of impending economic collapse. If the League and world fail in these tasks, 'we shall be failing in our duty, and failing cruelly and disastrously'. He concluded by stating Ireland's position, that she wanted peaceful coexistence. This was obviously aimed at Britain,

> In spite of the opinions you may have formed from misleading reports, I want you to know that our history is the history of a people who have

55 NA, D.F/A, P26/2.
56 *Report into the work of the League of Nations during the war* (League of Nations, Geneva, 1946), p. 5.

consistently sought only to be allowed to lead their own lives in their own way, in peace with their neighbours and with the world.

The draft conclusion was less flowery and gave a grave judgement on the future of the League. Referring to disarmament and the economic situation de Valera was scripted to conclude, 'The supreme test of the League is at hand. ... Now if ever, the League must live and act, or remain forever an idle aspiration.' His actual conclusion fitted well onto the unofficial one; in Irish he appealed 'may God assist in the exalted task before us, and may He not permit that we should fail'. De Valera's austere black figure combined with the feeling of chaos and international anarchy created an atmosphere that suited the tone of the speech. Ireland, despite press reports, had renewed its faith in the League, but had made clear, from the League's highest body that when all the cards were on the table, the future called for drastic action to save the League from international oblivion and disregard.

The tone and impact of this speech stand today as effectively as they did in 1932. Yet the speech has never been seen in context. The role played by Lester on the Council since September 1931 and his close co-operation with Cremins and Boland to prepare de Valera for Geneva have not been emphasised. De Valera was not a one-man-show at Geneva, he was a popular spectacle at the 1932 Assembly because of his background, but not yet a statesman of international repute. His performance greatly aided his transformation into the role. It was only in the wake of his speech that the view of the Irish Minister for External Affairs as an international statesman developed. Prior to this, it was the novelty value of the rebel turned constitutional politician and the 'unique spectacle in which John Simon represented Britain and over which presided eminent rebel Eamon de Valera'.[57] De Valera's international profile developed both as a result of his hard-hitting speech and his later performance as the impartial chairman of the Council as it dealt with the Lytton Commission report. Crucial to this was the preparation of Lester and Cremins, coupled with de Valera's own critical yet hopeful view of the League. De Valera was reassessed by the world community and seen to be a statesman of world stature. As the *New York Times* remarked, 'he has shown himself a resourceful and formidable statesman'.[58] De Valera's performance complemented Lester's policy of improving Ireland's reputation on the Council over Manchuria. The reaction to the speech put Ireland into the headlines of the world's press. The Assembly's lacklustre proceedings were enlivened by de Valera's outburst.

The press seized upon de Valera's argument that the League was at 'the bar of public opinion, with a burden of justification upon us that is almost overwhelming' and the lack of applause that greeted him on the conclusion of

57 NA, D.F/A, 27/18A.
58 27 September 1932.

his speech. This has been interpreted as a sign of condemnation founded on the uneasiness of hearing the truth[59] or it may simply be due to the Assembly not realising that de Valera, never a good public speaker, had in fact finished. It is more likely a sign of judgement suspended until a new figure on the international scene had been evaluated over a number of performances. Was this a one off maverick performance or the outlining of a considered and long-term approach?

The press were in no doubt as to the quality of the speech, yet they made a fundamental mistake: de Valera was not a critic of the League. Ireland was a supporter of the Covenant, but also a supporter of its active implementation. De Valera argued that the League could live up to international expectations if its members grouped behind it. He was not pronouncing a sentence of death, but calling for a brave and fresh return to the principles of the founders of the League before it was too late. It was a warning, it was in 1936 that the last rites were administered and in 1938 that de Valera pronounced the League dead in body, but not in mind. De Valera's speeches throughout the 1930s catch the mood of decline at specific points in the League's last years. De Valera remained an optimist in the League to the end, as did Sean Lester.

The impact of de Valera's speech ensured that he was the villain of Geneva. The Irish were enemies of the League in the minds of the idealists, critical supporters in the view of the majority of states and its executioners according to the hostile American press who were glad to see the League berated. De Valera made use of an inauguratory address at Radio Nations, the League radio station, to correct any misinterpretation that might have arisen from his speech:

> I spoke not as an enemy of the League but as one who wishes the League to be strengthened and developed, as the best visible means of securing peace among nations and of solving the major political and economic problems which face the world today.[60]

He argued that the criticisms he brought to notice were current criticisms that could not be ignored. Many of the criticisms were unjust and this could be shown by reference to the many successes of the League over the previous year he had mentioned in his speech. Yet it was factors such as the failure of the League's disarmament mission that were contributing to its growing credibility problem in the eyes of the watching world. He argued that if an effective League was the object of the international community, then there was no problem in these criticisms being voiced. The League could not expect to succeed if these difficulties were shirked. He concluded by making clear

---

59 See M.J. McManus, *Eamon de Valera* (Dublin, 1944) p. 162.
60 *Peace and War*, p. 18.

Ireland's support of the League to 'guarantee justice and provide effective protection against aggression'.

De Valera left Geneva the day after he made this broadcast. The normally wary Dominions Office heaved a sigh of relief that their bugbear had left town and that this troublesome Irishman had behaved himself. Price concluded that the 'opinion is generally expressed that Mr de Valera has carried out his duties as President of the Council very efficiently'.[61] De Valera would return to preside over the Council's deliberation on the Lytton report on 21 November. The ideals of his speech were reflected in de Valera's, Joseph Connolly's and Lester's actions in the final episode of what was fast becoming the Manchurian debacle.[62]

Ireland and the Lytton Report

The Lytton Report was published on 2 October. It recommended a joint regime in Manchuria that would ensure the sovereignty of China whilst ensuring Japanese security and economic interests. The Japanese remained intransigent, remarking that the recognition of Manchukuo was irreversible. Ireland would preside over the historic session at which the Lytton Report would be examined by the Council. De Valera, accompanied by Connolly, Cremins and Michael Rynne left Dun Laoghaire on 17 November. The delegation wished to arrive early in Geneva to meet the parties to the dispute.[63]

Between the Assembly and the re-scheduled commencement of the Council session on 21 November, Cremins sought reports from each Irish legation about their respective countries views on the impending report and Council meeting. Charles Bewley reported that the Holy See did not wish to get involved in the dispute and that it made few appearances in the Italian press. Leo McCauley reported how well disposed the Japanese Ambassador to Germany had always been towards the Free State in Berlin diplomatic circles where the British Ambassador was instead the figure to be courted. It was Michael MacWhite in Washington who had the high prestige task of entering into communications with the American Secretary of State, Henry L. Stimson, with the intention of securing America's viewpoint on the report. He found that whilst America could not associate herself with League affairs in Manchuria, the United States would support the Lytton Report as it paralleled United States policy of the non-recognition of Manchukuo. This was whole-

61 PRO, DO 35/184/5.6856/A, Price–Wiseman, 29 September 1932.
62 **Joseph Connolly**: Consul General in US, 1921–2; Fianna Fáil politician, member of Irish Free State Senate, 1928–36. On retirement from politics in 1936 became chairman of the Board of Public Works.
63 **Michael Rynne**: Joined External Affairs, 1932; Head of League of Nations Section, 1936–40; Legal Adviser, 1938–50; Assistant Secretary, 1951–3; Ambassador to Spain, 1954–61.

heartedly supported by Lester who wanted to bring the United States into line with the League to create a united front against Japan.

The greatest burden fell upon Lester. Along with the Council session he was also attending the Disarmament Conference and making preparations for the impending Special Assembly that would result when the Council passed the Lytton report on to the Assembly. He advocated a softly-softly approach to ensure that Japan and China were present at the Council session. Then he urged that 'the Council, or the Irish representative on the Council, should be inclined towards bringing the strongest pressure on Japan to accept the Lytton recommendations'.[64] If the Japanese, as he expected, did not accept the Lytton report, Lester felt that this was the end of the Council's involvement. The matter should then be turned over to the Assembly and thereafter to the Committee of Nineteen on which neither Japan or China sat. Japan wanted the Council, not the Assembly, to deal solely with the report.

The session opened on 21 November with de Valera chairing the meeting in a crowded Council chamber. Lester took on the role of intermediary between de Valera and the other small states on the Council. This allowed Ireland to act in concert with the representatives of Czechoslovakia, Spain, and Norway, during the meetings. The mood in Geneva was pessimistic, few expected a successful outcome. Matsuoka for Japan, and Dr Wellington Koo representing China, presented their respective cases. It was common knowledge that Japan would reject the Lytton report. China threatened to invoke Article 16 of the Covenant, the as yet untried sanctions article. With China and Japan at loggerheads and the near universal acceptance of the impartiality of the Lytton report, either the Japanese would have to leave the League or the principles of the Covenant would have to be ditched. The message of de Valera's September speech to the Assembly had centred on just such a crisis of confidence and a moment of reckoning. How could the League survive with credibility if it retreated and accepted a fait accompli in Manchuria?

Following a lengthy series of presentations by the parties, de Valera invited Lord Lytton to make any further points he and his team might have. This shook the Council into life and the Japanese protested at such a move, stating that the Lytton Commission had presented its final report. De Valera calmly responded that the Commission was still in being and that this was an opportunity for the members of the Commission to alter or modify their findings in light of the speeches they had heard at the Council meeting. Matsuoka maintained his objection. According to Lester, Sugimura, the Japanese Under-Secretary-General, felt that 'the President had been very fair'.[65] De Valera's handling of such situations contributed to his growing international image as a statesman. His ease and authority was such that, 'pro-

64 NA, D.F/A, 27/18A, Lester–Walshe, 3 November 1932.
65 Ibid., Lester–Walshe, 19 December 1932.

League elements came to regard him as one of the champions of the rule of law in international affairs'.[66]

Lord Lytton, representing his eponymous commission, stated that they had nothing to add to their report. The Council, despite Japanese objections, then moved to pass the dispute to the Assembly in line with Article 15 of the Covenant. De Valera hoped that the debate at the Council did not represent the final positions of both belligerents and that they would not turn down any just and permanent settlement to the dispute. The President asserted the key principle of Ireland's policy towards Manchuria since Fianna Fáil had taken office: 'it would be an 'intolerable defiance of public opinion' if, in a dispute such as this, 'the machinery of the League were not availed of to the full, or if the working of that machinery were impeded by any want of the necessary co-operation on the part of one of the states concerned.'[67] On 29 November the Council resolved to pass the report on to the Assembly without comment.

With the discussions on Manchuria finished, de Valera passed the chair onto Joseph Connolly and returned to Dublin. Speaking to journalists in Dublin, de Valera continued to believe that a solution was possible using the Lytton report and based on the Covenant and the principles of the peaceful settlement of international disputes and non-aggression. Ireland had made clear its belief in the primacy of the League for the solution of international disputes.

The Lytton Report at the Assembly: December 1932

The Extraordinary Assembly met on 6 December. With the British, French and German foreign ministers present, Matsuoka for Japan and Dr Yen for China again presented their cases. Joseph Connolly then spoke for the Free State. As the first speaker after the two parties the Free State held a position relative to their increased importance in the proceedings. Connolly's speech is an illustration of how the collective Irish response to Manchuria should be considered during 1932, and not solely the actions of de Valera. It has received less attention than de Valera's of the previous September. Connolly, after consultation with Lester, developed the Lester–de Valera line that was balanced between the two parties involved but stressed the primacy of the Covenant and the League. He tempered this with the warning that if the League:

> falters or hesitates, fearing lest its action may offend, then as an organisation, built up by moral support of what is right, it will not survive and will not deserve to survive.[68]

66 Ibid.
67 Quoted in *The Times*, 26 November 1932.
68 NA, D.F/A, 27/18A.

Returning to the report before him, Connolly used Ireland's prestigious position as first speaker after the belligerents to announce her refusal to recognise the Japanese puppet state of Manchukuo. To do otherwise would be to repudiate the Lytton report and the Covenant. Connolly linked this into Ireland's position in the League by stressing that 'we of the smaller states are vitally concerned to ensure that the principles embodied in the Covenant are steadfastly maintained'.[69] If the League failed over Manchuria, then its critics would be justified. The Assembly must uphold the Covenant and try to salvage the position of the League. Connolly concluded by emphasising that Manchuria was 'a supreme test of the League.' Ireland would accept the Lytton report:

> we intend to follow the advice of the Commission by *refusing to recognise a state set up under the conditions which have operated in Manchuria*. Having definitely made that declaration, we are willing to lend what aid we can in trying to find a solution on the basis of the Report, in the hope that justice to all interests concerned can be secured, and that the horrors and turmoil of war may be removed from the people of Manchuria, and the dangers to world peace be eliminated.

The massed delegates followed a similar line and the Assembly moved towards a declaration of the non-recognition of Manchukuo. Lester remarked that he received a great many personal congratulations on Senator Connolly's behalf after the speech. His speech had been, according to C.P. Price, 'the most anti-Japanese of those which have been delivered'.[70] The debate concluded on 8 December with a draft resolution bearing the signatures of the Irish Free State, Spain, Czechoslovakia and Sweden. It referred to the Lytton report and made four points:

1. The action of Japan was not legitimate self-defence.
2. That the establishment of Manchukuo was not a spontaneous movement;
3. That the present situation was not consistent with the Covenant of the League, the Kellogg Pact, and the nine-power Treaty; and
4. That the American and Soviet Governments should be invited to take part in the deliberations.[71]

Lester had linked Ireland to the resolution to make a place for Ireland in any drafting committee. Connolly had reserved the right for Ireland to put forward suggestions to the Assembly for the settlement of the dispute. Ireland was able to show her independent attitude and associate herself with the

69 Ibid.
70 PRO, DO 35/141/2/6010/366, C.P. Price–Clutterbuck, 7 December 1932.
71 Synopsis quoted in the *Irish Times*, 8 December 1932.

advanced line being taken by three of the most prominent small states. This action worried the Great Powers, Price agreed with Lester that,

> it does no harm, but on the contrary a good deal of good for the small states to express themselves pretty freely about Japan's actions. On the other hand, if they intend as seems likely, to carry this further and press condemnatory resolution on the Assembly, the effect of that can only be bad.[72]

Matsuoka called for the removal of the Irish-sponsored resolution, stressing that it might have unforeseen consequences; a statement interpreted to refer to a Japanese withdrawal from the League. The Assembly adjourned after the Japanese ultimatum. It reconvened that afternoon 'in an atmosphere of intense excitement.'[73] Frantic discussions had taken place between the signatories and the Secretary General. They refused to withdraw their document. The resolution was instead sent to the Committee of Nineteen. The resolution co-sponsored by Ireland was not voted upon and replaced by the less aggressive Czech–Swiss resolution which was approved by Japan. This suggested a less forceful resolution that the Committee of Nineteen, along with the United States and Soviet Governments, should devise the machinery of conciliation under Article 15 paragraph 3 of the Covenant. The carefully worded motion took in the Irish motion by calling on the Committee to look not only at the Lytton report, but also,

> the observations of the parties and opinions expressed in the Assembly, in whatever form they were submitted, to draw up proposals with a view to the settlement of the dispute.[74]

Thus the dispute went back to the Committee of Nineteen on 9 December; the committee would suggest a method of solution. The decision the committee reached would be referred back to the Assembly for a final vote. Lester felt that Ireland's 'decision to participate in the resolution kept us in the forefront of the fight'.[75] This reference to the Irish co-sponsored motion to the Committee meant that the official resolution would be much more far-reaching. The press lavished praise upon the four small powers:

> When the crisis comes we must look for aid to the smaller governments like those of Spain, Sweden and the Irish Free State, with whom liberty is more than a platform phrase.[76]

72 PRO, DO 35/141/2/6010/366.
73 *Irish Times*, 9 December.
74 Op. cit., 10 December 1932.
75 NA, D.F/A, 27/18B, Lester–Walshe, 19 December 1932.
76 *Manchester Guardian*, 12 December 1932.

At the Committee of Nineteen, which met from 13 to 20 December, a gap emerged between the powers who favoured conciliation and the smaller states, Ireland, Spain, Sweden, Norway and Czechoslovakia, who wanted to combine conciliation with a declaration of League principles along with a formal statement that the League did not recognise Manchukuo. Ireland was represented on the drafting sub-committee by Joseph Connolly. In these discussions, the Irish along with the other small powers present, urged the adoption of a strong line in the final resolution. The small states were insistent that the adoption of the report and the non-recognition of Manchukuo was more important than the consequences, even if these included Japan leaving the League. The Great Powers, especially British Foreign Secretary, Sir John Simon, did not subscribe to such a moral victory and called for continued efforts at conciliation. This incensed the Chinese, but Japan made it clear that she would leave the League if the resulting resolution was stronger than that of the March 1932 Special Assembly. Japanese opinion was moving against even a conciliation commission.

The final round of the Manchurian dispute

During January and February 1933 the Commission of Nineteen produced the League's final judgement on Manchuria. Lester worked within the Committee to strengthen the final report by including as many of the Lytton recommendations as possible. Lester also played a crucial part in careful negotiation with the Japanese and Chinese representatives. In the absence of Benes of Czechoslovakia, Lester was recognised as the spokesperson of the small states group. His impartiality was clear, he was supporting the application of League rules, this may have appeared as pro-Chinese in opposition to Japan when the dispute was viewed in inter-power terms. The Committee of Nineteen held its final meeting on 13 February at which it considered the text of its report to the Assembly. Lester here made re-drafting suggestions and at the end of the proceedings received congratulations for his stance by the representatives of the small states. The Committee of Nineteen reported to the Assembly the facts of the case and recommended a settlement under Article 15 paragraph 4.

The report incorporated the Lytton Commission's findings and recommended Manchurian autonomy under Chinese sovereignty combined with a Sino-Japanese non-aggression pact. It did not recognise Japanese rights in Manchuria. On 24 February 1933 the Assembly adopted the Committee of Nineteen's report and the Japanese delegates walked out. Japan was still in occupation of Manchuria, it was a hollow formal victory by the League. The Assembly set up an advisory committee to look at the Far Eastern question. On 27 March 1933 Japan announced its decision to withdraw from the League. The League had not recognised the puppet state of Manchukuo. Its impartial and authoritative verdict had given effect to the world's voice and moral warnings. The minor gains to the League outweighed the losses. Faith in the Covenant was severely shaken. The small states had recognised the weakness of the League but had not given in. The Council's power was shaken and the gap between small and large at League was increasingly apparent. After the May 1933 Tangku Truce the League ended its dealings with Japan.

South America: Lester, Chaco and Leticia

Affairs in Latin America began to spin out of control as the Lytton Commission delivered its report. A dispute flared between Bolivia and Paraguay over the Chaco region. In the same year Peru and Colombia were involved in hostilities over the disputed border area of Leticia. The Great Powers had no reason to get involved in these disputes and both were finally brought to the League Council. The Bolivia–Paraguay dispute simmered on until 1938 but the League successfully resolved the Leticia dispute by the summer of 1933.

Ireland's presidency of the Council between September 1932 and January 1933 brought Lester into committees of the Council dealing with both disputes. In September 1932 he became Chairman of a Committee of Three investigating Chaco and in January 1933 he became Chairman of a similar committee investigating the Leticia dispute. These two disputes show Lester metamorphosing into an international civil servant. Though his actions on both committees directly benefited the Free State in terms of international prestige, Lester's capability and presence within the League system was greatly enhanced. F.P. Walters refers to Lester's and his Spanish colleague and friend Madariaga's work over Leticia in glowing terms, 'the brilliancy and courage of the Spaniard being reinforced by the sound judgement and political flair of the Irishman'.[77] Following on from his role on the Committee of Nineteen and the two Latin American Committees, the metamorphosis was complete as Lester was appointed League High Commissioner in Danzig.

Peru–Colombia Leticia: 1932–3

Peru invaded and occupied the disputed border region 31 August 1932. It was not until January 1933 that the dispute was brought to the attention of the Secretary General by Colombia. Lester, representing Ireland as President of the Council, became involved.

Lester's actions were taken without seeking advice from Dublin; they were matters of League and not national policy. He was acting as President of the Council, not Irish Permanent Representative. On 14 January he despatched telegrams urging both sides to avoid escalation of the conflict. He then in-

---

77 Walters, *History*, p. 525.

formed Walshe of his actions. His pessimism about the League's ability to act was revealed 'it is doubtful whether a clash can be avoided, but it is necessary to do something'.[78]

By early February the parties had moved in favour of League based negotiations. The Council appeared to favour Colombia and war fever rose. The Council's Leticia committee met with the remit to follow the dispute and report back. The Committee consisted of Lester, Madariaga and Matos (Guatemala). Lester presided even though the Free State was no longer President of the Council.

Lester failed in his immediate objective to avoid further military clashes. Colombia appealed to the League under Article 15 and Lester called an extraordinary Council session for 21 February. Negotiations took place between the two parties at Geneva with Lester presiding. His objective was a lasting solution, as he informed Walshe, 'we were anxious not merely to lay down the law on the question, but to secure a settlement which would enable permanent good relations to develop between the two countries'.[79] The first step in this was to get Peru to evacuate the territory and put Leticia under League control and then to get the Colombians to reoccupy under League auspices. This met with Colombian but not Peruvian approval.

Lester relied on his wits and the Committee of Three's advice over Leticia. Dublin was informed as Lester happened to be Ireland's representative. Cremins's role as onlooker was apparent by a memo of 3 March when the Department of External Affairs quickly tried to bring itself up to date with the Leticia dispute to follow Lester's reports. Lester remarked in a report to Dublin that, 'this dispute continues to occupy a very large amount of my time. My committee meetings rarely finish earlier than 8pm or even later'.[80] Lester adopted a two-track strategy. He and Madariaga continued with the international force option, but in the event of Peru failing to accept it, proposed an arms embargo and possibly economic sanctions on Peru. The crucial aspect was to keep a united League–American front so as not to give the parties a way out.

The Council, under Article 15 paragraph 4, produced a report on the situation. The report favoured Colombia and offered a resolution of the dispute through a League commission. It was adopted at a Council session on 18 March and the Peruvians walked out. An Advisory Committee was set up that included the existing Committee plus representatives from Brazil and America with Lester as President. There was general approval of this move, with Lester reporting to Dublin that the South American states 'express appreciation and pleasure that I was to continue to be President of the Committee dealing with the dispute'.[81]

78 NA, D.F/A, 27/30, Lester–Walshe, 16 January 1933.
79 Ibid., Lester–Walshe, 23 February 1933.
80 Ibid., 9 March 1933.
81 Ibid., 18 March 1933.

As the enlarged committee met news filtered through of renewed naval confrontations. Lester proposed an arms embargo on Peru as the situation became more aggravated. Sean Murphy informed Lester that Ireland, though not an arms exporting country, would accept such an embargo. He warned Lester not to go too far and appear over-zealous, 'the Minister desires to avoid a situation in which the Irish Free State would be too prominent in the acceptance of an obligation the burden of which falls not upon the Irish Free State but upon other states'.[82] This is evidence of the clear difference between Lester's interpretation of his role and Dublin's. Lester saw himself representing the League and the Council first and foremost, Dublin continued to see him as Irish representative who happened to be presiding over an international dispute and who would have to follow Dublin's line. To Lester, the League line was paramount.

Lester, the committee, the Secretary General and the parties continued negotiations. The dispute had lost its military significance and was down to a question of national prestige. Lester attempted to reduce Peru's expectations so that she might accept a compromise solution, Colombia felt that it had compromised enough already.

The assassination of Peru's President, Colonel Sancho Cerro on 30 April changed matters completely. Lester called an emergency meeting of the advisory committee on learning that the late President had despatched a naval force which had passed through the Panama Canal on 3 May. The Advisory Committee recommended that countries on its route refrain from giving facilities to the convoy. Negotiations continued in Geneva.

On 10 May Lester put forward new proposals of a Colombian-financed League Military Commission to take over the territory for 12 months prior to its handing back to Colombia. This was a historic occasion, Lester wrote to Walshe that

> we have been making history in Geneva this week ... [A] committee of which I have been President, has proposed and the Council has accepted the formation of an international army to take over temporarily a disputed territory.[83]

The convoy continued to make progress towards the Amazon and British and Dutch colonies en route had refuelled it contrary to League recommendations. Peru used the threat of the convoy to back away from immediate acceptance of Lester's new solution. On 25 May the Peruvian delegate declared his agreement with the new solution and would sign. A cease-fire was declared. Lester remarked to Walshe that, 'I have been receiving personal felicitations and congratulations from scores of people and I think the success

---

82 Ibid., Murphy–Lester, 4 April 1933.
83 NA, D.F/A, 34/117, Lester–Walshe, 4 April 1933.

of our efforts will have effects out of proportion even to the nature of the dispute itself.'[84] On 25 May at a public session of the Council both Colombia and Peru signed the agreement. A League Commission with Colombian military support administered the Leticia area from June 1933 to April 1934 when the Rio Treaty passed the territory to Colombia. By this stage the Irish had left the Council, and Lester had resigned as President of the Committee of three and was on his way to Danzig.[85]

Lester had acted as a go-between and a mediator and so had allowed the League to show that it could work effectively and efficiently under Article 15. He had helped create an environment whereby Peru could back down without losing face and had shown that international administration and arbitration could resolve disputes peacefully and cool down conflicts. The dispute showed that contrary to the Manchurian debacle, the Council could act with speed and efficiency to resolve a dispute and without recourse to the Assembly. Lester's experiences with the Council's procrastination and his own inability to play a greater role over Manchuria determined his active stance over Leticia.

This time he did not seek directions from Dublin, he acted first and it was left to Dublin to react. Lester's confidence had grown enormously since September 1931 and he was relying on his own resources, ability and working relationship with diplomats such as Madariaga to work the Council. He was conscious that he was representing Ireland, but his actions more and more indicate he was beginning to think internationally before nationally. Lester's personal role through Manchuria, Leticia and later Chaco showed that Ireland was a capable and effective Council member.

Lester, far more so than de Valera, was Ireland's outstanding personality in practical terms at Geneva in the early 1930s. Lester achieved results that put into practice what de Valera had advocated through his September 1932 address to the Assembly and Presidency of the Council. De Valera might have been the enduring international and public image of Ireland at the League, but it was Lester who made sure that these declarations of intent counted and that Ireland was known for the work record of its Permanent Representative in addition to chilling speeches to the Assembly by its Minister for External Affairs. Lester is the neglected component of this very effective partnership at Geneva.

Bolivia–Paraguay, Chaco: The Council's moment

The League's ability to act was hampered in the case of the Chaco conflict by Washington's desire to keep the League out of the dispute. The sheer nationalistic pride of the parties concerned also contributed to the failure of interna-

---

84 NA, D.F/A, 27/30, Lester–Walshe, 25 May 1933.
85 Lester sent Secretary General Joseph Avenol his resignation from the Presidency of the Committee of Three on 18 December.

tional efforts at mediation. The League's Committee of Three looking into this dispute was again made up of Ireland, Spain and Guatemala. The area in question was a barren wasteland, but it gave land-locked Bolivia river access to the Atlantic Ocean. Skirmishes had first broken out in 1928, but the parties did not want recourse to the League as regional organisations were involved in seeking a solution. When hostilities were renewed in 1932 the parties and neighbouring states were more inclined to get the League involved in the dispute. Drummond, de Valera and the representatives of the small states on the Council were anxious for it to get involved. Madariaga first insisted that the League get involved and set up a Committee to investigate the dispute, if anything it would increase the League's prestige in Latin America.

Despite some complaints as to the suitability of the members, the aforementioned Committee of Three took the Chaco dispute on board. It kept in contact with the so-called Neutral Commission that was a Washington-led Latin American grouping also investigating the Chaco dispute. Ireland was represented on the League Commission by de Valera, Connolly and Lester respectively. De Valera began by despatching telegrams to both parties urging them to cease-fire and accept arbitration. The question of an arms embargo was then raised. Lester took over this policy of proposing arbitration and threatening an arms embargo. The multiplicity of groups involved in the efforts to solve the dispute was a considerable problem. Lester maintained contact with MacWhite in Washington to try to keep up with the Neutral Commissions views. MacWhite's reports suggested that the United States wished to sideline the League by putting off its involvement until a later date. This angered the Council as two League members were in conflict and it was being pushed aside.

By early 1933 the Council was merely keeping in touch with the matter. No formal appeal had been made to the League. The Council remained inactive until June 1933 as a great power brokered solution was attempted. Cremins remarked in a memorandum for de Valera how Lester's attempts at solving the dispute had failed because the parties would not accept a League-based solution. Lester wanted to invoke Article 11 of the Covenant to get discussion of an arms embargo underway. Cremins observed that this would require the unanimous vote of all members of the Council, including the parties to the dispute, for a recommendation under this article to have validity.

Guatemala, Spain and Ireland invoked Article 11 and made a formal request for information from the parties. Lester was extremely enthusiastic about its implementation. This was the first time the League was working towards an arms embargo. Murphy informed Lester that Ireland would accept such an embargo as it had over Leticia. Objections and problems were raised and the arms embargo question got caught up with these problems until May 1933.

Finally, in early May, Paraguay declared war on Bolivia. Paraguay had previously accepted proposed League efforts and Bolivia rejected them, thus the Committee was placed in a curious situation. It was now more uncertain just who would be judged to be the aggressor. By 19 May, after much discussion, the Council secured an agreed report on the Chaco situation. On 20 May an Irish call for a League Commission of Inquiry to organise an armistice, negotiate an agreement and submit the dispute to arbitration was accepted by Paraguay and reluctantly agreed to by Bolivia.

This Commission was appointed in July 1933 and reached Chaco in November. On 21 February 1934 the Commission held its last meeting with the two parties, found them to be totally obdurate and returned to Geneva to report to the Council. The result was not as effective as over the Leticia question. The report was prophetic in that it claimed, as happened, that the two sides would be forced to make peace due to exhaustion, fighting continuing through 1935 and eventually ending in 1938.

Ireland and the arms embargo: 1934–5

An arms embargo came into effect during the summer of 1934. It was Francis Cremins, who took over at Geneva from Lester, who gave Ireland's support to such a move. Ireland was by now simply an observer and an ordinary Assembly member. Her Council membership had ended in October 1933. However Lester's legacy was apparent through the implementation of the embargo. Due to Lester's initiatory role towards the embargo Ireland made sure she was seen to implement it. This was solely for political value and involved use of extant legislation under the 1925 Firearms Act. Walshe wrote to D.J. Browne, Secretary at the Department of Justice, that, 'it is desirable, having regard to the part played by the Saorstát in the initiation of this proposal, that such measures as may be practicable should be undertaken here without delay to make the embargo effective in this country'.[86] This was essentially a cosmetic exercise allowing Ireland to make definite her stance even though it was known that she was not an arms manufacturing country. Walshe's caution was apparent as he was careful to tell Cremins that though the League was dwindling as a force in world politics, the adherence to the embargo would have the effect of maintaining Ireland's adherence to the Covenant. Ireland had taken a strong line on these two conflicts, not to have followed the embargo would have been a noticeable omission. Ireland's belief in the League was more uncertain by now and it was realised that the embargo was full of loopholes and gaps. Some discussion appears to have taken place in the Department of External Affairs as to whether Ireland need align herself with and implement the embargo.

86 NA, D.F/A 34/117A, 27 July 1934.

De Valera spoke at the Sixth Committee of the 1934 Assembly that it was with great disappointment that the League was apparently impotent to end the war in Chaco. He argued that a change in League procedure was needed if the League was to have any kind of success. There were too many bodies involved in the search for a solution to the dispute. He seemed to be seeking a way out as he called for a sub-committee on Chaco to be formed with a limited time scale of operation. If this elapsed and there was no solution, then the matter should be handed over to the Assembly for a final judgement. De Valera was not only concerned with ending the conflict, but in arriving at a solution to the dispute. The short speech indicated how impotent the Council had become; the Assembly now holding more international prestige. Also apparent was that de Valera realised that at some time the League would have to admit it was powerless to deal with the Chaco problem until both parties wanted a solution and that the League would have to retire to the sidelines until needed.

The application of Article 15 to the dispute was finally accepted by Bolivia. Paraguay rejected it as its armed forces were on the offensive. The embargo was kept on Paraguay but removed from Bolivia. Ireland again changed its embargo to refer to Paraguay only. Walshe and de Valera discussed the embargo question in detail and it was minuted that, 'it has been decided that the Saorstát must fall into line with the other governments and accept the League's recommendations.'[87]

Despite Ireland's initiatory role in the half-heartedly enforced embargo, Walshe stuck to his line that Ireland should be implementing it only as a League member in response to League recommendations. As with Manchuria he made it clear that Ireland's lack of material interest or diplomatic representation in either country meant that 'our role in the efforts of the League to put an end to this dispute must be strictly limited to doing whatever is positively incumbent upon us, as a League member, to do'.[88] Ireland was to adopt all League measures but,

> for our representative in Geneva to take the initiative or to support proposals made by others before it had become clear that they commanded a substantial measure of support ... would be to misconceive completely our obligations and functions as a member of the League ... The assumption of an active role in the proceedings by Saorstát Éireann is entirely uncalled for. It could not enhance our national dignity or the prestige of the League. In fact it would make the entire proceedings appear unreal and ridiculous.

---

87 Ibid., 21 February 1935, my italics.
88 Ibid., Walshe–Cremins, 9 March 1935.

Walshe put forward geographical propinquity and interests in the region forward as criteria for the involvement of a state in the dispute. Walshe evidently did not believe that the problems of one member were the problems of all, he saw the world order in terms of powers and spheres of interest, not the view of the founders of the League that it was to form a global pan-national network. To Walshe the League was an adjunct to the balance of power system where states, especially small states looked after those factors which affected their national interests.

By summer 1935 fighting had stopped due to exhaustion. De Valera felt that the League had done all it could do and should now withdraw discretely. Murphy urged Cremins to associate himself with any delegates who were urging that the Advisory Committee be wound up. Ireland, along with other League members lifted the arms embargo in August 1935. The dispute spluttered on until July 1937. The League's involvement in the dispute attempted a brave departure in international relations but to no success. Lester's part in this was made clear by the Acting President of the Council on the occasion of Ireland's departure from its ranks; he praised Lester and 'his devotion to the League's ideals, his tact and his sound political sense'.[89] Ireland's role as an ordinary League member after the termination of Council membership was, by geographical position and Walshe's views on Ireland's limited international interests, of necessity lessened. The state continued to support League action in relation to Chaco as much as she could. It would have been more damaging to her prominent position at the League to have overstepped the mark through adopting policies she could not implement towards disputes in which she had no interests at stake.

The re-eligibility debate and Ireland's departure from the Council

The conclusion of Ireland's term on the Council in September 1933 led Lester, Walshe and Cremins to consider whether Ireland should seek re-election. By the 1926 rules Ireland would have to get a two-thirds majority vote in the Assembly before her name could go forward for election. She would then have to repeat the performance of 1930. Ireland's seat was a supposedly independent seat, but had from 1927 been occupied by Canada and in 1933 either Australia or Canada would stand for election. The seat was increasingly seen as the preserve of the Commonwealth, despite Ireland's independent Council position.

Cremins and Lester discussed re-eligibility in a preliminary manner in March 1933. Cremins urged Lester to 'do all in your power to prepare the ground'.[90] Lester remarked that 'our position here has been growing stronger

---

89 NA, D.F/A, 34/117C, 12 October 1933.
90 NA, D.F/A, 26/53, 20 March 1933.

(in spite of hardships not to be mentioned) but time would be invaluable'.[91] He also felt that 'the Irish Free State has done exceedingly well on the Council in a more than usually active period'.[92]

However two problems presented themselves almost immediately. Firstly, the group system against which Ireland had gone up for election in 1930 had become the accepted structure of the Council; Ireland would get no support for opposing this system and her successor would probably be a Commonwealth member. By replacing Canada, Ireland, despite her independence, had ironically ensured that the seat would become a Commonwealth seat. Secondly, re-eligibility was not only difficult but unpopular. Members of the Assembly would not make up their mind until the last minute who they would vote for and whether they would support a candidate's re-election. Lester recalled the situation in 1930 where China went up for re-eligibility; he had at the time feared that she might get her two-thirds majority, but that these might not translate into votes in the election. He considered the same might happen Ireland: 'I personally, think that our chances of obtaining the necessary majority are remote'.[93] Ireland had entered the Council promising to represent the Assembly and play by the rules, re-eligibility would look as if Ireland was solely after national prestige. There was definitely an element of this, but Lester's international viewpoint saw Ireland's re-election as a response to her active role as a non-permanent Council member. The end result, he feared, was that Ireland would damage her chances of future Council membership if a re-eligibility bid ended up as an embarrassing debacle.

Australia had announced her candidature on 16 June. Walshe informed Lester that de Valera was 'of the opinion that our chances of re-eligibility were very slight' and that consequently he was in favour of supporting Australia.[94] Lester agreed and suggested Ireland should run in 1934. He also suggested that Ireland should not vote for Australia as she would be completely under British influence and that it would look bad for the Free State's reputation as an outspoken and active League member. Dublin informed Canberra that the question would be given due consideration in September as the vote drew close. Irish support of Australia would be to the detriment of Ireland's own position. A return to the Council, after a lapse of some time, clearly figured highly in Lester's plans. Australia would be little more than another British vote, her membership would entitle the other Dominions and possibly India to a seat.

Two options faced Ireland. Re-eligibility could be floated and if this did not look like a possibility, then support could be given to Australia. The other possibility was to leave on a high note with Ireland's reputation intact and retire with a good record as a Council member. In that way the possibility was

91 Ibid., 7 July 1933.
92 Ibid., 13 July 1933.
93 Ibid.
94 NA, D.F/A, 26/60, 16 June 1933.

left open for a future candidature, a failed re-eligibility bid would rule out such a possibility.

At the 1933 Assembly, Ireland did not try to get the Assembly's vote for re-election. They instead flirted with the possibility of de Valera becoming President of the Assembly. De Valera's name had been mentioned and Finland and Hungary were known to favour his appointment. However, de Valera decided not to attend the 1933 Assembly. The Free State received much praise when it left the Council. The German paper *Der Bund* noted how the departure of Ireland and Norway would be met with 'deep regret in minorities circles whose interests were defended with extreme effort and untiring vigour by the representatives of the two countries'.[95]

Conclusion

Council membership saw Ireland mature within the League. It gave Irish diplomats and statesmen access to the highest body of the League within which they met and developed links with the leading diplomatic and political figures of the time. The effect this had on Irish diplomats is evident by comparing the development of Sean Lester from a rather uncertain Permanent Representative in 1929–30 to a respected, suave and efficient League official by his 1933 appointment to Danzig. Lester's promotion is a personal example of the overall impact of Council membership on Ireland.

By 1933 the League had become indispensable to Ireland and through Council membership she had created an advocacy role for herself within it. The League and the international environment had become Ireland's natural constituency. Sean Lester, considering a world without a League, wrote of this in early 1933:

> Since we began to take part again in international life the League has existed. I am sure you would have regard to what our international position would have been if it had not existed. If the League disappeared tomorrow something would have to take its place. Great powers would remain with their might in the international field. There might be concerted action between the great ignoring the views and actions of the small. There might be the withdrawal of the great into two camps preparing for a contest of strength, the small powers would return very largely to their pre-war state. Their rights and independence would be in very much greater danger than with the small and uncertain degree of protection they may count upon, through their shelter behind theoretical equality, and through the greater measure of publicity which this institution in Geneva gives to all.[96]

95 12 October 1933.
96 NA, D.F/A, 19/40 Geneva, 31 March 1933.

In this framework Ireland would have to send many representatives to all the major countries rather than being able to meet them through an institution like the League. Lester summarised what the League had become to the Free State by 1933:

> We are beginning slowly to make a small place for Ireland in that realm [Lester was referring to inter-governmental relations] also, and for that purpose the League gives our best and our only field for work, our best, if not our only platform; and one of the best, if not the best of the elements for our protection ... No reasonable person in Ireland should regard with equanimity the weakening or collapse of the League imperfect and weak as it may be, and that even if it is going to collapse it is our duty while it still remains to take out of the situation every ounce of prestige we can draw from it.

The League had become integral to Irish foreign policy and Ireland had used Council membership to show this. The not insignificant praise that the Irish received for their work on the Council shows that the members of the League, especially the small states, considered Ireland a small but important member. Irish policies on the Council had sought to preserve the rights and place of the small states and this had not gone unnoticed. The de Valera–Lester team at Geneva, advised by Cremins ensured also that Ireland was noticed by the wider world. The old policy goals of independence, sovereignty and prestige had been more than accomplished. Ireland emerged into the harsh international climate of the 1930s with a more respected position at Geneva. Lester's almost single-handed control of policy over Manchuria in late 1931 and into early 1932 was essential in this. Writing to de Valera in November 1933, Lester contrasted the League against the other areas where Ireland maintained a diplomatic presence: 'Washington and the Vatican have great importance, but for a small country Geneva offers opportunities which it would be regrettable to ignore'.[97]

Manchuria led to a change in overall Irish League policy. Prior to September 1931 and since 1923, the Irish had praised the League but stated that its role would diminish if the Covenant were not adhered to. The tone had now changed to one approaching failure as the League proved incapable of dealing with the Manchurian dispute. This belief that the League was in danger of becoming, as Francis Cremins was to remark, 'more a shuttlecock than a directing force' was as opposed to the belief in the 1920s that the League, if nurtured correctly, could become a directing force in international politics.[98] 1932 did not mark a change in support for the League, the changeover in administrations had little effect on League policy. Ireland remained a sup-

97 FLK, de Valera papers, file 1413, 2 November 1933
98 NA, D.F/A, 26/75, 20 July 1934.

porter of the League, the change was rather of emphasis. Ireland's term on the Council saw her become a more sanguine supporter of the League. Ireland's views were respected and at times sought out, but lacking international power and clout, they ultimately carried little weight in the foreign offices of the Great Powers. It was only amongst the group of small states that any heed was paid. Here Ireland hit a common cord amongst the weak who would suffer greatly in another world war and who saw strength in numbers.

A decade's theory of critical support was put into practice through the Manchurian dispute. Irish diplomats showed that they practised what they preached. Manchuria had allowed the Irish to fulfil their role on the Council and use it to prove their mandate. The theorising and calls for moral and physical support of the League, as de Valera had at the 1932 Assembly would have been simply a more forceful continuation of the line since 1923 had it not been for the Manchurian dispute. Manchuria allowed the state to put its money where its mouth was and actively support the League. Ireland showed that it would work by the philosophy it advocated. Hence the resolution of 9 December 1932 and Matsuoka's angry calls for its removal.

The Manchurian crisis epitomises the role played by Ireland on the Council between 1930 and 1933. It also defines the change in Ireland's position within the League by 1933. A crisis had rocked the League, it was having difficulty with its first power-oriented test of strength. Ireland, using the austere preacher-like figure of de Valera had shown that it could and would put the League first and that above all it was the League's future success that mattered. Lester's feelings on Manchuria put the theory of Ireland's policy of critical support into practice. In doing so it brought Ireland from a respected theoriser in the importance and value of the League to a valued forceful contributor amongst the small states who were coming to be considered as the League's only supporters and hope for its continued existence as a body of some stature in the world order.

CHAPTER 7

De Valera's Heyday at Geneva, September 1933–July 1936

The limits of Irish League policy: September 1933–September 1934

September 1933 marks a climactic point in Ireland's relations with the League. Membership of the Council, a goal of policy since 1926, was ending. The pressure of Council membership meant that, despite discussing re-eligibility, External Affairs had undertaken little forward planning on League policy. Because of personnel, time and financial constraints, Council policy remained a hand-to-mouth operation. In September 1933 it was uncertain how League policy would develop after Ireland's departure from the Council and with the Assembly.

During a discussion on cutting back External Affairs expenditure in May 1933, it was mentioned that Ireland's involvement in the League would decrease from the following September. This was over-interpreted by the parsimonious officials in the Department of Finance as a signal to close down the Geneva office. Drastic reductions in expenditure on the League were proposed by the Economy Committee of the Cabinet for the 1934–5 financial year. Cremins informed Finance that expenditure would decrease naturally after Ireland left the Council and it was here that savings would arise. In addition, he made perfectly clear that closing down the Geneva office was not an option: 'It is the policy of the Government that this country should take an increasing part in international affairs, and it is the considered opinion of the Minister that the maintenance of the permanent office at Geneva is central to this end'.[1] Without local representation it would be impossible to keep abreast of the activities of the League. Cremins forced the point home, remarking that 'if the permanent offices were withdrawn, it would be almost as well to withdraw from the League altogether, but this is a possibility which can not be contemplated even if the present critical conditions in the international political and economic affairs were non-existent'. This debate of summer 1934 shows that Ireland saw her international position within the League as essential to the development of her external affairs. Geneva was a crucial

1 NA, D.F/A, 26/51, 29 May 1934.

office when it came to monitoring the increasingly volatile political climate in Europe.

Lester felt that the proposed cost-cutting was a political move contingent on the Government's view of the importance of the League to Ireland. He wrote to Cremins that 'the proposal to close down the permanent offices here is in accordance with the spirit which has maintained the financial discrimination against Geneva'.[2] He taunted Cremins that the Government should close down the Geneva office if it was symptomatic of an intention to pay no attention to the League. There was no use making a pretence at League membership.

Lester's experiences on the Council had made him the most internationalist figure in the Irish diplomatic service. He felt that complete commitment to the League was required or none at all. He was disillusioned with Ireland's position within the League and the Government's inability to give him the resources to maintain an active position on the Council. Ireland was a prominent Council member, but Lester would have preferred a more interventionist stance. He had outgrown the small Irish presence at the League and indeed the entire Irish diplomatic service. His secondment into League service as High Commissioner to Danzig in early 1934 was a fitting promotion.

Since Manchuria, the Assembly had outshone the Council as the more prominent of the League's bodies. Ireland's departure from the Council coincided with this shift in the League's centre of gravity and as the world order changed in favour of the great powers who resorted increasingly to balance of power politics and alliances. From 1933 to July 1936 the League was on its last chance as a political institution. The immediate concerns were the failure of the Disarmament Conference which was precipitated by Germany's withdrawal from the League in the wake of Hitler's rise to power. These were compounded by the Polish-German Pact of January 1934 and increased Italo-German rivalry. With re-armament and the consolidation of Japanese control in Manchuria, the League had suffered a considerable blow.

The European system was moving away from Geneva towards the pre-1914 alliance system. Ireland would lose an important diplomatic foothold on the continent through any retreat from the League. In this uncertain international climate Ireland would fare best if it continued to support the bruised and battered League. The League gave Ireland a limited international position and limited international protection. Ireland's faith in the League was based on the primacy of the Covenant and the desired universality of the League. De Valera's antagonistic approach to Anglo-Irish affairs had distanced Ireland from the Commonwealth. Despite the League's less than favourable position, it was Ireland's only link with the wider international community outside its limited bilateral relations.

2 Ibid., Lester–Cremins, 1 April 1934.

The first analysis of Ireland's role in the League after September 1933 was undertaken by Francis Cremins after he took over the post of Permanent Representative from Sean Lester in May 1934. Cremins is one of Ireland's least known diplomats. From a post in the General Post Office he transferred to External Affairs in July 1922 as a Higher Executive Officer. He stayed in External Affairs before taking a four-year transfer to the Department of Lands and Fisheries. He returned to External Affairs in May 1929 as part of Patrick McGilligan's expansion of the department. For five years, from May 1929 to May 1934 he was head of the League of Nations section in Dublin. Here he was in constant contact with Sean Lester but never took Lester's internationalist outlook. In contrast to Lester's liberal internationalist stance, Cremins was much more of a realist in his views on foreign policy. To him power and the ability to use that power to attain international objectives was the basis of international affairs. As he became Permanent Representative his faith in the League greatly diminished as he saw the League lacked the ability to make the Covenant effective in the international order. Through the influence of his reports, Cremins provided the material out of which de Valera constructed his League policy for Ireland.[3] Cremins primed de Valera before his visits to Geneva and de Valera built his prominent position at Geneva on this base.

Cremins's realist critique of the League as an international body meant that Ireland had a unique diplomat at Geneva in the mid to late 1930s. He was extremely perceptive towards the development of the blocs in Europe and the decline to war. Cremins's belief that a European war was on the horizon seems to date from 1934, coinciding with his move to mainland Europe.

Lester criticised Cremins as over-cautious; but Cremins's caution was due to his belief that after 1934 it was the Great Powers who determined international affairs. Unlike Lester he did not feel that a small state always had a role in the international order. With his less than idealistic view of the League this explains Ireland's growing lack of faith in the League after 1935. Where Lester would have tried to forge a new place for Ireland, Cremins felt that the time for the small state to get involved in the world system was over. Cremins concentrated on mapping the European and League political environment of the thirties rather than developing a pro-active League policy for Ireland. His apparent caution is in fact discretion.

Cremins's review of Ireland's role in the League in 1933-4 provided an exhaustive list of Irish involvement in the League that mentions adherence to League conventions, attendance at Assembly, ordinary and extraordinary Council sessions with Ireland's duties as Rapporteur for minorities, sessions of the Disarmament Conference, Presidencies of the commissions looking into the South American disputes and Assembly committees on the Sino-Japanese dispute and numerous international conferences held by the League and un-

3 The memoranda quoted below formed the basis, almost word for word, for de Valera's 13 June 1934 speech on the League in the Dáil. See *Dáil deb*, 13 June 1934, vol. 53 Col. 286-7.

der League auspices in Geneva. The crowning moment was Lester's appointment as High Commissioner in Danzig. Cremins could write with no exaggeration that,

> our prestige and influence at Geneva increased more last year than during any previous year of our League membership. It is not possible, of course, to adduce concrete proof of the truth of this assertion, but evidence of it is furnished by the fact that Irish nationals were called upon to play a larger part in the service of League offices last year than ever before.[4]

Cremins argued that the League needed to involve small states because the greater the degree of political tension at Geneva,

> the greater is the importance of the action of states, such as the Saorstát, whose independence and sincerity are above question, and the more are their good offices and those of their representatives, in demand to supply that element of arbitrament which is necessary to prevent political tension developing into open hostility.

Ireland's impartial mediatory role as one of these small states was responsible for Lester's appointment to Danzig. This was besides the Presidency of the Commission of Three into the Bolivia–Paraguay and Colombia–Peru disputes, the appointment of an Irish jurist on the Bernheim Petition Committee, the appointment of an Irish corresponding member of the League economic committee, Irish involvement in the question of the Assyrian minority in Iraq, and the appointment of an Irish member of the League health committee. With each of these appointments made between 1933 and 1934, Cremins could write that, 'the Saorstát was thus intimately associated with every major question which came before the League during the last twelve months'. That this involvement was continuing was seen with the League's attempts to ensure an Irish judge would serve on the Saar Plebiscite Tribunal which would judge disputes arising out of the plebiscite to be held in January 1935 to decide whether France or Germany would govern the Saar region which was contiguous to both states.

Cremins argued that, 'there is probably no state which enjoys a higher degree of prestige as a member of the League than the Irish Free State and the policy of independence, frankness, and straight dealing which we have always followed at Geneva is now receiving due recognition'. As long as the League had a place in the international order, Ireland would remain an active and supportive member. Ireland's vote and veto in the Assembly allowed Ireland along with the other small states to exert limited influence if they

---

4 NA, D.F/A, 27/73, subsequent unattributed quotations are from this source.

could 'prevent unjust action being clothed with the mantle of legality, and to put states which follow certain courses in the position of the violators of the law and rebels against the international order'. This gave the small states slightly more protection than when war between parties was a private matter and when aggression could be committed in the name of the law. The League had become a standard of international order and it was unlikely that in the medium term the small states would give this limited protection up.

Cremins's final paragraphs reflected his desire to make the League a more effective institution. He argued three points of necessary reform: increasing the League's universality, breaking the link between the Covenant and the peace treaties and most difficult, trying to break up the political combinations within the League which were contrary to the Covenant. The League ought to be universal even if this meant reducing its powers. This would entail achieving Cremins's second point. If Germany was to rejoin the League then it would have to be a body separate to the Versailles Treaty. He felt that the organisation should be developed from the existing international climate, not that of 1919: 'it is absurd that the fate of the form of the organisation adopted for international society should be anchored to the destiny of political arrangements of doubtful justice'. Cremins was an outright revisionist of the peace-treaties. His objective was to ameliorate the complaints of Germany and try to re-forge her links with the League. He felt that Article 10 of the Covenant which safeguarded the existing territorial status quo had to go as it was 'ineffective in practice'. The League should at most provide a forum for the peaceful change of borders after discussion but should not guarantee existing borders.

Cremins's third point illustrated his clear perception of the European order. Groups within the League such as the Little Entente states of Eastern Europe were directly antagonistic to Germany and Italy. Germany and Italy were now the League's main detractors. The League was viewed by outsiders as being tainted by the external political considerations of its members. Freeing the League from such connotations and making it less a Franco-British institution would link in with Cremins first point of allowing universality.

The League was a pathway towards international concord if it was properly reformed. As it stood, the League was too deeply entrenched in the international confrontations of the period and the legacy of World War I to be an effective force in the world order without reform. Cremins felt that without these reforms there was no point in the League becoming anything other than a purely consultative body. Until it could do so, Cremins considered it would not be 'an effective instrument of world government and order'.

De Valera was far more positive in his outlook towards the League than the staff of his League of Nations section. Boland and Cremins held that the Assemblies were of increasingly academic importance and that accordingly de Valera should refrain from attending. De Valera remained a supporter of the League after his department made little secret of their lack of faith in the

League. Despite the importance of Anglo-Irish relations between 1932 and 1938, and the growing attitude of disillusionment with the League, what is remarkable is how important the League remained to Ireland and how important Ireland was to become within the declining League. In the thirties the state acted in tune with the Geneva system rather than attacking it with the youthful idealism of the 1920s. This was the key to mid-thirties League policy, a belief in the Covenant and that its articles should be followed to the letter of the law. National considerations should transcend the Covenant as it became the fundamental force of world politics.

Europe in the run-up to the 15th Assembly: July–September 1934

The drift from the League by the Great Powers made it difficult to anticipate the importance of the 1934 Assembly. The agenda might lack lustre, but the meetings taking place in hotel lobbies meant that the Assembly remained an important event. In July 1934, this was the problem facing the new head of the League of Nations section in the Department of External Affairs, Frederick Boland. Mentioning the Disarmament Conference's failure, the ongoing Bolivia–Paraguay conflict and the possible admission of the Soviet Union, he could offer no constructive analysis and wrote, 'if the Assembly decides to discuss these matters it will be the most important Assembly of recent years'.[5]

Cremins was soon able to brief Boland about the forthcoming Assembly. He took a wider perspective than Boland and placed emphasis on the need to lock China firmly into the League system by supporting her candidature for election to the Council in the forthcoming elections for three non-permanent seats. The League weakness in the Far East increased with Japan's departure from the League. Cremins felt that 'China needs every help and encouragement from the League organisation in the dangerous political conditions which exist and are developing in the Far-East'.[6] The need to have a China drawn into a closer relationship with the League was made imperative by Soviet Russia's probable admission to the League. Cremins urged de Valera to support the candidature, despite Ireland's acknowledged opposition to the system of semi-permanent seats.

With the rise of Hitler in Germany in 1933, German rearmament, her consequent departure from the League in reaction to the deadlock in the Disarmament Conference and the signature in January 1934 of a Polish-German pact, the Soviets decided to throw in their lot with Geneva. Japan's departure from Geneva and France's interest in Russian admission contributed to a growing mood amongst the permanent members of the Council that Russia should be admitted.

---

5 NA, D.F/A, 26/75 Memo by Boland, 18 July 1934.
6 Ibid., Cremins–Boland, 20 July 1934.

By late July the issue was not 'a live project' to quote Cremins and Ireland had time to develop her position. Cremins considered that 'on general grounds ... the inclusion in the League of every state in the world is desirable'. In Cremins's opinion, Russia should be admitted to the League, her Communism notwithstanding. Cremins was a devout Catholic and his favourable position on Russian admission was taken without ascertaining the Vatican's views. As the Vatican was not a League member, he considered that the Irish Minister to the Vatican might provide some information on the Vatican's view.

Hopes that Ireland would receive guidance or that Ireland could support the Vatican's line as a willing minion were halted when P.J. O'Byrne, writing in the absence of the Minister, William J.B. Macaulay, informed Boland that 'the Holy See prefers not to express an opinion on the question of the admission of Russia to the League of Nations as the Holy See is not a member'.[7] O'Byrne had approached the Curia on the matter and suggested a forward role for Ireland in championing the cause of freedom of worship in Russia. The Vatican had no such idealistic role in mind and said that the Soviets would use membership of the League as a mere propaganda tool. O'Byrne felt that despite this, the Holy See feared Russia's admission and would obstruct it if it could, but as it could not, would not.

This appears to be a snub to Ireland's self-conceived 'special relationship' with the Vatican, but there is a more subtle point. Without any ruling from the Vatican on the matter, and with the Vatican taking no active involvement, Ireland could take whatever line it wished over Russia's admission. O'Byrne's demarche had freed the Irish from having to take a definite Vatican line. De Valera was aware from O'Byrne's report that the Vatican was opposed to Russia's admission but would and could do nothing. He could now follow his own pro-League policies on the admission of Russia and do so without feeling that the Catholic church in Ireland would oppose him. If it did, he could respond that he had consulted the Vatican and whilst willing to follow their rulings, had found there to be no Vatican policy. This allowed de Valera to develop his desire for a universal League without the fear of an attack from Irish clergy or anti-Communist groups.

From 1934 Cremins's attitude to the League became increasingly cynical. He was supportive of international institutions if they were universal, had teeth and protected the interests of all. He was pro-League in his heart, but a realist in his head. Cremins considered the backroom dealing at the Assembly would revolve around the pressing international issues while the technical details of the Assembly were thrashed out in isolation. There was an enormous gap of perception between what could happen at the 1934 Assembly and what would happen. The League was no longer the master of its own destiny. Exogenous events were dictating its pace. Cremins wrote his epitaph

---

7 NA., D.F/A, 26/78, 4 August 1934.

for the League of the 1920s when as he reported to Boland that in the present state of the world, and of Europe politics in particular, 'the League is more a shuttle cock than a directing force'.[8]

By late August the vista was even more blurred. As the delegation of de Valera, John Hearne and Boland prepared to travel to le Havre from Cobh, Cremins, whom they would meet at Geneva, could write, 'The 15th Assembly meets with the clouds hanging over Europe almost as dark as those of August 1914'.[9] It was re-armament and the reconstruction of alliances that worried Cremins rather than the Council elections and the still indefinite admission of Russia. In a pessimistic tone he wrote of growing conflicts over spheres of interest as in 1914, the major difference being the partial degree of disarmament and that the League existed to try to secure peace and the resolution of disputes. The lack of weapons wrote Cremins, 'alone keeps the Europe of 1934 from being comparable to 1914'. He painted a picture of the defeated states of 1918 preparing for war again, pointing only to their 'unreadiness for adventures in the field [as] the main factor against the outbreak of hostilities'. With remarkable insight Cremins mapped out the course of Europe from 1934:

> [T]he outstanding feature of the political situation is that the belligerents of the war are sharply divided into those who are determined to keep what they won and those endeavouring to work up a situation in which by force if necessary they may be able to regain what they have lost. Relations between Germany and France are more strained than they have been since France invaded the Ruhr in 1924.

There were also problems over the Saar, the possibility of an Anschluss and Cremins even mentions the possibility of tension amongst the Sudeten Germans in Czechoslovakia. This 25 August memorandum sets the scene for World War II, noting that 'the major problems left by the treaties are as little likely to be solved peacefully as the problems of 1914'. War either sooner or later was Cremins fundamental belief. Any attempt to revise the status quo would be 'almost as sure to provoke an outbreak as the maintenance of the existing position'. Political and economic discontent in Europe made the abatement of these problems even more urgent. The Franco-German problem transfixed Cremins: 'unfortunately some of the Great Powers which seemed a year or so ago to be anxious for a détente find themselves almost forced back into a position of intransigence by methods pursued across the Rhine'.

Whilst de Valera concentrated on the Economic war with Britain and his redefinition of the Anglo-Irish relationship, Cremins paid close attention to events in Europe. De Valera spoke to the Assembly about the need for disar-

---

8 NA, D.F/A, 26/73 Cremins–Walshe, 20 July 1934.
9 NA, D.F/A 26/75, Cremins–Walshe, 25 August 1934.

mament, collective security and adherence to the Covenant. He was more in tune with Lester than the realist Cremins. Cremins had no place for the League in this memo. It was, as mentioned above, a shuttlecock. War was imminent and what stopped it was not the League, but the degree of preparation for that war in the international community: 'on the whole, the situation is as disturbed as it could be, but unreadiness seems at the moment to be a safeguard'. Effective international organisation or a return to balance of power politics was Cremins's line.

Awaiting the arrival of de Valera, the main powers in the Assembly and Council, remembering his speech of 1932, were eager to keep such a loose cannon as de Valera carefully under control. The admission of Russia was a very tricky issue, even more so than the admission of Germany. The powers, especially France, needed Russia in the League to bolster their own alliances and the League itself since Germany had withdrawn. In the run-up to the admission of Russia the powers did everything possible to keep de Valera from a position of prominence in the Assembly so that his speeches on the Russian issue were as low-key as possible.

The delegation arrived in Geneva on 7 September. They set about canvassing to see if there was support for de Valera to go forward for one of the Assembly's Vice-Presidents. Britain and India were also possible candidates, but Cremins noted how, 'we are not regarded as being quite the same as the other dominions or India, who always follow the Foreign Office'.[10] Nonetheless, he urged that there were still difficulties of recognition to be overcome and that it might not look good for Ireland. If Ireland could appear on the same stage, holding the same offices as a British and an Indian delegate and not be seen as a stooge of the Empire, then the independence of Irish foreign policy would be shown. A chairmanship might otherwise be possible or one of the smaller offices. The Presidency of the Assembly was a long shot for Ireland, despite de Valera's performance in 1932. The Presidency of te Walter of South Africa in 1933 made Ireland's chances of obtaining the Presidency remote.

The allocation of offices at the 1934 Assembly shows de Valera's growing popular position at Geneva. Ireland's increasing participation in League affairs made it likely that the Assembly would look to an Irish delegate as President for its 1934 session. On his arrival at Geneva, de Valera had considerable support. The leading candidate, the Swedish Foreign Minister, Sandler, had stepped down and pledged his support to Ireland. Cremins had received other pledges from Madariaga of Spain and Hambro of Norway. Support was also promised from the main League groupings. With the opening of the Assembly the prospects looked bright. The Acting-President made his opening address and then there was a surprise adjournment for about fifteen minutes. The powers and the Eastern-European states were hunting for a

10 Ibid., Cremins–Boland, 27 August 1934.

candidate to oppose de Valera. Pressure was brought on Sandler to stand from the French Foreign Minister Barthou with the connivance of the British. Sandler, despite all assurances to the contrary, eventually stood for election and de Valera withdrew his candidature accordingly.

Denying de Valera the Presidency was a strategic move as the great powers did not have 'the necessary degree of confidence that the President [i.e., de Valera, the President of the Executive Council] could be relied upon to see eye to eye with them on various matters which will come before the General Committee of the Assembly in connection with the admission of Russia, from this fact the conclusion may be drawn that our prestige in the Assembly is extremely high'.[11] This view was boosted as de Valera had never announced he was going to stand, there had been no explicit canvass and support had developed spontaneously with de Valera's arrival at Geneva. Cremins optimistically read the best possible interpretation into the election: 'the result may be regarded as highly satisfactory. We have had the next best thing to the honour of the Presidency of the Assembly, i.e., the fact of not being asked to run in order to make possible the election of the person who was ultimately elected'. This may be something of the Irish triumph of failure mentality. Ireland's prestige might be high, but it did not translate into any high office at the 1934 Assembly. This was a backlash by the powers to de Valera's aggressive stance as champion of the small states in 1932.

The admission of Russia: September 1934

The majority of League members favoured the admission of Russia. Her candidature was supported by Britain, France, the Little Entente, Turkey and the Scandinavian and Baltic states. Switzerland and Holland were strongly opposed. The opposition manifested itself around the question of the freedom of religious liberty in Russia. Before Russia was admitted, the need arose to define the admission procedure. Those supporting the candidature would attempt to circumvent the opposition by manipulating the rules of admission. They wanted to invite Russia into the League. This would shield her from any attacks and forego the possibility of a hitch which might cause the Russians to leave Geneva.

On 12 September de Valera spoke out against the proposed admission procedure. He took a middle ground between the issue of religious freedom and Ireland's desire for universal League membership. The negotiations behind the scenes in hotels to pave the way for Russian admission were at a delicate stage. De Valera did not wish to derail these negotiations, but wished to draw attention to the need to keep the League at the forefront of the admission process as it was the institution to which Russia was being admit-

11 Ibid., Cremins–Boland, 10 September 1934.

ted. All previous new admissions had first been discussed in committee before the vote on admission was taken. League members ought to have the right to discuss this issue and not be presented with a fait accompli.

De Valera took a twin-track approach to Russian admission. In his main address to the Assembly on 12 September he stressed procedure whilst he saved the religious freedom issue to immediately before Russia's admission on 18 September. He was not seen immediately to be confessional. The admission of Russia was more important; it was in line with Ireland's universalist view of the League. As illustrated above, de Valera had freed himself from following an explicit Vatican line. Though the speech of 18 September was undoubtedly pro-Vatican in its concerns, his initial pronouncements were on the role of the League Assembly, the home of the small states which he represented, in the admission of a new member to their ranks.

He began his September 12 speech by playing down his remarks to the 1932 Assembly. Russia was a more important area and was 'even more delicate'.[12] De Valera made clear that he favoured plain speaking in the Assembly and not in the Council or in private negotiations. He did not want the admission of Russia stitched up beforehand feeling that no League member should have special entrance privileges. He understood the fear of rejection. No state would accept an invitation if there was a possibility that it would be rejected. However, those not prepared to support Russia's admission should have the right to express their views.

In de Valera's opinion, League machinery had to be used for the admission of a member, even if there were negative votes. The speech was impartial, with de Valera urging simply the primacy of the League: 'there is no humiliation to Russia in coming along in the ordinary way, having been assured that there is no intention on the part of the majority of delegates to attempt to humiliate her in any way'. League members, as well as prospective members had rights too. Their views should be respected and so the admission should take place by way of the Sixth Committee and not hotel rooms. The world needed Russia in the League to safeguard world peace, but Russia must enter the League without any specialised position. De Valera did not hide how Ireland would vote: 'I represent a country which, if you consider its political and religious ideals, is as far apart as the poles from Soviet Russia; but I would be willing to take the responsibility of saying openly and frankly here that I would support and vote for the entry of Russia into the League on account of the considerations I have mentioned'.

De Valera made clear that he would like Russia to grant greater religious rights to its citizens. However, this was a secondary point to the immediate concern of Russian admission. The Assembly should take the admission in its stride, frankly and forthrightly, paying little heed to the over-cautious and

---

12 All quotes from de Valera's speeches, unless otherwise referenced are from the versions contained in Eamon de Valera, *Peace and War* (Dublin, 1944).

getting down to the procedural matter of admitting Russia. This would give states the right to criticise Russian admission if they wanted to. Would Russia really feel accepted into the League if the hotel method were adopted? De Valera was certain 'It is important that it should be understood that she comes in through no specially privileged position'. If there was not unanimity, then let that be so; attempts at an appearance of unanimity should not be tried at the expense of procedure. Ireland would in any event vote for the admission of Russia despite misgivings over how this came about.

The speech was well received, but the British Foreign Secretary, Sir John Simon, in a private personal meeting with de Valera attacked him for not acknowledging the complexity of the situation. De Valera's speech was made at a strategic moment: the negotiations for Russian admission were moving to a climax. The astute Frederick Boland felt that the general feeling in Geneva was that the speech was 'bound to exercise a strong influence over the future course of the negotiations in connection with the admission of Russia'.[13] Frank Walters makes the Irish initiative a crucial turning point in the admission of Russia in his history of the League; he writes, 'Barthou was vexed and anxious, but once again the great powers, including Russia, found it necessary to give way, and it was agreed that the question should be referred, as usual, to the Sixth Committee'.[14]

The delegation, after their rebuff from the Vatican over Soviet admission, were quick to consult the Roman press after de Valera's speech but found it completely impartial. Ireland's consistent policy since 1923 of making the League more democratic was seen to be working with Russia's successful admission. De Valera took a middle way between supporting the League and the Vatican. Russia would still be invited to join the League by its members. This removed the need for a formal resolution which needed the unanimous vote of the Assembly. The matter would instead go to the Sixth Committee. It would then go to the Assembly where only a two-thirds majority vote was needed to secure Russian admission. In political terms it had a favourable impact in that it relaxed the strained atmosphere caused by the fact that the other states in the Assembly felt that the hotel negotiations were neglecting them. The speech contributed to reducing the levels of anxiety and created a détente between the powers negotiating in the hotels and the states waiting for Russia's admission to the Assembly. Such interventions also brought Ireland to the attention of the widest audience as an active player in League affairs; Lester, writing from Danzig, felt that 'Ireland is counting more every year in European affairs and consequently appears less as a small island beyond Great Britain whose affairs from the European point of view do not concern other nations'.[15] In the same letter Lester passed on a comment from

---

13 NA, D.F/A 26/75. Boland–Murphy, 13 September 1934.
14 Walters, *History*, p. 582.
15 FLK, de Valera papers, file 1413, Lester–de Valera, 8 October 1934.

Phelan that ' "Dev" has put himself right in the middle of the front row with a series of remarkable speeches'.

Thirty-four League members signed a petition inviting Russia to Geneva. In line with his equivocal speech, de Valera did not sign the invitation; the Irish were desperately trying to reconcile their anti-communism with their support of the League. The Russians replied favourably and agreed to comply with all international obligations under the Covenant. The admission details went to the Sixth Committee and on 18 September 1934 to the Assembly where Russia was admitted by 38 votes to three with seven abstentions. It was also unanimously agreed that the USSR would get a permanent seat on the Council.

In the Assembly debate before the vote, de Valera spoke about Russia's internal religious policies. Though willing to support Russia's admission, the lack of religious liberty in the country was one of de Valera's main misgivings. He continued his twin-track strategy by speaking on the religious issue as Russia was being admitted. In no way then could he be misrepresented as being against Russia's admission. It was a matter of great 'importance and seriousness'. Assurances of religious freedom to her population were seen by de Valera as a show of goodwill by Russia on her admission. A show of goodwill was necessary for world peace and the integrity of the League. However, it was not religion for the sake of religion. De Valera drew a crucial link between religion and politics. Christians would be watching how the League dealt with Russian admission and the associated issues and would judge the League and give their continued support for the League accordingly: 'if Christians lose confidence in the League of Nations—there are six hundred millions of them, remember ... if they lose confidence in the League of Nations as a means for promoting peace in this way, then the League of Nations cannot possibly succeed.'

Cremins felt that the speech made a good impression in Catholic circles and had pleased everybody, both those against and those in favour of Russia's entry.[16] Pius XI expressed his gratitude to de Valera over the speech.[17] De Valera's ability to say all things to all at the League paid handsome dividends. Ireland again cast herself as a supporter of the League system and its primacy in the international order but had also pleased the Vatican. The speech was timed to placate those in Ireland and abroad who were concerned over the religious issue. Its timing, when Russia's admission was certain, illustrates how de Valera was willing to use religious issues to his own benefit, but not let them dictate the overall direction of policy which in this instance was securing the admission of Russia to make the League more universal.

16 NA, D.F/A, 26/75 Cremins–Walshe, 17 September 1934.
17 See Dermot Keogh, *Ireland and the Vatican: the politics and diplomacy of church–state relations, 1922–1960* (Dublin & Cork, 1995), p. 125.

Abyssinia: 1934–6

December 1934–October 1935: Armed stand-off

An armed border clash at Wal-Wal between Italian and Abyssinian forces in December 1934 was the harbinger of the Italian invasion of Abyssinia in October 1935. The failure of the League to deal with this breach of the Covenant compounded the failures of 1933 and effectively killed the League. On 3 January 1935 Abyssinia appealed to the League under Article 11 of the Covenant. The Council asked the parties to try to solve their differences and find the basis of a solution. Mussolini considered a League sponsored solution was beneath his dignity. He also realised that Britain was not concerned over Italian action in Abyssinia. Irish Minister to the Vatican, William J.B. Macaulay reported that a foreign adventure would suit Italian domestic policy as it would divert attention away from the poor state of Italy's economy and would be a focus for national regeneration.[18]

Francis Cremins brought de Valera up to date with the League's role in brokering a solution. The Council set up a Committee of 5 to look into the dispute. It would report at the September 1935 Assembly. By late May, Cremins could report that though 'there appears to be universal criticism of the high-handed attitude of Italy'; it was 'almost certain that Italy intends to make war regardless of the repercussions and consequences'.[19]

Sean Murphy had mentioned to Cremins that, 'the Minister is anxious to follow the development of this question as closely as possible'.[20] Cremins continued to comment on events as they unfolded. He lunched regularly with Anthony Eden, then British Foreign Office Minister for League Affairs, with whom he was very friendly. These conversations with Eden must have been of great use to Cremins. Through June 1935 Cremins reports are a catalogue of increasing pessimism. He wrote to Walshe and Boland how, 'in League circles there is a feeling of complete depression now regarding the Italo-Ethiopian trouble, and it is generally accepted that war is almost inevitable'.[21] Cremins later reported that 'France now relies so much on Italy as an ally in European troubles, that she is prepared, if necessary for the purpose of retaining Italian friendship, to let Italy go ahead in Africa'.

Boland remained as pessimistic as Cremins, writing that 'the only thing that is now uncertain about the Italo-Abyssinian war is the date on which it will commence ... rifles are being carried in Abyssinia very much as umbrellas

---

18 NA, D.F/A, 27/95, Macaulay–Walshe, 21 May 1935. **William J.B. Macaulay** (1892–1964): Former British Naval officer, resigned commission to join Irish civil service, Secretary of Washington Legation, 1925–9, Counsellor, 1929, Consul General, 1930–4. Minister to Vatican 1934–41.
19 Ibid., Cremins–Walshe, 23 May 1935.
20 Ibid., Murphy–Cremins, 18 May 1935.
21 Ibid., Cremins–Walshe, 22 June 1935.

are in Ireland'.[22] In a rather tongue-in-cheek mood Boland referred to the area of Abyssinia as being 'by a happy coincidence, equivalent to that of Manchuria—about 360,000 square miles'. He considered that the Abyssinians were rather foolhardy about their military ability and that they 'will soon succumb to machine-gunning, and the bombing of their villages from the air'. Boland poured cold water upon Macaulay's reports of disturbances in Italy and stated that Mussolini had made the Abyssinian adventure a test of Italy's 'strength and discipline. With the whole Fascist "mystique" thus staked on the outcome, the Duce is not likely to leave much to chance.' Boland discounted any role for the League brokering a compromise in the dispute: 'the safest proquostic is that Italy is aiming at, and will be satisfied with nothing less than, what the Japanese achieved in Manchuria'. Boland felt that the Manchurian episode was a major influence on the method that Mussolini used to define his objectives towards Abyssinia. Like Japan, Italy had no regard for international morality which Boland felt Mussolini regarded 'as hypocritical humbug'.

Boland supported Cremins's line about France's willingness to betray the Covenant in favour of an alliance with Italy: 'France will not allow Abyssinia to come between herself and Italy, and thus vanishes the one hope—the adoption of a firm attitude by France and Britain in common—of checking the Italian designs'. He concluded that this would ruin Britain's pro-League foreign policy: 'the Italian annexation of Abyssinia will knock the bottom out of the foreign policy (personified by Mr Anthony Eden) which the government proposed to submit to the country at the next election'. It was doubtful if behind the pro-collective security facade of Britain's foreign policy there lay any in-depth commitment.

Macaulay reported that the Vatican responded to the Abyssinian dispute with 'a clear refusal to discuss it at all'.[23] Macaulay fared better with Italians outside the Vatican who he felt spoke to him because he was 'such an avowed admirer of the regime'.[24] He considered that they 'deplore the situation which has arisen between Italy and Great Britain and admit that Mussolini's impetuosity has landed him in a diplomatic cul-de-sac'. The Irish Minister felt that Mussolini had made up his mind and that his course of action was inevitable, 'he has now admitted that the actual conquest of the territory is in his mind.'[25] Macaulay felt that Mussolini had almost been goaded into going ahead with his invasion by Britain's ambiguous policy over Italy and Abyssinia. The same mood of pessimism pervaded Macaulay's despatches, the League's Committee of Five would soon be exhausted and Mussolini hoped that the League would then not embarrass Italy further and allow her conquest to continue.

22 Ibid., Memorandum by Boland dated 25 June 1935.
23 Ibid., Macaulay–Walshe, 6 June 1935.
24 Ibid., Macaulay–Walshe, 15 June 1935.
25 Ibid., Macaulay–Walshe, 8 July 1935.

Britain's Foreign Secretary, Sir Samuel Hoare with Eden had been trying to keep Britain's Abyssinian policy nominally within the realms of the Covenant. John Dulanty, Irish representative in London had kept in reasonable touch with the Foreign Office.[26] He told Hoare that Ireland was 'most anxious to see the position and prestige of the League supported'.[27] Dulanty launched a new perspective to Ireland's views on the League. He told Hoare that it had taken many years for the principles of law to be accepted in national law and that 'the wide acceptance of the same principle in international affairs clearly could not be achieved in the comparatively few years of the League's existence'.

This is one of the first references to Ireland's retreat from the League. Where in the 1920s the League was a centre of Ireland's foreign policy and internationalism remained a key theme and influence to the admission of Russia in 1934 and beyond, the Italo-Abyssinian dispute is taken as a turning point. July 1936 and de Valera's speech to the Assembly is normally taken as the beginning of the overt turn to neutrality. Dulanty's conversation with Hoare precedes this by almost a year and marks the beginning of a trend away from the League far earlier than previously supposed. With the major Irish diplomatic figures growing increasingly pessimistic over the future of the League, it was only de Valera who continued to have any lasting faith in the Geneva process.

Such faith became increasingly difficult as reports from Geneva that opinion in the Secretariat 'could scarcely be more pessimistic'.[28] Dulanty reported from London on how an Abyssinian national approached him about acquiring arms and ammunition from Ireland. Walshe curtly replied that Ireland did not manufacture warlike materials. The downward spiral towards war elicited a blunt appraisal from Cremins. Referring to the popular notion that if the League had existed in 1914 it would have prevented World War I, he thought it, 'open to doubt whether the existence of the League would have prevented the clash, as states which are bent on trouble decline to use the safeguards, and there is not sufficient cohesion amongst the other states to impose in time their authority on the aggressive state'.[29] The same, he realistically argued, could be said for the League and Abyssinia.

August was as always quiet in Geneva as the holiday season prevailed. Boland and Cremins remained in constant touch through the holiday as they prepared for the September Assembly. With conflict in Abyssinia likely to break out shortly after the Assembly, with the end of the seasonal rains, and with the Council commission on the Abyssinian crisis likely to report, Boland hedged his bets and concluded, 'I don't think that the possibility of its prov-

26 **John W. Dulanty** (1881–1955): Irish Trade Commissioner in London, 1926–30; High Commissioner, 1930–50; Special Counsellor, London, 1950–1.
27 NA, D.F/A, 27/95, Dulanty–Walshe, 29 July 1935.
28 Ibid., O'Byrne–Walshe, 18 July 1934.
29 Ibid., Cremins–Walshe, 23 July 1935.

ing a very important and interesting one [Assembly] could be safely left out of account'.³⁰

Following the debacle over Assembly offices in 1934, Cremins and Boland pushed that Ireland should go forward for the Chairmanship of the Sixth Commission which dealt with political questions. Cremins, in conversation with Under-Secretary General Frank Walters found that there was general agreement within the Secretariat. They felt that de Valera was a 'champion of the League' and someone who would be well suited to the Sixth Commission, especially if the Abyssinian dispute came before it.³¹ The Irish were determined to get a high office in the Assembly. Cremins felt that at least a Vice-Presidency, definitely the Presidency of the Sixth Commission and possibly even the Presidency. Cremins was making the Dominion representatives aware of Ireland's plans. The Abyssinian dispute surrounded these calculations and its development through September and October was still as perplexing as it ever was.

De Valera made clear to the Secretary of State for Dominion Affairs that Ireland would retain its policy of official reserve to Commonwealth meetings at the forthcoming Assembly. Ireland would support moves by Britain to solve the Abyssinian problem, but Ireland's attitude would primarily be determined by support of the Covenant. De Valera was determined to stick by the League, even when confidence in its ability was dwindling. Cremins reported that it was expected at Geneva that de Valera was returning to the Assembly with the intention of making clear that Ireland supported the Covenant and was fully behind the League's efforts towards a solution.

The Executive Council met on 30 August and took the unprecedented decision of agreeing the attitude to be adopted by de Valera over Abyssinia.³² Important League matters were normally settled between De Valera, Walshe, Boland and Cremins. Involving the Cabinet in League policy had not figured in de Valera's League policy since 1932. De Valera, Hearne, Boland and new recruit to the department, Denis Devlin, left for Geneva on 3 September with Cabinet backing for the pro-League stance de Valera was to take.³³

The 1935 Assembly: Prelude to invasion

Before the Assembly opened the Irish delegation undertook rounds of meetings and interviews to get up to date information on Abyssinia. A rumour

30 NA, D.F/A 26/94, 23 May 1935.
31 Ibid., Cremins–Boland, 6 August 1935.
32 NA, Cabinet Minutes, CAB 1/6 (7/256), 30 August 1935.
33 **Denis Devlin** (1908–59): Poet and Diplomat. Left a junior Lectureship in English in UCD to join External Affairs in 1935. First Secretary, Rome, 1935; Washington, 1938–46, Counsellor at High Commission in London, 1947; Minister and later Ambassador to Italy, 1950–8, also accredited to Turkey, 1951. Devlin was a major figure in the Irish modernist poetic movement along with Brian Coffey and Samuel Beckett.

developed that de Valera would stand for President of the Assembly, but that the Great Powers felt him to be 'too forceful a nominee for the post'.[34] Boland was less sanguine about the Presidency, writing to Cremins that he considered that 'the important thing is not to endanger our claim for an elected Vice-Presidency, or in default of that the Chairmanship of a Committee by allowing ourselves to be led away into a campaign for the Presidency which may ultimately have to be abandoned'.[35] Anthony Eden had let it be known that Britain would not favour de Valera's Presidency as 'he would be likely to make use of the office to make attacks on imperialism generally'.[36] It appeared that the ailing Benes of Czechoslovakia would become President on humanitarian grounds because he was not expected to make another Assembly. Cremins was unimpressed, writing to Murphy that this was 'rather an undiplomatic reason'.[37] De Valera again stepped down and let Benes stand for the Presidency unopposed. De Valera had the support of the Scandinavians and other Small States, but 'as there seemed to be a strong desire among the other delegations to pay a personal tribute to Dr. Benes by electing him to the presidency, Mr de Valera decided that he would prefer that his name would not go forward'.[38]

The Czechoslovaks proposed de Valera for the Presidency of the Sixth Commission to which he was elected on 10 September. De Valera thanked the delegations for the honour and 'recognised the gravity of some of the matters which might come before the commission, and he trusted that he would discharge the duties of the office to their satisfaction'.[39] The Sixth Committee which dealt with political questions became de Valera's favourite office at the Assembly. It allowed him to keep his finger on the pulse of political questions before the League such as Abyssinia.

Macaulay wrote from Rome that the atmosphere was highly charged over Abyssinia: 'the tension is too great here and it can be relieved only by definite action within four or five weeks'.[40] The *Irish Times* of 11 September spoke of 'deep gloom' at Geneva. The Assembly disposed of its routine work and turned its attention to the Abyssinian dispute. On 11 September Hoare spoke to the Assembly and stressing the possibility of sanctions, put Britain at the forefront of the League's resistance to Mussolini. Britain's stand for the Covenant had a huge psychological impact. A new confidence appeared in the Assembly and Hoare's speech coincided with the arrival of a British fleet off Gibraltar. However Britain would only go so far as other states would. This meant as far as France was prepared to intervene. It appeared that the League

34 NA, D.F/A 26/94, Boland–Cremins, 2 September 1935.
35 Ibid.
36 Ibid., Boland–Walshe, 10 September 1935.
37 Ibid., Cremins–Murphy, undated, September 1935.
38 *Irish Times*, 6 September 1935.
39 Ibid.
40 NA, D.F/A 27/95, 5 September 1934.

was going to put up a fight. French Foreign Minister Pierre Laval made a similar speech two days later. War scares pervaded the Assembly; the delegates at Geneva simply watched and waited.

De Valera had the opportunity to broadcast to the United States from Geneva on 12 September. The speech was a mish-mash of de Valera's hopes for the League and the views expressed by Cremins through 1934 and 1935. De Valera opened by making clear to his American audience his hopes that the universality of the League would one day be accomplished. Then it would become a parliament of the world. Unlike a national parliament it lacked the ability to make binding decisions; de Valera stressed that 'this power is absent because the will to have it otherwise is absent'. Chiding the slowness of states who failed to fully embrace the Covenant he spoke of how 'they desire security but are not willing to make the sacrifices necessary to achieve it'. These points were allusions to the League's failures since his last radio address in 1932. De Valera made plain his disagreement with states which subscribed to the Covenant in theory but displayed an unwillingness to put collective security into practice. This became a central theme of de Valera's during the Abyssinian crisis. He was certain that sometimes force was the only way to solve international disputes, as long as it was force under an international mandate. This was a sparsely veiled reference to the dislike of the great powers to act through the League and the increasing normality of resorting to private discussions rather than the open diplomacy of the Assembly. The admission of Russia and the attempts by Eden to broker a solution to the Abyssinian dispute outside the Assembly were all too clear and recent examples of this tendency.

The development of de Valera's disillusionment with the League since 1932 is obvious. Where in 1932 he could speak of positive achievements to dispel his many criticisms, by 1935 de Valera seemed to be diagnosing the patient terminally ill with no chance of a reprieve: 'this League of Nations ... would now appear to be in imminent peril of splitting on the rock on which previous attempts at international organisations of a similar character have perished'. He wondered aloud if 'there be another war to convince the world that sacrifices must be made for peace'. Only then would the selfishness and self-interest shown since Manchuria be seen to be in vain. Removing self-interest was the key to effective world order.

The speech marks the first sign of a public change in Ireland's views on the League. For the first time, the Irish, who had been such stalwart supporters called for a new Covenant, a 'more flexible instrument'. De Valera also indicated that unanimity in voting must go to free up decision making. Most strikingly, de Valera advocated appeasement or revisionism in European affairs. He spoke of how 'the rights of haves and have nots need to be adjusted from time to time ... and when a wrong cries out for redress or an evil for a cure, there must be some means for providing them in time without waiting for a threat of war to compel attention'. De Valera was advocating outright treaty revision to ameliorate Germany. This is a prototype of his 'general settlement' policy of a peace conference before, rather than after, the war. To the ever logical de Valera it seemed that the obvious way to settle grievances was to do so before the points of contention led to conflict.

De Valera had built his speech on Boland and Cremins's views, but he had a greater sense of hope in the League idea. The League might be 'a precarious and imperfect instrument', but it was also 'a beginning, a real effort on the part of many to order international affairs by reason and justice instead of by force'. Cremins and Boland saw their hopes vanish after Manchuria and the retreat from the League into armed camps. De Valera wished to develop the League so that it began to approximate to the unselfish ideal he spoke of. To him it was still incomprehensible that the League should collapse. His closing remarks to his American audience still resonate with the incredulity that de Valera felt as he saw the powers deserting the League and only the small states pledging continued if uncertain support: 'to destroy it now would be a crime against humanity. To maintain it we must live up to its obligations. The alternative, so far as Europe is concerned, is a return to the law of the jungle. What philosophy of life can make us believe that man is necessarily condemned to such a fate.' The League was flawed, but half a League was better than total war. The seeds of Ireland's retreat from the League had been sown in this speech to the United States.

This speech was overshadowed by de Valera's momentous address to the Assembly on 16 September. It was uncertain to the last moment if de Valera would speak. He did not want to over-politicise his chairmanship of the Sixth Commission but wanted to make sure that the Assembly was not adjourned without discussing Abyssinia. Boland reported to Dublin how 'the President has at present an open mind as to whether he will speak in the Assembly at all and, if so, as to what he will say'.[41] What he had to say provoked a storm of controversy as the League waited, apparently helpless, as two League members prepared to go to war.

The palpable sense of depression in Geneva was overwhelming as de Valera opened by contrasting the ideals of the League and the Covenant with the all-pervasive expectancy of conflict that filled Geneva in September 1935. It was the beginning to a depressing speech which asked only questions about why the world order had come to the brink of a new conflict, and, unlike his 1932 speech, it provided no answers. A 'Functionalist' League wherein, 'by loyal co-operation, first in the smaller things, the nations would be led to realise that the highest good of each was best secured by devoted service to the common interests of all' was de Valera's ideal. However, he spoke of how the cynic was now the League's teacher as one League member was about to be invaded by another and the League appeared powerless, a victim of its own indecision. This indecision was the prologue to another world conflict if states

41 NA, D.F/A 26/94, Boland–Walshe, 12 September 1935.

did not act immediately in terms with the Covenant. The speech argued this was better than the terrible price of war. It was better to support collective security now than fight later: 'It is a hard price, but harder still and more terrible is the future in store for us if we should fail to be ready to pay it. The final test of the League and all it stands for has come.' The League's conduct in the coming weeks would show if it was worthy to survive or should disappear from the international order. Ireland was ready to forgo the League in 1935 if Articles 15 or 16 were not invoked. There was no shirking as Ireland realised that this test of the League would be strenuous; de Valera's support for collective security was not a lightly taken decision.

The speech argued that collective security must be universal to work. All must be given equal protection. If the League did not excel over Abyssinia then the world order would and should revert to a system of alliances. De Valera's incomprehension at the chain of events and the future conflict was obvious. Echoing Neville Chamberlain's 'in war, which ever side may call itself victor, there are no winners, but all are losers', de Valera argued 'Why cannot the nations put into the enterprises of peace the energy they are prepared to squander in the futility and frightfulness of war'.[42]

This led into the novel idea that was a mix between appeasement in its 1930s style and the preventive diplomacy later championed by United Nations Secretary General Dag Hammarskjöld. 'We', de Valera argued, should 'deal with wrongs when we perceive them ... not every demand for change deserves to be listened to ... must we wait until the wronged have risen up in armed revolt before we grant him the redress to which we know he is entitled'. This developed into de Valera's 'general settlement' policy. Perhaps this was no more than wishful thinking in a speech which was resigned to war.

The tone was consistently questioning; always asking 'why?', but giving no answers, 'Why can we not endeavour to forge an international instrument, not merely for settling international disputes when they arise, but for removing in advance the causes of those disputes'. It is a resigned hope that states can group together in crisis. De Valera's only grain of hope was that 'the solidarity of which we have had, happily, such a manifestation within the past few days is an earnest that the goodwill of the nations can in the last resort be depended upon for the fulfilment of the obligations into which they have entered freely'. He concluded by hoping that the current crisis would bond the nations together and that it would at last appear clear to them that self-preservation was essential. There was no flourishing conclusion, only a despairing prayer that reason would prevail: 'God grant us the will and wisdom to avail ourselves of it'. It was not de Valera's usual rousing speech as an under-dog champion of the small states in the League. It simply despaired, asking why the existing League did not work. It was almost funereal.

---

42 Chamberlain quoted in Duncan Keithshaw, *Neville Chamberlain* (London, 1939, p. 111).

Observers did not see that Ireland was noticeably preparing to distance herself from the League; that de Valera was moving Ireland away from the League. His hope in vain that collective security would prove a useful weapon caused a major sensation as it was interpreted by the press as simply support for Britain. His only message was a plea to follow collective security now rather than later because of the terrible price of war. The *Irish Times* opened its report on the speech quoting de Valera: 'The Irish Free State will fulfil its obligations under the Covenant of the League of Nations in the letter and the spirit'.[43] Because Britain, through her Foreign Secretary Samuel Hoare, appeared as a champion of the League and a supporter of sanctions and de Valera had also taken this line it was narrowly defined within the bounds of Anglo-Irish relations. The *Washington News* could interpret no further into de Valera's speech than 'Ireland supports Great Britain in League stand over Ethiopia'.[44] Michael MacWhite was instructed to counter this notion with a press release that, 'the fact that both Ireland and Great Britain have taken a similar line is due to the fact that the British policy at the moment is in support of the Covenant. The President's first speech at Geneva in 1932 equally supported the Covenant'.[45] Because Ireland and Britain both stood behind the Covenant, it was mistakenly interpreted by the press that Ireland stood behind rather than alongside Britain and the other League members in their support of the League. Public confusion whether Ireland stood behind Britain or behind the League is misleading. Ireland was backing the League, and to quote the Secretary of the Irish Legation in Washington, Robert Brennan, 'Ireland was, for once, in the same boat as Great Britain'.[46] What is clear from the speech is that Ireland was now reserving its support for the League contingent on its ability to deal with the Italo-Abyssinian dispute if a serious conflict were to break out.

Invasion and sanctions: October–November 1935

Events moved swiftly towards conflict as Italy rejected the League's attempts to broker a solution. On 27 September the dispute was brought under Article 15 paragraph 4 of the Covenant which for the first time brought in the possibility of sanctions. Speculation grew over the Free State's involvement in sanctions. The *Irish Times* concluded that the Government could hardly remain neutral and would have to participate in the imposition of sanctions, possibly even military sanctions.[47] A dispatch from Boland to Walshe catches the mood of the final weeks before the conflict:

---

43 *Irish Times*, 17 September 1935.
44 *Washington News*, 17 September 1935.
45 NA, D.F/A 26/94, Walshe–MacWhite, 17 September 1935.
46 Ibid., Brennan–Walshe, 18 September 1935.
47 *Irish Times*, 20 September 1935.

most people here seem to think that nothing further is likely to be done either by the Council or by the Assembly before the Italian invasion of Abyssinia, which is now said to be fixed for the second week of October.[48]

Boland felt that the powers were allowing a slide to war to allow Article 16 to be implemented and bring sanctions into play. De Valera disliked this war by stealth and desired that the Covenant should be followed by Article 15 being fulfilled to the letter and a report into the situation being published and a 'resolution re-affirming the intention of the League to resort to sanctions if Italy invaded Abyssinia, or the constitution of a committee of the Assembly to follow the development of the dispute and to convoke the Assembly again in case of necessity'.[49] In any attempt to coerce Italy, Ireland's attitude would be, 'strictly determined by their obligations under the Covenant'.[50] As de Valera returned from Geneva on 2 October, Europe prepared for war in Africa and the Anglo-French response of League sanctions against Italy.

After an absence of a month a tired de Valera returned to Ireland with public expectation rising about Ireland's place in any sanctions against Italy. Much of this focused around opposition claims that Ireland had committed herself to fighting in a British war. United Irish Party politicians and extreme Republicans criticised de Valera for subserviently following Britain. Commandant Cronin of the League of Youth and Blueshirt T.F. O'Higgins criticised de Valera's not using the League as a bargaining force in the Economic War.[51] General Eoin O'Duffy had requested that Rome allow Irish Blueshirts to help Italian troops in their 'struggle of civilisation against the barbarism with which all the hidden forces of retrograde materialism and anti-fascism are today allied'.[52] De Valera planned a series of national addresses to snuff out domestic opposition and make his position clear. He would address the nation by radio and make a speech from his constituency base in Ennis.

On 2 October, Italian forces began their invasion of Abyssinia. Macaulay reported a mood of pessimism in Rome. He spoke of fears in Italian diplomatic circles of eventual open war with Britain and France supported by America against Italy. However public opinion remained buoyant.[53] Charles Bewley reported that the Berlin press saw the developing conflict in national terms between Britain and Italy, with no mention of the League.

De Valera addressed the nation from Dublin in the immediate aftermath of the invasion. He stressed that it was the role of the League to end this dispute. However, his references to Ireland's distancing herself from the League

---

48 NA, D.F/A 27/95A, Boland–Walshe, 25 September 1935.
49 Ibid.
50 Ibid., undated draft despatch to Hoare
51 For a greater illustration of the domestic background see Keogh, *Europe*, pp. 57–61.
52 NA, D.F/A 27/95B, press report from *Il Journale d'Italia*, 13 September 1935.
53 NA, D.F/A 27/95C, Macaulay–Walshe, 3 October 1935.

had multiplied. If the League failed again it should 'disappear' before it becomes 'a trap for states trusting in it, leading them to neglect adequate measures for their own defence.' Ireland would take an independent position, 'its attitude will be determined by its desire to see the League of Nations preserved as an effective guarantee of peace ... that was our attitude and it remains our attitude'. De Valera was putting a brave face on a nearly hopeless situation. The Covenant should and would be enforced. Ireland's faith in the League might be dwindling, but that would not stop the state giving support when the need arose. Ireland would support economic sanctions, but de Valera made it clear that military sanctions would need the consent of the Oireachtas under the constitution. He concluded by calling for reform of the League so that society was not 'doomed to remain forever subject to brute force and passion'. It was a call to make the League more effective. Behind the enthusiasm at each speech de Valera made in late 1935, the swing to neutrality was being developed steadily. Current support for the League was in no doubt, but the speech makes clear that this could not be expected to be ongoing if there was a failure of the League to effectively grasp the Ethiopian dispute.

On 7 October 1935 the Council voted that Italy had resorted to war in breach of Article 12 of the Covenant and a clear cut act of aggression in violation of Article 16 existed. De Valera prepared to return to Geneva to the reconvened Assembly. On 10 October the Council voted for sanctions to be imposed upon Italy with the Assembly concurring the following day. Fifty-one out of the 54 states represented at Geneva agreed that sanctions should be implemented.

Sanctions were to be organised by a Co-ordination Committee. Initial sanctions, adopted on 11 October, were to prevent the export of arms and warlike materials to Italy.[54] Sanctions evolved so that states were to break all economic, trade and financial links with Italy. Governments were to impose sanctions individually rather than under League auspices. De Valera made certain that religious orders in Italy were not affected by sanctions and that these bodies would be covered under the area of humanitarian bodies. Te Water of South Africa and the Aga Khan along with Anthony Eden approached Cremins to see if de Valera would take up a position on the Co-ordination Committee because of his chairmanship of the sixth Committee of the Assembly. De Valera could not take up the post as domestic business called him back to Dublin.

Britain followed a policy of cautious support of League through minimal sanctions. Cremins wrote to Walshe how Lester's friend de Madariaga was 'pessimistic about the whole situation and said that nothing but a big gesture from Britain would save it'.[55] Sanctions were eventually agreed to cover military supplies, finance and credit, with a ban on imports and exports. The Co-

---

54 The existing 1925 Firearms Act covered the Free State in this case.
55 NA, D.F/A 27/95C, 18 October 1935.

ordination Committee was to be kept informed of their implementation at national level. Cremins wrote of how 'the application of measures will be slow to take effect ... there will be many gaps.'[56] 28 October was the last day for notification by states of their intentions to implement sanctions. A timetabling problem over the re-assembly of the Dáil meant that the necessary legislation had not been passed and only armaments sanctions were being imposed by the Free State. Financial and economic sanctions would come into operation on 18 November 1935; there was still time for the Free State to catch up.

Departmental discussions took place in Dublin how Ireland would conform with League sanctions. On the advice of John Leydon, Secretary of the Department of Industry and Commerce, legislation to conform with the import and export restrictions was considered necessary.[57] It would be brought into force on a date fixed by the Co-ordination Committee. Sanctions on arms and finance were already in practical operation under existing legislation. New legislation to cover import and export restrictions would be introduced into the Dáil on 29 October.

The bill to implement sanctions was passed by the Dáil on 6 November. Domestic opposition within the Dáil and by pro-Italian figures was disorganised, based on crude racism and over-zealous Catholicism. However, it was not significant enough to be a threat. De Valera let the various loose cannons fire off harmlessly. His parliamentary control of League of Nations policy and his certain pro-sanctions line at Geneva meant that fickle public opinion would not influence his line.

Italy sent a note of protest to all states imposing sanctions on 11 November and later threatened counter-sanctions. Murphy informed Cremins that de Valera considered that, 'our participation in sanctions is exclusively due to the necessity of fulfilling obligations devolving on us as a member of the League of Nations'.[58] The official reply to Italy was phrased in the courtesies of diplomatic language, but the primacy of Ireland's support for the League was evident.

The sanctions episode shows that Ireland would still go as far as others to implement League policy. In striking contrast to Manchuria, Ireland did not play a central role to the development of policy. The return to the Assembly had lessened Ireland's ability to play an active part in the development of sanctions, though de Valera's unwillingness to hold office on the Co-ordination Committee also contributed to this situation. From the ranks of the Assembly Ireland threw its lot in with the League hoping that the rule of international law and the efficacy of the League would be shown through the operation of sanctions.

On 18 November 1935 the League of Nations (Obligations of Membership) Act came into operation to implement sanctions by Ireland within the

56 Ibid., Cremins–Walshe, 21 October 1935.
57 Ibid., Leydon–Walshe, 25 October 1935.
58 NA, D.F/A 27/135, 19 November 1935.

international framework of the Co-ordination Committee. The Department of External Affairs acted as a conduit to inform other departments of the introduction and operation of the bill. The Co-ordination role gave External Affairs a greater profile in the civil service and an extra degree of importance. With sanctions in place it was now up to international opinion to try to force Italy out of Abyssinia by economic pressure.

The Hoare–Laval pact: December 1935

By December 1935, Italy was suffering under League imposed sanctions. Financial difficulties were increasing and restrictions to export and import trade were leading to internal confusion while criticism and discontent were spreading. This was not helped by Italian forces getting bogged down in Abyssinia. Britain and France had kept up their policy of negotiations with Italy towards a compromise solution. The Italian Government did not want any solution except Italian colonisation. On 7 December 1935 Hoare met Laval in Paris. They agreed a plan to partition Abyssinia giving the majority of the territory to Italy and the rump Abyssinia a corridor to the sea. Britain and France were willing to make a deal with Italy at Abyssinia's expense. Abyssinia would lose more than half her territory. Italy would be told first and then Abyssinia. The plan was leaked by the French press on 9 December.

Public opinion was horrified that the League should be sidelined. Cremins had little to say on the pact; he was officially in the dark and was getting meagre information from the lobbies. Cremins became increasingly worried as the proposals emerged. He wrote of how 'the proposals were a blow to the League, and a very severe blow to British prestige'.[59] With the publication of the plan League opinion turned against Britain. Cremins felt that Britain had fallen from grace and League officials were 'at pains to give the impression that they would like to see the proposals dead and buried.'[60] British diplomats were very irritable at Geneva; Cremins met Strang after a meeting of the Co-ordination Committee and Strang immediately confronted him: ' "are you going to attack me, too?" I said "no—what's going to happen now, are the proposals largely to be accepted by the Council?" He replied that he though the proposals were dead.' Cremins felt that 'people seemed to have the feeling that they had been "had".' Strang was in agreement: 'yes, that's the worst of it'. With British prestige at Geneva 'about as low as it could be', Cremins considered the other members of the League to be 'in the fog'. Eden was 'ill at ease, quite different from Mr Laval who is calm as usual'.[61]

Opinion was outraged at this breach of faith towards the League and Abyssinia. Cremins noted that 'a feature of the situation here is the open

---

59 NA, D.F/A, 27/141, Cremins–Walshe, 12 December 1935.
60 Ibid., 14 December 1935.
61 Ibid., Cremins–Walshe, 14 and 18 December 1935.

condemnation of the British Government by the British—even by British League officials here'.[62] Sean Murphy wrote to John Dulanty in London and asked him to transmit to the Foreign Office Ireland's view that, 'peace on the terms suggested will be regarded by the peoples of all countries as a failure of the League of Nations'.[63] Hoare was forced to resign. Anthony Eden became Foreign Secretary and began to pick up the pieces. The Hoare-Laval pact was the end of Locarno and the death of the League. Public expectations of the League had been carried high and the League would correspondingly fall further. Macaulay in Rome reported that, 'the Geneva front is broken beyond repair ... it was thought that having voted for the application of all kinds of sanctions few states would have the courage or the interest to go on and run the risk of becoming involved in war. Something like erosion was anticipated, a gradual crumbling away.'[64] Sanctions had been slowly becoming more effective as 1935 drew to a close; Hoare–Laval robbed them and the League of any credibility as it was apparent that the powers were willing to operate secretly behind the League.

The impact of sanctions in an Irish context

By mid-1935 Irish–Italian trade was minimal so the impact of sanctions was going to be slight. Nonetheless the effect is interesting and Ireland's participation was in any case part of a wider operation. Table 1 shows that the European depression gravely hit Irish–Italian trade after 1930. By 1931 a substantial trade surplus had become a considerable deficit. Irish exports to Italy declined phenomenally through the thirties.[65] With the imposition of sanctions it was expected that the average amount of lost export earnings to Ireland would be £3000–£4000 per annum, based on 1935 figures.[66] This sum was mostly made up of animal exports and the export of scrap iron and steel.

Irish imports from Italy declined from 1929, but remained reasonably constant compared to the huge decline in exports. Total Irish imports, based on country of origin, from Italy from April to September 1935 amounted to £82,554, a quarter of which was made up of agricultural and horticultural imports. All of these products could be imported from elsewhere. Sanctions

62 Ibid., Cremins–Walshe, 18 December 1935.
63 Ibid., Murphy–Dulanty, 18 December 1935.
64 Ibid., Macaulay–Walshe, 17 December 1935.
65 The method of collecting trade statistics changed on and from 1 April 1937. Imports were compiled by country of origin where previously it was by country of consignment. The statistics were published with an explanatory note that in some cases aggregate totals will not always be equal to the sum of the published monthly figures. Though this is apparent in the data used, figures in each table are consistent, except where stated, but cross table comparisons are affected.
66 All figures are from data contained in *Department of Industry and Commerce Monthly Trade Statistics* (Monthly, Dublin) supplemented by figures from NA, D.F/A 26/103 and 27/158.

did not pose a serious burden on the Irish economy. During the same period for 1935 imports from all other countries, based also on country of origin, amounted to £18,220,138. The Italian figure roughly accounted for a half of one per cent of these imports.[67]

When it comes to the imposition of sanctions the trade pattern is visibly affected. From the figures in table 2 it can be seen that sanctions brought already negligible Irish exports to Italy down to almost zero. It is in imports that the real impact can be seen. There was a lag in the impact of sanctions. Existing contracts had to be fulfilled and orders completed. It is in January 1936, after the debacle of the Hoare–Laval pact that sanctions began to have an impact. Ireland was not a significant trading partner of Italy's and sanctions were not on essential items in general, but their impact is immediately apparent from the accompanying graphs. By June 1936 sanctions had reduced Irish imports from Italy to 12 per cent of their September 1935 figure. Multiplied over the total number of states implementing sanctions, and given time, sanctions would have had a significant impact on Italy's economy. However, the backlash to Hoare–Laval and the sense of depression following Italy's eventual conquest of Abyssinia meant that sanctions were removed too soon. The first imposition of sanctions on a major power was not given enough time to trickle down into the Italian economy. Ireland successfully implemented the limited import and export sanctions that the League had imposed on Italy until their removal in July 1936. With the removal of sanctions, Ireland's imports from Italy again rose through the remainder of 1936. On a yearly basis it is here that the differences between the two methods of collection of trade statistics make precise comparisons difficult. Though not directly comparable, both figures 2 and 3 show that Irish imports from Italy were significantly affected by sanctions while they were in operation. This is most obvious from figure 3.

Ireland's trade with Italy was minimal, so the imposition of sanctions, though effective as the graphs and tables show, was more important as a moral point and as part of a collective action by all League members. Cremins wrote to Walshe in late January 1936 that the collective impact was promising because, 'the population are very disheartened ... unemployment is growing and tourist numbers have fallen. There is no sign whatever of any break ... even the existing sanctions without any addition will eventually break Italy if continued.'[68]

Speculation focused on an oil embargo. Macaulay felt that Italy could hold out over a year under a blockade. Supplies had not been cut, rather price had been increased to limit consumption. Cremins caught the mood of the moment when he spoke of 'a crop of rumours ... next steps are canvassed from

---

67 Other imports for 1935 included £12 cotton seed cake, £236 soup and purees, £726 wheat products, £2 rosaries. *Figures from Department of Industry and Commerce Monthly Trade Statistics* (Monthly, Dublin).
68 NA, D.F/A 27/158, Cremins–Walshe, 23 January 1936.

Table 1: Irish–Italian trade: 1929–37

Year	Imports (£)	Exports (£)
1929	89,626	174,379
1930	80,984	113,483
1931	73,217	40,198
1932	61,475	25,879
1933	49,487	16,154
1934	50,315	12,863
1935	52,153	3215
1936	37,972	762
1937*	171,319	1271

Source: *Trade and shipping statistics* (Yearly, Department of Industry and Commerce Dublin)

* Figures for 1937 are by country of origin, other years by country of consignment.

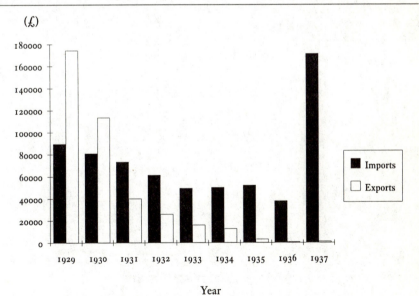

Figure 2: Irish–Italian Trade, 1929–37

Table 2: Irish–Italian trade: September 1935–December 1936

Month	Imports (£)	Exports (£)
September 1935	18,095	274
October 1935	18,980	23
November 1935	18,601	335
December 1935	13,926	23
January 1936	7353	29
February 1936	3600	23
March 1936	4098	19
April 1936	2251	8
May 1936	2743	16
June 1936	2329	19
July 1936	3088	9
August 1936	9651	192
September 1936	9137	139
October 1936	21,394	68
November 1936	7902	22
December 1936	19,687	213

Source: Monthly trade statistics (Department of Industry and Commerce, Dublin). All figures by country of origin

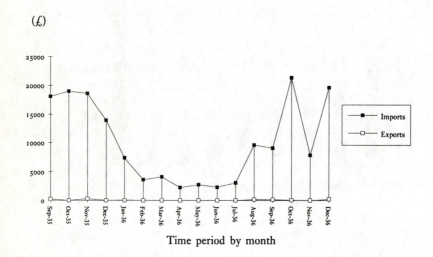

Figure 3: Irish–Italian trade, September 1935–December 1936

every angle, everybody sounding everybody else'.⁶⁹ Cremins felt that oil sanctions had 'really entered the bounds of probability, if present efforts at negotiation draw a blank'. The mood for spring 1936 vacillated between peace and the further imposition of sanctions. Events in Abyssinia brought the conflict closer to a cessation. Organised resistance was expected to be crushed by the end of April. By that point, Macaulay felt, 'the League will then not be in a position to maintain its opposition'.⁷⁰

On 7 March 1936 German forces remilitarised the Rhineland. The League was further hit, though indirectly. The powers were now resorting to balance of power politics; collective security was dead. The impact on the Abyssinian Crisis was that oil sanctions, nearing a possibility, were dropped. France could not divert Italy irrevocably into German arms through the imposition of oil sanctions. Britain dropped her commitments to Abyssinia to free her hands to deal with Germany. On 17 April the Council Committee into Abyssinia heard the Spanish representative, de Madariaga, read a report that the League could no longer expect a negotiated solution between the parties. Hostilities would have to end by military victory. In the aftermath of these statements Cremins sent another failure-ridden report to Dublin:

> The resolution of the Council is regarded as being completely anaemic. In the lobbies, after the meeting it was clear that amongst lovers of the League (and they are legion here!) there was *nothing* but depression ... the Rhineland governs the whole position.⁷¹

The end of sanctions: May–July 1936

The flight of Emperor Haile Selassie to Palestine on 1 May 1936 and the proclamation of an Italian Empire in Ethiopia on 9 May showed the failure of collective security. The May 1936 Council session did not lift sanctions, but the sanctions front began to dissolve. Macaulay reflected on the League's lack of effectiveness after the Council session: 'the League in its present form has failed ... with the elimination of Articles 10 and 16 it should be preserved as it may still fulfil a useful function'.⁷²

The final act of the Abyssinian drama would take place with the reconvening of the 16th Assembly on 30 June. Macaulay expected that the denouement was imminent: 'Mussolini has at last made up his mind to leave the League unless he gets satisfaction next month. Hitler is believed to be stringing him along waiting for the development. Next month should be a crucial one for Europe.'⁷³

69 NA, D.F/A 27/95D, Cremins–Walshe, 4 March 1936.
70 Ibid., Macaulay–Walshe, 8 April 1936.
71 Ibid., Cremins–Walshe, 21 April 1936.
72 Ibid., Macaulay–Walshe, 8 May 1936.
73 NA, D.F/A, 27/95C 26 May 1936.

De Valera, Devlin and Dr Michael Rynne comprised the Free State delegation to the reconvened Assembly. Boland had moved to the Department of Industry and Commerce to become head of the foreign trade division and Rynne, who had joined External Affairs in 1932, became the new head of the League Section. The Assembly initially was concerned with whether the Ethiopian Emperor Haile Selassie could address the League as Ethiopia had been conquered. The League had not yet recognised the Italian conquest. De Valera, supported by the British delegate, intervened on Haile Selassie's behalf stating that the Ethiopian Emperor had a right to speak under the Covenant.

On 30 June Haile Selassie made an impassioned speech 'defending the cause of all small peoples who are threatened with aggression'.[74] He mentioned alleged Italian atrocities on his people and condemned France's obstruction and pro-Italian stance. Begging sanctions be kept he concluded:

> I ask the Great Powers, who have promised the guarantee of collective security to small states—those small states over whom hangs the threat that they may one day suffer the fate of Ethiopia: What measures do they intend to take? Representatives of the world, I have come to Geneva to discharge in your midst the most painful duties of the head of a state. What answer am I to take back to my people?

The Mexicans walked out in protest to the Great Powers, arguing that Ethiopia would remain 'as Banquo's ghost to disturb the tranquillity of Geneva's conscience'.[75]

Eden and the French Prime Minister Blum had both accepted in their speeches that the League, through economic sanctions, had failed to prevent aggression in Abyssinia. De Valera was scheduled to speak on the afternoon of 3 July. His message would be directed to the case in hand, but it would make clear how Ireland viewed her international position following the failure of the League. Rynne mentioned to Walshe that 'it seems possible ... that the neutral intentions of Saorstát Éireann in the event of a future European war will be made apparent in the course of the Presidents' speech'.[76] De Valera had been a willing supporter of the League, his September 1935 speeches made it clear that Ireland would be prepared to leave the League if it could no longer effectively contribute to her international security. De Valera would make it clear that Ireland was now prepared to fend for herself in the international order. The speech is a watershed, but it did not come out of the blue. Cremins had been sending accurate assessments of the European situation to de Valera from his appointment in May 1934 and from September 1935 de

---

74 Quoted in Elmer Bendiner, *A time for Angels* (London, 1975) p. 375.
75 Ibid., p. 376.
76 NA, D.F/A, 26/94, 2 July 1936.

Valera had been preparing to distance Ireland from the League if there was a collapse over the Italo-Abyssinian question. This had come to pass and de Valera was acting on his word. His speech to the Assembly on 2 July was not a bolt from the blue, it promoted to centre stage a movement in Irish League policy that was apparent from 1935 in speeches and 1934 in confidential reports. The Irish foreign service realistically saw that Ireland could no longer expect support from the League if she needed it. Lester's internationalism of the early thirties had been replaced by Cremins's realism blended with de Valera's pragmatism. Ireland would support the League as long as it was an effective international force and it was in Ireland's interests to do so. The speech analysed below is a turning point, but it was no sudden shift of policy. Neutrality did not emerge overnight as a policy option as opposed to a romantic Irish ideal. Ireland was not opting out when the going got tough. Ireland had supported the League and championed its cause. Now it seemed there was little to do but retreat.

De Valera's sentiments from September 1935 had proved correct. He forlornly spoke of how despite the efforts of the League, 'we have come here to confess that we can do nothing about it ... we must abandon the victim to his fate. It is the fulfilment of the worst predictions of all who decried the League and said it could not succeed.' The tone of his address to the Assembly had become increasingly grave from 1932. Where once there was a call for reform, a salutary reminder of public opinion, there was now an announcement of full blown failure. Ireland, a small state, feared it could well share Ethiopia's fate 'should the greed or the ambition of some powerful neighbour prompt its destruction'. The League could no longer inspire confidence to Ireland and the other small states. De Valera made it clear that he supported military sanctions: 'let us face the fact that economic and financial sanctions can be made effective only if we are prepared to back them up by military measures'. In line with the reports he was getting from Ministers abroad de Valera regarded this failure as bringing closer the threat of a war in Europe.

The danger to Europe and the need to prevent a conflict, rather than the development of the League, was de Valera's main theme: 'let us, thinking only of the future, set about the urgent task of preserving peace in Europe, and leave aside for the moment such questions as to how the Covenant should be altered to make it effective and universal'.

If the statesmen of Europe could not solve Europe's problems peacefully then Europe was bound for war. De Valera could not understand how statesmen would willingly take this course: 'no losses could be heavier than those which the preparation for war and war itself entail'. In now famous words he reminded the Assembly that disputes must be dealt with in time: 'two miles above Niagara ... it is possible to land, but wait until you are a hundred feet from the Falls and you are lost. How much nearer is Europe to the Falls?' Evidently de Valera thought it was very close; his conclusion was a sorry commentary on the ability of the League to provide collective security for the small states and their powerlessness: 'all the small states can do, if the statesmen of the greater powers fail in their duty, is resolutely to determine that they will not become the tools of any great Power, and that they will resist with whatever strength they may possess every attempt to force them into a war against their will'. The League had failed, Ireland would have to provide for her own international security. The curtain had come down on 13 years of Irish foreign policy where the Geneva umbrella, imperfect as it was, was a factor in Irish security policy. Neutrality was a chimerical presence in Irish foreign policy up to 1936. Ireland actively promoted a policy of non-involvement in any conflict after 1936. Ireland was now discarding a belief in the fundamental articles of the Covenant. The League could not work for international security, but it remained an international meeting place of some importance. Ireland's small foreign service could not afford to leave Geneva, it was not only their central meeting place, but was fast becoming a cockpit from which to view the burgeoning conflict in Europe.

Rynne considered that the speech had been 'very well received, considering its rather general tone'.[77] De Valera immediately left Geneva for Zurich and Cremins and Rynne stayed on to attend the meetings of the Assembly.

On 6 July 1936 the Co-ordination Committee unanimously voted to lift sanctions against Italy on 15 July. Ireland accordingly revoked the League of Nations (obligations of membership) Act. There were no qualms about this. Though Ireland supported the League it was realised that the conquest of Abyssinia made sanctions worthless. By the time of the Italian conquest, opinion in Dublin was that sanctions were detrimental to a solution to the conflict: 'the longer sanctions are allowed to continue, the weaker will become certain states, near neighbours of Italy, on whom so much will depend if pressure has to be brought by the League to bear on Italy at any future date'.[78] Support for sanctions was contingent on the effectiveness of the policy. When the international effectiveness diminished, so did the policy.

Conclusion

With his acceptance by the international community as a statesman of ability and presence after his September 1932 Assembly speech, de Valera embraced the League wholeheartedly. His pragmatism knew no bounds. The erstwhile critic of the League had been transformed into the ultimate supporter. The admission of Russia, with de Valera balancing his Catholicism and internationalism, and the Abyssinian debacle with de Valera championing collective security and sanctions, were the pinnacles of his League of Nations appearances. They have stuck in the public mind; occupying even a place in Irish folk memory.

77 Ibid.
78 NA, D.F/A 27/158, memo on removal of sanctions, dated 21 May 1936.

De Valera's ability lay in his austere presence and his ability to sculpt words to suit the mood. The keynote addresses analysed above fitted closely to their surrounding international environment. De Valera had an uncanny ability to become the man of the moment. From determined neophyte to mature champion de Valera caught the mood of the League.

This presence at the League obscures two essential points. The hard slog of League policy, so evident in the 1920s, was absent from 1933 on. At the League de Valera was lucky. Ireland had achieved a respected position at Geneva by 1932, de Valera simply reaped the benefits. Ireland's position at Geneva was ready-made for de Valera to develop.

Secondly, the delegation and Permanent Representative spent their time creating an environment where de Valera could posture on the international stage. His appearances at Geneva were the tip of the iceberg of Irish League policy. It was Boland and Cremins that were the nine-tenths below the surface. To mix a metaphor, Irish League policy was like a swan, de Valera was the serenity apparent on the surface, it was the League of Nations section of External Affairs that was paddling like hell below to keep de Valera going.

De Valera appears as the most prominent member of the delegation in the thirties because the Cumann na nGaedheal practice of including members of the Executive Council was dropped by de Valera. With the exception of Assemblies at which he was not present, only at the September 1932 Assembly did de Valera include another member of the Executive Council: Senator Joseph Connolly. Officials from External Affairs, particularly legal and League staff made up the bulk of de Valera's delegations. The effect of this was to increase his pre-eminence as the master of League affairs. The tactic of including only civil servants instead of politicians did not end the continuity of League delegates. John J. Hearne, later Michael Rynne and of course Francis Cremins, made up the core of de Valera's League delegates. The practise of including junior members from External Affairs was continued. Future senior diplomats such as F.H. Boland, Denis Devlin, William Warnock and Denis R. McDonald all served diplomatic apprenticeships on League delegations. The Assemblies were valuable training grounds and meeting points for such junior diplomats.

It has been fashionable in Ireland to attack de Valera in recent years; this analysis instead critically suggests that whilst de Valera was a one-man-show at Geneva in his and his department's eyes, this show was a re-interpretation based solidly on that of 1923–32. It might not have been an ensemble piece on stage, but behind the scenes the solo performer was prepared, advised and initially supervised by the staff of the Department of External Affairs. De Valera was certainly not their mouthpiece, but neither was he performing all his own work. A solid base to work from, de Valera's inspiration and the Department of External Affairs perspiration and expertise, were the significant factors behind Ireland's position in the League in the 1930s.

De Valera spent only one month of the year at Geneva. For the remainder of the year he immersed himself in Irish or Anglo-Irish matters. It is mere popular fantasy that de Valera could be master of all trades unaided and simply change his persona when he entered the Assembly Hall. The tendency has been to view de Valera as a polymath, with an all-encompassing scope to his actions. At Geneva he relied heavily on the support of his Permanent Representative and Assembly delegation. Without them, he would have been at a complete loss when in the company of Foreign Ministers who held no other portfolio and could devote themselves all year round to their Foreign Affairs portfolio.

The years 1932 to 1938 are popularly perceived as Ireland's 'Golden Years' at the League with de Valera championing both collective security and the League itself. The picture now appears somewhat different. From 1933 to 1936 Ireland's participation in the affairs of the League outside the Council and the Assembly was certainly at it widest. Ireland was also a favoured small state at the Assembly and within the Secretariat. However well presented it was, de Valera's belief in the League idea is not as overwhelming as has previously been argued. From as early as 1935 Ireland was increasingly distancing itself from the League. This is veiled under supportive speeches. However that support was contingent on the success of the League in future ventures. De Valera's support for sanctions was a last ditch effort to prove the League effective. He was more than willing to let Ireland look after her own international security if the Abyssinian episode proved that the League could not actively ensure collective security. The Hoare–Laval Pact and the retreat from sanctions at the July Assembly were interpreted by de Valera and External Affairs as signs of failure and so Ireland moved her national security policy away from Geneva towards non-involvement in any future bilateral conflicts. This did not reduce the importance of the League as an international meeting place or as a central part of the Irish diplomatic network as will be shown in the next chapter.

The mid 1930s are nonetheless 'de Valera's years' at Geneva. They are a period of personal success and achievement and as such rather different to the collective success of the late 1920s and the period of Council membership. Whereas McGilligan, O'Sullivan, FitzGerald, MacWhite and Lester to name a few, could each be apportioned a share in making Ireland a going concern at Geneva, de Valera was rather different. His policy is a personal one, despite Cremins's input and influence. The other members of the delegation played a supportive role to de Valera who held centre stage. In the 1920s it was Ireland's role at the League; by 1934, when de Valera's tutelage at the League was complete, it was simply de Valera's role. Hearne, Rynne, Devlin and even Lester and Cremins were simply voices in the wings aiding and assisting de Valera's personal League policy. From 1934 to 1936 de Valera was champion of the small states and a keen supporter of collective security.

De Valera's' League policy was based on universalism and support of the Covenant. This is strikingly apparent from his stance over the admission of Russia. He saw that Russia became a League member to bolster her international position, but that it also allowed the continued operation of the League. However he was realistic enough to see that once the Covenant had failed, the League's importance to Ireland was limited and reduced. Before the failure of sanctions on Italy, de Valera had decided that Ireland would de-prioritise Geneva if the League could not effectively solve the Abyssinian crisis. Abyssinia was not a turning point in itself, the decision had been reached sometime beforehand. It was a testing ground. The League's failure in Africa turned de Valera away from the League as an institution that could provide for Ireland's security. Rather it would become, as the next chapter will show, an international meeting place and an essential post from which Dublin's knowledge of the slide to war was comprehensively enhanced.

The realism underlying League policy through Cremins's reports from Geneva changed the terms of Irish support for the League from 1934. Lester's internationalism might be the initial basis of de Valera's League policy as evidenced in Ireland's last year on the Council. Cremins's arrival at Geneva changed the scope of policy completely. No longer did the Irish Permanent Representative see increased support for the League as the key to a more effective League. Cremins saw that the League was flawed because the tenor of world affairs was unsuited to it. Lester felt that the League was a collective body especially for the small states; Cremins viewed the League in the global concerns of power politics and felt that the world order had moved away from the internationalism of the 1920s and towards armed camps and bilateral alliances. He moved Ireland's League perspective out of the Geneva-centric stance of Lester and into the realm of Europe. From 1936 Cremins was to pay more attention to European affairs in total rather than League affairs in particular. The League was increasingly becoming academic. Ireland was realistic enough to realise that the League failed as a security weapon over Abyssinia, but was not foolish enough to withdraw from the international arena. Support still existed for the idea of the League within Irish foreign policy circles. The League now occupied a different place in Irish foreign policy; it was important but not seen as effective. The League was de-prioritising itself in Irish minds. It now lay third behind the United States and Britain in importance in Irish foreign policy. Certainly there is no longer the League-Commonwealth axis in Irish foreign affairs that one observes in the 1920s. Nonetheless de Valera still continued to support its ideals in his heart even if in his head he realised they were futile and the private opinion of his department was increasingly lacking in interest in the Assembly. Geneva's place in Irish foreign policy remained undiminished, even if its central importance was decreasing.

CHAPTER 8

The Retreat from Geneva, 1936–46

In the wake of Abyssinia the League diminished as an active factor in Irish foreign policy. Ireland's Permanent Representative at Geneva, whilst nominally accredited to the League, became a diplomatic representative without portfolio for European affairs. Cremins's confidential reports to Dublin paid less attention to the disintegrating League and began to chronicle the final events on the road to war. Ireland abandoned the League in practice, but never formally withdrew from Geneva after 1936. From 1936 to 1939 Ireland slowly re-centred her foreign policy around neutrality. Irish participation in the League was limited to the Assembly. Without a seat on the Council and with Cremins preferring European political affairs to League affairs the scope for action was limited.

After the July 1936 Assembly, the League sought to redefine itself by halfhearted reform of the Covenant and by emphasising itself as a social and economic institution. The League struggled on through World War II, though it was politically redundant and by-passed by the powers. Sean Lester took over from Joseph Avenol as Acting-Secretary General in 1940.[1] Lester safeguarded the League through the war and kept it functioning on a limited scale. The United Nations came into existence on 24 October 1945, after the San Francisco Conference of April of that year. The League held its final Assembly in April 1946. At this gathering, Lester was retrospectively made Secretary General from 1940.

The 1936 and 1937 Assemblies: A League without sanctions?

Through 1936 many states reconsidered the role of the League in their foreign relations. Russia and France wanted to give the League the power of automatic sanctions so as, if need be, to use against Germany. The Scandinavian

---

1 Joseph L. Avenol: took up post of Deputy Secretary General of the League of Nations in 1923 after a career in the French Finance Ministry. Secretary General of the League of Nations, 1933–40.

states and Canada wanted to accept the failure of sanctions and confine the League to functional and consultative rather than security issues. De Valera stood somewhere between the two extremes, but favoured the Scandinavian approach.

Opening the June 1936 External Affairs estimates debate de Valera made his position clear. The League had failed to provide collective security and would 'have to set itself an humbler task ... the question of compelling other states to maintain their obligations will have to be abandoned'.[2] In future some more adventurous scheme could be attempted and de Valera suggested going beyond the range of mere economic sanctions to consider whether military sanctions were necessary. De Valera felt that after their unwillingness to enforce oil sanctions on Italy, states were not ready for military sanctions. Ireland would therefore support reform of the League as 'a forum for the consideration of such questions as might otherwise lead to war, using it as a conciliatory machine, perhaps on occasion as an arbitration machine'.[3] This was not deserting the League but wishing to see it adopt a lower profile in world affairs. The speech showed how de Valera had reconsidered his views on the League and that idealistic as he might be, the course of events indicated that an effective League was not possible in the immediate European circumstances.

De Valera did not attend the 1936 Assembly. It was a sign of the dwindling importance of the League to Ireland. Cremins forwarded some points that any Irish speech to the Assembly might include, starting with the Scandinavian policies on reform that were the most appropriate for Ireland. Cremins felt that 'in view of the increasingly menacing international situation, he [de Valera] may consider it well to make a reservation regarding the future application of article sixteen'.[4] Cremins picked up on the general settlement idea that had surfaced in de Valera's speeches since 1935. He argued that it was impossible to conceive of an effective League:

> until the states, especially the states in Europe arrive at some sort of normal basis in their political and economic relations, and until the obstacles in the shape of political, territorial and other grievances arising out of the peace treaties are frankly faced and removed.

Cremins's point was that the League could only work in a suitable international climate. That climate had to be created before reform of the League could be considered. The general settlement policy, similar to appeasement, became more important to Irish views on Europe and the League than the 'critical support' approach. The European crisis was a cause of the League's failure, not a symptom.

2 *Dáil deb*, 62: 2655, 19 June 1936.
3 Ibid., 62: 2656–7.
4 NA, D.F/A 26/119, Cremins–Walshe, 12 September 1936.

The Seventeenth Assembly opened on 21 September and spent its first days deciding if an Abyssinian delegation could be admitted. When the Abyssinian delegation finally took its seats, despite the best attempts of Eden to prevent this, it was universally felt that the League had negotiated itself out of a major crisis. This had a palliative effect on the Assembly, in which according to Rynne,

> no-one seems to be troubled by the fears of an early war, of the immediate withdrawal of Italy from the League, and of the imminent fall of Madrid ... The morale of the League is becoming higher accordingly as its activities lose interest.[5]

Rynne was thoroughly bored by the proceedings, writing to Walshe that 'the Minister need have no regrets that he is not here'.[6] Rynne paid close attention to Eden's speech calling for League reform, calling it a 'spiritual defence of democracy which no Irish delegation speech could be expected to improve upon'.[7] The Assembly continued to new depths of boredom and futility. Writing again to Walshe, Rynne told how after the admission of Abyssinia, the Assembly passed through 'a temporary state of mild elation, [and] lapsed into a condition which can best be described as the doldrums'.[8]

A Reform Committee was set up by the 1936 Assembly. The central question was whether to re-build collective sanctions or to use the Covenant as a consultative framework within which to peacefully settle international disputes.[9] The dilution of the coercive features of the Covenant and the watering down of Article 16 and its enforcement were likely results. By September 1937 its discussions had been 'desultory and unfruitful', leading Cremins to feel that, 'the Eighteenth Assembly is therefore, unlikely to achieve much in the domain of League reform'.[10]

Ireland's changed perspective of the League, a factor in League policy since 1935, became publicly apparent in May 1937. De Valera brought the development of Irish League policy to a standstill when he confirmed that Ireland would await the report of the Reform Committee, 'before committing Saorstát Éireann to any new policy with regard to the League of Nations'.[11] For the time being Ireland would not leave the League and would continue to work within its reduced framework. Ireland would tread water at the League

---

5 Ibid., Rynne–Walshe, 29 September 1936.
6 Ibid.
7 Ibid.
8 Ibid., Rynne–Walshe, 29 September 1936.
9 These discussions were tedious, but their results can be seen in the 1945 United Nations Charter with the separation of the Charter from the post-war settlements, the increasing use of preventive diplomacy in the United Nations and the increased role of regional bodies in the Charter.
10 NA, D/F/A, 126/37, Cremins–Murphy, 16 August 1937.
11 *Dáil deb*, 66: 801–2, 19 May 1937.

and future policy would depend on the outcome of the reform process. De Valera's disillusionment with the League was obvious. Mentioning Ireland's possible withdrawal from the League if international circumstances required it, de Valera said he 'was one of those who believed there were great possibilities for the League of Nations'.[12] His concluding sentence was ominous, 'I hope the changes will be of such a character as will commend themselves to us and enable us to recommend to the House a continuance of our membership'.[13]

De Valera spoke guardedly on the method of reform that Ireland would favour: 'the first thing that we have got to do is to try to get all the important states of Europe in a group, meeting together even for relatively trifling purposes to start with'.[14] The League as it stood did not retain Ireland's confidence and the state would await the reform programme before re-defining its League policy. In the meantime Ireland would, as a formality, continue its support of the League. Though the League Section in External Affairs remained in operation and de Valera kept up his policy of support for the ideal of a league of nations, Ireland progressively saw the League of Nations as a spent force. The League ceased to have a practical importance for Ireland after May 1937.

The speech was well timed in the run-up to an Extraordinary Assembly that was to admit Egypt in the last week of May 1937. Cremins monitored the proceedings as no Irish delegation attended. Many delegates mentioned to Cremins that they were bewildered by the Dáil speech and 'wanted to know exactly what it meant'.[15] Evidently the Irish Permanent Representative was not briefed, either before or after, on the contents of his Minister's speech. This was a lamentable gaffe considering the impact of the speech in the European press. Cremins found diplomats at Geneva 'somewhat mystified regarding our League attitude ... a French journalist said to me that the League was serious enough to enter, but not serious enough to quit'.[16] There was growing speculation in Europe and Ireland in the summer of 1937 that Ireland was preparing to leave the League and isolate herself in the world order.

This mood continued during the preparation for the September 1937 Assembly. The *Irish Press* reported somewhat unusually in normal circumstances that 'an Irish delegation will be sent to the eighteenth Assembly of the League of Nations'.[17] The agenda for the 1937 Assembly was a mere formality. Cremins, writing in late July mentioned the Spanish Civil War, the renewed Sino-Japanese conflict, re-armament and general unrest in Europe and

12 Ibid., 803.
13 Ibid., 804.
14 Ibid., 819.
15 NA, D.F/A, 126/35, Cremins–Walshe, 28 May 1937.
16 Ibid.
17 *Irish Press*, 24 August 1937.

told Rynne that, 'anything may happen between this and September'.[18] Cremins still felt that de Valera ought to attend the Assembly even if solely to meet the other foreign ministers present. With Europe 'within measurable distance of finding itself another Spain', Cremins considered that de Valera would have much to contribute, especially as his policy of preventive diplomacy needed to be publicised when 'the alternative is almost certain war, where everybody will lose'.

Cremins and Rynne remained unsure of de Valera's intention to attend the 1937 Assembly. Rynne felt that he should not as the Assembly agenda was not important and went as far as recommending that no member of the Government should attend. In Rynne's opinion the only reason de Valera should attend was if there was any chance of a good office for the taking. Cremins was urged to quietly sound out the possibilities.

Rynne's comments were part of a telling personal letter. His mood was upbeat but the letter reads as if he was putting on a brave face considering increasing irrelevancy of the League. Cremins was to 'prepare for the best and expect the worst'. Rynne reflected, with rose-tinted glasses, on the changes in the League section since Cremins had been 'running the show from the home front'. The workload had increased as Rynne found himself 'suddenly confronted three weeks before an Assembly with a lot of documents ... of minor importance ... which have to be mastered "tant bien que mal" in a rush'. The more optimistic days of the early thirties were also a more relaxing time; by 1937 the 'days are past when the "League Section" was a special branch full of maps and French newspapers and peace'.

At the last moment, de Valera decided he would attend the Assembly. Rynne was caught off-guard and quickly contacted Cremins as he was 'liable at any moment to be put through the third degree on the matter' by de Valera.[19] Rynne felt that the Minister was 'in the mood for taking definite decisions' and so he needed up to the minute information to satisfy de Valera. The pressing concerns were the situation in Spain and in Palestine.

Cremins response was a list of possible areas 'as it occurs to me'.[20] Conscious of the growing inevitability of war, it was 'the dangerous international situation and the deterioration since the last Assembly' that was of most concern to Cremins. This revolved around renewed conflict in the Far East and the Spanish war. The brooding catastrophe which was the 'general malaise in central Europe which is a result of the peace treaties of 1919, and of the will during the past seventeen years on the part of some of the states who won the war to continue the penalties and the effects of the treaties'. Cremins felt that it was this underlying cause which was running contrary to the aims of the League and diminishing its value.

In his despatches during the late 1930s Cremins constantly wrote of the

18 NA, D.F/A, 126/37, Cremins–Rynne, 23 July 1937.
19 Ibid., Rynne–Cremins, 26 August 1937.
20 Ibid., Cremins–Walshe, 4 September 1937.

destructive capacity of the coming conflict being 'infinitely more disastrous to civilisation than the last'. Cremins was advocating appeasement with territorial transfer to ameliorate grievances. He considered that governments should 'be prepared to make sacrifices if their peoples are to be spared. I have in mind even the return of some territories.' The General Settlement concept that was central to de Valera's European policy in the late 1930s may appear naive. Cremins was aware of its idealism, and felt such a policy was difficult to put in practice. The difficulties were nothing compared to those that would follow another global war and Cremins wondered, 'will the next generation have to face another catastrophe as a result'. No longer could Ireland call for mere reform of the League. The climate on the continent had outgrown the Geneva organisation; the possibility of war had spread continent wide and was threatening to engulf Europe. The League was only as effective as its members wanted it to be and was a reflection of the world environment in which it existed. There could be no hope for the League in the climate of 1937 and Cremins, with growing despair, thought that appeasement was the only way out. The powers had to meet to thrash out the 'root cause of the malaise in Europe' but Cremins could not conceive of a world that wished to envelop itself in a renewed global war: 'these are matters for statesmen and not for soldiers'. There was little role for the League in the settlement of these disputes. 'It would of course', Cremins later argued, 'have been all to the good if they could have been settled long ago within the League context, but what does it matter now how they are settled, if they are settled'.[21] Such sentiments were the basis of Ireland's perspective on the European crisis of the later thirties.

The memorandum may indicate more about Cremins's pessimism than his desire to give de Valera a frame of reference from which to devise a speech. Rather than repeat the same general speech that he had made in July 1936, de Valera, who was elected one of the Vice-Presidents of the Assembly, felt compelled to deal with the Spanish question. After Russian, German and Italian involvement in the war, the internationalisation of the conflict in Spain became a growing concern through the year. The 1937 Assembly saw for the last time nearly all of Europe's foreign ministers present at Geneva as the Spanish question dominated the Assembly. They attempted in vain to effect a settlement of the question of foreign intervention.

The League sidelined: The Spanish Civil War 1936–9

The Spanish Civil War began on the 18 July 1936.[22] The British Government feared that international intervention would lead to chaos and conflict across

21 NA, D.F/A 126/73, Cremins–Walshe, 29 August 1938.
22 Non-intervention was carried out outside the framework of the League of Nations and so will only be dealt with insofar as it impinges on Irish activities at the League.

the continent. Blum, the French Prime Minister proposed an international Non-Intervention Committee to prevent the Spanish conflict spreading. An Anglo-French Non-Intervention Committee was set up. The Spanish Civil War was outside the League's framework; to quote Walters, 'only at intervals, and incompletely' was it brought within the field of action of the League.[23]

On 18 August de Valera told the Cabinet that the French Minister in Dublin had informed him about the Non-Intervention proposals. De Valera then mentioned that he had informed the French Minister that the Free State agreed in principle with the terms.[24] There was no Cabinet discussion, the letter to Pierre Guerlet, the French Minister in Dublin informing him of Ireland's acceptance had been sent on 14 August. This caused consternation in the Irish Legation in Paris as the French press were aware of Ireland's adhesion before the Irish Minister.[25] On 23 August 1936 Ireland publicly announced its support for non-intervention. Ireland did not want to make foreign enemies and simply wanted to keep out of the conflict. The Dáil would pass legislation that would prohibit the export of arms and ammunition to Spain. Later a fine of £500 or two years in jail was imposed on persons volunteering for service in Spain. There was much domestic discontent that Ireland did not break diplomatic relations with the Madrid Government. Ireland refused to alter the diplomatic status quo and resolutely determined to stick to a policy of non-intervention.

The February 1937 Dáil debates on the Non-Intervention Bill were bitter, invoking base religious and political insults that showed the levels of misunderstanding, supported by passion, amongst TDs. The bill was passed by 77 votes to 50 on 24 February. De Valera showed his complete mastery over external affairs in his handling of the issue and Ireland continued to preserve strict impartiality.

The international blockade of Spain and the Pyrenees, controlled by the Non-Intervention Committee, began in March 1937. Observers were placed on all ships sailing to Spain. The Free State passed the Merchant Shipping (Spanish Civil War) Act to enforce the scheme in Irish law. Ireland supplied maritime and land officials to police the scheme and was prepared to contribute £2000 towards the costs. De Valera was not going to give in on non-intervention. He would not reverse his policy to appease domestic interests.

For a general account of Ireland's stance towards the conflict in Spain see J. Bowyer Bell 'Ireland and the Spanish Civil War', *Studia Hibernica*, Vol. 7 (1969), pp. 137–63, and Keogh, *Europe*, chapter 3.
23 Walters, *History*, p. 721.
24 NA, Cabinet Minutes, G2/12 C7/300, 18 August 1936.
25 Non-intervention policy was solely in de Valera's hands; on 22 December 1936 when discussing the extension of non-intervention to the despatch of volunteers and financial assistance the Cabinet decided that the, 'decision as to the policy to be adopted in regard to this proposal was left to the President'. NA, D.F/A, 227/87.

Ireland would stay with the non-intervention powers. However the Non-Intervention Committee did not stop Germany and Italy helping Franco's Nationalist rebels. The Spanish Government argued at the League that the fair conduct of war in Spain was impeded by the arms embargo. Though the Spanish civil war first appeared on the Council agenda in December 1936 and from then on to 1939 was a common feature at the Assembly and the Council, only at the 1937 Assembly was the matter fully faced up to by the League.

France and Britain admitted that though the conflict had been localised, non-intervention was a farce and was openly violated. Along with the Republican Spanish representative there was a movement to end non-intervention unless all foreign combatants were withdrawn immediately to allow the Spanish Government forces to import arms. A resolution to this end was constructed at the Sixth Committee. It was unlikely that foreign forces would be withdrawn and the days of the non-intervention agreement looked numbered.

The resolution was welcomed by Russia and resented by the Axis powers. It was an issue which presented de Valera with a dilemma when the draft resolution came up for discussion in the Sixth Committee on 30 September. Ireland approved of the removal of foreign forces from Spain, but disagreed with the formulation of the resolution which could be construed as a threat to end non-intervention. Ireland would always support non-intervention. De Valera wanted the draft resolution to be amended to read that 'certain members' would be prepared to reconsider non-intervention. This would let Ireland vote for the resolution, the general aims of which they supported, but not to be implicated in the ending of a policy they approved. When the sponsoring powers made it clear that the resolution was a unit and could not be revised further, Ireland had no option but to, 'abstain from voting as the only way to avoid a misrepresentation of our attitude and the attitude of our Government'.[26] De Valera considered that even if various subtleties were contained in the resolution's wording to show that it was not a threat, the general public would regard its acceptance as an end to non-intervention. De Valera abstained from voting and said that he would make a public presentation of his Government's case to the Assembly.

On 2 October de Valera told the Assembly that 'We believe in the policy of non-intervention, because that policy respected the right of the Spanish people to decide for themselves how they should be governed and who should be their rulers ... We deplore the interventions and the counter-interventions which make Spain a cockpit for every European antagonism.'[27] Ireland would not accept the resolution because it would misrepresent Ireland's support for non-intervention. Only certain of the parties to the non-intervention agreement were prepared to let it lapse. De Valera made it clear that 'the Irish Government will not be one of those to take any share in that responsibility

---

26 Eamon de Valera, *Peace and War* (Dublin, 1944), p. 61.
27 Ibid., pp. 61–2.

... [O]ur Government is not being committed to any policy of action which might result from the termination of the Non-Intervention Agreement.'[28]

The resolution was put to a vote, only Portugal and Albania voted against it, thirty-two states voted in favour, and Ireland, though in favour of the portion of the resolution calling for the removal of foreign forces, abstained with many others. These states could not bring themselves to vote for a policy which Russia would approve and Italy resent and which in addition would escalate the conflict in Europe. Spain vanished from the League agenda and non-intervention remained, though increasingly a dead letter.

The 1938 Assembly: Munich

The League simply noted the Anschluss between Germany and Austria. All eyes turned to Czechoslovakia, now caught in the jaws of the Reich. The negotiations between Britain, France, Italy and Germany over the fate of the Sudetenland showed the League's redundancy. No one turned to Geneva to involve the League during the Sudeten–Czech crisis. It was on Nuremburg, Prague, Berchesgaden, and finally Munich, that attention centred.

During July 1938 Cremins urged Murphy to suggest that de Valera attend the September Assembly. De Valera's increased international prestige in the wake of the 1938 Anglo-Irish agreements would be a useful starting point for a campaign for the Presidency of the Assembly. The formal agenda might look less interesting than usual, but with the volatile climate in European politics anything might come before the Assembly. The League might be redundant, but its high offices still gave a good vantage point for a small state to observe the European crisis.

Cremins did not rate the chances of League reform very highly: 'practically nothing of a constructive character has so far emerged'.[29] During the 1938 Assembly the remaining 43 members of the League freed themselves from the obligations of the Covenant. They argued that the Covenant was a good idea but was not practical in the present circumstances. Henceforth, they would look after their national security by their own methods. Ireland had, for practical purposes, followed this line since 1936.

The 1938 Assembly was de Valera's swan-song at the League. Though openly lacking faith in the League, he returned to Geneva to see it through its dying days. The dire prophesy of de Valera's 1932 speech was in the process of being fulfilled. His election as President clashed with Hitler's speech at Nuremberg recounting the grievances of the Sudeten Germans. The announcement of German mobilisation and the invasion of Czechoslovakia were expected to follow.

28 Ibid., p. 63.
29 NA, D.F/A, 126/73, Cremins–Murphy, 26 July 1938.

De Valera's opening address to the Assembly was one of platitudes. It focused on the worsening Czechoslovak crisis. The selfishness of national interests was the theme of the speech. States were incapable of implementing just international settlements because of national interests. De Valera considered that 'to be just is to be truly wise' but considered that states were neither wise nor just. He urged the states to cling to the League and use it 'as an instrument for the righting of international wrong wherever it exists'.[30] However it was to cling as to the mast of a sinking hulk. De Valera's concluding hope that 'this Assembly [would] close with the immediate dangers passed and a beginning made for the coming together of that conference for peace upon the basis of justice' made it clear that the League would have no part in resolving the crisis.

As the Assembly worked through its weary agenda, the Sudeten Crisis reached its climax. Chamberlain met Hitler at Berchesgaden and Godesberg and with no solution in sight war appeared the only way to solve the Sudeten problem. De Valera, though President of the Assembly, had no mechanism by which to involve himself or the League in the moves that led to the Munich meeting. All he could do was to speak of his hope that the crisis would resolve itself peacefully. The Assembly continued about its business with the real attention being paid to the meetings between Hitler and Chamberlain. Cremins felt that, 'in Geneva generally opinion seems to be more calm than it was a year or so ago, although everyone realises the danger of the situation. There seems to be a feeling that war is not imminent, but military preparations for defence are said to be proceeding all around the frontier.'[31]

As President of the Assembly, de Valera sent a personal note of support to Chamberlain. Chamberlain and de Valera had developed a good relationship as they negotiated the 1938 Anglo-Irish agreement. De Valera's 'General Settlement' policy was very close to Chamberlain's own ideas on appeasement and de Valera clearly hoped that the Munich agreement could be built upon.[32] Sean Lester, now Deputy Secretary General, was aghast at Chamberlain; writing in his diary Lester recorded that 'what Chamberlain has done is a logical sequence of the policy pursued by Britain and France during the past two years; they paralysed the League of Nations; they gave no help to the weak attacked by the strong; they ran away every time a threat was uttered'.[33]

Unwilling to hamper Chamberlain and aware that Germany and Italy had no time for the League, de Valera did not attempt any initiative as President of the Assembly. There was no precedent for the President of the Assembly taking such an initiative. It would have been up to Secretary General Joseph Avenol who hankered after the re-admission of Germany and Italy to the

30 Eamon de Valera, *Peace and War* (Dublin, 1944), p. 68.
31 NA, D.F.A. 19/40, Cremins–Walshe, 1 September 1938.
32 *Irish Press*, 1 October 1938.
33 Sean Lester diary, 10 October 1938, quoted in Elmer Bendiner, *A time for angels* (London, 1975) p. 394.

League and would not have wished to endanger his chances. Deirdre McMahon has commented that de Valera did not consider any initiative as Taoiseach because of its potentially detrimental effect on Ireland's neutrality.[34] The impotency of the office of President of the Assembly, the low prestige of the League itself and national concerns about the impact of such an appeal on Ireland's neutrality led de Valera to discretely support Chamberlain, but not involve himself either as a League office holder or as an Irish statesman in the crisis. De Valera's telegram to Chamberlain of 27 September simply urged Chamberlain to 'let nothing daunt you or deflect you in your effort to secure peace' and to remember that there were tens of millions of people praying for the success of his approaches to Hitler.[35] The Taoiseach had written to Archbishop John Charles McQuaid that 'the League has lost whatever moral authority it had'; evidently de Valera did not expect the League to make much of a contribution to the Sudeten Crisis. Though he did continue that he felt that 'because of its promise for the future ... I am convinced that we should not abandon the existing League however ineffective it may be'.[36] Clearly the League ideal remained important to de Valera to the last. De Valera's only active involvement was sponsoring a unanimously accepted resolution in the Assembly that it had observed the crisis 'with deep and growing anxiety' and were certain that the crisis would be solved by peaceful means.

In a broadcast to the United States de Valera made no secret of the League's impotency, speaking of the delegations 'following with anxiety, but with hope, the effort that is being made on Mr Chamberlain's initiative to obtain a just and peaceful way out of the present situation'.[37] His sentiments made it clear that he would not attempt any personal initiative. De Valera spoke of the feeling in a schoolroom at the end of term when 'the business is being got through as a mechanical task, whilst the minds of those engaged in it are far away, distracted by the urge of a more compelling interest'. His hope that Governments would see the catastrophic impact of a continental war was falling on deaf ears. He again called for the voluntary grouping of nations in the cause of peace but only once 'the soul of Europe is at peace'. His conclusion was an acceptance that his idealism for an international institution was in vain by the standards of the time. Not until 'the Great Powers of Europe have come together to settle their differences and establish some modus vivendi for themselves' could an ideal like the League operate effectively. As if aware that time was running out for the League and for peace he concluded ominously: 'I have not time to say more'.

The four great European powers met at Munich and on 30 September an agreement to cede the Sudetenland to Czechoslovakia was reached without

---

34 Deirdre McMahon, 'Ireland, the Dominions and the Munich crisis', *ISIA*, Vol. 1 No. 1, pp. 30-7.
35 NA, D.F/A 126/73, de Valera–Chamberlain, 27 September 1938.
36 FLK, de Valera papers, file 451.
37 Eamon de Valera, *Peace and War* (Dublin, 1944), pp. 69-70.

the involvement of the Czechs. Cremins, writing in late August 1938 felt that, 'it is incumbent on any state, the continuity of whose existence in case of serious conflict is dependent on other states to make all necessary sacrifices for the removal of sources of trouble in order that those other states also concerned should not be needlessly involved in conflict'.[38] It is not difficult to see that Cremins was referring to the Sudeten Germans. The Assembly closed on 30 September, the same day as the Munich agreement was signed.

At the close of the Assembly de Valera wondered whether Europe 'having gazed over the brink, shrank back appalled by the ghastly prospect of what it saw in the abyss'. He spoke of the League's inability to influence events: 'while these events were taking place and these efforts were being made, we in the Assembly were performing the task which lay immediately to our hands'.[39] He referred to the growing social and humanitarian activities of the League 'there is hardly a domain of human life or action in which the League does not take an interest and cannot play an effective part'. All, that is, except the most pressing political event of the time. It had been the most extraordinary of Assemblies, opening on the day of Hitler's Nuremberg speech and closing as the Munich agreement was signed and yet the Assembly was involved in none of the power-brokering. For the first time since Locarno neither the French nor the British Foreign ministers were present and there was ' "a tragic air of unreality" hanging over the proceedings'.[40] Europe breathed a sigh of relief as it gained a respite from war thanks to Munich. De Valera left Geneva for the last time.

The descent to war

Cremins weekly reports to Dublin read as a fascinating first-hand account of the final months of peace in 1939. The expectations and rumours of peace and war ebb and flow to be replaced by new concerns over the intentions of Hitler and the fate of remaining Czechoslovak territories and Poland. Swiss domestic affairs took up more of Cremins's attention. The Swiss were concerned that when Hitler was contented in Eastern Europe he would turn west. Cremins felt that they were quietly confident of their military capabilities if there was an invasion, having fortified their borders. With a military build-up evident there were 'what are said to be anti-tank devices are to be seen in the neighbourhood of Geneva and other roads and passes in the Jura'.[41] At the centre of Europe, Swiss opinion was a good barometer of

---

38 NA, D.F/A, 126/73, Cremins–Walshe, 29 August 1938.
39 Eamon de Valera, *Peace and War* (Dublin, 1944), pp. 76–80.
40 NA, D.F/A 126/73 copy of letter sent to Lester by a friend and forwarded to de Valera.
41 NA, D.F/A, confidential reports, Geneva 19/40, Cremins–Walshe, 22 February 1939. Subsequent unattributed quotations are from this source.

continental opinion. Cremins's reports are remarkably perceptive. In February 1939 he felt that 'there is little disposition to regard the outbreak of a European war as being in any way imminent'.[42] The real concern for Switzerland and western Europe was 'long distance preparation in case an excuse should ever have to be found to break through the small countries at either end of the Maginot line, rather than an immediate menace'.

The immediate menace was still in Eastern Europe. On 15–16 March German troops occupied the remaining Czech territories and set up the German protectorates of Bohemia and Moravia. The reaction in Switzerland was to be expected: '[A] state amounting to alarm prevails among the population here, in Switzerland in general'.[43] They increased the political temperature on the continent and made clear 'the diminishing possibility of a peaceful settlement, and therefore the increasing danger in which the small western states would find themselves in the event of war'.

Many of his diplomatic colleagues in Geneva felt that there was no cause for alarm, but few would divulge their views on Poland. Cremins spoke to Sean Lester on the situation in Poland and found Lester less than optimistic. Cremins had heard confidentially from his former colleague:

> that the situation in Danzig is serious, and that developments provoked by Germany may be soon expected there. The position of Poland *vis-à-vis* Germany has been distinctly weakened by the acquisition of Czechoslovakia by the Reich, by much the same way as Czechoslovakia has been weakened by the annexation of Austria.

Events were moving towards a denouement in Europe, but Hitler played his cards close to his chest and the question in Geneva was where would Germany's next move be. Some thought that Memel would flare up. Others that the ball would be passed to Mussolini:

> It is said that amongst the population of Italy that the *axe* is not at all too popular and the Italian people will not appreciate being dragged to the verge of war for gains which always seem to go to Germany. Italy therefore may be tempted to take a risk in order to have something to show for her membership of the axe. Snr. Mussolini's speech on the 26 March is looked forward to as an indication of possible developments in the Mediterranean.

Opinion in Switzerland returned to the calm of February and waited the next moves which it seemed would be in Eastern Europe or the Mediterranean. On 1 April, in the aftermath of the Anglo-Polish Guarantee, Cremins reported

---

42 Ibid.
43 Cremins–Walshe, 20 March 1939.

the general impression amongst his colleagues as one of 'the greatest relief that Great Britain has broken away from tradition by giving, along with France, the guarantee to Poland'. The barometer again pointed to war, though Cremins found:

> the general situation is regarded here today as an improvement, although of course all the main problems remain unsettled. I should add however that on Thursday Mr Jacklin, the Treasurer of the League told me that he found international financial circles pessimistic, and he said that in London the view which formerly was 'war possible, but appeasement probable' was now reversed 'appeasement possible but war probable'.

It is important to see this ebb and flow to get a picture of how rumours and stories in diplomatic circles were developed by actual events and occurrences in the final months of peace in 1939. Cremins's reports picture the uncertain state of Europe on a month to month basis through 1939. These coupled with Cremins's everyday meetings and activities give a more human picture of the diplomatic representative of a small state trying to decipher the cryptic events of an uncertain world. Cremins could only rely on his contacts, many of whom were also from small states and had little access to first hand information from the Chancelleries of Europe. The Anglo-Polish Guarantee had a short-term calming effect, though 'opinion continues calm in regard to the present situation, but no-one would venture to prophesy regarding the eventual outcome'.[44]

On 7 April Italy invaded Albania, Cremins wrote how:

> the mild optimism which existed here regarding the immediate future has been replaced by something like the alarm that was evident a couple of weeks ago. What has greatly added to the shock here, and is the subject of general comment, is that Italy, a Christian and Catholic nation, should have selected Good Friday for the start of such measures.

It did not seem that the invasion of Albania would lead to a European war. However Italy's actions did contribute to the increasing of tension on the continent and:

> the actions of the western powers and Hitler's next move as a counter-action to the British–Polish agreement are looked forward to with anxiety. I share the general view that it is becoming exceedingly difficult to foresee any outcome except war. Germany and Italy are now at the

---

44 Cremins–Walshe, 1 April 1940.

stage when they will be forced more and more to gamble on uncertainties, for any more serious upset to the equilibrium in Europe or the Mediterranean must eventually produce military reactions from Britain and France.[45]

With a degree of humanity, Cremins concluded that he was afraid that 'my report is in a more pessimistic strain than usual, but I am not alone in my pessimism'. His Argentinean and Bulgarian colleagues felt the same way. Cremins showed his lack of understanding of the Dictators, a common error amongst democratic statesmen before the war when he tried to put on a brave face by hoping 'that a world war would be so disastrous for winners and losers that it would not make common sense, and that must be evident to all in whose hands the decisions lie'. Tragically, this was not the case.

By late April the pessimism and gloom had not abated. News was filtering through of a possible attack on Denmark. Cremins met the German Consul and casually asked him his opinions on the international outlook. He blamed Britain and France and did not feel that war was imminent. Cremins then asked him 'whether he really felt that nothing which would result in war was likely to happen in the near future. He said, something will come, but not now. I thought that he had lost a great deal of the sang-froid which he had displayed on the previous occasion.'[46] Cremins did not believe that in any quarter there was a hankering for a European war. He urged Walshe to persuade de Valera, still President of the Assembly, to try some last minute appeal to the democracies. This received short shrift from External Affairs. Boland doubted 'whether the course suggested by Mr Cremins is really politic'.[47] Rynne considered that the idea was:

> no doubt admirable, [but] it is hard to see what benefit this country would receive out of a demarche by the Minister such as he suggests. Unless we could be sure that such a demarche would result to our international prestige (and not the contrary) it had better not be tried out at present.[48]

On his return from leave in late August, Cremins reported the shock of the Molotov–Ribbentrop Pact of 23 August. The terms were regarded:

> as a cynical performance, and as a serious let down for Britain and France and their Allies on the one hand and for Japan on the other, the balance being against the western powers. No doubt Russia felt it

---

45 Cremins–Walshe, 8 April.
46 Cremins–Walshe, 28 April.
47 Boland–Rynne, May 1939.
48 Rynne–Boland, May 1939.

highly desirable in her weakened situation to relieve her western frontier in case of possible trouble in the far east.[49]

Cremins felt that:

In the present crisis public opinion in Geneva remains remarkably calm. Practically every one clings to the hope, that, despite the measures that are being taken in Germany against Poland, and the countermeasures in other countries, the actual outbreak of war may even yet be avoided.

By 31 August the situation was:

regarded today as being much more tense than during the past few days. The opinion is in fact freely expressed that war may break out at any moment ... In the international circles, hope has almost reached vanishing point. I myself consider the situation as being extremely grave, the chief danger being that the position of Danzig may precipitate events in the pursuit of the Nazi programme.

Cremins gave a vivid picture of preparations in Switzerland with emergency measures in increasing evidence. Public buildings, bridges and railways were being guarded by the military and food controls had come into operation. All these measures he felt, brought home to the population the seriousness of the situation. There was no chance of a settlement. On 1 September German forces began their invasion of Poland. Cremins reported to Dublin how:

rumours that the Germans had crossed the Polish frontier at 5.45 a.m. began to circulate and some time later it was confirmed that the expected emergency had actually arisen. The wireless news gave no indication that hostilities had begun. General mobilisation in Switzerland was preparing to take effect from today.[50]

Most people, he continued, 'are now satisfied that a European war had practically begun ... a fight to the finish as being the only possible solution, as in the war of 1914–18, and in Spain etc'. As President of the adjourned 19th Assembly de Valera informed Avenol 'that in his opinion a state of emergency had arisen such as to necessitate the bringing into force from 2 September the Assembly's resolution of 30 September 1930 conferring on them special powers'.[51]

49 Cremins–Walshe, 26 August 1939.
50 Cremins–Walshe, 2 September 1939.
51 NA, BE, S Gen 1/5, 2 September 1939.

Swiss neutrality and public opinion were the central theme of Cremins's late 1939 reports. Public opinion was high and talk of resistance if Swiss territory was invaded resonated through the press. The Swiss Government was carrying out a strict policy of neutrality, though with the fighting taking place in Eastern Europe Switzerland was breathing easily. Cremins felt that this would be short-term and had 'no doubt that the situation may yet be serious for small countries at the end of the Maginot line'.[52] Daily life in Geneva was,

> much quieter than usual, with so many men withdrawn for military shortage, there is no shortage of food, but people are using their reserve stocks of commodities such as sugar, rice and certain cereals, etc., which have been temporarily withdrawn from the market. The restaurants function as usual. Petrol has been rationed during the past couple of weeks, 60 litres a fortnight are allowed and apparently this will be continued. There have been no blackouts at night so far, but the lighting up and down has been reduced and France across the lake seems to settle down each evening into complete darkness.

Everyday life for Cremins took on a new meaning as war decrees took effect. His reports manage to merge the events of high politics with everyday life to give an overall account of day-to-day life in Europe on the outbreak of the war. At the Irish Legation preparations were made for the destruction of confidential records. Some preliminary weeding and burning took place. Many confidential reports from MacWhite and Lester's years were destroyed.

By November it seemed that events were soon to hot up on the western front. 'The Belgians and the Dutch here', Cremins reported,

> have become, in the last few days, extremely anxious, as they seem to expect a German attack at least on Holland at any moment. The view is held that the Germans cannot remain still indefinitely, and that they will try for success with their overwhelming force in the hope that they might be able to consolidate any position gained.[53]

The Swiss authorities were stepping up air defences but remained optimistic as long as Italy did not enter the war. For the remainder of the year Cremins paid attention to the Russo-Finnish war and the moods in Geneva and across the continent. He paid little attention to the on-going struggle between Lester and Avenol to keep the League going and did not appear to file a report on the December session of the Assembly. The 20th Session, to open on 11 December 1939, had been put off from September and was the last time the

---

52 Cremins–Walshe, 11 September 1939.
53 Cremins–Walshe, 11 November 1939.

Assembly met before the fall of France and the Low countries in May 1940. It adjourned and did not meet again until April 1946.

De Valera, despite convoking the meeting and requests from the League, did not attend the Assembly. Lester was gravely disappointed and considered the failure to attend a grave error on de Valera's part. Cremins instead attended in de Valera's place. The Taoiseach had important business to attend to at the Fianna Fáil Ard Fheis. Lester felt that Ireland was reneging on its international duty by not attending. He was also deeply critical of Ireland's failure to take on board the allied cause and considered that Dublin was being pressurised into neutrality by Germany. He was not against Irish neutrality when it was announced, but rather was critical of its implementation.

As 1940 began rumours continued to circulate about a German outflanking attack on the Maginot line through Switzerland and the Low countries. Cremins paid little attention to them and the pressure lightened for the Swiss when Germany invaded Denmark and then Norway in April 1940. Anxiety soon grew in Geneva at the possible fate of the European neutrals as 'the feeling is growing that the turn of Switzerland will come eventually'.[54]

On 10 May 1940 Germany invaded France through the Low Countries. A month later Italy entered the war. France surrendered on 22 June and on 10 July Pétain became head of state in Vichy France. Cremins's reports for this period have not survived and were probably incinerated. Cremins wrote to Boland on 31 May: 'I have burned also all the confidential reports I could trace. I had already the vast majority of them separated. The term ' "confidential files" includes all papers, publications, which would embarrass governments'.[55] With the League defunct and being run-down for the course of the war, Cremins's need to remain in Geneva diminished. On 11 October 1940 Francis Cremins ceased to be Irish Permanent Representative to the League of Nations and became Chargé d'Affaires at Berne. Ireland's official involvement with the League of Nations, except for a cosmetic yearly contribution, was at an end.

Cremins at Berne: 1940–6

In Berne Cremins was nominally responsible for League of Nations affairs, but his main task was to keep Dublin informed of the operation of Swiss neutrality and to report on the progress of the war from a Swiss perspective. Walshe was particularly keen on infringements of neutrality urging Cremins to 'report fully all infringements of Swiss neutrality by air or otherwise stating action taken by Swiss govt and reply made by offending belligerent'.[56]

54 Cremins–Walshe, 10 April 1940.
55 NA, D.F/A, BE, S Gen 1/6, Cremins–Boland, 31 May 1940.
56 NA, D/F/A, Secretary's Files, P12/7, Cremins–Walshe 18 November 1940.

Through November 1940 there was, Cremins reported, speculation in the Swiss press about the fate of the former Irish Treaty ports, focusing on the question from Britain's perspective and her defence needs. In general, the Swiss were impartial towards Ireland's neutrality.

Opening a new legation meant a round of the diplomatic community in Berne. Through December and November Cremins met its various members, neutral, allied and axis, and reported on his conversations to Dublin. The Papal Nuncio thought an 'attack on [Irish] ports was improbable owing to the reaction of the United States and the Dominions'.[57] The Italians were friendly and the French and the Germans respectfully and positively referred to Irish neutrality. 'All gave me', Cremins reported, 'a very friendly welcome and displayed interest in policy and conditions in Ireland ... I find that people generally consider danger to Ireland comes from one side or the other according to their own predilections'.[58] General opinion was that the war would be long and drawn out and would not end without a clash between Germany and Russia. Cremins's reports concentrated on the progress of the war, Swiss troop movements, and security measures such as blackouts and frontier defence.

In early 1941 Cremins submitted a yearly report for the previous year. He mentioned the reduced number of Irish citizens in the country, there were only 3 to 4 Irish students at the University at Fribourg, and tourist traffic had diminished. Cremins's main duties centred around trade relations and repatriating Irish citizens. References to the League are few and sparse in these reports. Edward Phelan had departed with the ILO to Montreal, but Lester remained in the Palais des Nations. There were other Irish nationals of lower rank among the greatly reduced staff of the Secretariat, but Cremins spoke vaguely of them, 'when the League of Nations was active there was a fair number of Irish at Geneva, but these, for the most part, have now left Switzerland'.[59] Strangely he never mentions Lester though, as we will see, the two men remained in contact through the war. Cremins was very correct in his interpretation of his mandate and official reports were not the place to mention such contacts.

Cremins and Lester wrote to each other weekly and the friendly banter of the letters adds a great depth to the historian's understanding of their friendship. When Lester was moving into a new house in the spring of 1941 he offered Cremins, a keen gardener, free range through his plants to take what he liked. Lester invited Cremins down to stay as he would 'enjoy wandering around the grounds'.[60] When Cremins was in Geneva on League business connected to his post on the League pensions board, he an Lester would

57 Ibid., Cremins–Walshe, 13 December 1940.
58 Ibid.
59 NA, D/F/A, Confidential Reports, 313/5, Cremins–Walshe, 10 January 1941.
60 NA, BE, C1, Lester–Cremins, 19 March 1941.

meet, as they would also in Berne when Lester was passing through. Lester referred to this as Cremins, 'coming home' to Geneva.[61]

Lester's wartime years in Geneva have been characterised as rather a lonely vigil.[62] Cremins's personal papers bring out Lester's frustration at Ireland's neutrality and her failure to adequately pay her League contribution, they do not show the definite strain on his personal life that separation from his wife and children must have led to, but they do show that he had a regular, if unofficial stream of Irish visitors. William Warnock, who represented Ireland in Berlin during the war, Gerald O'Kelly de Gallagh, Sean Murphy, and Denis McDonald, to name a few had occasion to pass through Switzerland and would call in on their former colleague. O'Kelly de Gallagh wrote to Cremins in October 1941 thanking Cremins for the hospitality he had shown to him whilst he was in Berne, and in passing mentioning he had found Lester 'in good form' when they lunched at Geneva's Cornavin railway station.[63] Cremins personal papers show a great degree of interaction on a personal level between the Irish diplomatic community on the continent during World War II. The need to pass through neutral Switzerland meant that Cremins was in continuing contact with his colleagues; there was a steady stream of visitors to the Berne legation. Thanking Cremins for his cordial welcome for them whilst passing through Berne in late December 1942, Denis R. McDonald, then Secretary of the Irish legation in Rome, wrote of how he and his wife, Una, owed Cremins 'a lot of thanks for pleasant memories of the Grill Rooms'![64]

The League's operations had now been run down by Lester. Cremins sole reference to the League in January 1941 was that 'this legation remains the channel of communication with the League of Nations and the International Labour Office, though in the existing circumstances the communications with these organisations are not numerous'.[65] The League was no longer of importance. There is a sad irony that at the moment when an Irish national was in charge of the organisation that Ireland had put so much into between the wars, Ireland had no need of the League or the Covenant. Introducing the League estimate of a symbolic ten pounds in the Dáil in July 1941, de Valera noted that the League's political functions had ceased to exist but that its technical activities were continuing at a reduced pace. Politically, Ireland had little use for the League, but de Valera argued that the technical activities and functions should be kept in the post-war world. Ireland, he made clear, would not leave the League. Neutrality had isolated the state, termination of League membership would further increase this isolation. Irish censorship, of which

61 Ibid., Lester–Cremins, 22 September 1941.
62 See Elmer Bendiner, *A time for angels* (London, 1975), pp. 379–406, for such an analysis.
63 NA, BE, C1, O'Kelly de Gallagh–Cremins, 7 October, 1941.
64 Ibid., 28 December 1941.
65 NA, D/F/A, confidential reports, 313/5, Cremins–Walshe, 10 January 1941.

as a former journalist Lester was highly critical, meant that it took some time for the news to filter through about the reduced estimate. Lester was furious at this 'symbolic' estimate and wrote to Cremins that 'such a decision would have the appearance of a political decision'.[66] Cremins sent Lester the Dáil debates for the estimate as the newspapers were highly censored. On reading de Valera's speech accompanying the estimates, Lester found it 'sound and reasonable'.[67] Lester commented in a later letter how these parliamentary debates gave him 'some glimpse behind the curtains drawn over Ireland'.[68] Cremins had been passing on old newspapers, but Lester, though he read them for 'personal snippets', found them to show 'a complete absence of mental pabulum' due to the heavy censorship of the Irish press. Lester saw the need for such censorship during wartime, but felt that the degree imposed upon Ireland was 'undignified and unworthy of a people with any degree of political responsibility, dangerous for the present and dangerous for the future'.[69] Cremins did his best to pass on material relating to Ireland to Lester so as to give him a greater insight into the domestic situation in which Lester never lost interest.

Cremins increasingly dealt with enquiries from Irish nationals in Eastern Europe asking for information regarding their relatives in Ireland, or raising questions regarding passports or citizenship. Berne also became the channel of communication between the Irish legation in Vichy and the Irish Legation in Berlin. Lists of foreign airmen interned in Ireland were passed on to Cremins by Dublin for transmission to the Red Cross. Cremins's post remained very much an international one in the same vein as his posting at Geneva. Berne became a key part of the Irish diplomatic framework on the continent during the war.

Reference to the League continued to be minimal. In July 1942 the possibility arose of the League Supervisory Commission, which ran the organisation through the war, meeting in Ireland. Cremins had returned to Dublin on leave and floated the possibility with Boland. He brought with him Ms Rohde of the League Secretariat, who was in Dublin seeing him on the business of staff pensions at the League. Boland spoke to Walshe, who 'agreed that I [Boland] should tell Ms Rohde that we couldn't make any definite statement without speaking to our Minister but if the case arose we would be prepared to submit the matter to him and we thought it unlikely that he would see any objection'.[70] Rohde made clear that there was no present intention of holding a meeting of the Supervisory Commission in Dublin, but that the Treasurer of the League foresaw a possibility in future that it would be desirable to hold a meeting on neutral territory. Ireland's relations with the League might have

66 NA, BE, C1, Lester–Cremins, 5 August 1941.
67 Ibid., Lester also thanks Cremins for, 'remembering me when at your tobacconist'.
68 Ibid., 30 September 1941.
69 Ibid.
70 NA, D.F/A 226/75, Memo by Boland, 12 July 1943.

been reduced to the bare minimum, but there was still a degree of residual co-operation between the two.

After the Moscow conference of December 1943 talk of a new international organisation to replace the League grew. De Valera evaded answering questions in the Dáil about Ireland's attitude to such plans. In August and September 1944 at the Dumbarton Oaks Conference plans for the Charter of what became the United Nations were drafted.

John Hearne was now Minister to Canada and met Edward Phelan shortly after the Dumbarton Oaks Conference. Hearne reported to Walshe his conversation with Phelan: ' "I avoided Dumbarton Oaks" he said with a smile which seemed to convey the idea that, in his view, the Dumbarton Oaks Conference was one to be avoided'.[71] Phelan did not see how the ILO could have been represented at that conference. The old institutions of inter-war Europe were by-passed in the plans for post-war international organisations. Lester was sidelined in Geneva, Phelan knew his place, it was the superpowers and their closest allies, the powers of the Cold War that held sway. Ireland was not invited to the San Francisco Conference of April 1945 that set up the United Nations. Irish nationals might have helped preserve the League and the ILO throughout the war, Ireland herself might have been an avid supporter of the League, but there was no place for such beliefs in post-war Europe.

The birth of the United Nations

Excluded from the creation of the United Nations by her neutrality, Ireland was in the dark about the development of the new international organisation. With no staff in External Affairs dealing with what became the United Nations, Rynne by default as former head of the League of Nations section, began dealing with United Nations matters. Through 1945 and on to the first Assembly of the United Nations in London in January 1946 Cremins sent a series of commentaries on the new organisation comparing it to the League and speculating on its place in the post-war order.

The growing split in the wartime allies weighed heavily in Cremins's analysis of the effectiveness of the United Nations. He did not yet see the world in bi-polar terms and spoke of three or five great powers, but it was evident that, 'if their interests clash seriously, they will eventually come into armed conflict, and their immediate satellites will have to take sides, League or no League'.[72] The war had seriously affected Cremins's optimism and he felt that the lessons of 1919–45 had not been appreciated. Events in Poland,

---

71 NA, D.F/A, 417/1, Hearne–Walshe, 17 October 1944.
72 NA, D.F/A, 417/12, Cremins–Walshe, 30 June 1945. I would like to thank Dr Joseph M. Skelly for pointing out these files to me.

Greece, Iran and the Far East spelt disaster to him. Pearl Harbor meant that nations would remain armed in fear of a surprise attack; Cremins felt that disarmament did not stand much chance of success in the United Nations. The 'senseless cruelties of the present war in camps and otherwise' would hopefully spur the United Nations on to greater humanitarian actions than the League. The growing controversy in the nascent United Nations over the use of the veto made Cremins think that the organisation would be effectively paralysed. He considered that the development of regional pacts might alleviate this problem. A greater degree of international order was Cremins's basic concern, without this 'there is little hope that the world ... will not again blunder into experiences similar to those of the past years'.[73]

Writing in early July 1945, Cremins suggested that an organisation of sovereign nations was his hope for the United Nations. He felt that 'it will be very difficult to improve the new institution, if by improvement is meant a surrender of any rights retained by a member under the charter as now drawn'.[74] He was still concerned about the scope of the veto and wished to see the Great Powers views on it before considering whether the new international institution 'is likely to be a safeguard of world peace'.

By November 1945 Cremins had seen the draft charter and had time to consider it. He immediately hit on the issue that was to divide the United Nations through the Cold War:

> the effectiveness of the organisation in the case of a major dispute would be altogether dependent on the aggressor *not* being one of the five Permanent Members of the Security council, nor one of the satellite States of those members. In cases where the aggressor was one of those powers, or a satellite of one of them, the new organisation could be rendered inoperable under the right of veto accruing to the Permanent Members of the Security Council.[75]

The issue of whether absence constituted a veto or abstention constituted a blocking action also perplexed Cremins. This would keep the United Nations outside any future conflict which Cremins felt was probable 'from a development of a clash of interests which is unfortunately already visible between the Great Power members of the Security Council'. From the growing likelihood of this possibility Cremins concluded that the United Nations would probably remain ineffective. The 'Uniting for Peace' resolution of November 1950 eventually managed to break the impasse of the Superpower veto on United Nations actions. Cremins overall felt that the United Nations 'would be a distinct advance on the League of Nations for the maintenance of peace, if a

---

73 Ibid.
74 NA, D.F/A 417/12, Cremins–Rynne, 5 July 1945.
75 Ibid., Cremins–Walshe, 1 November 1945.

fairly equitable basis for peace were assured, and if the five Great Powers, members of the Security Council, continued their collaboration'—the likelihood of which he was now beginning to doubt.[76]

Ireland held back from immediate membership of the United Nations. Rynne wrote a revealing personal note to Cremins thanking him for his reports on the United Nations. He mentioned how External Affairs did 'not take to the UNO for many of the reasons which seem to endear it to you (that's a hard one!)'.[77] Ireland feared that the United Nations would be a tool of the victors, as in a sense it was to the mid 1950s. Ireland supported the United Nations because 'the new organisation, unlike the old one, possesses "teeth".' What External Affairs feared was that chapter seven of the Charter would prove to be ' "dragon's teeth" which will eventually be employed to grind up (1) the ex "enemy" states (2) the ex-neutrals and (3) the small nations, in that appropriate order'. Ireland clearly feared for her sovereignty in the United Nations as it initially appeared. Many of Ireland's national interests would be compromised. Rynne wondered whether Ireland would 'have to refuse to salute neutral Catholic Spain and have to take up arms every time a small state refuses to be bullied by a fellow who can veto action against himself?' There were many questions that Ireland would have to sort out before defining its attitude to the United Nations. In the new world order, reference to the state's experience at the League counted for nothing. The burgeoning Cold War was a new international order with new rules, as Ireland was to find when her request for United Nations membership was rejected in August 1946 after a Russian veto. Critical support and support for the League did not pay dividends in the United Nations.

The League was due to be dissolved during its final Assembly in the first week of April 1946. Cremins prepared for the dissolution in his work on the League staff pensions board and attended the Assembly as sole Irish delegate. He was taken under the wing of the British delegation who were determined to build relations with Ireland and help re-integrate Ireland into the world order. The proceedings were calm and paid tribute to the League. Cremins served on the nominations committee, but played little role in the Assembly. He did not make a valedictory speech on the League as many other states present did. All eyes were on the future and not the past. Cremins hoped for early United Nations membership for Ireland. The newly appointed Secretary General of the United Nations Trygve Lie had recently visited Lester and had 'expressed his urgent and keen desire that Ireland and Sweden, "two decent little countries" should as soon as possible become members'.[78]

76 Ibid.
77 Ibid., Rynne–Cremins, 15 January 1946.
78 Ibid., Lester–Walshe.

Conclusion

From 1936 to 1946 Ireland's slow dislocation from the League took place. Ireland paid less attention to the League from July 1936. It is difficult to speak of any definite League policy after de Valera's May 1937 speech on League policy to the Dáil other than idealised support. The public perception, based on de Valera's speeches to the Assembly, was of support for collective security. Greater attention was paid to the looming clash between the forces of Fascism and Democracy. Cremins was ideally placed in Geneva to get an overview of the late thirties European crisis.

De Valera paid less attention to external affairs in the late thirties and was more concerned about Anglo-Irish affairs until the signing of the 1938 agreements. In an interview with Lester in 1938 de Valera 'confessed that he had been following international affairs very little during recent months'. Lester was highly critical, writing that 'he is the Minister for External Affairs and we have been passing through grave international crises, but of course he was absolutely absorbed in the Anglo-Irish settlement'.[79] Lester and de Valera now had very different outlooks on the international situation. De Valera was determined to keep Ireland out of the looming conflict whereas Lester was hoping to band nations together to resist Fascist aggression. The remarks do throw some light on the low esteem that the League was held in after 1937. De Valera had other things on his mind, but Lester's criticism that this was not a moment when the portfolios of Taoiseach and Minister for External Affairs should have been combined on account of the sheer weight of each portfolio is one which has a degree of truth to it. De Valera's single-mindedness and stubbornness coupled with his apparent mastery of the portfolio to the exclusion of all others meant that Lester's criticisms would remain idle thoughts.

By the outbreak of the war the League mattered little except in the formal sense of the diminishing yearly contribution. By 1946 it was history. Ireland's rehabilitation in the international arena was now crucially important. Six years of war had effectively destroyed the benefits of League membership. It was to take Ireland more than a decade to recover the position she had lost in the League due to wartime neutrality.

---

79 Diary entry by Lester, quoted in Barcroft, p. 230.

CHAPTER 9

The League, Europe and Irish Foreign Policy Between the Wars

The Free State's actions at the League shed a wider and brighter light on the murky shapes and occasionally well-defined patches that until recently made up the historiography of Ireland's pre-1945 foreign policy. The broadest conclusion one can draw from the Free State's position within the League is that Ireland had more than a one track foreign policy. Irish foreign policy in the inter-war period emerges as a more complex issue than the simple pro-forma of describing all in terms of Anglo-Irish relations. The dyad of League and Commonwealth had by the late 1920s become a triad, by including bi-lateral relations. This is the basic picture of the state's position in the multi-dimensional and multi-power international network of the inter-war years; though the Commonwealth dimension was to give way to an intensified Anglo-Irish dimension in the 1930s. The pre-eminence of the Anglo-Irish leg of the triad and the powerful influence exerted by neutrality in the popular mind has, until the release of archival evidence on the internal working of the Department of External Affairs, been the enduring mental picture of Ireland's foreign relations.

Previous accounts have argued a narrowly defined Irish foreign policy based around the Treaty and resultant considerations. It was therefore possible to detach Ireland from Europe and the complex events of the 1914–45 period which Winston Churchill referred to as the years of 'another Thirty Years' War'.[1] It has been a great error of twentieth-century Irish historians to see the Irish national revolution and the period of state building and consolidation following it between 1919 and 1939, overwhelming as it was, in insular national terms divorced from concurrent events in Europe and a wider world which was going through a period of crisis.

The revolutionary years of 1914–23 period imbued Irish diplomats and her more internationally minded statesmen with idealism and a belief in the peaceful settlement of international disputes through the League. The Treaty-split and the resultant civil war showed that violence solved nothing. It may even have led Irish statesmen towards favouring compromise in the solution

[1] Winston S. Churchill, *The Gathering Storm* (Boston, 1948), p. 1.

of disputes. The destruction of World War I, the 1916 Rising and events from 1916–23 in Ireland, meant that this generation of Irish statesmen was antiviolence; they had seen the destruction of war and its impact on the world; from these ideas and shared experiences the League of Nations emerged. The Irish held the same hopes for it as their European neighbours; they had both been through the same chaos between 1914 and 1918. In a domestic context, Ireland too had its birth throes of internal chaos and civil war like Weimar Germany or Finland or even Russia, though of course on a smaller but as divisive scale. The shared heritage of domestic and international destruction meant that Ireland put the same faith in the League as a means of securing world peace and co-operation as its other members.

Irish diplomats of the 1920s and 1930s were thinking, acting and operating in tandem with their continental counterparts. The Army Mutiny, Boundary Commission, Shannon Scheme, land reform, etc., that filled the domestic agenda were born out of 'Independence' and the Treaty, but they are part of the era of military versus civilian unrest in Britain and Germany, of widespread boundary changes following the Paris Peace Conference—partition in the Irish case not withstanding—and of reconstruction and reform of political, social and economic matters continent-wide.

Though Ireland might in many ways have been an inward-looking and insular state, as the lack of press and public interest in foreign relations bears out, its diplomatic service was in no sense provincial. Diplomat Denis Devlin's poetry is itself a curious allegory for the mindset of his department and colleagues.[2] It was self-confident, definitely Irish, though unquestionably international. It sought to experiment with new ideas; as such it also mirrors what Irish diplomats were undertaking at the League. The League gave Irish diplomats wider international experience, exposure to a wider international community that could never have come about through bi-lateral links alone. It imbued them with the spirit of the age: *l'Espirit du Genève*. Diplomats with long-term League experience tended to be more international and in tune with events on the continent. The astute Cremins, especially the pragmatic internationalist Lester and probably Boland, though his career movements through the 1930s obscure this, were definitely much more in tune with European affairs than their minister whose prime concern was within a British Isles context until April 1938. Belatedly, de Valera then cleared his Anglo-Irish desk and faced the coming onslaught.

The study of Irish foreign policy in the inter-war period is thus of particular importance historiographically, as it illustrates the fallacy of Irish historians who have until the very recent past treated Ireland's history as divorced from that of the European continent. That is not to say that the specific contours of Irish history should be 'revised' to downgrade the 'Anglo-centric' origins of the Irish Free State. The Irish Free State followed European trends

---

2 See J.C.C. Mays (ed.), *Collected poems of Denis Devlin* (Dublin, 1989).

with its foundation in liberal democracy, its flings with Keynesianism, Corporatism, frugality (comparable to the Nazi 'Volk' concept), to a small extent Fascism and the experiments of many small groups such as Saor Eire and elements of the IRA with Communism, not to mention the quasi-fascist Blueshirt experience.[3] Ireland's League policy shows that while there was a specific Irish agenda, it was part of a wider European agenda; a re-definition in response to the confusion of the Great War. Ireland of the 1920s was Ireland of statebuilding and reconstruction, but through this it was participating in the birth pangs of the 'modern age'. The common bond between Ireland and the European continent that is seen through an analysis of Irish League policy provides a basis for this insight.

Too often Ireland's international role from 1922 to 1945 has been portrayed as an attempt to posture at greatness or an ill-defined and underfunded pipe-dream. Fear of foreign relations since the Treaty split have also led to some unease about external affairs. This is to under-estimate the players involved. Ireland possessed a dedicated cadre of diplomats who desired to play an active role in the League to defend Ireland's limited national interests and her international interests for peace, security and the rule of international law.

Foreign relations are a crucial factor by which the independence of a nation can be gauged. Ireland's performance in practical terms at the League of Nations shows that between the wars the state's diplomats secured Ireland's international position by the early 1920s and then began looking, thinking and ultimately acting beyond national boundaries as they were to do for the 1930s at the League. They were not insular figures banging the partitionist or narrow nationalistic drum on the world stage. They were in tune with the Zeitgeist of the 1920s and 1930s and their support for the League is itself a monument (albeit a tragic one) of those fatal and fated decades. Irish involvement in the League of Nations shows how early in its existence, by 1923, the Irish state, born in such turbulence, had gained international legitimacy. The success of Ireland's foreign relations in securing the state's international position through the League and the development of Dominion status is undoubtedly a sign that the Treaty had secured Ireland's place amongst the nations. Despite the begrudging attitude of the public and many public representatives, Ireland's foreign relations between the wars are a success story. The Irish state's degree of integration into the world community between the wars was blunted and ultimately destroyed by the Eire's wartime neutrality.

The relationship between League and Commonwealth policy is an area of peculiar subtlety. Simply because the Irish used the League to play a part in the re-establishment of the Commonwealth and Dominion status on a demo-

---

3 Professor J.J. Lee's assertion that the Blueshirts were a manifestation of the death throes of violence in Irish politics rather than Fascism outright does not deny them a part in a European trend. See J.J. Lee, *Ireland 1912–1985: Politics and Society*, pp. 179–84.

cratic basis does not mean that the area of Dominion status was singularly the most important area of Free State foreign affairs. The Irish used the League in a flexible way. Its domain was far wider than it at first appears. We saw how League policy could be used to the benefit of the Commonwealth and how the Commonwealth could in part be useful for the League. Ultimately it might be said that though this was a bilateral process, the League was of more use in the development of the Free State's Commonwealth policy than vice-versa.

Ireland did not adopt a holier than thou attitude at Geneva; she simply wanted the League to work and to defend the rights of small states. However this did lead to tensions. Walshe did not want Ireland to overstep its limited capacity, whereas Lester felt that Ireland could punch above its weight to get others to act, especially if Ireland acted in concert with other non-permanent members of the Council and not on her own. Rarely did Ireland ever act on its own, usually it was representing the combined interests of the small states of the League with which its interests coincided, even if such a group was initially notional and though by the 1930s it did have some shape, it was never to have such an intermediary position as the Non-Aligned Movement had in the United Nations.

Irish participation in the League has given another angle on the tense Anglo-Irish relationship of the 1930s. During the 1920s League policy had some impact on Ireland's desire to develop the international autonomy of the Commonwealth, but this ended in 1932 with the conscious move away from the Commonwealth by the de Valera administration. Thereupon it is plausible to suggest that the League environment provided a neutral and non-partisan meeting place for Irish and British diplomats during a stormy period of Anglo-Irish relations. The League was never, however, considered as a body through which to solve outstanding Anglo-Irish grievances, though de Valera did consider using League machinery as a method of solving the annuities problem. Such moves came to nothing and the bilateral Dublin–London axis was from where the 1938 Agreements materialised.

Many of the old certainties of Irish nationalism are curiously absent from League policy. England's difficulty is no longer Ireland's opportunity. Within the League context, the Anglo-Irish relationship is merged, though not submerged in the whirlpool of 1930s Europe.

Partition is noticeably absent. Northern Ireland is rarely mentioned. In the 1920s this was probably due to the Boundary Commission fiasco and the resultant decision to letting sleeping dogs lie. In the 1930s de Valera was more concerned about sovereignty than about partition. For the totality of Irish League membership there was a lack of a role for partition in League policy. Partition was never formally raised at Geneva, though it was at times referred to in cryptic terms. Simply, the League of Nations was judged not to be the place to raise such questions. The Irish objected to the partition plans for Palestine, but had no problem with the partition of Silesia, or the partitioning of Czechoslovakia to cede the Sudetenland to Germany. If anything they welcomed the Munich agreement. Though de Valera was seen as having views on minorities, the issue played little part in plans for League policy under either Cumann na nGaedheal or Fianna Fáil. The decision not, under any circumstances, to refer the Boundary Commission to the League possibly means that it was felt that partition would be solved or dealt with in other spheres, on a direct Dublin–London basis and not in any case, on an international level. Partition is simply never mentioned. The pragmatism of the statesmen involved led to the realisation that such claims would ruin Ireland's international image at the League. They did not want to bring in what was seen as a different agenda that was not compatible with League policy.

The supposedly neutral tradition in Irish foreign policy is compromised by League membership. Ireland did not declare her neutrality until it was necessitated by the state of the world order. Therefore it did not exist in the League context until a need was found for it. This was only when the League was seen to be redundant as an international instrument and an international actor. Ireland supported League sanctions, de Valera made positive references to military sanctions under Article 16 and was prepared to send Irish troops to Saar to police a League-sponsored plebiscite there in January 1935, when neutral Switzerland made clear that her own neutrality prevented this.[4] Most significantly, the League of Nations Guarantee Act of 1923 contains no restrictive covenants that refer to Irish neutrality. Thus Ireland was undertaking to comply with League obligations concerning military and economic sanctions, should the need occur to initiate them. This is not the stance of a neutral state. Had World War II been in any sense a League of Nations war, as was periodically considered, rather than a Great Power war, it is interesting to consider what Ireland's actions might have been.

The League was made for states like Ireland; after a slow start, Ireland used her membership to the best of her limited ability. Her rise in the League's hierarchy to 1934–5 is a sign that other League members noticed and approved of this. Irish links with the Commonwealth bloc, the Scandinavian states and the small states of Europe, her common birth with them in the aftermath of World War I and her historical links with the Latin American states meant that she had limited links with the majority of the amorphous groupings in the League. Britain respected if not always agreed with Ireland's policies. The grudging acceptance of the registration of the Treaty, support for Ireland's Council candidature in 1930 and Anglo-Irish co-operation at Geneva in the 1930s are signs of this. France and Germany were similarly respectful of Irish diplomats, if not of Irish policies.

Ireland's position in the Geneva system was no small achievement for a small weak state. However one must be aware that these achievements were of limited value outside the Geneva system. The failure of the League in the late

---

4 I hope to deal with this issue in a forthcoming article.

1930s is also a parameter within which to keep any interpretation of Irish league policy. Small nations do have a role in the international order; they cannot always fulfil it because they have little control over that order. So though Ireland had a prominent place in the League system, it is important not to over-emphasise that role. Ireland's policy was one of limited autonomy within the global system. That limit was her small state position. Small states can try to act independently of the Great Powers, but ultimately they need to depend upon these powers to support and give life to international institutions like the League. Small states must realise that the Great Powers have the world order at their mercy. As Ireland did on the Council, the small must try to curry the favour and the intentions of the large in the hope that the powers will ultimately act in favour of the international community. Ireland was thus not acting independently within the League to bolster its own interests. Rather, Ireland was trying to sell the League system as the method of settling international conflicts. Irish League policy and participation in the League was not a skilful public relations exercise or merely declaratory. The intentions and consequences of Irish actions, as part of the small states loose grouping, bear this out. The state was not just acting to enhance her own prestige or international position. Ireland was not playing to the gallery, but trying in a limited manner to prevent another war breaking out. Its diplomats were playing a minor role with limited power as best they could. Ireland's national interest was to preserve and develop the League as an instrument to safeguard world peace; this was in the interest of all states, especially the smaller ones.

The legacy of Ireland's years in the League of Nations can be seen in her United Nations policy between 1955 and 1969. Boland and Costello, both League of Nations veterans were involved in the development of United Nations policy, as was Eamon de Valera, before turning the External Affairs portfolio over to Frank Aiken. Though there was a conscious desire in the United Nations to forget the League, and the Cold War climate of bi-polarity was very different to the multi-polarity of the inter-war period, Ireland's policy of a belief in international law and order and need to safeguard the small against the powerful remained.

The League gave international confidence to the new Irish state. It embraced the League system and acted within it, with the self-confidence never to punch above its weight due to the need to hide any inadequacy. Ireland was small, effectively powerless, with the exception of some moral standing, and its impact on the League was moderate in terms of the League environment. Few exogenous factors existed to deflect Ireland from its desired League policy. Anglo-Irish relations rarely affected League policy as is seen in the close links retained by Eden and Cremins through the height of the Economic War. Similarly, bilateral relations never upset moves within the League of Nations as the League of Nations was in one sense a massive interwoven set of bilateral relations. It was a pre-eminent area, perhaps the forgotten area of the dual foundation of the Commonwealth/Anglo-Irish and League of Nations basis of inter-war Irish foreign policy.

Ireland's contribution to the League of Nations is not unimpressive considering her small size and limited international position. The League was there for states such as Ireland to make the most of. This Ireland did. Ireland received recognition and thus international sovereignty through the League. The League gave Ireland a place in the international system and however weakly and feebly, provided a degree of protection for Ireland that she herself could not provide. Gaining a small international role and niche was no small achievement by the administration of a newly independent state that was plagued by civil war, reconstruction and the need to build a domestic, not to mention an international, programme and policy. Fragile as the Geneva system was, between 1923 and 1946 it had allowed the integration of the new entity of the Irish Free State, and later Éire, into the European and world environment. Thus it widened the scope of Irish foreign policy. The League of Nations gave an international identity, purpose and sense of place to Ireland.

APPENDIX I

The Covenant of the League of Nations

The High Contracting Parties, in order to promote international co-operation and to achieve international peace and security
    by the acceptance of obligations not to resort to war,
    by the prescription of open, just and honourable relations between nations,
    by the firm establishment of the understandings of international law as the actual rule of conduct among Governments,
    and by the maintenance of justice and a scrupulous respect for all treaty obligations in the dealings of organised peoples with one another,
Agree to this Covenant of the League of Nations.

Article 1
1. The original Members of the League of Nations shall be those of the Signatories which are named in the Annex to this Covenant and also such of those other States named in the Annex as shall accede without reservation to this Covenant. Such accession shall be effected by a Declaration deposited with the Secretariat within two months of the coming into force of the Covenant. Notice thereof shall be sent to all other Members of the League.
2. Any fully self-governing State, Dominion or Colony not named in the Annex may become a Member of the League if its admission is agreed to by two-thirds of the Assembly, provided that it shall give effective guarantees of its sincere intention to observe its international obligations, and shall accept such regulations as may be prescribed by the League in regard to its military, naval and air forces and armaments.
3. Any Member of the League may, after two years notice of its intention so to do, withdraw from the League, provided that all its international obligations and all its obligations under this Covenant shall have been fulfilled at the time of its withdrawal.

Article 2
The action of the League under this Covenant shall be effected through the instrumentality of an Assembly and of a Council, with a permanent Secretariat.

Article 3
1. The Assembly shall consist of Representatives of the Members of the League.
2. The Assembly shall meet at stated intervals and from time to time as occasion may require at the Seat of the League or at such other place as may be decided upon.
3. The Assembly may deal at its meetings with any matter within the sphere of action of the League or affecting the peace of the world.
4. At meetings of the Assembly, each Member of the League shall have one vote, and may have not more than three Representatives.

Article 4

1 The Council shall consist of Representatives of the Principle Allied and Associated Powers,[1] together with Representatives of four other Members of the League. These four Members the League shall be selected by the Assembly from time to time in its discretion. Until the appointment of the Representatives of the four Members of the League first selected by Assembly, Representatives of Belgium, Brazil, Spain and Greece shall be Members of the Council.
2 With the approval of the majority of the Assembly, the Council may name additional Members of the League Representatives shall always be Members of the Council;[2].the Council with like approval may increase the number of Members of the League to be selected by the Assembly for representation on the Council.[3]
2bis[4] The Assembly shall fix by a two-thirds majority the rules dealing with the election of the non-permanent Members of the Council, and particularly such regulations as relate to their term of office and the conditions of re-eligibility.
3 The Council shall meet from time to time as occasion may require, and at least once a year, at the Seat of the League, or at such other place as may be decided upon.
4 The Council may deal at its meetings with any matter within the sphere of action of the League or affecting the peace of the world.
5 Any Member of the League not represented on the Council shall be invited to send a Representative to sit as a member at any meeting of the Council during the consideration of matters specially affecting the interests of that Member of the League.
6 At meetings of the Council, each Member of the League represented on the Council shall have one vote, and may have not more than one Representative.

Article 5

1 Except where otherwise expressly provided in this Covenant or by the terms of the present Treaty, decisions at any meeting of the Assembly or of the Council shall require the agreement of all the Members of the League represented at the meeting.
2 All matters of procedure at meetings of the Assembly or of the Council, including the appointment of Committees to investigate particular matters, shall be regulated by the Assembly or by the Council and may be decided by a majority of the Members of the League represented at the meeting.
3 The first meeting of the Assembly and the first meeting of the Council shall be summoned by the President of the United States of America.

Article 6

1 The permanent Secretariat shall be established at the Seat of the League. The Secretariat shall comprise a Secretary-General and such secretaries and staff as may be required.

---

1 The Principal Allied and Associated Powers are the following: States of America, the British Empire, France, Italy and Japan.
2 In virtue of this paragraph of the Covenant, Germany was nominated as a permanent Member of the Council on 8 September 1926.
3 The number of Members of the Council selected by the Assembly was Increased to six instead of four by virtue of a resolution adopted at the third ordinary meeting of the Assembly on 25 September 1922. By a resolution tabled by the Assembly on 8 September 1926, the number of Members of the Council selected by the Assembly was increased to nine.
4 This Amendment came into force on 29 July 1926, in accordance with Article 26 of the Covenant.

2   The first Secretary-General shall be the person named in the Annex; thereafter the Secretary-General shall be appointed by the Council with the approval of the majority of the Assembly.
3   The secretaries and staff of the Secretariat shall be appointed by the Secretary-General with the approval of the Council.
4   The Secretary-General shall act in that capacity at all meetings of the Assembly and of the Council.
5[5] The expenses of the League shall be borne by the Members of the League in the proportion decided by the Assembly.

Article 7
1   The Seat of the League is established at Geneva.
2   The Council may at any time decide that the Seat of the League shall be established elsewhere.
3   All positions under or in connection with the League, including the Secretariat, shall be open equally to men and women.
4   Representatives of the Members of the League and officials of the League when engaged on the business of the League shall enjoy diplomatic privileges and immunities.
5   The buildings and other property occupied by the League or its officials or by Representatives attending its meetings shall be inviolable.

Article 8
1   The Members of the League recognise that the maintenance of peace requires the reduction of national armaments to the lowest point consistent with national safety and the enforcement by common action of international obligations.
2   The Council, taking account of the geographical situation and circumstances of each State, shall formulate plans for such reduction for the consideration and action of the several Governments.
3   Such plans shall be subject to reconsideration and revision at least every ten years.
4   After these plans shall have been adopted by the several Governments, the limits of armaments therein fixed shall not be exceeded without the concurrence of the Council.
5   The Members of the League agree that the manufacture by private enterprise of munitions and implements of war is open to grave objections. The Council shall advise how the evil effects attendant upon such manufacture can be prevented, due regard being had to the necessities of those Members of the League which are not able to manufacture the munitions and implements of war necessary for their safety.
6   The Members of the League undertake to interchange full and frank information as to the scale of their armaments, their military, naval and air programmes and the condition of such of their industries as are adaptable to warlike purposes.

Article 9
A permanent Commission shall be constituted to advise the Council on the execution of the provisions of Articles 1 and 8 and on military, naval and air questions generally.

Article 10
The Members of the League undertake to respect and preserve as against external aggression the territorial integrity and existing political independence of all Members of the League. In case of any such aggression or in case of any threat or danger of

---

5   This Amendment came into force on 13 August 1924, in accordance with Article 26 of the Covenant.

Appendices

such aggression the Council shall advise upon the means by which this obligation shall be fulfilled.

Article 11
1 Any war or threat of war, whether immediately affecting any of the Members of the League or not, is hereby declared a matter of concern to the whole League, and the League shall take any action that may be deemed wise and effectual to safeguard the peace of nations. In case any such emergency should arise the Secretary-General shall on the request of Member of the League forthwith summon a meeting of Council.
2 It is also declared to be the friendly right of each Member of the League to bring to the attention of the Assembly the Council any circumstance whatever affecting international relations which threatens to disturb international peace or good understanding between nations upon which peace depends.

Article 12
1 The Members of the League agree that if there should arise between them any dispute likely to lead to a rupture will submit the matter either to arbitration or judicial settlement or to enquiry by the Council, and they agree in no case to resort to war until three months after the award by the arbitrators or the judicial decision or the report by the Council.
2 In any case under this Article the award of the arbitrators or the judicial decision [6]shall be made within a reasonable time, and the report of the Council shall be made within six months after the submission of the dispute.

Article 13
1 The Members of the League agree that whenever any dispute shall arise between them which they recognise to be suitable submission to arbitration or judicial settlement, and which be satisfactorily settled by diplomacy, they will submit whole subject-matter to arbitration or judicial settlement.
2 Disputes as to the interpretation of a treaty, as to any question of international law, as to the existence of any fact which, if established, would constitute a breach of any international obligation, or as to the extent and nature of reparation to be made for any such breach, are declared to among those which are generally suitable for submission to arbitration or judicial settlement.
3 For the consideration of any such dispute, the court to which the case is referred shall be the Permanent Court of International Justice, established in accordance with Article 14, or any tribunal agreed on by the parties to the dispute or stipulated in any convention existing between them.
4 The Members of the League agree that they will carry out in full good faith any award or decision that may be rendered, and that they will not resort to war against a Member of the League which complies therewith. In the event of any failure to carry out such an award or decision, the Council shall propose what steps should be taken to give effect thereto.

Article 14
The Council shall formulate and submit to the Members of the League for adoption plans for the establishment of a Permanent Court of International Justice. The Court shall be competent to hear and determine any dispute of an international character

---

6 The Amendments printed in italics relating to these Articles came into force on 26 September 1924, in accordance with Article 26 of the Covenant.

which the parties thereto submit to it. The Court may also give an advisory opinion upon any dispute or question referred to it by the Council or by the Assembly.

Article 15
1 [7]If there should arise between Members of the League any dispute likely to lead to a rupture, which is not submitted to arbitration or judicial settlement in accordance with Article 13, the Members of the League agree that they will submit the matter to the Council. Any party to the dispute may effect such submission by giving notice of the existence of the dispute to the Secretary-General, who will make all necessary arrangements for a full investigation and consideration thereof.
2 For this purpose the parties to the dispute will communicate to the Secretary-General, as promptly as possible, statements of their case with all the relevant facts and papers, and the Council may forthwith direct the publication thereof.
3 The Council shall endeavour to effect a settlement of the dispute, and if such efforts are successful, a statement shall be made public giving such facts and explanations regarding the dispute and the terms of settlement thereof as the Council may deem appropriate.
4 If the dispute is not thus settled, the Council unanimously or by a majority vote shall make and publish a report containing a statement of the facts of the dispute and the recommendations which are deemed just and proper in regard thereto.
5 Any Member of the League represented on the Council may make public a statement of the facts of the dispute and of its conclusions regarding the same.
6 If a report by the Council is unanimously agreed to by the members thereof other than the Representatives of one or more of the parties to the dispute, the Members of the League agree that they will not go to war with any party to the dispute which complies with the recommendations of the report.
7 If the Council fails to reach a report which is unanimously agreed to by the members thereof, other than the Representatives of one or more of the parties to the dispute, the Members of the League reserve to themselves the right to take such action as they shall consider necessary for the maintenance of right and justice.
8 If the dispute between the parties is claimed by one of them, and is found by the Council, to arise out of a matter which by international law is solely within the domestic jurisdiction of that party, the Council shall so report, and shall make no recommendation as to its settlement.
9 The Council may in any case under this Article refer the dispute to the Assembly. The dispute shall be so referred at the request of either party to the dispute provided that such be made within fourteen days after the submission of the to the Council.
10 In any case referred to the Assembly, all the provisions of this Article and of Article 12 relating to the action and powers of the Council shall apply to the action and powers of the Assembly, provided that a report made by the Assembly, if concurred in by the Representatives of those Members of League represented on the Council and a majority of the other Members of the League, exclusive in each case of the Representatives of the parties to the dispute, shall have the same force as a report by the Council concurred in by all the members thereof other than the Representatives of one or more of the parties to the dispute.

Article 16
1 Should any Member of the League resort to war in disregard of its covenants under Articles 12, 13 or 15, it shall ipso facto be deemed to have committed an act of war

---

7 The Amendment to the first paragraph of this Article came into force on 26 September 1924, in accordance with Article 26 of the Covenant.

against all other Members of the League, which hereby undertake immediately to subject it to the severance of all trade or financial relations, the prohibition of all intercourse between their nationals and the nationals of the covenant-breaking State, and the prevention of all financial, commercial or personal intercourse between the nationals of the covenant-breaking State and the nationals of any other State, whether a Member of the League or not.
2 It shall be the duty of the Council in such case to recommend to the several Governments concerned what effective military, naval or air force the Members of the League shall severally contribute to the armed forces to be used to protect the covenants of the League.
3 The Members of the League agree, further, that they will mutually support one another in the financial and economic measures which are taken under this Article, in order to minimise the loss and inconvenience resulting from the above measures, and that they will mutually support one another in resisting any special measures aimed at one of their number by the Covenant breaking State, and that they will take the necessary steps to afford passage through their territory to the forces of any of the Members of the League which are co-operating to protect the covenants of the League.
4 Any Member of the League which has violated any covenant of the League may be declared to be no longer a Member of the League by a vote of the Council concurred in by the Representatives of all the other Members of the League represented thereon.

Article 17
1 In the event of a dispute between a Member of the League and a State which is not a Member of the League, or between States not Members of the League, the State or States not Members of the League shall be invited to accept the obligations of membership in the League for the purposes of such dispute, upon such conditions as the Council may deem just. If such invitation is accepted, the provisions of Articles 12 to 16 inclusive shall be applied with such modifications as deemed necessary by the Council.
2 Upon such invitation being given the Council shall immediately institute an enquiry into the circumstances of the dispute and recommend such action as may seem best and most effectual in the circumstances.
3 If a State so invited shall refuse to accept the obligations of membership in the League for the purposes of such dispute, and shall resort to war against a Member of the League, the provisions of Article 16 shall be applicable as against the State taking such action.
4 If both parties to the dispute when so invited refuse accept the obligations of membership in the League for purposes of such dispute, the Council may take such measures and make such recommendations as will prevent hostilities and will result in the settlement of the dispute.

Article 18
Every treaty or international engagement entered into hereafter after by any Member of the League shall be forthwith registered with the Secretariat and shall as soon as possible be published by it. No such treaty or international engagement shall be binding until so registered.

Article 19
The Assembly may from time to time advise the reconsideration by Members of the League of treaties which have become inapplicable and the consideration of international conditions whose continuance might endanger the peace of the world.

Article 20
1 The Members of the League severally agree that this Covenant is accepted as abrogating all obligations or understandings inter se which are inconsistent with the terms thereof, and solemnly undertake that they will not hereafter enter into any engagements inconsistent with the terms thereof.
2 In case any Member of the League shall, before becoming a Member of the League, have undertaken any obligations inconsistent with the terms of this Covenant, it shall be the duty of such Member to take immediate steps to procure its release from such obligations.

Article 21
Nothing in this Covenant shall be deemed to affect the validity of international engagements, such as treaties of arbitration or regional understandings like the Monroe doctrine, for securing the maintenance of peace.

Article 22
1 To those colonies and territories which as a consequence of the late war have ceased to be under the sovereignty of the States which formerly governed them and which are inhabited by peoples not yet able to stand by themselves under the strenuous conditions of the modern world, there should be applied the principle that the well-being and development of such peoples form a sacred trust of civilisation and that securities for the performance of this trust should be embodied in this Covenant.
2 The best method of giving practical effect to this principle is that the tutelage of such peoples should be entrusted to advanced nations who by reason of their resources, their experience or their geographical position can best undertake this responsibility, and who are willing to accept it, and that this tutelage should be exercised by them as Mandatories on behalf of the League.
3 The character of the mandate must differ according to the stage of the development of the people, the geographical situation of the territory, its economic conditions and other similar circumstances.
4 Certain communities formerly belonging to the Turkish Empire have reached a stage of development where their existence as independent nations can be provisionally recognised subject to the rendering of administrative advice and assistance by a Mandatory until such time as they are able to stand alone. The wishes of these communities must be a principal consideration in the selection of the Mandatory.
5 Other peoples, especially those of Central Africa, are at such a stage that the Mandatory must be responsible for the administration of the territory under conditions which will guarantee freedom of conscience and religion, subject the maintenance of public order and morals, the prohibition of abuses such as the slave trade, the arms traffic and the liquor traffic, and the prevention of the establishment of fortifications or military and naval bases and of military training of the natives for other than police purposes and the defence of territory, and will also secure equal opportunities for the trade and commerce of other Members of the League.
6 There are territories, such as South-West Africa and of the South Pacific Islands, which, owing to the sparseness of their population, or their small size, or their remoteness from the centres of civilisation, or their geographical contiguity to the territory of the Mandatory, and other circumstances, can be best administered under the laws of the Mandatory as integral portions of its territory, subject to the safeguards above mentioned in the interests of the indigenous population.
7 In every case of mandate, the Mandatory shall render to the Council an annual report in reference to the territory committed to its charge.
8 The degree of authority, control or administration to be exercised by the Mandatory shall, if not previously agreed upon by the Members of the League, be explicitly

defined in each case by the Council.
9 A permanent Commission shall be constituted to receive and examine the annual reports of the Mandatories and to advise the Council on all matters relating to the observance of the mandates.

Article 23
Subject to and in accordance with the provisions of international conventions existing or hereafter to be agreed upon, the Members of the League:
(a) will endeavour to secure and maintain fair and humane conditions of labour for men, women and children, both in their own countries and in all countries to which their commercial and industrial relations extend, and for that purpose will establish and maintain the necessary national organisations;
(b) undertake to secure just treatment of the native inhabitants of territories under their control;
(c) will entrust the League with the general supervision over the execution of agreements with regard to the traffic in women and children, and the traffic in opium and other dangerous drugs;
(d) will entrust the League with the general supervision of the trade in arms and ammunition with the countries in which the control of this traffic is necessary in the common interest;
(e) will make provision to secure and maintain freedom of communications and of transit and equitable treatment for the commerce of all Members of the League. In this connection, the special necessities of the regions devastated during the war of 1914–18 shall be borne in mind;
(f) will endeavour to take steps in matters of international concern for the prevention and control of disease.

Article 24
1 There shall be placed under the direction of the League all international bureaux already established by general treaties if the parties to such treaties consent. All such international bureaux and all commissions for the regulation of matters of international interest hereafter constituted shall be placed under the direction of the League.
2 In all matters of international interest which are regulated by general conventions but which are not placed under the control of international bureaux or commissions, the Secretariat of the League shall, subject to the consent of the Council and if desired by the parties, collect and distribute all relevant information and shall render any other assistance which may be necessary or desirable.
3 The Council may include as part of the expenses of the Secretariat the expenses of any bureau or commission which is placed under the direction of the League.

Article 25
The Members of the League agree to encourage and promote the establishment and co-operation of duly authorised voluntary national Red Cross organisations having as purposes the improvement of health, the prevention of disease and the mitigation of suffering throughout the world.

Article 26
1 Amendments to this Covenant will take effect when ratified by the Members of the League whose Representatives compose the Council and by a majority of the Members of the League whose Representatives compose the Assembly.
2 No such amendments shall bind any Member of the League which signifies its dissent therefrom, but in that case it shall cease to be a Member of the League.

APPENDIX 2

Letter of Application by the Irish Free State to the League of Nations

17 April 1923

To/
The Honourable Sir Eric Drummond,
Secretary-General to the League of Nations,
GENEVA.

Sir,
    In accordance with the terms of Article 1 of the Covenant of the League of Nations, I have the honour to request that the Free State of Ireland may be admitted as a Member of the League of Nations, and that this request may be placed on the agenda of the next meeting of the Assembly of the League.
    The Government of the Irish Free State is prepared to accept the conditions laid down in Article 1 of the Covenant, and to carry out all the obligations involved in Membership of the League.
    The Government will send representatives, empowered to give all necessary explanations, to the Assembly, and it will be glad in the meantime to give any information relevant to this application which may be required.
    It is requested that this application may be brought without delay to the knowledge of all Members of the League.

I have the honour to be,
Sir,
Your Obedient Servant,
(Signed) DESMOND FITZGERALD
            Minister for External Affairs.

APPENDIX 3

Delegation Personnel, 1923-46

1923
W.T. Cosgrave, President of the Executive Council — Primary Delegate
Desmond FitzGerald, Minister for External Affairs — Delegate
Eoin MacNeill, Minister for Education — Delegate
Hugh Kennedy, Attorney General — Delegate
The Marquis MacSwiney of Mashonaglas — Substitute Delegate
Ormonde Grattan Esmonde, TD — Substitute Delegate
Kevin O'Sheil — Substitute Delegate
Michael MacWhite, Representative to the League of Nations — Delegation Secretary

1924
Desmond FitzGerald, Minister for External Affairs — Primary Delegate
Patrick McGilligan, Minister for Industry and Commerce — Delegate
John Byrne, Attorney General — Delegate
James MacNeill, Free State Representative in London — Substitute Delegate
John M. O'Sullivan — Substitute Delegate
The Marquis MacSwiney of Mashonaglas, MRIA — Substitute Delegate
Michael Heffernan, TD — Substitute Delegate
Joseph Walshe, Secretary, Department of External Affairs — Delegation Secretary
Michael MacWhite, Representative to the League of Nations — Technical Adviser

1925
Desmond FitzGerald, Minister for External Affairs — Primary Delegate
Kevin O'Higgins, Minister for Home Affairs — Delegate
Diarmuid O'Hegarty, Secretary to the Executive Council — Delegate
Michael MacWhite, Representative to the League of Nations — Delegate
Joseph Walshe, Secretary, Department of External Affairs — Delegation Secretary

March 1926 (Extra-ordinary Assembly)
Desmond FitzGerald, Minister for External Affairs — Primary Delegate
Michael MacWhite, Representative to the League of Nations — Delegate

1926
Desmond FitzGerald, Minister for External Affairs — Primary Delegate
Ernest Blythe, Minister for Finance — Delegate
Eoin MacNeill — Delegate
Daniel Binchy, Professor of International Law (NUI) — Substitute Delegate
Michael MacWhite, Representative to the League of Nations — Substitute Delegate
Joseph Walshe, Secretary, Department of External Affairs — Delegation Secretary

1927
John A. Costello, Attorney General	Primary Delegate
Michael MacWhite, Representative to the League of Nations	Delegate
Diarmuid O'Hegarty, Secretary to the Executive Council	Delegate
Joseph Walshe, Secretary, Department of External Affairs	Substitute Delegate and Delegation Secretary

1928
Ernest Blythe, Vice President of the Executive Council and Minister for Finance	Primary Delegate
Desmond FitzGerald, Minister for Defence	Delegate
John M. O'Sullivan, Minister for Education	Delegate
John A. Costello, Attorney General	Substitute Delegate
Michael MacWhite, Representative to the League of Nations	Substitute Delegate
Sean Murphy, Assistant Secretary, Department of External Affairs	Substitute Delegate

1929
Patrick McGilligan, Minister for External Affairs	Primary Delegate
John M. O'Sullivan, Minister for Education	Delegate
John A. Costello, Attorney General	Delegate
Sean Lester, Representative to the League of Nations	Substitute Delegate
Sean Murphy, Assistant Secretary, Department of External Affairs:	Substitute Delegate
F.T. Cremins, Department of External Affairs	Delegation Secretary

1930
Ernest Blythe, Vice President of the Executive Council and Minister for Finance:	Primary Delegate
John M. O'Sullivan, Minister for Education	Delegate
John A. Costello, Attorney General	Delegate
Daniel Binchy, Free State Representative in Berlin	Substitute Delegate
Sean Lester, Representative to the League of Nations	Substitute Delegate
Count Gerald O'Kelly de Gallagh, Free State Envoy Extra-Ordinary in Paris	Substitute Delegate
F.T. Cremins, Department of External Affairs	Delegation Secretary

1931
Patrick McGilligan, Minister for External Affairs and Minister for Industry and Commerce	Primary Delegate
Daniel Binchy, Free State Envoy Extra-Ordinary in Berlin	Delegate
Sean Lester, Representative to the League of Nations	Delegate
Sean Murphy, Assistant Secretary, Department of External Affairs	Substitute Delegate
J.J. Hearne, Legal Adviser, Department of External Affairs	Substitute Delegate
John Leydon, Department of Industry and Commerce	Substitute Delegate

March 1932 (Extra-ordinary Assembly)
Sean Lester, Representative to the League of Nations	Primary Delegate
J.J. Hearne, Legal Adviser, Department of External Affairs	Delegate

1932

Eamon de Valera, President of the Executive Council and Minister for External Affairs:	Primary Delegate
Joseph Connolly, Senator and Minister for Posts and Telegraphs	Delegate
Conor Maguire, Attorney General	Delegate
Sean Lester, Representative to the League of Nations	Delegate
Sean Murphy, Assistant Secretary, Department of External Affairs:	Substitute Delegate
J.J. Hearne, Legal Adviser, Department of External Affairs	Substitute Delegate
John Leydon, Department of Industry and Commerce	Substitute Delegate
Francis T. Cremins, Head of League of Nations section, Department of External Affairs	Delegate
F.H. Boland, First Secretary, Paris Legation	Delegate
T.J. Coyne, Secretary, Geneva Legation	Secretary
Kathleen O'Connell	Secretary to the President
Shiela G. Murphy, Department of External Affairs	Secretary

November 1932 (Extra-ordinary Assembly)

Joseph Connolly, Senator and Minister for Posts and Telegraphs	Delegate
Sean Lester, Representative to the League of Nations	Delegate
Francis T. Cremins, Head of League of Nations section, Department of External Affairs	Delegate
Michael Rynne, Assistant Legal Adviser, Department of External Affairs	Secretary

1933

Sean T O'Kelly, Vice-President of the Executive Council and Minister for Local Government and Public Health	Primary Delegate
Sean Lester, Representative to the League of Nations	Delegate
Francis T. Cremins, Head of League of Nations section, Department of External Affairs	Delegate
T.J. Coyne, Secretary to Geneva Legation	Substitute Delegate
John A. Belton, Department of External Affairs	Substitute Delegate
Shiela Murphy, Department of External Affairs	Secretary

1934

Eamon de Valera, President of the Executive Council and Minister for External Affairs:	Primary Delegate
Francis T. Cremins, Representative to the League of Nations	Delegate
J.J. Hearne, Legal Adviser, Department of External Affairs	Delegate
F.H. Boland, First Secretary, Paris Legation	Substitute Delegate/Secretary
Kathleen O'Connell	Secretary to the President

1935

Eamon de Valera, President of the Executive Council and Minister for External Affairs:	Primary Delegate
Francis T. Cremins, Representative to the League of Nations	Delegate
J.J. Hearne, Legal Adviser, Department of External Affairs	Delegate
P.J. O'Byrne, Secretary, Geneva Legation	Substitute Delegate
Denis Devlin, Department of External Affairs	Secretary

June–July 1936 (Extra-ordinary Assembly)
Eamon de Valera, President of the Executive Council — Primary Delegate
   and Minister for External Affairs
Francis T. Cremins, Representative to the League of Nations: — Delegate
Michael Rynne, Assistant Legal Adviser, — Delegate
   Department of External Affairs
Denis Devlin, Department of External Affairs — Secretary
Kathleen O'Connell — Secretary to the President

1936
Francis T. Cremins, Representative to the League of Nations — Delegate
Michael Rynne, Assistant Legal Adviser, — Delegate
   Department of External Affairs
Denis Devlin, Department of External Affairs — Delegate/Secretary

May 1937 (Extra-ordinary Assembly)
Francis T. Cremins, Representative to the League of Nations — Delegate

1937
Eamon de Valera, President of the Executive Council — Primary Delegate
   and Minister for External Affairs:
Francis T. Cremins, Representative to the League of Nations — Delegate
J.J. Hearne, Legal Adviser, Department of External Affairs — Delegate
Michael Rynne, Assistant Legal Adviser, — Substitute Delegate
   Department of External Affairs:
William Warnock, Department of External Affairs — Substitute Delegate/Secretary
Kathleen O'Connell — Secretary to the President

1938
Eamon de Valera, Taoiseach and Minister for External Affairs — Primary Delegate
Francis T. Cremins, Representative to the League of Nations — Delegate
J.J. Hearne, Legal Adviser, Department of External Affairs — Delegate
Michael Rynne, Assistant Legal Adviser, — Substitute Delegate
   Department of External Affairs:
Denis R. McDonald, Department of External Affairs — Substitute Delegate/Secretary

1939 (December)
Francis T. Cremins, Representative to the League of Nations — Delegate

No Assembly took place between December 1939 and April 1946

1946
Francis T. Cremins, Chargé d'Affaires, Berne — Delegate

APPENDIX 4

Conventions Acceded to and Ratified by the Irish Free State, 1922–32

Convention/ Date	Irish Ratification Deposited/ Date of Accession
The Obscene Publications Convention, 12 September 1923	15 September 1930
The International Convention Relating to Dangerous Drugs/ 19 February, 1925	1 September 1931
Geneva Gas Protocol/ 17 June 1925	24 August 1930
Slavery Convention/ 25 September 1926	18 July 1930
Pacific Settlement of International Disputes: General Act/ 26 September 1928	26 April 1931
International Convention relating to Economic Statistics and Protocol/ 14 December 1928	15 September 1930
International Treaty for the Limitation and Reduction of Naval Armaments/ 22 April 1930	31 December 1930
The International Convention for Limiting the Manufacture and Regulating the Distribution of Narcotic Drugs and Protocol of Signature/ 13 July 1931	11 April 1933

Bibliography

A NOTE ON SOURCES

The bulk of the primary material for this thesis came from Department of Foreign Affairs and Department of the Taoiseach collections at the National Archives, Dublin. These provide the basic departmental and official accounts of League policy. They have been consolidated by use of the collections of personal papers in the University College Dublin Archives Department and the Trinity College, Dublin Manuscripts Department. Along with those mentioned above, these sources provide the main documentary framework of primary sources. They combine to give a reasonably clear picture of how Free State League policy was formulated and executed. Other smaller collections have been used to provide an insight into particular areas or particular one-off events. This was the case with the D[áil] E[ireann] series files needed to develop a deeper insight into very early involvement with the League. Similarly, Cabinet Minutes allow one to see that League affairs were dealt with at high level, and were not then dealt with on an ad hoc manner.

Particularly useful were collections that contained private letters from Irish delegates in Geneva. Too often in this kind of thesis dealing with 'high politics' one gets drawn into a grey-world of 'Protocol' and 'Officialdom'. The League was also a prime social occasion and with these letters we can inject some feeling into League affairs if not capture *L'Espirit du Geneve*. They also provide a fascinating insight into the views of the Irish abroad and their rather conservative frame of mind.

Printed sources tend to be incredibly dull. Both official Irish and League publications contain none of the sparkle that many of the manuscript sources abound with. The League published so many documents that were merely for advice that integrating them into state policy is fruitless. The most useful League publications are the Special Supplements to the Official Journal containing the Assembly and Council records and debates. Printed League sources are primarily utilitarian and as such provide little insight into the formulation of League policy at any level.

Secondary sources on Irish foreign policy are a reasonably new phenomenon. With specific regard to League policy, they are practically non-existent. The main texts such as those by Keatinge and Harkness are strongly based on an Anglo-Irish footing. What journal articles exist suffer also from this outlook. Recent books on Irish foreign affairs such as those by Dermot Keogh, have taken a broader more 'European' outlook.

Secondary sources on the League itself are only marginally better. The League has become a historical curiosity and serves merely as an introduction to the United Nations. It is badly in need of a re-appraisal in light of the European Community's increasing role as a 'civilian power'. Not since F.S. Northedge's 1985 survey of the League of Nations has there been any up to date reappraisal of the League's role or work in its widest sense. The sources on the League provided an admirable account of its working, mechanisms and actions, but were very short on any original interpretations.

The particular quirks of the Department of Foreign Affairs Archives have been documented before. This aside, the sources used provided an in-depth, though not inexhaustible resource. Gaps, man-made or purely accidental are the biggest hindrance along with the increasingly dated secondary material.

Sources at the League of Nations Registry, Palais des Nations, Geneva
There are two predominant strains of information/sources at the League of Nations archives in the United Nations Library at the Palais des Nations in Geneva. The first, by far the largest number, are the everyday documents of the League's work. They contain the transmission of international information and statues from international organisations and conferences to the Free State. These provide evidence of the League in action and the many unsung ways in which it was successful before the crisis of the thirties.

The second type, by far the more important for the historian, are those documents dealing with the areas where the Free State and the League came into direct conflict. This is somewhat different to League policy on a national perspective. It refers to the thoughts of the League of Nations about the Free State. How it, as an international organisation felt that it should respond to specific matters. For example how it should treat what Britain felt were *inter se* agreements between Commonwealth members and what the Free State instead perceived as 'international agreements'.

These smaller number of documents provide the key to how the League itself saw the Free State as a state in the international milieu. But they can never provide the full story. The League was not a 'supranational' institution in the way the European Community is. It was little more than the manifestation of the international will of its collective members. The League was a 'forum' but it was not always an actor in the play. It provided and pervaded the setting and created the drama.

PRIMARY SOURCES: MANUSCRIPT

National Archives, Dublin
Dáil Éireann Papers
Department of the Taoiseach
   S Series files
Department of Finance
   E Series files
Department of Justice
   General files
Department of Industry and Commerce
   General files
Cabinet Minutes
Department of Foreign Affairs
   League of Nations Series (LN)
   GR Series
   EA Series
Number Series
   'Pre 100' Series
   100 Series
   200 Series
   300 Series
   400 Series

Secretaries Files
   Confidential Reports
   Letter Books

Embassies Series
   Berne Embassy Series
   Geneva Embassy Series
   Paris Embassy Series

Dáil Éireann/ Provisional Government/
Irish Free State Series
   League of Nations (Miscellaneous Papers)
   Ministers Office Papers
   Geneva Correspondence

Francis T. Cremins, personal papers (stored in Iveagh House)

Bibliography

University College Dublin Archives, Dublin
Ernest Blythe Papers
Desmond FitzGerald Papers
Hugh Kennedy Papers
Patrick McGilligan Papers
Richard Mulcahy Papers
Michael Tierney Papers

National Library of Ireland, Dublin
George Gavan Duffy Papers
Irish League of Nations Society Papers

Manuscripts Department, Trinity College, Dublin
Frederick H. Boland Papers

Military Archives, Cathal Brugha Barracks, Dublin
Department of Defence Collection

Franciscan Library, Killiney, Co. Dublin
Eamon de Valera Papers

Public Record Office, London
Cabinet Office Papers
Colonies Office Papers
Dominions Office Papers
Foreign Office Papers

League of Nations Registry, Palais des Nations, Geneva
General Registry Collection

Michael MacWhite papers
In private possession

PRIMARY SOURCES: PRINTED

Department of External Affairs Treaty Series (Government Publications Office, Dublin)
League of Nations Council Reports (Government Publications Office, Dublin)
League of Nations Assembly Reports (Government Publications Office, Dublin)
The aims and origins of the League of Nations (League of Nations Secretariat, Geneva, 1929)
Ten years of international co-operation (League of Nations, London, 1930)
The League hands over (League of Nations, Geneva, 1946)

The League idea (Irish League of Nations Society, Dublin, Undated)
Dáil Debates
Seanad Debates
League of Nations Official Journal (League of Nations, Geneva)
Special Supplements to the League of Nations Official Journal (League of Nations, Genevao
Public Statutes of the Oireachtas (Government Publications Office, Dublin)

Newspapers
Concord (Journal of the Irish League of Nations Society), Bray
Irish Statesman, Dublin
Irish Times, Dublin
Irish Independent, Dublin
Freeman's Journal, Dublin
The Times (London)
The Manchester Guardian

SECONDARY SOURCES

Armstrong, David, *The rise of the International Organisation*, London, 1982
Baer, George W., *Test-case, Italy, Ethiopia and the League of Nations*, Stanford, 1976
— *The coming of the Italo-Ethiopian war*, Cambridge, Mass., 1967
Barcroft, Stephen A., 'The International Civil Servant, The League of Nations career of Sean Lester', Unpublished Ph.D. Thesis, Trinity College, Dublin 1972
— 'Irish foreign policy at the League of Nations: 1929–1936', *Irish Studies in International Affairs*, Vol. 1, No. 1 pp. 19–29
Barros, James G., *Betrayal from within, Joseph Avenol, Secretary General of the League of Nations, 1933–1940*, Yale, 1969
— *The League of Nations and the Great Powers: The Greek–Bulgarian Incident of 1925*, Oxford, 1970
— *Office without power: Secretary General Sir Eric Drummond, 1919–1933*, Oxford, 1979.
Bendiner, Elmer, *A time for angels, The tragicomic history of the League of Nations*, London, 1975
Benes, Eduard, 'Ten years of the League of Nations', *Foreign Affairs*, Vol. 8, No. 2, 1929, pp. 212–24
Bewley, Charles, *Memoirs of a Wild Goose*, Dublin, 1989
Bliss, Tasker H., 'What is Disarmament?', *Foreign Affairs*, Vol. 4, No. 3, April 1926, pp. 353–68
Bowman, John, *De Valera and the Ulster Question, 1917–1973*, Oxford, 1982
Canning, Paul, *British policy towards Ireland: 1921–1941*, Oxford, 1985
Carlton, David, 'Great Britain and the League Council crisis of 1926', *The Historical Journal*, XI, 2, 1968
Carr, Edward H., *The twenty years crisis 1919–1939*, second edition, London, 1946
Carroll, Francis M., *American opinion and the Irish Question, 1910–1923*, Dublin, 1978
— 'Protocol and international politics, 1928; the Secretary of State goes to Ireland', *Éire-Ireland*, Vol. 26, No. 4, 1991
Claude, Inis L., *Swords into ploughshares (The problems and progress of International Organisation)*, Third edition, London, 1964
Colliard, C.A., *Institutions Internationales*, Paris, 1967
Coogan, Timothy P., *Ireland since the Rising*, London, 1966
Cosgrave, Ann Carol, and Twitchett, Kenneth J., *The new international actors*, London, 1970
Crawford, James, *The creation of states in international law*, Oxford, 1979
Cronin, Michael, 'The League of Nations Covenant', *Studies*, Vol. 8, March 1919, pp. 19–34
Curran, Joseph M., *The birth of the Irish Free State*, Alabama, 1980
Daly, Mary E., *The social and economic history of Ireland since 1800*, Dublin, 1981
Dawson, Robert MacGregor, *The development of Dominion status: 1900–1936*, London 1937
Davies, David, *Nearing the Abyss: the lessons of Ethiopia*, London, 1936
De Vere White, Terence, *Kevin O'Higgins*, London, 1948
Drudy, P.J. (ed.), *Irish Studies 5, Ireland and Britain since 1922*, Cambridge, 1986
— and McAleese, Dermot, *Irish Studies 3: Ireland and the European Community*, Cambridge, 1984
Dudley Edwards, Owen (ed.), *Conor Cruise O'Brien introduces Ireland*, London, 1969
Dulles, Alan W., 'Some misconceptions about Disarmament', *Foreign Affairs*, Vol. 5, No. 3, April 1927, pp. 413–26
— 'The Disarmament puzzle', *Foreign Affairs*, Vol. 9, No. 4, July 1931, pp. 603–16
Dunbabin, J.P. 'The League of Nations' place in the international system', *History*, 1993, Vol. 78

Duncan-Hall, H., *The British Commonwealth of Nations*, London 1920
Fanning, Ronan, *Independent Ireland*, Dublin, 1983
— *The Irish Department of Finance 1922–1958*, Dublin, 1978
— 'Irish neutrality a historical view', *Irish Studies in International Affairs*, Vol. 1, No. 1, pp. 27–31
Farrell, Brian, *Chairman or Chief? The role of the Taoiseach in Irish Government*, Dublin, 1971
Finnegan, Robert B., *Ireland: The challenge of conflict and change*, Colorado, 1983
Foster, R.F., *Modern Ireland, 1600–1972*, London, 1988
Gallagher, Tom and O'Connell, James (eds), *Contemporary Irish Studies*, Manchester, 1983
Galthorne-Hardy, G.M., *A short history of international affairs, 1920–39*, Oxford, 1960
Golding, G.M., *George Gavan Duffy 1882–1951: A legal biography*, Dublin, 1982
Grigg, Edward, 'The merits and defects of the Locarno Treaty as a guarantee of world peace', *International Affairs*, Vol. XIV, No. 2
Gwynn, Denis, *The Irish Free State, 1922–1927*, London, 1928
Hancock, W.K., *Survey of British Commonwealth affairs. volume one: problems of nationality: 1918–1936*, London, 1937
Harkness, David W., *The Restless Dominion: The Irish Free State and the British Commonwealth of Nations 1921–1931*, London, 1969
Henig, Ruth B. (ed.) *The League of Nations*, Edinburgh, 1973
Hilmer, Norman and Wigley, Philip (eds), *The First British Commonwealth, essays in honour of Nicholas Mansergh*, London, 1980
Hudson, W.J., *Australia and the League of Nations*, Sydney, 1980
Hudson, Manley O., 'The Geneva Protocol', *Foreign Affairs*, Vol. 3, No. 2, December 1924, pp. 226–35
Joannon, Pierre (ed.), *De Gaulle and Ireland*, Dublin, 1991
Keatinge, Patrick, *The formulation of Irish foreign policy*, Dublin, 1973
— *A place amongst the nations: issues in Irish foreign policy*, Dublin, 1978
— 'The Irish Free State and the League of Nations', *Studies*, 1970, pp. 133–47
— 'The formative Years of the Irish diplomatic service', *Éire-Ireland*, Vol. 6, No. 3, 1971, pp. 57–71
Keith, A.B., *The sovereignty of the British Dominions*, London, 1929
Kelen, Emery, *Peace in their time: men who led us in and out of war, 1914–1945*, London, 1964
Kennedy, Kieran, Giblin, Thomas & McHugh, Deirdre, *The economic development of Ireland in the twentieth century*, Dublin, 1988
Kennedy, Michael, 'The Irish Free State and the League of Nations: the wider implication', *Irish Studies in International Affairs*, Vol. 3, No. 4, 1992, pp. 9–24
— 'The Irish Free State and the League of Nations: 1922–1932', Unpublished Ph.D. thesis, University College, Dublin, 1993
— 'Candour and chicanery, the Irish Free State and the Geneva Protocol', *Irish Historical Studies*, No. 115, May 1995
— 'Principle well seasoned with the sauce of realism: Sean Lester, Joseph Walshe and the definition of the Irish Free State's policy towards Manchuria', *Irish Studies in International Affairs*, Vol. 6, October 1995
Keogh, Dermot, *The Vatican, the Bishops and Irish politics, 1919–39*, Cambridge, 1986
— *Ireland and Europe, 1919–1989, A diplomatic and political history*, Dublin, 1990
— 'Profile of Joseph Walshe, Secretary, Department of Foreign Affairs, 1922–1946', *Irish Studies in International Affairs*, Vol. 3, No. 2, 1990, pp. 59–80
— *Twentieth century Ireland*, Dublin, 1994
— *Ireland and the Vatican*, Cork, 1995
Kitchen, Martin, *Europe between the wars: a political history*, London 1988

Larus, Joel (ed.), *From collective security to preventive diplomacy*, London, 1965
Le Roy Bennett, A., *International organisations. principles and issues*, New Jersey, 1977
Lee, Joseph, *Ireland 1912–1985, politics and society*, Cambridge, 1989
Long, Eric, 'Dáil Éireann's attempts at international recognition: 1919–1921', unpublished M.A. Thesis, University College, Dublin, 1984
The Earl of Longford and O'Neill, T.P., *Eamon de Valera*, Dublin, 1970
Lowell, A. Laurence, 'The future of the League', *Foreign Affairs*, Vol. 4, No. 4, July 1926, pp. 525–34
Luard, Evan (ed.), *The evolution of international organisations*, London, 1966
— (ed.), *The international regulation of frontier disputes*, London, 1970
— *A history of the United Nations*, 2 Vols., London, 1982 & 1989
Lyons, F.S.L., *Ireland since the famine*, London, 1971
Macartney, M.H., and Cremona, Paul, *Italy's foreign and colonial policy, 1914–37*, London, 1938
MacDonagh, Michael, 'Ireland's attitude to external affairs', *Studies*, Spring 1959, pp. 78–83
MacDonnell, A.G., *England, their England*, London, 1933
McMahon, Deirdre, *Republicans and Imperialists, Anglo-Irish relations in the 1930s*, London, 1984
MacQueen, Norman, 'Eamon de Valera, the Irish Free State and the League of Nations, 1919–1946', *Éire-Ireland*, Vol. 17, No. 4, pp. 110–27
McSweeney, Bill, *Ireland and the threat of nuclear war*, Dublin, 1985
Maier, C., *Recasting Bourgeois Europe*, Princeton, N.J., 1975
Manning, Maurice, *The Blueshirts*, Dublin, 1971
Mansergh, Nicholas, *The Commonwealth experience*, London, 1969
Marks, Sally, *The illusion of peace: International relations in Europe 1918–1933*, London, 1976
Martel, Gordon (ed.), *The origins of the Second World War reconsidered*, London, 1986
Martin, F.X. and Byrne, F.J. (eds), *The scholar revolutionary: Eoin MacNeill, 1867–1945, and the making of the new Ireland*, Dublin, 1973
Munch, P., *Les origines et l'oeuvre de la Societe des Nations*, Two volumes, 1923–4, Copenhagen
Nicholas, H.G., *The United Nations as a political institution*, 5th edition, Oxford, 1975
Nicolson, Harold, *Diplomacy*, Third edition, London, 1965
Northedge, F.S., *The troubled giant, Britain and the Great Powers, 1916–1939*, London, 1966
— *The League of Nations, its life and times, 1920–1946*, Avon, 1986
O'Sullivan, Daniel, *The Irish Free State and its Senate*, London, 1940
Phelan, E.J., 'Ireland and the International Labour Organisation: Part One', *Studies*, March, 1926, pp. 1–18
— 'Ireland and the International Labour Organisation: Part Two', *Studies*, September, 1926, pp. 381–98
Prill, Felician, 'Sean Lester: High Commissioner in Danzig, 1933–1937', *Studies*, Autumn 1960, pp. 261–7
Reynolds, P.A., *An introduction to international relations*, London, 1973
Robinson, Lennox, *Bryan Cooper*, London, 1931
Ross, Graham, *The Great Powers and the decline of the European states system: 1914–1945*, New York, 1983
Rovine, Arthur W., *The first fifty years: The Secretary General in world politics, 1920–1970*, Leyden, 1970
Ryle-Dwyer, T., *De Valera, the man and the myths*, Dublin, 1991
Salmon, Trevor C., *Unneutral Ireland: an ambivalent and unique security policy*, Oxford, 1989

Scelle, Georges, *Une crise dans la Societe des Nations. (la reforme du Conseil et l'entree de l'Allemagne a Geneve*, Paris, 1927
Schaefer, L.F., *The Ethiopian crisis, touchstone of Appeasement*, Boston Mass., 1961
Scott, George, *The rise and fall of the League of Nations*, London, 1973
Sharp, Paul, *Irish foreign policy and the European Community*, Aldershot, 1990
Taylor, A.J.P., *English history: 1914–1945*, London, 1965
— *The origins of the Second World War*, Harmondsworth, 1964
Thomas, Hugh, *The Spanish civil war*, 3rd ed., London, 1990
Tierney, M. (ed. F.X. Martin), *Eoin MacNeill: scholar and man of action*, Oxford, 1980
Tierney, Michael, 'Some thoughts on the League of Nations', *Studies*, Vol. 25, 1936, pp. 226–38
Walters, F.P., *A history of the League of Nations*, Vols one and two, London, 1952
Wheeler-Bennett, John, *Disarmament and security*, London, 1932
Wright, Quincey, The Manchurian crisis', *The American Political Science Review*, Vol. 26, No. 1, February 1932
Zimmern, Alfred, *The League of Nations and the rule of law*, London, 1936

Index

Note: entries in bold type signify a biographical footnote.

Abyssinia, 13, 16, 84, 224, 224–6; Italian invasion of, 202–22
Amery, Leopold, 67
Anglo-Irish Agreement (1938), 165
Anglo-Irish Treaty (1921), 15, 23–4, 34–5, 42–3, 48, 121, 251; registration of, 53–72
Article 393 (Treaty of Versailles) issue, 46–8, 53
Anschluss, 234
Anti-Treaty elements, 43
Australia, 73, 124, 130–4, 140, 148, 184–5
Austro-German Customs Union Plan, 155
Avenol, Joseph, 226, **226**, 235, 241–2

Balfour Declaration (1926), 94, 99
Batterbee, Harry, 135
Bewley, Charles, 130, **130**, 140, 171, 211
Binchy, Daniel, 77, **77**, 88–9, 106–7, 130, 140, 143, 157; on Irish candidature for Council (1930), 131–2; approaches German Foreign Office about Irish candidature for Council, 138
Blythe, Ernest, 77, 84–5, 88, 102, 103, 118, 121; at 1926 Assembly, 77–82; on policy options after 1936 Assembly, 91–5; speaks to Assembly in late twenties, 106–9; and Free State economic policy at the League, 111–14; on General Act, 124–5; at 1930 Assembly, 143, 147, 149
Boland, F.H., **151**, 151, 156, 167, 169 223, 240, 243, 246, 252, 256; on Irish League policy, 193; on European political situation (1934), 194, 208; on admission of USSR to League of Nations, 200; on Italian invasion of Abyssinia, 202–5, 210–11; moves to Industry and Commerce, 220
Boundary Commission, 24, 28–9, 53, 56–7, 59, 254–5
Brennan, Robert, 210
Briand, Aristide, 80, 89, 140, 147, 153, 157–8, 167
Briand Plan, 147, 154

Cadogan, Alexander, 135, 155
Canada, 97–9, 128–9, 132, 134, 137, 141, 145, 148, 184–5, 227
Cecil, Sir Robert, 123, 135, 142
Chaco dispute, 177, 180–4
Chamberlain, Austen, 48, 50, 82–3, 88–9, 96–8, 100
Chamberlain, Neville, 209, 234–7
China, 133, 135–6, 139–40, 142, 146–7, 185; and Manchurian dispute, 156–77
Civil War (Irish), 25–6, 28, 35, 56, 251
Clemenceau, Georges, 19
Cockram, Ben, 165
Codification of International Law, 114–16, 152
Collins, Michael, 22
Concord, 153
Connolly, Joseph, 171, **171**, 173–4, 176, 181, 223
Cooper, Bryan, 48
Cope, Alfred, 26
Corfu Crisis, 41, 44–6
Cosgrave, W.T., 26–8, **27**, 30, 36, 150, 167; at 1923 Assembly, 39–45, 49; and registration of Treaty, 58–61, 63, 65–6

281

Costello, John A., 103, 103, 115, 120, 152, 256
Council of Europe, 29
Craig, Sir James, 29
Cremins, Francis T., 16, 104, **105**, 105, 106; and General Act, 125; and 1930 Council elections, 133, 137, 139, 141, 145–6; and 64th Council Session, 156; at 13th Assembly, 164, 166–7, 169; and Manchuria, 171; and Leticia, 178; and Chaco, 181–2, 184; views on Irish re-eligibility to Council, 187; opinions on League of Nations, 184, 195–6; on Irish League policy, 189, 191–4, 198, 225; importance as a diplomat, 191, 223–4, 252; comparison with Lester, 191; on admission of USSR to League, 194–5, 201; views on European political situation in mid-thirties, 196–7, 204, 207, 220, 226; on Abyssinian Crisis (1935–6), 202–5, 212–14, 216, 219, 222; friendship with Anthony Eden, 202, 256; and 1936 Assembly, 227–8; and Ireland's distancing from League, 229; and 1937 Assembly, 229–30; and European political climate 1936–9, 230–1, 250; and appeasement, 231, 237; and 1938 Assembly, 234; and Munich, 235; and build-up to war, 237–43, on first months of World War II, 242–3; Chargé at Berne during war, 243–7, and destruction of Geneva Legation reports, 242–3; correspondence with Lester during war, 244–6; and United Nations, 247–9; and Final League Assembly, 249
Cronin, Michael, 24
Curtis, Lionel, 30–1, 39, 44–5

Dalton, Hugh, 134–5
Danzig, 16, 186, Sean Lester's appointment as League High Commissioner, 104
Devlin, Denis, **205**, 205, 220, 223–4, 252
Disarmament, 106, 121–4, 150–4, 168, 170, 190
Dixon, C.W., 165
Douglas, James, 32, 34
Drummond, James Eric, 21, 21–2, 36, 64, 67, 70, 98, 116, 132, 134, 158, 181

Dulanty, J.W., **204**, 204, 215

Economic War, 17, 165, 254
Eden, Anthony, 165, 202–4, 206–7, 212, 214–15, 220, 228, 256
El Salvador, 130–1, 139, 141
External Affairs, Department of, 13, 16, 28, 36, 42, 47–8, 53, 55, 58–9, 75, 81, 93, 103, 130, 143, 149, 178, 182, 189, 214, 223–4, 229, 240, 251, 253

Figgis, Darrell, 59–60
Finance, Department of, 93–4, 103, 137, 189
Firearms Act (1925), 182
FitzGerald, Desmond, **23**, 143, 167, 224; views on League, 15; appointment and role in first attempt at Irish admission to League, 23–7; on application and admission, 23, 31, 36, 39, 40, 43; on Geneva Protocol, 48, 51–2; on registration of Treaty, 57–64, 70–1; at 1926 Assembly, 73, 75, 77–9, 81–90, 94; and March 1927 Council session, 96–8; 103–4, 109, and Disarmament, 122; and development of External Affairs, 128
France, 48, 50, 115, 132, 139, 148, 198, 203, 206, 214, 220, 226, 239, 255

Gavan Duffy, George, 19; at Paris Peace Conference, 19; and first Irish attempt at admission to League, 21–3; resignation and legacy to Irish League policy, 23–7, 57
General Act, 115, 124–7
Geneva Protocol, 48–53, 66, 124
Germany, 50, 73–4, 79–80, 115, 123, 132, 138–40, 148, 154–5, 171, 190, 193, 226, 234–7, 252, 255
Grattan-Esmonde, Ormonde, 39
Griffith, Arthur, 21

Hackett, Francis, 29
Harding, E.J., 83
Hayes, Michael, 57
Hearne, John J., **143**, 143, 148, 161–2, 223–4, 247
Henderson, Arthur, 119, 134, 153
Hoare, Sir Samuel, 204, 206, 210, 214–15
Hoare–Laval Pact, 215–16, 224

Index 283

Imperial Conferences of, 1923, 55; 1926, 94, 98; 1930, 143
Industry and Commerce, Department of, 103, 213
Irish Independent, 141
Irish Press, 229
Irish Race Convention (1919), 19
Irish Times, 147–8, 206, 210
Italy, 13, 16, 115, 132, 140, 148, 193, 227, 239; Corfu Crisis, 44–6; invasion of Abyssinia, 202–22

Japan, 16, 107, 132, and Manchurian Crisis, 156–77
Justice, Department of, 182

Keith, Arthur Berriedale, 70
Kelen, Emery, 38, 90
Kellogg–Briand Pact (Pact of Paris) 1928, 118, 122, 157
Kennedy, Hugh, 26, 35, 59, 62

Laval, Pierre, 207, 214–15
League of Nations Conventions, 116–18
League of Nations Guarantee Act (1923), 34–7, 255
League of Nations Obligations of Membership Act (1935), 213–14, 222
Lester, Sean, 16, 104, 104, 109–10, 118, 224, 242, 243, 252, 254, 256; and preparation for Council elections 1930, 129, 132–4; and expansion of Geneva Legation, 136–7; and canvass for Council elections, 139–44; and January 1931 Council session, 151–3; and Council session 64, 156; and Manchuria, 157–76, 187–8; and 13th Assembly (1932), 166–70; and Leticia, 177–80; and Chaco, 181–2, 184; views on Ireland's re-eligibility to Council, 184–5; impact of Council membership on, 186; views on Ireland's role in League, 186–7, 190, 200, 225; appointment to Danzig, 186, 192; comparison with Cremins, 191; appointment as Acting Secretary General, 226; and Munich, 235; conversations with Cremins during World War II, 238, 244; and struggle with Joseph Avenol, 242; as Acting Secretary General during World War II, 244–5, 247; on Irish wartime censorship, 246; and Trygve Lie, 249; on de Valera, 250
Leticia, 177–80
Leyden, John, 103, 156, 213
Lie, Trygve, 249
Lloyd George, 19, 21
Lytton Commission, 161, 163–4, 166, 169, 171–4, 176

Macaulay, W.J.B., 202, 202–3, 206, 211, 215, 219
Madariaga, Salvador de, 160, 163, 178, 180–1, 197, 212, 219
Manchurian Dispute, 16, 107, 127, 150, 156–77, 183, 187, 203, 207, 213
Manchukuo, 166, 171, 174, 176
Matheson, Arthur V., 34
McCauley, Leo T., **155**, 155, 171
McDonald, Denis R, 223, 245
MacDonald, Ramsay, 48, 65–6, 119
McGilligan, Patrick, 77, 99, **99**, 167, 224; and re-appraisal of League policy, 101–5; speaks at League assembly in late twenties, 106; and League economic policy, 112–14; on ratification of League Conventions, 116–17; regarding 'optional clause', 119–21; and Disarmament, 121–3; and General Act, 125–7; and expansion of External Affairs, 128; announces candidature of Irish Free State to Council, 129; and candidature for Council, 135–6, 138, 144–5; and January 1931 Council session, 151–3; and Council session 63, 154–5; and Council session 64, 156; and Manchuria, 157–61
MacNeill, Eoin, **37**; and admission of Free State to League 37–40; speaks on Corfu Crisis, 43–5; and registration of Treaty, 58; and 1926 Assembly, 77, 82
McQuaid, John Charles, 236
MacWhite, Michael, 20, 48, 109, 242; posting to Geneva, 20; conversations with Eric Drummond, 21; and first Irish attempt at admission, 22–3, 25–6; and re-launch of League policy, 31, 34; and 1923 Assembly, 39–40, 42–3, 45; on Geneva Protocol, 50, 53; and registration of Treaty, 58–61, 64, 69, 71–2; and 1926 Assembly, 73–5, 82, 89, 94; and March 1927 Council

MacWhite, Michael (contd)
  incident, 96–8; role in re-appraisal of League policy, 101–4; role in Council elections (1930), 130, 134, 146; and Manchuria, 171; and Chaco, 181; and Abyssinia, 210
Molotov–Ribbentrop Pact, 240
Morning Post, 40
Murphy, Sean, 102–3, 103; and Council elections, 129, 137; and Council session 64, 156; and Leticia, 179; and Chaco, 181, 184; and Abyssinia 202, 213, 215, 245

Neutrality, 35, 221–2, 243–5, 247, 250, 255
New Zealand, 132, 134, 148
Noel-Baker, Philip, 135
North Eastern Boundary Bureau, 28, 56
Northern Ireland, 28–9, 56, 254
Norway, 57, 186

O'Byrne, P.J., 195
O'Duffy, Eoin, 211
O'Hegarty, Diarmuid, 39, 49, 62, 75–6
O'Hegarty, P.S., 24–6
O'Higgins, Kevin, 27, 53, 55
O'Kelly, Sean T., 19, 19, 29, and General Act, 127
O'Kelly de Gallagh, Gerald, 129, 129–34, 138–41, 143, 145, 245
O'Rahilly, Alfred, 61–2
O'Sheil, Kevin, 28–9, 39, 44, 46, 57
O'Sullivan, John Marcus, 103, 103, 112–14, 120, 143, 224
Optional Clause, 116, 118–21, 147

Palestine, 254
Paris Peace Conference, 19
Passfield, Lord, 134–5
Phelan, Edward J., 36, 36, 46, 60, 70–1, 89–90, 97, 159, 201, 244, 247
Portugal, 145–7
Price, C.P., 171, 174–5

Radziwill, Princess, 15
Rhineland, re-militarisation of, 219
Rynne, Michael, 171, 171, 220, 223–4, 228, 230, 240, 247, 249

Saar, 192, 255

Siam, 139–40
Silesia, 150, 152, 254
Simon, Sir John, 163, 169, 176, 200
Sinn Fein, 13, 18–21
Smiddy, Timothy A., 72, 72, 130, 133–5, 138
South Africa, 73, 83, 128, 134, 141, 144, 148, 197
Spain, 73–4, 81, 86, 148, 172, 174, 179, 181
Spanish Civil War, 229–34
Spanish Civil War (Non-intervention) Act, 232
Spanish Civil War (Merchant Shipping) Act, 232
Statute of Westminister, 145
Stimson, Henry L., 171
Sudetenland, 234–77

Thomas, J.H., 66–7, 136
The Times, 59, 163

United Nations, 247–9, 254, 256
Uruguay, 130
USSR, 123, 159, admission to League, 194–201; 226, 252

de Valera, Eamon, 16, 18, 18, 20, 24, 27, 29, 186–7, 191, 193, 240–1, 243, 245, 247, 252, 254–5; and Manchuria, 162, 164–6, 172; and Thirteenth Assembly, 164–73, 188; addresses Radio Nations, 170–1; comparison with Sean Lester, 180; and Chaco, 181, 183–4; on Irish re-eligibility to Council, 185; admission of USSR to League, 194–5, 197–201, 225; denied Vice-Presidency of 1934 Assembly, 197–8; and Abyssinia, 202, 204–13, 220–1, 225; 1935 Assembly, 206–10; and appeasement; 207–8; and General Settlement, 209; on League in mid-thirties, 222–5, 250; and League failure over Abyssinia, 227; and Ireland's distancing from League, 227–9; and 1937 Assembly, 230–1; and Spanish Civil War, 232–4; and Munich Agreement, 234–7;
Vansittart, Sir Robert, 155
Vatican, 130, 171, 187, 195, 199–200, 203

Waller, Bolton, 28–30, 34, 55
Walshe, Joseph, 20, 23, 31, 34, 38, 48, 57, 59, 60, 62–3, 67–70; views on MacWhite, 20; on Geneva Protocol, 49–50, and Council, 75–8, 83, 94–5, 97–102, 104–5, 107, and Council, 1930, 129, 132–9; on Silesia, 150–1, and Council Session 63, 154–5; and Manchuria, 157–63; and Thirteenth Assembly, 164; and Leticia, 177–81; and Chaco, 182–4; views on Ireland's re-eligibility to Council, 184–5

Warnock, William, 223, 245
Whiskard, G.G., 65–6
Wicklow, earl of, 32–3
Wilson, Woodrow, 15, 19